T0290172

A
RUDE
LIFE

A RUDE LIFE

THE MEMOIR

VIR SANGHVI

PENGUIN

VIKING

An imprint of Penguin Random House

VIKING

USA | Canada | UK | Ireland | Australia
New Zealand | India | South Africa | China

Viking is part of the Penguin Random House group of companies
whose addresses can be found at global.penguinrandomhouse.com

Published by Penguin Random House India Pvt. Ltd
4th Floor, Capital Tower 1, MG Road,
Gurugram 122 002, Haryana, India

First published in Viking by Penguin Random House India 2021

Copyright © Vir Sanghvi 2021

All rights reserved

10 9 8 7 6 5 4 3

ISBN 9780670095391

Typeset in Minion Pro by Manipal Technologies Limited, Manipal
Printed at Thomson Press India Ltd, New Delhi

www.penguin.co.in

For my parents
Vimoo and Ramesh Sanghvi

CONTENTS

ONE

'WHO DOES THE QUEEN GO TO?'

I am always astonished by people who can remember their childhoods with remarkable clarity. Almost everything I know about my early years comes from conversations I had with my parents in later years.

My mother came from a rich mill-owning family in Ahmedabad. They owned several textile mills and at one stage, in the 1950s, they were in the same league as the Sarabhais and other top industrial families in Ahmedabad. I always thought of her parents as being relatively progressive because they let her go to America on her own, in the mid-1940s, to study at the University of Michigan. She made a success of her studies but once confessed to me—with a certain amount of bitterness—that the reason her parents had agreed to let her go abroad for studies was because they thought she was dark.

In those days, she said, fair girls were married off early while dark girls were told to study hard because they couldn't be expected to find rich husbands.

My father came from a middle-class family in Rajkot. Or, more correctly, they would have been middle class if my grandfather had not had thirteen children from two wives (he wasn't a bigamist; his first wife died young). No middle-class person can stay middle class for very long with those many children, so lower middle class may be a more accurate description.

Certainly, my father was left pretty much on his own, which may or may not have been a good thing because he took to reading

1

Das Kapital and assorted lefty treatises. He travelled all over India ending up in Bombay where he went to Elphinstone College. He did very well academically and then (in my view) threw it all away by becoming a full-time worker of the Communist Party of India (CPI).

I later asked him why he gave up all hope of a proper career by working in a CPI cell and often remaining 'underground' because the CPI was illegal. (Well, its official policy was to overthrow the legally elected government of India.)

His response was simply that he cared about India. Along with many young people of his generation, he worried that post-independence India would be colonized once again by our own fat cats and that the poor would just get poorer. In those days, the CPI was considered to be the idealists' option and there was a certain glamour attached to being a theoretical revolutionary.

My mother later told me that he had been like that for much of his life. (They first met in Ahmedabad, where my father was visiting, even before he went to college in Bombay.) Her first memory of him, she recalled, was of a charming and deeply charismatic boy who knew that he was always the brightest person in the room. He brought everyone he spoke to around to his view. But he never seriously entertained the possibility that he might be wrong or that he was throwing his future away.

My father was enough in love with the cause to ignore my mother's obvious adoration of him and to marry a fellow party worker. They had hardly been married when the police picked him up and put him in jail along with scores of other CPI activists. He said afterwards that the jail part wasn't so bad but he was less-than-delighted to be visited in prison by his bride along with a party comrade.

Was he doing okay, they asked.

He said he was fine.

Oh good, they said, because we have something to tell you.

My father realized that the conversation was not headed to a happy place.

We have fallen in love, the comrade said. My father's wife added: 'And I am going to have his baby!'

The communist party did not believe in private property but this, my father later said, seemed to be taking things too far.

Divorce papers were drawn up and by the time my father was released (after eleven months in jail), he was ready to look for something new.

He had an added motive. The CPI threw him out for some ideological deviation and in a manner that he had come to expect, the commissar who drew up the chargesheet against him was his own younger brother.

At this stage, my mother re-appeared in his life. My father had been friends with her cousins and she told him that she had been in love with him since they were teenagers. Her parents hated him, of course. Not only was he from a lowly middle-class family from Rajkot but he was a communist, the sort of chap who wanted to take all their money away.

To the dismay of my mother's family, her cousins also became communists. (One of them gave away property that would be worth hundreds of crores today to the party.) They blamed my father for that (probably accurately) and regarded him as a malign influence on their family.

Once my father was free of everything—jail, his now ex-wife and the party—my mother decided that she would tell her parents to take a flying leap and marry him. She was thirty-one and not prepared to wait.

This was easier said than done.

My father had brains but no money. He persuaded R.K. Karanjia, editor of a left-leaning weekly tabloid called *Blitz*, to give him a foreign affairs column (though my father had never been abroad). But that was not going to be enough. So, while he looked for something else to do, my mother, who always had a slightly secretive streak, hatched a plan.

By then, she was living in Mumbai and earning her own money as an industrial psychologist. (I still don't know what that is but it was the subject of her American degree.) She stayed in a very nice three-bedroom apartment in Churchgate, bought for her by her father.

Her plan was as follows. The United Nations was being set up in Paris in 1951. My father would persuade *Blitz* to send him to cover it. She, herself, would take a ship to France. They would meet in Paris and would get married as soon as possible. Apparently, my father was a little taken aback by the audacity of the scheme. But my mother had lived in America for four years (as a student), had travelled there by ship and assured him that she knew her way around 'abroad'.

It worked, despite a few hiccups. She booked her ticket, helped my father get a passport and sent him on ahead. In the manner of some rom-com movie, her father found out that she was leaving and rushed men to the docks to stop her. As it happens in the movies, they arrived just as the ship was sailing away, too late to prevent her departure.

My grandfather was incandescent with rage. But all he could do in those days was send a telegram which would be delivered to her when the ship next docked.

When the boat stopped in Suez, the telegram was waiting. 'If you marry Ramesh,' it said, 'I will shoot you!' It was signed by my grandfather. My mother ignored the cable and kept going. I asked her later if the tone had frightened her.

'Aww no,' she replied dismissively. 'My father was one *vanya sheth*. If he ever even saw a gun, he would have been so scared that he would have run away. Ha.'

This was a very disrespectful attitude. But it was entirely accurate and valid.

My father picked up my mother at the docks in Paris and they set about planning their wedding. At that moment, my mother suddenly decided to be awkward. She wanted a traditional Indian wedding, she said, with a sacred fire and *pheras*.

My father, with his communist background had no time for ritual or even religion. But my mother would not be swayed. He was flummoxed. Where were they going to find a pandit in Paris in 1951?

In desperation my father turned to the Indian delegation to the UN. They didn't know of a pandit either. P.N. Haksar, later to become a very famous civil servant, told me the story. When my father came to him, he said, he told him not to worry. He would arrange everything. Another member of the delegation, Appa Pant (later to be high commissioner to London) said he was a Brahmin and he would preside over the ceremony. And so, my mother got a Hindu wedding after all.

After that, my parents moved to London. My mother got a managerial job (her American degree helped) and put my father through the bar.

She had been right about my grandfather. Once he realized that he had been presented with a fait accompli, he put away his imaginary Colt 45 and welcomed my father (with a slight grimace perhaps) as his son-in-law. My grandmother, a warm and loving person in whose eyes my mother could do no wrong, had always been of the view that if it made my mother happy, she would be happy too.

My parents came back to India after my father became a barrister, moved into my mother's Churchgate flat and set up his law practice. In those days, law was not a big-money profession. There was no corporate law as such so my father took whatever work he could get: murders, divorces, etc.

But he remained devoted to his family. He made it his mission to educate and settle his many brothers and sisters. He put some through medical school and helped them all to go and live abroad. His own parents had died while he was still at Elphinstone College, so the family really had no one else to turn to. Why my father (who had two older brothers and two older sisters) believed that the family was only his responsibility has never been clear to me. But it remains one of the kindest and most selfless things he did in his life.

My grandfather didn't really care about my father's career or his dedication to his brothers and sisters; all he wanted was a grandson. Alas, this was not to be. My mother miscarried. My parents went to Dr Shirodkar, then one of the world's best regarded obstetricians. My mother miscarried again.

By 1955, when my mother was thirty-five (considered too old for a safe delivery in those days) and got pregnant again, my grandfather was not prepared to take any chances. My mother would go to the best doctor in the world, he declared.

This was grand but nobody in Ahmedabad or Mumbai knew who the best doctor in the world was.

'Who does the Queen go to?' my grandfather asked.

My parents did some quick research and discovered that Prince Charles had been delivered by Sir William Gilliatt. (By some coincidence, he handled Camilla Shand's delivery, too, at a time when nobody could guess that Charles and Camilla would marry one day.)

So my parents were despatched to London.

What Sir William made of this couple from Mumbai who announced that they were going to stay in London till their baby was born, I do not know. But my mother remembered him as being thoughtful and kind, with none of the airs you would expect from the Queen's doctor.

And so, on 5 July 1956, I was born at King's College Hospital in London. My mother remembers counting all my fingers and toes after they brought me to her and being relieved to find that I was not lacking in any way. Her only comment though was less than flattering. 'He looks like a mouse,' she said.

Photos were despatched to Ahmedabad from where a week later, my grandfather called. 'Ha Ha,' he said. 'He looks just like me: bald and dark.'

My mother, I am told, handed the phone back to my father and refused to continue the conversation.

In India, jibes about complexions never really go away.

TWO

'I CAN PUT YOU IN JAIL AGAIN'

All of this comes from my parents' accounts of their wedding and my birth. For the period from 1956 to 1963 or so, I have no real memories.

I vaguely recall going to a nursery school on Marine Drive called Casa Montessori. In 1964, over my father's objections, I joined Campion School in Bombay, which my mother said, accurately, was regarded as one of the city's best schools. My father said it was a religious racket run by unscrupulous *padris*. (His lefty prejudices never really went away fully.)

He was not entirely wrong, though. Each day, the Society of Jesus would send us out at lunch to raise money from passing strangers for assorted Catholic causes. We were taught to be worshipful of the Jesuits which further angered my father who took to being brusque or borderline rude to the Fathers and Brothers. He would say things to me like, 'Who is that fat little Spanish grocer in a white dress? Gosh! This joker is your principal?'

It was inevitable that I would be pulled out of Campion sooner rather than later and in the late summer of 1965, when my father visited Jaipur and was taken by a friend to see Mayo College in Ajmer, he decided that I should move there.

He never explained to me why he sent me to boarding school. But I suspect the reasons had to do with my mother's health.

In 1965 she suddenly fell very ill and was sustained by regular blood transfusions. The doctors suspected leukaemia, then a death sentence. Eventually it was diagnosed as a severe form of anaemia but for weeks it was touch and go. She never went to hospital but I have many memories of round-the-clock nurses and of doctors bustling around the house while I cowered in my room. I remember my father crying and my grandparents who were then too unwell to travel from Ahmedabad to Bombay calling several times a day.

I imagine that my father wanted to take me out of this environment but I was not thrilled to go to a boarding school. In my first week I tried to run away twice from the school. Both times, the school found me and brought me back. (Clearly, I wasn't much of a runner even then!)

Rajasthan seemed like a very different place from Mumbai. Many of the boys chatted to each other in Hindi which had never happened at Campion. The food was revolting and unfamiliar (I had never heard of paneer or rajma before) and the teaching staff in the junior school was useless—wives of masters from the senior school trying to earn some extra money. Looking back, none of them had any business being a teacher.

Middle school and middle house were marginally better and I was in a much better frame of mind during that phase: my mother had recovered; and my father had rented a very nice flat in London where we spent our summer holidays.

I only really came into my own during senior school when I was allowed to do the subjects I enjoyed and began to do better academically. I was never top of the class but always in the first four or so in my last years at school; never school captain but always a monitor—a pattern that has probably recurred throughout my life.

It wasn't until I was thirteen or fourteen that I began to ask questions about my parents' financial circumstances. By 1965 my father had given up the law and decided that he would try and make his fortune abroad. So, he was away for long periods (not that I noticed from my boarding school). As far as I could tell, he had two basic skills—the law and an ability to write well. Neither was going to make him a fortune. And as time went on, I had the distinct sense that he was bored of the law.

He made, I guess, a good enough living but from time to time, my mother's family would have to chip in. They bought the large flat on Carmichael Road in Mumbai that we still live in. My grandfather had a *pedhi*, a kind of treasury which handled financial affairs for the whole family and paid my school fees. (I remember it as being the Gujarati equivalent of a modern accounts department. Scores of *dhoti*-clad men would sit on *gaddi*s or mattresses hunched over ledgers. There were no credit cards in those days but the *sheths* never touched cash. Every bill went to the *pedhi*.)

My father's lifestyle was, for want of a better word, international. Not many Indians travelled in the 1960s but my father had the unique ability to seem as much at home at the Excelsior Hotel in Rome or the George V in Paris as he did in Ahmedabad or Rajkot. How he did it remains a mystery. By the early sixties, he had taken over from my mother as the parent who was more at home abroad. Some of it was probably due to his annual trips to New York to cover the UN General Assembly. And then, he made himself available to businesses that needed an international legal consultant.

I imagined, therefore, that money was not a factor in our lives. If we travelled to Delhi we stayed at the Ashoka. In London it was Grosvenor House (before we leased the flat). In Geneva, it was The President. And so on.

And besides, my parents had a life that (unless they travelled) called for relatively little expenditure. My mother had trained in England as a potter (when I was four, I spent four months in Devon with her, living on a farm while she trained with Marianne de Trey, one of the top potters of the time) and enjoyed the company of artists. My father didn't hang around too much with lawyers and journalists but was a part-time member of what used to be called the progressive set. These were former communists, fellow travellers, crypto communists and general all-purpose lefties who had a world view that was probably overly simplistic.

They liked Jawaharlal Nehru but they hated the Congress. In those days the Congress was the overwhelmingly dominant party. But it was, in Nehru's words, a banyan tree giving shelter to lefties and to old-style party bosses. Most people supported the Congress for the lack of a viable alternative. But they chose a faction within the Congress to back.

The progressives looked for lefties within the Congress's ranks to support. This led to a slightly bizarre situation where *Blitz* could claim to fight the Congress ('King Kongress' was the paper's name for the party monolith) but praise individual Congressmen. The Congress strongmen of Maharashtra (S.K. Patil, V.P. Naik, etc.) were anathema to *Blitz* and other progressives. They also loathed Morarji Desai ('Morarjehar' as *Blitz* called him) whom they saw as a stooge of big business.

In my father's case, it was personal. Morarji hated communists and my father hated Morarji. On one occasion it got openly nasty.

My father went to call on Morarji in Delhi.

'Did you find the house easily?' Morarji asked.

'Yes,' said my father. 'I just looked for the house where all the Mercedes and big cars were parked.' (This was a reference to the industrialists who hung around Morarji.)

'Careful, I put you in jail once. I can put you in jail again.' Morarji was not amused.

The progressives loathed Indian big business and the Indian press (except the papers they wrote for). They called it the *jhoot* press, picking up on Nehru's dig that so much of it was owned by Marwaris from the jute business. Their reference points were American or British but they opposed the foreign policies of both countries. (Though I guess everyone opposed the Vietnam War, anyway.) The Russians were supposed to be our pals but nobody wanted to go to Russia or even see a Russian movie.

During the 1965 war with Pakistan, my father wrote (in *Blitz*) 'An Open Letter' (a fashionable genre at the time) to British Prime Minister Harold Wilson who had clearly backed Pakistan. I no longer remember the letter but I remember the photo captions. One was 'Wilson: hypocrite and humbug'. There was not a lot of room for subtlety in those days. But the letter to Wilson was a big hit; strangers would come up to my father and congratulate him for writing it. So we went to London on holiday but also managed to hate the British at the same time.

The hero of the progressives was Krishna Menon. My father had known him since his London days (Menon was the high commissioner) and they struck up a friendship. (Menon generously helped to get my father's younger brother—yeah, the same commissar who had him thrown out of the CPI—admitted to Cambridge as a favour to my father, from where my uncle went on to join the UN.) Menon and my father worked together to set up a small publishing house (which mainly published books by Menon and my father, or so it seemed to me) and each time Menon came to Bombay, our house was his first stop.

Till 1962, Menon was the defence minister so he would arrive with a large motorcade with police outriders. Everyone in the building would gather in the compound to watch and often I would be despatched to receive him downstairs and to take him up to our fourth floor flat. I have to say, I loved it!

In 1962, Menon fell from grace. It's a long story with many versions but it centred around India's border dispute with China. Menon was no China lover but Nehru was. It was Nehru's idea to accept the Chinese annexation of Tibet. Once this was done, China cited several instances where India had encroached on Tibet's (now China's) borders.

The Chinese did not worry too much about many of these disputes but they did care about those borders where they wished to build arterial roads and the like. Menon suggested compromise solutions (like leasing the deserted area where the road was to be built) but these were rejected.

Nehru hoped to use friendship to get the Chinese to give up their territorial claims. When this did not work he instituted a Forward Policy which came perilously close to provoking the Chinese. Eventually he declared that he had asked the army to throw the Chinese out.

The Chinese then aggressively protected what they claimed was their territory, inflicting a crushing defeat on the Indian army.

Most of this was quite clearly Nehru's fault. Even the military victory had been handed to the Chinese by B.M. Kaul, Nehru's favourite general.

Menon was also to blame. As the defence minister he had failed to treat the army with respect. Morale was low and the generals squabbled when they should have been strategizing.

After the defeat, everyone recognized that it was unthinkable to ask Nehru to take the blame. So Menon bore the brunt of the attack and eventually Nehru sacrificed him.

R.K. Karanjia, my father and various other progressives stood by Menon, even arranging for him to stand from his old North Bombay constituency in the 1967 General Election as an independent. (Indira Gandhi had denied him re-nomination from the Congress.) Menon lost to a little-known Congressman called Barve, much to the disappointment of the progressives.

My father then wrote a piece called 'A Political Obituary of Mr Barve' which I thought (even then) was in dodgy taste considering that Barve had actually won the election. When Barve then actually dropped dead a short while later, the piece seemed in even more bad taste than it had at first. (My father's thesis, in the original piece, was that Barve had fulfilled his purpose for the Congress and would now amount to nothing. He may or may not have been right but obituary was an ill-chosen word.)

The progressives asked Menon to stand again. He would surely win the by-election they said. The Congress put up Barve's sister and ran a sentimental campaign. Menon huffed away (in English; he spoke no Hindi) about national issues, and of course, he lost yet again.

Despite these electoral humiliations, my father stayed friends with Menon. His explanation was 'if you are friends with somebody when they are up, you must stay friends with them when they are down'.

I didn't see the point at the time but I recognize now that it has actually been one of the guiding principles of my own life too.

With my father's political friends (mostly from all factions of the Congress) came the odd dose of glamour.

Dilip Kumar and my father were close friends. It all began when the censors raised innumerable objections to his film *Ganga Jamuna*. They demanded cuts in nearly every scene. Dilip asked my father to represent him. The negotiations went on and on and finally the film was passed with hardly any cuts.

Then, around 1964, Dilip Kumar was accused by the police of being a Pakistani spy. The allegation was ridiculous but the police actually raided his house looking for a transmitter he used to communicate with his Pakistani controllers!

Even now I find it hard to believe that a man like Dilip Kumar who had done so much to create a secular climate in India could have been harassed in this manner.

It started when the Calcutta police arrested a young man on espionage charges. The police claimed to have found a diary which contained several names including Dilip Kumar and some other Muslims (one or two of whom were friends of my parents).

Based on this tiny bit of 'evidence' the Calcutta police arrived in Bombay, enlisted the help of the local constabulary and went around raiding innocent people and looking for evidence of Pakistani links.

As young as I was, I was incredulous. Could anyone really believe that Dilip Kumar was a Pakistani agent? I could not understand why my father took the charges so seriously or why Dilip Kumar seemed so shaken. It was only much later when I was older that I realized how easy it could be to question a Muslim's loyalty or how communal the mindset of many of our law enforcement agencies is.

The charges eventually collapsed, but for a week or so it seemed possible that Dilip Kumar would actually be arrested for treason. Years later, when I interviewed Dilip Kumar about the incident he shrugged it off and was unwilling to say much. To his credit, he exhibited no bitterness.

Even when Dilip Kumar was not in legal trouble, he stayed friends with my father and I grew up idolizing him because of his intellect, charisma, warmth and charm. (The only Dilip Kumar films I saw during that phase were *Ganga Jamuna*—which I had to—and *Mughal-e-Azam* so no, I wasn't star struck.)

There was enough happening to keep a young boy entertained so I never thought about money but my mother later told me that by 1966, my father was already living beyond his means (suites at Grosvenor House which we could not really afford) and by 1967, he was beginning to wonder if perhaps he should come back to India full-time and start going to court everyday rather than just accept the cases he enjoyed.

Then, in 1967, my grandmother and grandfather died within a month of each other. My grandparents had a relationship that always struck me as different from anything I had seen. They lived in a huge house in Ahmedabad and each had his or her own areas and their own servants. They did not even eat their meals together. My grandfather never used my grandmother's name. He would always say something like '*Sambhlo chho*?' in Gujarati which translates as 'are you listening?' And she would always know that he was talking to her.

My grandfather was a bumptious fellow which I guess came from having to play the big *sheth* at his mill. But beneath that exterior he was a shy and sentimental man, quick to anger and quick to forget. My grandmother, on the other hand, was quiet and introverted and happiest on her own. I would often find her on the porch of the bungalow gently rocking on a swing looking past the garden, staring at the open gate.

Every time I asked her what she was doing, she would say, '*Manaa jowuchhu*' which translates as 'looking at people'. There was not much to see through the gate and in any case there were few pedestrians in Shahibagh where she lived so I imagine she just liked being on her own.

Somehow I had never thought of my grandparents as being particularly close to each other. But when my grandmother died in 1967 my grandfather was shattered. He died just twenty days later.

While my mother was clearing out my grandmother's effects, she came upon several bundles of notes that the old lady had salted away for a rainy day. I forget now how much it was, but my guess is that it was two or three lakhs, a fortune at the time.

My mother's family had always believed that my grandmother was the Lakshmi of the house. (Indeed, they lost their mills after she died.) My mother stuck to that belief, and told my father to use the money in a last-ditch approach.

My father went to Teheran where he had previously worked as a legal adviser on a business deal and was introduced to the Shah of Iran. From all accounts, the two men hit it off and the Shah commissioned him to do a book on Iran.

From there my father went to London, where he looked for some way of establishing a base there. The Shah suggested he set up a global consultancy. This struck my father as being overly ambitious.

Then, my father had a thought. What if the Iranian government provided him with a couple of clients? He could produce the inflight magazine for Iran Air. He could consult for the state-owned Iranian oil company.

The Shah agreed and, with the Iranian business assured, my father bought Clark Hall, an old British PR firm, and went on to win such global clients as Canada Air and the Continental Oil Company. He took over Clark Hall's office, two floors on Clifford Street (between New Bond Street and Savile Row) and took a lease on a three-bedroom apartment.

The old lady's money had done the trick.

He was flusher than he had ever been.

THREE

'YOU ARE MY LINK WITH THE FUTURE'

If you were to ask me what the happiest years of my childhood were, I would have to say 1967–70. It is probably because those were the years when I really got close to my father. By 1967 I was eleven years old and able to have reasonably adult conversations with him. And let's be honest here—because those were the years when we were rich and I lived an impossibly glamorous life that I never lived again.

We usually spent summer in London but in 1967, shortly after my grandparents had died, it seemed better to stay on in India. However, later in the year, after my father had leased a flat in London, we went there for Christmas.

Truth be told, Christmas was never a big deal in India. But I had read enough about English Christmases in Enid Blyton and wanted the full Noddy experience. It was too much to expect my parents to arrange snow on Christmas Eve or to expect Santa to come down the chimney. (The flat did not even have a chimney!) But I still had expectations. The day we arrived, I demanded a Christmas tree. (It was a nasty artificial thing with plastic branches and a retractable steel base.)

Then we went for Christmas Eve dinner with English friends of my parents. (Nice enough but not quite Toyland.) By the time we had got to a New Year's Eve party where we held hands and sang *Auld Lang Syne* (many people did not know all the words—but I hadn't even heard of the song) I was beginning to wonder what the fuss was about.

The Christmas may have been underwhelming without snow or Santa but there were lots of holidays (France, Switzerland, Italy, Scandinavia, America, etc.) and I tried as best as I could to immerse myself in the Swinging London scene to the extent that it was possible for a fourteen- or fifteen-year-old to do. Mostly, this consisted of going to Carnaby Street or the King's Road and buying clothes at the trendy shops of that era: John Stephen, Mr Fish, Granny Takes a Trip, Lord John, etc. Sergeant Pepper came out in 1967 and the next three years were a great time for music.

My father seemed to become more and more prosperous: first class on flights, an account at Harrods, an account at a limo company, and so on.

As I grew a little older, he began talking to me about the future. His business in London worked, he said, because he knew how to write well and had the ability to make an impression on people. He was confident, he said, that I had inherited those abilities (I am not sure what he based this confidence on—I was a thirteen-year old-schoolboy!) but I must never let my success in school (at this stage, I was winning all the school debates, editing *The Mayoor*, the school magazine, etc.) go to my head. Instead I should always follow his policy: allow yourself to believe that you are only slightly above average. The rest is hard work.

He had plans for me. I would finish at Mayo in December 1972, then I could either go directly to college in India or come to England and spend two years earning A Levels. After that I would go to Oxford or Cambridge. After I got my degree, I would join him at work.

This was heady stuff. The sense that a future had been mapped out for me and the implication that a life of privilege would continue were both exciting prospects. By the beginning of 1971, I was in a state of optimistic self-satisfaction.

In March, that year, I was called to the principal's office at school. My father had called, the principal said. He was in a hospital called the London Clinic and would be there for a while. So he thought it might be a good idea for his family to join him. Could I prepare to leave at once for London?

This was easier said than done. I could take a night train from Ajmer to Ahmedabad. Then the following day, my uncle's office would arrange to send me to Mumbai. And I would leave that night for London. My mother and my uncle Siddharth (my father's younger brother) would be on the same flight.

As I began my journey on the Ahmedabad train, I was filled with misgivings. Nobody pulled you out of school if your father had a minor ailment. Why was my uncle, a brilliant doctor, also flying out?

On the other hand, I told myself, my father was only fifty. How serious could any ailment be?

I got to Ahmedabad and discovered that my uncle's office had failed to secure me a seat on the plane to Mumbai. I would have to take the night train. This meant I would miss the flight my mother was on and would be able to leave only the next night.

I spent an anxious day alone at home in Mumbai but I did get to speak to my mother who had reached London and who assured me that it was just jaundice. But this meant that my father would be in bed for two weeks so he thought it would be nice not to be alone. She had spoken to his doctors (some Harley Street types) who had assured her that my dad was fine.

This seemed to be an accurate assessment. When I finally got to my father's hospital bed at the London Clinic, he was sitting up and reading. His skin had a yellow pallor but, in all other respects, he was fine. They would do an operation tomorrow just to rule out complications, he told me. And then it was two weeks of bed rest.

The operation seemed to go well. Nobody said anything to suggest the contrary. Then, late at night, after dinner, my mother said she had something to tell me.

My mother had no small talk. So she got right to the point. 'Your father has cancer,' she said. 'But don't worry. His family are all doctors. He will be fine.'

But would he?

I sought out my uncle Siddharth who told me the whole story. When he had heard about my father's jaundice, he had asked for more details. These included an X-ray from his last medical check-up which showed a shadow in his lung. The hospital had sent him a reminder to come in again so they could examine his lungs.

When my uncle heard all this, he came to two worrying conclusions. One: it was entirely possible that the shadow was a malignant tumour. (My father was a two-packs-a-day man.) Could the cancer have spread to his pancreas? Or his liver? In either case, the most likely prognosis (in 1971) was death.

My uncle had gone to see my father's Harley Street physician who had laughed at him and said, 'You better stop spreading these silly stories around or they will take away your FRCS. Ha, ha ha!'

My uncle had insisted. As it was hard to check the liver in those days, they decided to operate. My uncle asked for the best surgeon they could find and the London Clinic contacted Mr Rodney Smith (in the UK surgeons are Mr not Dr), who later became the president of the Royal College of Surgeons, if I remember correctly.

Smith found the problem easily. My father had a large malignant tumour in his liver. He was a goner.

They shifted my father to St George's Hospital (which is now, bizarrely, The Lanesborough, a luxury hotel) and the cancer specialists came to examine him. They were clear. There was nothing more to be done. He should go home and die in his own bed, in peace.

It is very hard to be told that a peaceful death is the best option for someone you love.

So my father's family gathered from all over the world and decided they were going to fight the cancer. All the brothers and sisters he had helped educate and sent abroad had done very well for themselves. Many were doctors.

A top New York doctor who was an old friend of my father's was flown in. He advised shifting him to New York. So, they took over the first-class cabin of an Air India plane and turned it into a mini hospital.

In New York, my father was admitted to the New York University Medical Center while his brothers and sisters looked after him. (My mother and I were looked after wonderfully by my father's brother Indoo, who, with his wife Jasu, did their best to make us feel better.)

They put catheters, chemotherapy tubes and God alone knows what else into my father. There were two more operations.

Nobody asked my opinion. (If they had, I would have opposed the shift to New York and let him die in his own bed, his dignity intact.) But I could see him shrinking before our eyes. Finally, at the beginning of July, my father's sister Sudha (a doctor herself) took me aside, said she had looked at the reports and that it was now only a matter of time.

I had guessed as much already. But what could one do?

I sat quietly (and for the most part, alone) in the hospital cafeteria waiting for the inevitable.

My father must have realized that he was dying despite the cheerful things they told him because he called me into his room once and asked everyone to leave.

'You are my link with the future. There is enough money for the future. Look after your mother. You will do much better than I could ever do.'

Of course I protested. Nothing was going to happen to him. I could never achieve a millionth of what he had. And so on. But that was to be our final conversation.

On 25 July, as I sat in the waiting room, they told me he was gone. I didn't cry (from what I remember). I walked out of the hospital and wandered the streets of New York on my own for several hours.

My life had changed. Forever.

FOUR

'YOU CAN BATHE ON MONDAYS AND FRIDAYS'

Once the funeral was over, my mother spoke to my father's younger brother who had taken leave of absence from his job at the UN to try and keep my father's office running.

His efforts didn't work for many reasons. The business was too dependent on my father for anyone else to run it. My uncle was not very good at anything other than the mathematical economics he had studied at Cambridge and which he now used to evaluate projects for the UN. And he said he was cheated by many of the people my father did business with, and large sums that were owed, never actually arrived.

My uncle met my mother and gave her the bad news. My father's treatment in New York had been ruinously expensive.

The business would not run. There was no money left. My father had exaggerated, in his own mind, the value of his holdings. There was just about enough money left to pay for me to go to school and university in England. He would look after this money and ensure that my fees were paid.

By the time we returned to India, my mother was convinced we were now broke. I pointed out that she still had her own money—the flat in Churchgate where we had once lived, our own large apartment on Carmichael Road and her inherited investments and shares. Nor did we have huge expenses. I had just three terms left to go at Mayo and then my education in England seemed to be taken care of.

She calmed down a little but for the rest of her life (another forty years or so), she never recovered from the shock of being told that the money she thought was in my father's London account, simply wasn't there. She became miserly, mean and money-minded.

I didn't mind. In the circumstances, it was understandable. But I knew, from the age of fifteen, that I was now on my own with no one to really count on.

I went back to Mayo where my academic performances improved further largely because I thought it did not matter. ('I am going to do A levels anyway. So I don't need ISC results to get into college'.) I rarely work well under pressure and usually thrive where there is none.

I did okay in the ISC (95 per cent in four of the five subjects, let down by 69 per cent in geography!) and in April, I went back to London where our old flat remained, pending a final disposal of my father's affairs. My father's sister Sudha and her husband Soham were living there.

The problem was that I had not secured admission at any school in the UK for my A levels. Moreover, I was also quite clear about the kind of school I wanted to attend. After Mayo, I felt I was done with strict schools (my contemporaries in India were all in college) and wanted a more relaxed experience.

I went out and bought myself a copy of the Public Schools Handbook and went through the list of schools. I picked a first choice and a few back-ups. One of my aunts (my father's sister) lived in Manchester so we went to a place called Cheadle Hume which was kind enough to accept me. I wrote off to Clifton College in Bristol which had offered me a place on the basis of my ISC results.

But I really wanted to be in a boarding school in London. According to the Public Schools Handbook, there was a place called Mill Hill with acres and acres of grounds in North London. For me what was more important was this: it was twenty minutes on the Tube from Euston, in the centre of London. So I called the Mill Hill admissions office and discovered that they were overly bureaucratic. It was already June. Did I realize that term began in September? They were full up, etc. There were no vacancies.

So, on the grounds that I had nothing to lose, I called the switchboard and asked for the headmaster. To my surprise they put me through. I explained who I was and said that I was looking for a place.

The headmaster, Michael Hart, sounded intrigued. 'Come and see me,' he said.

And so, I took the tube to Mill Hill, met Mr. Hart who asked various probing questions. 'Why are you doing this yourself? 'Why isn't there an adult who could do this for you?' 'Why have you left it so late?' And so on.

I explained my situation and he was entirely reasonable. He sent me off to be interviewed by the heads of his history and English departments, both of whom must have said nice things because he then offered me a place on the spot.

Then, a thought struck him. 'Who will pay your fees?'

'I will,' I said, pulling out a cheque book for an account that my uncle had set up for me in London.

'Will you do this every term?' he asked.

'I don't see why not, sir.'

He was pleased. 'Very good,' he responded.

And so I was in. As irritating as it was to wear school uniform and to explain why I needed to bathe everyday ('We are happy to let you have a bath on Mondays and Fridays', the matron said), it was an academically liberating experience.

The Indian education system, in those days, was based on mugging. For instance, it was a safe assumption that every single history exam paper would contain a question about Ashoka. No matter what the question said, most boys (under the guidance of their teachers) wrote the same essay about Ashoka, usually with flowery quotes from eminent historians. Most of these quotes were cringe-making. 'If the history of India were a hall of pillars, then the pillar of Emperor Ashok would stand the tallest.' (So, not just silly, but also needlessly phallic.)

So-called ideal answers were passed around and boys were encouraged to memorize them. Obviously, I refused to be part of this foolish exercise and wrote my own answers to the questions.

This worked less well in school than it did at the final ISC exam where I topped the school in history. But at least I had the satisfaction of knowing that I was doing more than just mugging. (In 1999, I went back to Mayo as the chief guest at the prize-giving ceremony for the girls' school. I met two enthusiastic boys who told me with great pride. 'Sir, we still use your history answers!' One of them had a faded exercise book with my name on it. I had left Mayo in 1972. If they were still copying my answers twenty-seven years later, then this was a sad commentary on the Indian education system.)

Mill Hill was nothing like that. Class sizes were small: just five of us in the politics class and fifteen for English and economics. The books didn't matter so much. The prescribed textbook for my English class was *Victory* by Joseph Conrad. But before we got there we read *Lord Jim* and other books by the same author to give us a background of who he was and what he was trying to say.

During the British Miners' strike of 1973-74, my politics class mainly discussed current events and what they told us about the workings of the system. The US politics class was especially fascinating because it was the time of Watergate.

Mill Hill was good to me. I won every academic prize that I was eligible for. They made me a monitor in my third term there so I didn't have to wear the uniform. And I went to central London at least twice a week.

I did well in my A levels because, once again, I felt there was no pressure, reckoning that I would take a different exam to enter Oxford that winter and that the A levels would be irrelevant.

But, of course, they weren't. Early in my Oxbridge term (in those days if you wanted to go to Oxford or Cambridge you had to come back for an extra term after your A levels and take an entrance exam), one of my teachers told me that he had met a don from Brasenose College and had told him about me. Would I like to go to Oxford and have tea with him?

Why the hell not?

I took the train to Oxford for what I thought would be a 'good chap' interview where the don would offer me a cup of tea and talk about his college (about which I knew nothing).

Instead I was ushered into a room where five people were sitting in a semi-circle. I was made to face an open window so I could see only silhouettes and had to wonder who the dons were. The questions came fast and intense. They were of a high academic level and some were, I thought, faintly shocking; considering that I had not been asked to prepare.

'So would you say that you were a Keynesian or a monetarist, Mr Sanghvi?'

I told the truth. 'My teachers are Keynesians. I have no strong views on the subject. I am hoping to make up my own mind once I get here and discuss it with economists like you.'

There were lots more of the same kind.

It did not go well. They shook hands grimly with me as I left for the station.

The following day, the teacher who had sent me there asked how it went. I remonstrated with him and accused him of sending me there under false pretences: 'You should have told me it was an academic interview with a full panel! At least I would have prepared something.'

The teacher looked apologetic but offered his own explanation. 'Whenever you are under pressure, you tend to overwhelm yourself. So I thought it was better to keep you relaxed.'

'Relaxed? I was a total wreck.'

Two days later, there was a letter from Brasenose College in my pigeonhole. The dons had been delighted to meet me, they said, and were pleased to offer me a place to read politics, philosophy and economics.

I was in.

I showed the letter to the teacher. 'Well,' he said, triumphantly, 'I told you that you tend to overwhelm yourself.'

But had they admitted me on the basis of my shambolic performance at the interview?

'Yes,' he said. 'You had the best A level results of anyone in the school. That got you through the door for the interview. The rest was just the way you spoke.'

I wrote back to Brasenose accepting the offer and asking if I could now go home. Did I still need to take the exam? Unfortunately

I did, they said, the system at Oxford was that even though I had a place at Brasenose, other colleges could 'buy' me by giving me a scholarship (an award, in Oxford terms).

I didn't really give a damn about an award which only gave you the right to wear a more elaborate gown and a token sum of money (£40, if I remember correctly, every year).

So I stopped working for the exam, went out to London as much as I could, saw lots of rock concerts and had a good time. The only moment of tension came when I realized that my interview date at Oxford (to allow another college to buy me with an award) conflicted with a Paul Simon concert I had already bought a ticket to.

So I went to Oxford with my fingers crossed, hoping that nobody would want to interview me. I was lucky. No other college seemed interested so I took the train back to London and caught Simon during his Still Crazy tour.

Later, I discovered that Brasenose had already given me an award so that no other college could steal me.

It was not the life I had imagined for myself. When I went to England in 1973 to try and find a school for my A levels, I stayed once again at our flat in London. Though my relatives tried their best to keep my spirits up, it felt cold and empty. It was hard to believe that this was the place I had spent some of the happiest times of my life in.

And all of what followed was challenging. I put on a brave face but I had never imagined that at seventeen I would have to find my own school and handle my own affairs. But the thing about recognizing that you are on your own is that you grow up quickly. You realize that you have no choice.

And no matter how lonely and alone I felt I also recognized that I was incredibly fortunate. Most of my Mayo contemporaries would have done nearly anything to go to school in London and then university in Oxford. I had no real reason to feel sorry for myself.

And through it all I was very lucky. Strangers helped me in ways that I could never have imagined. Michael Hart had no reason to admit me to Mill Hill when the school was already full. My teacher had no reason to push Brasenose to interview me and then, recognizing how bad I was under pressure, to play down the importance of the interview.

It taught me a life lesson that I have tried to remember: help people even when you know they will never be able to repay you.

It was only because of help given to me by people who knew they would lose touch with me in a year or two but still put themselves out anyway that I sailed through that difficult period.

FIVE

'ISN'T THERE ANYTHING BRITISH ABOUT YOU?'

At this stage in a memoir of this sort, it is traditional to say how Oxford changed your life, or what a huge success you were: president of the union, editor of *Cherwell*, a congratulatory First, etc.

Well, sorry, but none of that was true in my case.

My life did change. But that happened during my gap year and while I was studying at Oxford—but was not actually at Oxford.

Let me explain. Because Oxbridge entrance exams were in December and the university term only began in October, you had ten months off. I spent the first part of my gap year going back to teach at Mayo. When I was a student there, many English 'school leavers' had come and taught for a term. I thought it might be nice to turn that around with an Indian school leaver and fortunately S.S.N. Ganju, who was the principal in 1976, was kind enough not just to invite me to teach but also to give me a room in his own house for me to stay.

I taught one senior class and several junior classes but somehow it is the junior classes I remember better. Periodically, these days, some elderly gent comes up to me and says something like 'Hello Sir! You taught me English!' while my friends look at me quizzically.

I was this nice old man's teacher? How old am I really?

It is too much of an effort to explain that I only taught for a term when I was nineteen and was still to go up to university. So I offer no explanation and let them come to their own conclusions. ('Is it just the hair dye? Has he had a facelift?')

28

Mayo was fun but it was the second half of the gap year that changed my life. My best friend all through school was a boy called Nikoo Bhullar (Chander Uday Singh to use his full name). Nikoo had lived in Delhi while we were at school but he had now moved to Bombay, which was home for me. We spent most of our time together when I was in Bombay on vacation and he was at HR College, which I guess, is nearly the same thing.

Nikoo's mother, Mohini Bhullar, worked for Thomson Press and when the owner started magazines (through a sister concern called Thomson Living Media) she was entrusted with looking after the Mumbai office. In late 1975, *India Today* was launched and she was asked to help out before a proper bureau chief could be found. In 1976, when I got involved, the Emergency was still on, political journalism was not possible and most established journalists did not understand the sort of writing a newsmagazine needed.

In that era, everyone tried to write like Khushwant Singh: 'I told Sanjay Khanna (I'm making up the name) that I would be in Mexico and that as our Ambassador there, he should keep my spirits up by sending over two bottles of Black Label. They were delivered the day I landed by a buxom lass from the Embassy . . .' and so on.

This style worked when Khushwant Singh did it but seemed hopelessly dated when his imitators copied it. So *India Today* found it impossible to get the right kind of contributions, ones that did not rely on buxom lasses or free booze.

In Delhi, it relied on a tiny hardcore staff of Sunil Sethi, Shirley Joshua, Dilip Bobb and Mandira Purie. But there was no one in Mumbai.

As Nikoo and I were always hanging around her house, Mohini asked us if we would like to write for *India Today*. There was no money to speak of. We would get Rs 150 for an article and between Rs 25 to Rs 50 for a small item on the 'People' page.

We had nothing to lose so we cheerfully agreed and in that period it was impossible to write about politics, so we wrote about everything else. We even wrote about the collapse of the textile industry and the boom in the garment export business. None of it was particularly interesting but I realize (in hindsight) that the best training for journalism is to try and make a dull subject sound interesting to an audience that cares as little about it as you used to before you wrote the article.

We learnt on the job by perusing back issues of *Time* and *Newsweek* and by experimenting with various opening lines that were stolen from (or inspired by) the pages of *Time*: 'It is a boom that nobody saw coming.' Or 'The collapse of the textile industry is a metaphor for the collapse of the old bania/merchant families that have dominated Indian industry for a century . . .'

There were lighter items for the 'People' page too. We wandered around studios, doorstepping movie stars and other famous people and tried to turn authors into celebrities.

By the time I was ready to go up to Oxford, I must have had something like twenty-five bylines already; not bad for a guy who hadn't even become an undergraduate yet!

Oxford had a different kind of charm. There was the sense of history, of knowing that the room you were sleeping in had been in existence for centuries and of recognizing (as I did immediately) that no matter how special you felt then, you would be out of there in three years' time and be completely forgotten.

At the dinner at which he welcomed us, H.L.A. Hart, the great legal and moral philosopher who was the principal of our college warned us, 'You think you will be here for three years and indeed you will. But never forget that an academic year at Oxford consists of three terms of just eight weeks each. For six months of the year, you won't be at Oxford!'

Others looked downcast when Hart said this but it was a bit of a Eureka moment for me. This meant that I could spend half the year in the UK pursing my studies (well, sort of, anyway) and the other six months making a life for myself.

People often ask me if I ever considered staying on in the UK given that I had a legal right to a British passport by virtue of having been born there. It is a legitimate question but the answer is an emphatic no. I always knew that India was my home. I had nothing against NRIs (three quarters of my father's family lived abroad) but I believed that I would never truly feel part of any country except India.

But being born in England did give one certain advantages. (They still do: I don't need a visa for the UK and have right of residence there). At the start of the term, when the senior tutor was getting our details, I told him that I would be paying the overseas fee (about double of the UK student's fee) because I had an Indian passport.

'We can't have that,' he said. (The dons were bitterly opposed to the overseas fee.)

'Isn't there anything British about you?' he asked.

'Well, I was born in London.'

'Great, that's all I need,' he said and put me down for the UK fee. Later, he asked to see me.

'Aren't you getting a grant from your local council?' he asked.

In those days, if you wanted to go to university, not only would the local council of the area you lived in pay your fee but they would also give you a maintenance grant to help you support yourself at university.

'I don't have a local council,' I replied. 'We gave up our flat in 1973.'

'Oh hell,' he looked disappointed. 'Any other relatives here?'

'Yes,' I responded, 'my father's sister has lived in the Midlands for over a decade.'

'Have her children ever applied for a grant?'

'No. She doesn't have children.'

'Well, she's been paying taxes for years. Time she got something back. Why don't you call her local council?'

Though I was incredibly sceptical, I got the number of the grants department at Sandwell Council, which was my aunt's local council. I called, more as a gesture than anything else.

A very nice man answered the phone. I gave him my aunt's details, told him I was born in London and that she was listed by my college as the person to call in case of emergency. (This was true but nobody ever called her.)

'Which university is it?' he asked.

'Oxford.'

His tone changed. 'Well, if it is Oxford, then it can't be a grant. It is an award.'

I was delighted by his sudden display of respect for a university I had only just joined and promised to send him the details.

Within a week, Sandwell Council had written to my college to say they would pay my fees. Another week later, a cheque arrived in my pigeonhole. And they were giving me a maintenance grant to pay my living expenses.

God Save The Welfare State!

The don who had suggested I take this route was happy and relieved. Others were, I thought, needlessly unkind.

'They probably never had anyone go to Oxford from Sandwell before,' one said. I am sure that wasn't true. I am certain that Sandwell (it is near Birmingham) sent dozens of students to Oxford every year.

I asked one of my tutors why Oxford colleges were so opposed to the overseas fee and so determined to help foreigners get grants. His answer was that a) if education is free then getting into Oxford is truly competitive. Any bright student can get in. At Harvard, on the other hand, you had to apply for financial assistance or get a scholarship. In the UK, they believed that education should be a right. (We follow the same principle in India where government-run institutions of higher learning, such as the IITs are so heavily subsidized that education is almost a fundamental right.)

And b) the tutor said, the UK was a small country of no great importance. If it could educate the global elite and ensure that the elite's reference points were British, then the relatively small amount it would spend on education/grants, etc. would be a far better investment than say its nuclear arsenal which Britain really didn't need. (In those days, Britain had over 500 nuclear warheads!)

The UK has since changed its policy on financing higher education to bring it more in line with the US. But I think the old policy was much more effective and benefitted Britain more. (Well I would say that, wouldn't I?)

You can argue about the ethics and desirability of this policy but what it meant was that apart from the money that my uncle had held in reserve for my fees, I now had extra maintenance money. And I had no fees to pay.

My education was not only free, they were paying me to study at Oxford!

What a wonderful world this could be!

SIX

THE GREAT UNDERGRADUATE
EXTRAVAGANZA

The immediate consequence of my new-found prosperity was that instead of putting my little legacy away for later use as any good Indian boy should do, I decided to spend it all.

It wasn't as stupid a decision as it may sound. My father's money had been put aside in 1971. In 1973, massive inflation hit the world economy. The inflation rate in the UK between 1971 and 1977 was 122 per cent. You could have bought quite a lot with, say, a thousand pounds in 1971. By 1977, you would have needed £2220 to buy the same amount of goods or services.

Given that I only had three years at Oxford my choice was: should I make the most of those years or should I salt the money away only to see its value decreasing year by year?

It was a no-contest.

A second question also bothered me. The vast majority of Indians I knew at Oxford were graduate students studying for MPhils or DPhils. Many of them were brilliant. But their advanced intelligence meant that they were chained to the library day and night, happy one day to land a job at the International Monetary Fund or the World Bank.

Relatively few Indians came to Oxford directly from school to have what Oxford likes to call The Great Undergraduate Experience. Now that I had the money and the opportunity, what was I going to do?

Naturally, I opted for the Oxford experience.

When I think back to my Oxford years, they seem to pass in a blur. I suppose I had already decided that as I was going to go back to India, any decisions about my future would be made there. As for Oxford, it was what H.L.A. Hart had said. You were only there for six months of the year. Might as well make the most of it! (I am not sure Hart meant it that way though.)

When I look back, I suspect that my love for food and wine developed at Oxford. At most (perhaps all) Oxford colleges, the dining room ('Hall') had an elevated section with a large table where the dons and their guests sat. This was called High Table and it was served completely different food from the swill that was served to the students. Brasenose had a reputation for the best High Table food in Oxford. But any Michelin inspector would have passed out if he had tried the student food.

Though dinner in Hall was free (included in the fee) most of my friends had too much respect for their stomachs to eat there. So we ate our way around Oxford's restaurants and bars. The European food could be good though, looking back, I am not sure we could tell. The top restaurant was The Elizabeth. I went back there some years later and thought the food was mediocre. A young French chef called Raymond Blanc had just opened his first restaurant and we didn't think much of it. In fact, Blanc went on to win two Michelin stars and become one of the UK's best chefs!

Most British students drank beer. This was generally true of Oxford undergraduates as well but I think we also drank more wine and champagne than they did at other universities. There was an Oxford tradition that, after your final exams, you would walk out into the street where your friends would be waiting with bottles of champagne. (I got very drunk after my finals though this could have been because I realized I had thrown away the First my dons had expected me to get by messing up one of my papers.)

There were innumerable dining societies and wine clubs and though Oxford had the same level of drunkenness as most other universities, at least the stuff we got legless on was Appellation Contrôlée.

You could argue that the interest in eating, drinking and living well was actually an excellent preparation for one of my later vocations: writing about food and the good life!

When I was finishing at Oxford, the tutors asked me what I would do after university. I said I already had a job in India. (More about that later.)

But why did I want to go back immediately, they persisted. Why couldn't I stay on in the West for a few years? India could wait. I responded that as I was going to be a journalist, I thought it was important that I wrote about a country I really cared for. And as much as I loved England, I didn't really care what happened to it. (This was borderline offensive but they took it with good grace.)

Why journalism? They were not giving up. Just because it came easily? Why not a career where I could make some money? Wasn't there anything else I wanted to do?

Mainly to put them off, I retorted: Yes, the music business. I wouldn't mind a job that involved rock and roll.

The tutor looked rather shocked. After all, he had just suggested things like working for the Swire Group in Hong Kong, merchant banking, etc.

'Give me a couple of days', he said.

I giggled (a little childishly in retrospect) when he left, convinced that he would now give up on me.

But Oxford never gives up.

A few days later, he was back.

Had I heard of a man called Bhaskar Menon?

Oh fuck, I said to myself. These guys have won this round.

Anyone with a serious interest in the world of music knew about Menon. He had gone to Doon School and then Oxford before joining EMI, the record company that had signed The Beatles. EMI sent him to India to run its subsidiary, the Gramophone Company, later recalling him to the global parent. In the early seventies he rescued EMI from bankruptcy with his astute management and by 1979, when this conversation took place, he was the most powerful man in the global music business.

'His background is just like yours,' the tutor said. 'I have got in touch with his tutor, you know from the days he was at Oxford, and we are going to recommend you highly.'

It was mad but it worked. Bhaskar Menon wrote me a very nice letter suggesting that I follow the path he had taken, working first for the Gramophone Company of India and then moving abroad. That December I met him in Mumbai and thought he was a remarkable man.

But as tempting as the offer seemed, I eventually turned it down.

By some co-incidence I bumped into Bhaskar Menon a few years ago at dinner at a mutual friend's house. He was good enough to remember our brief interaction which was gratifying. And he was also kind enough to say that he thought I had made the right decision. There was no record business left. Once great companies (like EMI) were now in tatters.

This was true, I said. But it looked to me like the media business was in as bad a shape. Newspapers were dying and I didn't think that TV channels would necessarily survive either.

So, all that mattered was: where would I have had more fun in the years before the collapse? London, Los Angeles or here, as a journo in India.

I thought a lot about that.

Bhaskar was right. I had made the right decision.

If I have given the impression that Oxford meant very little to me in my growing years then perhaps I'm just downplaying its impact (possibly, because so many people make such a big deal of having studied there).

In fact, I have a lot to thank Oxford for. At that time, the learning system there was two-fold. You had lectures and seminars delivered or moderated by some of the greatest minds in the world. Not only were these optional, they were also open to all.

I could attend a lecture on nuclear physics and a chemistry student could attend one on Shakespeare. In my first term I went to a few and except for the ones on moral and ethical philosophy and a few by Amartya Sen, most were hardly riveting. (Which may say more about me than it did about the lectures.) So I stopped going.

The second and more important part of the system was the tutorial principle. Each college had tutors. (Some of whom also gave lectures; being a tutor was how you got into the system and then worked your way up.) In your first year, if you studied politics, philosophy and economics, you had one tutorial in each subject every week with a don, usually alone or with one other student. Typically, the tutor would give you a subject (say 'The Prime Ministerial system should be abolished; it is turning into a Presidential system anyway').The tutor gave you a reading list, you decided whether you agreed with the proposition and then wrote an essay defending your view.

At your next tutorial, you read out your essay and the tutor took your arguments apart while you tried to argue your case. It didn't matter which side you took or what the tutor himself believed. It was the quality of the arguments themselves that mattered. By the second year, tutorials were always one-on-one, your tutor and yourself. You always called your tutor by his first name and he would try to make it convivial by producing a bottle of sherry or even whisky.

It was a great way of learning because most tutors were brilliant and you had to hold your own against them week after week. It is not surprising that so many people who read PPE go on to become politicians or journalists. (David Cameron read PPE at Brasenose with some of the same dons who had tutored me.) It's a good course for a general education—and it teaches you how to take apart any argument. (Or it just teaches you how to bullshit about anything, no matter how much or how little you know.)

I enjoyed the tutorials and the conversations with the dons. But I didn't do much work or spend too much time in the libraries. I reckoned that I would forget everything I had learned in a few years anyway. (Do you remember much of what you learnt at school or college?)

The best thing Oxford had to offer was a chance to pit my wits against great minds, to learn to analyse things the way they did, and give me an edge when it came to sophisticated thinking.

When I went up to Oxford the dons told me that I was there not to gather information but to learn how to think.

It was a nice line, I thought, but a bit of a cliché.

I was wrong. In fact the one thing I will always thank Oxford for is the order it brought to my thinking. It taught me how to cut the crap and to get to the heart of the issue.

And yes, it taught me how to think.

SEVEN

'BACKWARD RAN SENTENCES
UNTIL REELED THE MIND'

While the Oxford part of my life was coasting along, I spent the other six months of the year doing more and more journalism. By early 1977, the Emergency had ended in India, a new government was in place and the press was obsessed with the misdeeds of Sanjay and Indira Gandhi, leading to a boom in sensational political journalism.

India Today benefitted the most from this boom. Aroon Purie, who was owner-editor-publisher, decided that he would ride the boom but would handle it with responsibility and professionalism. *India Today* became more and more like an American newsweekly ('India's *Time* magazine' was what it was called by its admirers) and we were encouraged to write even more in *Time*-language. ('Backward ran sentences until reeled the mind' as Wolcott Gibbs said of the original *Time* style.)

I enjoyed it. I liked writing and I hadn't been at it for so long that I objected to having to use only one style. But many of the things Aroon insisted on were good training. ('Don't say big, say 1009.2 feet. Give details. Be specific!')

But, in the age of political journalism what was a magazine to write about from Mumbai? I begged not to have to do stories about the textile industry again. Which left films. But Aroon had killed all film gossip stories arguing that they were not suited to a great newsmagazine.

Since the model was *Time*, I decided that the best way to find
story ideas was to look at back issues of *Time* and think of stories I
could put forward. Aroon was probably doing the same thing because
he came up with many *Time*-like stories including a national survey
about sex at Indian universities. I was assigned to look at the results
submitted by the polling agency and to turn them into a cover story,
presumably on the grounds that I was the only contributor to the
magazine who was actually still at university.

When the survey, titled Sex on the Campus was turned in, it had
one dramatic revelation.

There was No Sex on Campus.

Or, to put it more accurately: the surveyors had failed to figure out
how much sex there actually was. I forget the exact numbers now but
only a few males (around 15 per cent or so) admitted to ever having
had sex. Who they were having this sex with was not clear because
only 2 per cent of the female students admitted to ever having had sex.

I protested that the survey only reflected the lies Indians told
when it came to sex. The figures for men seemed low and either the
2 per cent of sexually active women were covering more of the male
population than seemed probable, or they were lying.

You didn't need to pay lakhs to a survey agency to discover that
Indian women were prevented from being candid about sex by the
double-standards and hypocrisy of our society.

But the agency had been paid and I wrote a story that reflected
both the figures and my scepticism about them. The issue sold out
and since then *India Today* has done regular sex surveys, presumably
to the delight of their circulation managers.

If not sex, then cinema?

The big film of the era, the one that everyone was talking about
was *Satyam Shivam Sundaram*, a big-budget blockbuster being
made (largely in secret) by Raj Kapoor, the great movie mogul who
was the darling of the film trade after the superhit *Bobby* which he
had made after a series of flops.

The interest peaked when photos from the shoot location were
leaked. They showed the heroine, Zeenat Aman, wearing blouses
that revealed much more of her bosom than had ever been shown

before in Hindi cinema. Raj Kapoor got angry, sued the publication that had run the pictures and the film became the subject of even more public interest.

So, here was my idea. *Time* had done a story on the American director Stanley Kubrick while he was shooting *Barry Lyndon*. It was called 'Kubrick's grandest gamble.'

I took the issue to Aroon and suggested that we do the same sort of story on Raj Kapoor. If *Time* could do it, why couldn't *India Today*? I knew how Aroon's mind worked by then and reckoned that the *Time* parallel would do the trick.

It did.

I got the go-ahead. But as Aroon pointed out, Raj Kapoor had not spoken to anyone. Why would he speak to us?

'Because of you, Aroon,' I said and saw him wince.

There was a backstory to this. Long before he moved to Delhi, V.V. Purie, Aroon's father, had been a film financer. He had financed most of Raj Kapoor's films till he gave up on the film finance business in the sixties. Raj Kapoor, I argued, could not say no to the Puries. Aroon was sceptical but saw the point. He spoke to his father and to Mohini Bhullar and our Raj Kapoor chase began.

It was a frustrating experience because, in that pre-mobile phone era, Raj Kapoor was never available. He was always out shooting. (This was true. But he could have called back . . .)

Finally, with our deadline approaching, we had to think of a plan B. I suggested that we do a cover story on Zeenat Aman instead. She was the hottest heroine in Bollywood and was currently shooting in Bangalore with Rex Harrison for an international film called *Shalimar*. (You may not have heard of it though; it would easily win a place on any list of the Worst Films Ever Made.)

This time, I took the initiative. I called the Ashoka hotel in Bangalore where Zeenat was staying. It took only two tries and she took my call. Yes, she said. She would do an interview. But how? She had no plans to return to Bombay.

I would fly to Bangalore, I told her.

'Really? Just to interview me?' she asked, delightedly.

'Yes. Just for you.'

It is a measure of how badly off the media were in those days that the notion that a journalist would fly to Banglaore just for an interview (with the film producer not paying for the ticket) was so startling. But Aroon recognized that good journalism cost money. So I flew to Bangalore and spent two days at the Ashoka interviewing Zeenat—who, by the way, was lovely and charming.

I got back to Bombay, thrilled that we had a story only to discover that V.V. Purie had finally got through to Raj Kapoor and he had agreed to not only do the story but also to give us stills from the movie. I decided to put together a *Time* magazine–like package: the main story on Raj Kapoor, a second article on Zeenat and a guest column by Devyani Chaubal, the leading gossip columnist of the day.

I went to brief Devyani at the National Sports Club of India where she had taken a room. I imagine that she had once lived in a home of her own but for several years she had lived out of the club in a messy, slightly musty room. I never found out why.

She was clearly not in great health but eager to talk. She had known Raj Kapoor for years, she said. (Probably true.) He was a breast-obsessive. (Well, maybe.) In fact, every time he got drunk, he fondled her. In fact, just the other day . . . (I quickly commissioned the column and got the hell out of there.)

A few days later her column arrived. It led with—no surprises!— how much Raj Kapoor was obsessed with breasts. 'The giant Shiva on the wall of R.K. Studios has huge busts . . .' (I checked it out later; the Shiva had no breasts at all.)

Worse still, she thought bust meant a single breast and kept referring to right bust and left bust.

We cleaned up her copy as best as we could (she was a big name). But we were still on tenterhooks till the time the Raj Kapoor interview came through. Raj Kapoor would meet visitors in a little hut on the grounds of R.K. Studios. It was called his cottage. He would sit on a *gaddi*; cross-legged like a Russian Buddha (he was fair enough to pass for a European), drink endless cups of tea and hold forth.

I was lucky to find him in a good mood. He was witty, charming, and once he dropped his guard, quite mesmerizing because he had been everywhere, done everything and told fabulous stories.

He saw *Satyam Shivam Sundaram* in philosophical terms. 'Take a stone,' he said. 'It is just a stone. But put some religious markings on it and it becomes God. (I assume he meant a Shiv Ling.) It is how you see things that matters. You hear a beautiful voice. But only later do you discover that it comes from an ugly girl . . .'

He paused.

'Take out the thing about ugly girl,' he commanded. 'Lata will get upset.'

I knew what it was he was talking about. In the early publicity for *Satyam Shivam Sundaram*, he had declared that he had been inspired to make the movie by the contrast between Lata Mangeshkar's face and voice. She had (understandably) flown into a rage and refused to sing playback for the movie. The songs had been picturized on Zeenat and Shashi Kapoor (the hero) with other singers providing the voices. At the last minute, Raj Kapoor had met Lata (the two had a history) and she had agreed to record them leading him to wipe out the tracks they had used for the shoot.

Then he produced what we had come for: stills. The Zeenat Aman shots were even more bosom-focused than the ones that had been leaked to the press.

I pointed this out. He hummed and hawed but finally said, 'Let them come to see Zeenat's body. They will go out remembering my film.' A discussion about what Devyani Chaubal would have called 'busts' followed and the great man lapsed into Hindi, making many references to 'teetiyan', which confused me at the beginning, and then shocked me.

We had it all: a great interview, great photos and great stories. And the issue sold out in something like twenty-four hours.

India Today had discovered that it could do film stories without getting into gossip and still sell the issue out.

After that, the film cover story became a regular at the magazine (at least two or three a year).

And I, who had no real interest in Hindi movies, became the go-to guy. It was a strange balance. Eight weeks at Oxford discussing Karl Marx and Immanuel Kant. And then eight weeks of journalism about film stars and celebrities.

I guess it gave me a well-rounded perspective.

EIGHT

'MY SWEET LORD'

Once we had perfected the newsmagazine-style film story, I suggested to Aroon that perhaps we should do a director from the world of alternative Hindi cinema. At that stage, Shyam Benegal was shooting *Junoon*, set during the 1857 War of Independence for producer Shashi Kapoor, so we had a perfect peg.

Plus, I added, we could use the story for a look back at Shyam's influence on Hindi cinema. He was shooting a big-budget movie now (the battle scenes for *Junoon* were shot on a larger budget than the whole of *Ankur*, the film that made his reputation) but he had started out small, making avant-garde movies when he did not need to. (He was a top director of commercials in those days.)

Aroon thought it was a good idea but believed that we needed a question to hook the readers with. I agreed and said I was thinking of an angle. By this time, *India Today* was better known so Shyam (whom I did not know) not only agreed to the interview but, when he realized I hadn't actually seen any of his movies, hired a preview theatre and made me watch *Ankur*, *Nishant*, *Bhumika* and *Kondura* back to back. (*Kondura* may be his least known film but I have always thought it was one of his best.)

I met his regular stars, Smita Patil and Shabana Azmi (who has remained a friend to this day). And eventually I went to Jaipur where they were shooting the horse-battle scenes and, like everybody else in that era, I was swayed by Shashi Kapoor's charm.

Shashi was both producer and star and said that he was sick of making the standard Hindi movie. So he would put his own money into producing pictures with talented directors. (It was a noble idea but eventually cost him his fortune.)

The cover story turned out well but Aroon still needed a question to hook the readers. I hadn't been able to come up with one, so Aroon thought of one himself: 'Is Shyam A Sham?' it said on the cover. That wasn't what the story was really about but it might have been the right way to shift copies because the issue did very well; much better than anything about art movies and their directors was expected to do.

Not everything I did was about movies. We heard from an indiscreet lobby manager at the Taj that a really big rock star was checking in the following day. We asked the PR lady if she could set up an interview for us with 'you know, the rock guy' when he checked in.

'Oh George Harrison?' she responded. 'He has told us not to even put his name on the check-in list. He won't give you an interview.'

Nikoo Bhullar, my old friend (and Mohini Bhullar's son) and I used to work as a team those days. The Beatles had only broken up about six years ago. George Harrison was a big deal for us (though, admittedly John or Paul would have got us even more excited) and we decided that we would crack the secrecy of his India trip and get him to talk.

I found out his room number and called him. He hung up on me. I called again. Olivia Arras, his girlfriend (they later married) picked up and was polite but would not put us through to him. I called a day later. He answered but seemed annoyed (well, fair enough) and said, 'I haven't come here to do any interviews.'

I tried again the following day but instead of calling, we slipped a note under his door. We said we didn't want a why-did-the-Beatles-break-up kind of conversation. We wanted to talk about Indian music, we wrote solemnly, our noses growing longer by the minute. Just before we slipped the note under the door, I added a postscript.

'PS: I really loved Thirty Three & ⅓ (his latest album which had come out the previous month) especially This Song.'

We waited fifteen minutes and called again. This time, he answered. We asked if he had read the note. He had.

'Did you really like Thirty Three & ⅓ ?' he asked. 'How did you hear it in India?'

I lied a bit more and said that I heard it in London (well, this at least was true) and that it was his best work since All Things Must Pass. (Actually, the album was rubbish.)

I knew we had him when he said, 'What did you think of This Song?'

I knew the background. Harrison's biggest solo hit had been a song called My Sweet Lord. The chorus was clearly plagiarized from a song called He's So Fine by a girl group called The Chiffons. The original writers had sued. Harrison had lost. And This Song was his take on the episode.

It helped to be a rock nerd when you were dealing with rock stars!

I said, insincerely, that 'This Song' summed up how unfairly he had been treated in the My Sweet Lord case.

That did it. He invited Nikoo and me to his suite the next day for 'a cup of tea'.

We stayed for over an hour.

The interview would have been an achievement even if George had not said much. He had steadfastly refused to say anything much about the Beatles since the breakup of the band. But here in Bombay, thousands of miles from home, he felt free to open up.

He started on Paul McCartney whom he clearly loathed. He talked about how much money he had been cheated of during the Beatles phase. There were lots of details that seem unimportant now but mattered to rock nerds like me: What Allen Klein was really like; how Robert Stigwood ('Stiggy' he called him) had tried to take over the Beatles after Brian Epstein died but 'we told him to fuck off'. And more of that sort of stuff.

We spent ten minutes discussing the My Sweet Lord controversy. He conceded that the chorus was the same but said the plagiarism (if any) was unconscious. He felt he had been treated badly by the Court. At the end of the trial, the judge had tried to finish on a happy note and said, 'Actually, I like both songs.'

Harrison's lawyer objected. 'You just ruled it was the same song. What do you mean both songs?'

We talked about the then current music scene and he was scathing. 'David Bowie should make up his mind what sex he is before deciding what kind of music he wants to make.' On Rod Stewart: 'The guy has a brain the size of a marble.' On Pete Townshend: 'You know the guy talks about God but every time I have seen him he has just been so drunk or stoned.'

As he grew more relaxed, I ventured to ask him about his ex-wife Pattie Boyd. For years, George, Pattie and Eric Clapton had been involved in a complex relationship. George and Clapton were best friends. George and Pattie also seemed to be a happy couple: he wrote Something for her. Eric wrote Layla about a woman he was in love with but who didn't seem to love him. Then Pattie ran off with Eric and the world realized the song was about her. They became a couple and Eric wrote Wonderful Tonight for her.

George took it all rather badly and recorded a bitter cover of the Everly Brothers' Bye Bye Love with the lyrics twisted ('There goes my baby /with you know who . . .'). People speculated about what had happened but nobody was really sure. (Since then Clapton and Pattie have written autobiographies telling their sides of the story.) And here I was, all of twenty years old, listening to a Beatle telling me how his wife had cheated on him with his best friend.

It was heady stuff.

Either the guy on the desk at *India Today*'s Delhi office had no interest in music or he was an idiot (I am inclined to the latter explanation) but he was unwilling to give the interview much space. I remember Nikoo calling him up and saying angrily, 'Do you realize that George Harrison is the most globally famous person *India Today* has ever interviewed?'

Was Nikoo right, I sometimes wonder.

On balance, I think he was. Indira Gandhi was arguably more famous but she had certainly never deigned to give *India Today* an interview. And at a global level, the Beatles were much more famous.

We got some space in the magazine but most of the fun bits were lost. For many years afterwards I did not see a single interview where

George discussed the break-up of either the Beatles or his marriage. We had it all—on record—and we wasted it.

Now I console myself by recognizing that journalism is ephemeral. Does anyone care that I had one of the few interviews where a member of the Beatles discussed the break-up?

It may have mattered in 1976-77. But it probably stopped mattering a few years later. And would people in India have cared if *India Today* had run a longer interview?

I think they would have. Certainly more than they cared about the textile industry or the other things the magazine made me cover at such length.

But you win some. And you lose some.

NINE

'A LITTLE RUSSIAN BOY'

It was inevitable that at some stage I would get into some kind of political journalism. There were not that many big stories coming out of Maharashtra in those days so I usually had to contribute to national stories.

In those days, the prime minister of India was the same old Morarji Desai whom I had been brought up to despise. Morarji had been wheeled out of retirement to take over when Mrs Gandhi lost. He had already retreated to his flat on Marine Drive in Bombay when he was pulled out to become prime minister at the age of eighty-two. He was a useless prime minister (my upbringing may have biased me against Morarji), unable to keep the Janata coalition together, and in 1979 when his government collapsed, he retired to Marine Drive again and leaked government papers that he had stolen from the PMO. (More about those papers later!)

At the time, however, he was best known for two things. The first was his advocacy of prohibition. The second was his preference for drinking his own urine every day. This led to many jokes about how he had given the phrase 'getting pissed' a new meaning, etc.

India Today asked its correspondents to compile a nationwide survey of how prohibition would be rolled out. I was put on the job and discovered early in my research that Maharashtra still had a well-staffed (and one that was paid for by the taxpayer) prohibition department where several self-righteous men were supposed to tell us about the terrible effects liquor had on society.

The prohibition commissioner himself sat in a very nice office decorated with posters warning of the dangers of drink. He gave me a lecture on how there was, apparently, no such thing as social drinking or a nice glass of wine with dinner. Anyone who touched any kind of alcohol was a moral reprobate.

The prohibition commissioner was of no use so I tried my luck with the prohibition minister. (Yup. Maharashtra had a minister for this too.)

He was a young and friendly guy who said that I should interview the chief minister as well. I looked dubious. Why would Vasant-dada Patil waste his time talking to me? 'Arre, just try, na!' said the minister.

'What you do,' he added, 'is that you first ask him how bad alcohol is. After ten minutes, you say, "But Vasantdada if it is so bad, then how is it that you own an alcohol distillery yourself?"' he laughed. 'Let us see what he says.'

It was my introduction to the world of Indian politics. A minister was encouraging me, a young journalist he had never heard of from a publication he had also never heard of, to embarrass his own chief minister!

Anyhow I requested an interview with the chief minister. To my great surprise it was granted—politicians were not so inaccessible then.

I asked Vasantdada whether the Congress would support Morarji's mad scheme. 'It is not Morarjibhai's scheme,' he said. 'In 1976, it was Indiraji who had promised total prohibition in the country. It is our scheme and we will implement it.' (I looked this up. Yes, Mrs Gandhi had indeed made such a promise.)

After about ten minutes of this, I asked the question.

'Dada, if you are so convinced that liquor is bad, then why do you own a distillery yourself?'

There was only a slight and almost imperceptible change in Vasantdada's manner.

'I don't own the distillery,' he said, evenly. 'It is owned by a sugar cooperative that I am a part of.' (In actual fact, he controlled the so-called cooperative.)

'If there is prohibition, then we will close down the cooperative,' he concluded.

He continued the interview without the slightest trace of annoyance and by the time I left his office I had realized that politicians were very different for the rest of us. They had no hesitation in stabbing each other in the back. And even when they were confronted with proof of their hypocrisy, it didn't really bother them.

Obviously, I had a lot to learn.

Rajni Patel had been a friend of my father's so it was only natural that I would tap him for stories. He was unfailingly polite and helpful (I later discovered that he did his best to help everyone). His political trajectory had been unusual. He was a freedom fighter who became a communist and then later, became a major figure in the Progressive Lobby. He was close to the Russians, and as a great Progressive, had been a supporter of Krishna Menon.

My father's progressivism did not extend to much Russian love (he never once visited a single Soviet Bloc country in my lifetime despite his global travel). His only Russia story had to do with visiting Moscow as a young CPI activist in a delegation led by S.A. Dange, the greatest CPI leader of all time.

Late one night, he recalled, a group of secret policemen arrived at the building where the Indians were staying.

'Which one of you is Dange?' they asked.

Dange told them who he was.

'Put your clothes on, quickly,' they told him rudely.

Dange hurriedly slipped into some formal clothes before he was frog-marched out of the building, while the CPI delegation looked worried. Would they ever see Dange again?

A few hours later, the same men brought Dange back. The Indian contingent looked concerned but Dange was ecstatic.

'Comrade Stalin had sent for me,' he said proudly.

After he had fallen out with the CPI, which he felt (perhaps unfairly) took its orders from the Kremlin, my father had as little to do with Indo-Russian friendship as was possible in Progressive circles.

The one memory I have of a Soviet-related event was a dinner thrown at a flat on Marine Drive (I think it belonged to Dr Baliga; a noted Progressive of that era) for Yuri Gagarin, the first man in space. Nobody had invited me but I insisted on attending and my mother dressed me in silly clothes (a bandi, a cap, etc.). Then my father coached me. The chief guest's name was Yuri Gagarin not, as I kept saying, Urine Gagarin.

I have dim recollections of the dinner. Gagarin wore military uniform, shook hands bemusedly with many Soviet-lovers and was surprised to see a young boy there. He knelt down and asked in Hindi '*Kyon Captaan! Kya haal hai?*' Obviously he had been well coached in PR. (And Hindi.)

We left before dinner was served because I had to get to bed. On my way out, we ran into a gaggle of excited fans who wanted to shake hands with the first man in space. Gagarin was still upstairs so they contented themselves with calling out to whoever left the dinner.

As I passed, a woman called out, 'Oh look! A little Russian boy! Is that Russian dress? So sweet.'

I went home humiliated and told my mother that I would never ever wear her idea of appropriate dress again.

And that's pretty much all I know about Indo-Russian friendship and Urine Gagarin.

Rajni Patel had also left the CPI but, unlike my father, he was a friend of Russia. He was already Bombay's leading lawyer when his moment came. From 1966 or so Indira Gandhi's political strategy had been largely determined by P.N. Haksar, a former diplomat with a strong leftist streak (and the man who had helped organize my parents' wedding). Haksar, Mohan Kumaramangalam and many other leftists and former communists were allies of Indira Gandhi.

When Mrs Gandhi split the Congress in 1969, the Progressives were delighted. Years of having to distinguish between Good Congressmen and Bad Congressmen were finally over.

Mrs Gandhi's (mostly bogus) rationale for the split was the answer to any Progressive's prayers.

The party had been hijacked by bosses (like Morarji Desai) and had become corrupt and was in thrall to big business, she said. She was breaking free of them to implement a socialist agenda which included nationalizing India's largest banks and imposing more regulations on business. The rich had it easy for too long. Now it was time for the poor to benefit.

It was all very leftist without being communist. Her policies condemned the neo-colonialism of the West but took care to do so in good English. Best of all, she echoed the Progressive line that Nehru (and therefore his daughter) was wonderful while the Congress's senior leaders were evil.

Left without an organization (which went with the other faction of the Congress run by the senior leaders she had denounced), Indira Gandhi looked around for new organizers and new advisers.

Mrs Gandhi had known Rajni Patel for years and when she came up against the old Congress establishment in Maharashtra (which hated her), she turned to Rajni Patel to re-organize the new Congress unit. His title was President of the Bombay Pradesh Congress Committee (BPCC) but because he had Mrs Gandhi's ear, he soon became one of India's most powerful men.

All went well, till the Emergency when Sanjay Gandhi took over.

Sanjay hated his mother's advisors. Too many of them were 'Commies', he said. And he hated 'Commies'. I don't think Sanjay ever had an evolved ideological world view so it has been suggested that his hatred of 'Commies' may have originated in his desire to separate his mother from her closest (left-leaning) advisors. So great was Sanjay's malign influence on his mother that one by one, they were all dropped. In the case of Haksar, the man who had created the Indira Gandhi of legend, his family was actually humiliated.

By the time I reconnected with Rajni Patel, Mrs Gandhi had lost the 1977 election and Patel was trying to help put the Congress together again without her. Because he was both a criminal lawyer and a politician, you met everyone at the Cuffe Parade flat he had converted into an office. (He lived in Worli.)

It was there that as a young journalist I first met Sharad Pawar, many union ministers and the top criminals of that era: Haji

Mastaan, Yusuf Patel and Datta Samant. (Though notionally Datta Samant was a trade union leader.) Of all the politicians I met with Rajni Patel, Sharad Pawar made the strongest impression. He was young at the time (in his thirties) but exuded authority. He rarely said very much but you had the sense that he missed nothing.

And he was totally pragmatic. He broke a Congress government in Maharashtra to tie up with the opposition Janata and become chief minister. And yet, because you always expected him to do these things, nobody held it against him. I had the sense that it did not matter which party Pawar was in, he would always be in it for himself and would know how to get people to follow him. Almost every other Maharashtra politician I met at the time is now forgotten. But Pawar continues to be a major figure with no need to follow the dictates of any party other than his own.

It was through Patel and the people he introduced me to that I began to understand a little more about the Maharashtra political scene.

I made one other unlikely pal: Bal Thackeray.

The Shiv Sena had been created by Thackeray to fight for the rights of Maharashtrians in Bombay. But its creation had been blessed by the Congress bosses of that age: V.P. Naik, S.K. Patil, etc. It served the Congress in two ways. One, it beat up Malayalis who wanted to vote for Krishna Menon (who was fighting the Congress candidate) in the 1967 General Election. And two, it battled the communist trade unions in north Bombay's industrial belt where their influence was growing.

Thackeray's politics were an anathema to me. Part of this was personal. He thought that Gujaratis controlled too much of Bombay's wealth, and would routinely urge Maharashtrians to fight us. And part of it was political: how could you not condemn somebody who believed in violence and spread sectarian feeling?

None of that changed over the years.

But somehow, we got along. I had dinner at his home several times, we joked about his politics and I discovered to my horror that he was one of the few politicians I enjoyed spending time with!

This had something to do with his ability (rarely credited) to talk to people of all ages in the same way. Even when I was in my early twenties he treated me exactly as he would a senior editor. He was also able to detach himself from his politics and take jokes at his own expense.

For instance, he was old school enough to see you to your car if you had dinner with him. Just before you closed the car door he would say, matter-of-factly 'Jai Maharashtra'.

To tease him I would often respond 'Jai Gujarat'.

He would laugh and eventually we agreed on a compromise: 'Jai Mumbai.'

When people write about Thackeray they also miss how important his identity as a cartoonist was to him. Walt Disney was his idol. I remember meeting him (in 1980, I think) after he had just returned from a holiday in America. The high spot of his trip, he said, had been a visit to Disneyland.

'We met them all,' he said, 'Mickey, Goofy, Donald! It was wonderful!'

None of this is to support the kind of politics he favoured. But he was a much more complex man than many people seem to think.

TEN

'THERE IS A MAN IN A 'DOE-TEE' AT RECEPTION'

As my journalistic career with *India Today* chugged along in eight-week intervals, Aroon began to consider expanding. Just as *India Today* had successfully adapted the *Time* magazine format to Indian conditions, Aroon wondered if the same could be done for *New York* magazine. Why not start a city magazine for Bombay?

It was a good idea and Mohini Bhullar who handled marketing for the group was asked to develop the concept. She saw an immediate potential because more and more advertisers wanted to place ads in colour and were short of options. A Bombay city magazine would allow them to target higher income readers. (Just as *New York* was aimed at Manhattan, *Bombay* would be aimed at south Bombay.)

Together, Aroon and Mohini hired an editor, Minhaz Merchant (a bright young journalist from the *Times*), and he was put to work to think of ideas. I did my own thing at *India Today*. I still had over a year to go at Oxford and promised to help Minhaz with the project.

When I next returned to India, Mohini told me that there had been a change of plan. Minhaz would now be *India Today*'s bureau chief and I would be the editor of *Bombay*.

I had been a journalist (of sorts) for less than two full years and still had a long time to go before I took my finals at Oxford. No matter, Mohini said, I could start hiring a team and planning the magazine now. I was due to be back in June/July having earned my degree and we could publish the first issue the fortnight after I came back. In the interim I could get the issues ready during my vacations from university.

It was a slightly bizarre situation that left everyone a little unsettled. Minhaz soon left to head a publishing empire of his own (The Gentleman group). Aroon said that I would be called managing editor. In those days, *India Today* followed the *Time* magazine principle. There was one editor-in-chief whose name appeared on every masthead. Individual magazines were run by managing editors. At *Time*, the editor-in-chief was on par with the CEO. At *India Today*, Aroon was both editor and owner so parity was not a problem.

Whom would I report to? I asked. Well, the editor-in-chief, of course, like all editors, he said.

But what of Mohini? Well, she became editorial director, a post created for her which allowed her to handle the business side as well as get involved in the editorial. This was clearly not an arrangement with as much clarity as we needed but it worked because Mohini and I were close and she told me how she had gone out on a limb to push my candidacy over Minhaz's (who had already been promised the job). So I was hardly in a position to demand clarity.

For the first year or so, the arrangement worked well. We designed a format that borrowed liberally from *New York* magazine, with a first section that had lists of restaurants, movies, plays and other things. Unlike *New York*, we varied them from issue to issue, reviewing new books, different restaurants and even records.

I wrote most of this section every issue: books, restaurants, records, English movies, etc. It was often the most reader-friendly part of the magazine and probably the most controversial because we were consistently rude about everything.

Nobody in India had ever been nasty about hotel restaurants before.

We went for the Oberoi at Nariman Point saying how bad the coffee shop food was. Ragini Kakkar, the smart Marketing Manager, took it in the right spirit, got the restaurant to redo many dishes and the next time I went (our office was also at Nariman Point), she came to the restaurant to check what I thought of the changes. This sounds normal now but in that era, it was unheard of. I thought then that Ragini would go far and she did. She headed all of the Oberoi Group's PR & marketing before leaving to do the same job at Jet Airways. (She became Ragini Chopra after she married a naval officer.)

I always assumed that nobody read the book reviews (they were two para blurbs anyway) and so I went a little berserk. A big local Mumbai celebrity of the time was Dr Rusi Dastur who spat out popular medicine paperbacks of a generally trashy quality every year. I was scathing in my review of his latest book: 'Hard work never killed anyone, as Dr Dastur points out in this book. But clearly he is taking no chances judging by the sloppiness with which this book has been put together . . .'

A month or so later, I bumped into a man in a safari suit at a dinner thrown by Rajni Patel. 'Do you know Rusi Dastur?' he asked genially.

Dr Dastur eyed me warily.

In an effort to make conversation I asked, 'Are you the Dr Dastur who writes all those books?'

'Which you review,' he responded shortly.

No further conversation was possible.

We had a lot of fun in the *Bombay* magazine days. All kinds of people would drop in. We were only a few months old when one of the very nice (but somewhat snobbish) Goan Christian secretaries came to my office and whispered, 'There is a man in a dhoti asking for you at reception.' (She pronounced it doe-tee so I had to get her to repeat what she had said.)

I went out to find Subramanian Swamy sitting near the reception desk. I had never met Swamy but he was an MP from Bombay and already nationally famous.

When I had taken him in and found him a chair, Swamy explained why he was here. Sharad Pawar had told me, in an interview, that nobody took Swamy seriously. Now Swamy wanted right of reply. Would I refuse it? Swamy demanded. Was I being nice to Pawar only because he was Chief Minister and Swamy was only an MP?

Not at all, I said. Would Swamy like a guest column? He would and the following fortnight, much to Pawar's disdain ('Why are you wasting time on that fellow?') we ran Swamy's guest column: 'Maharashtra needs a Pawar-cut'. (It would get one soon.)

On another occasion just after Zeenat Aman alleged that she had been assaulted at a party by friends of Sanjay Khan's wife (and also disclosed that Sanjay and she had been married), Sanjay turned up unannounced at the office. (Neither Mohini nor I knew him well.) Zeenat was lying, he said, and spent two hours giving us his version of the relationship which involved famous Bombay industrialists and serial infidelity.

Smita Patil stormed in once to complain about a small item on the People page which insinuated that she was having an affair with Vinod Khanna. (She was, so we didn't know what to say.)

We wanted *Bombay* to be like *New York* where you could have the Mayor on the cover one week and Candice Bergen the next. It was a difficult balance but I think we pulled it off.

The film business began to take us seriously. I remember covering Rishi Kapoor's wedding where the groom sat on a horse and took large gulps from a bottle of Black Label whisky while Raj Kapoor and his son, Daboo chased away gate crashers. (Years later, I had lunch with Rishi Kapoor and his son Ranbir before our session at the HT Summit. I reminded him of the wedding and he began the session by saying that 'Kapoors are supposed to have blue eyes and black hair. I don't have blue eyes. So I have Black Label.')

I did a story on *Qurbani* and Feroz Khan invited me home. He was regarded (by *Stardust* at least) as being the most anglicized and sophisticated star in the industry. He lived up to his image when he welcomed me to his house and offered me a drink ('I have a choice of champagnes') and spoke throughout in an Americanized drawl that I couldn't quite place. All went well till he discussed motor racing and his film (*Apradh* or something, I think it was called) which was about racing. 'I just love grand pricks,' he drawled languidly.

It took me a second to work out what he was talking about.

There were lots of older stars too. Dilip Kumar was back on form, making *Kranti* for Manoj Kumar and as is always the case with him, rising above the script and the movie. (I might be biased because of my childhood connections.) Dev Anand's career had revived with

Des Pardes, released around the same time as Raj Kapoor's *Satyam Shivam Sundaram* ('It is a dirty film,' Dev said solemnly about *Satyam Shivam*. 'Did you notice how the camera kept focusing on Zeenat's body? Dirty!')

But *Des Pardes* had been followed by flop after flop after flop mainly because Dev directed the movies himself and believed that the perfect shot was a close-up of his own face, bent slightly to one side while he twinkled (or leered) into the lens.

At a personal level though, he was immensely likable (if unreasonably obsessed with seeming young) and did not have the arrogance of other stars. After Janata collapsed, he tried to get the film industry to form its own political party saying to me (I was twenty-three at the time) that 'We young people must get together!' (He was fifty-six.)

The star of our journalistic involvement with the movies was, of course, Raj Kapoor. I remember going back at least thrice to that 'cottage' at R.K. Studio and sitting late into the night as he narrated anecdote after anecdote: how smart and fashionable Nargis had been. How, unlike today's heroines, she had brains and class. How of his kids, Daboo had got used to him but Rishi was still scared of him. How Rajesh Khanna had come to see him along with Dimple to say that they could star in *Satyam Shivam Sundaram* together. How much he hated the cinema of the 1970s with its angry young men and its plots about smugglers and policemen. How overrated Satyajit Ray was. ('Unlike him I don't make films for the New York film critics.') How he had no real affinity with communism though he was such an icon in the USSR. ('They buy my films. So I like them. Nothing more.')

I've met lots of movie figures since then but Raj Kapoor was different. He really was the Last Mogul.

ELEVEN

'DON'T SING SO CLOSE TO ME'

I came back to my office at *Bombay* magazine after lunch one day to find a message asking me to call Miles Copeland back. I knew of two Miles Copelands. One was a former CIA officer who had written a book about his time at the agency. The other was his son who managed rock bands including Squeeze and, most famously, the Police.

The Police were kind of special for me. In my last months at Oxford in the summer of 1979 I had fallen in love with a song called Roxanne. It was by a new band, The Police, and I was blown away both by the song, and the album it was on, titled Outlandos d'Amour. It was unlikely that their manager would be in Bombay just as their new album Reggatta de Blanc was at number one all over Europe (I had reviewed it for the records section at the front of the book that fortnight) and two massive hit singles had been pulled from it: Message in a Bottle and Walking on the Moon.

The caller was either the author-spy promoting some new book or my secretary had just got the name wrong. The phone rang again. It was Miles Copeland calling from his room at the Taj.

I took the call and knew in seconds which Copeland it was. 'I really liked your review of the album,' a loud (but young) American voice said. 'You got a minute?'

You bet!

I rushed over to the Taj to meet Miles Copeland who told me his tale of woe. The Police were now the best-selling band in the UK.

They needed to do something different. So they were embarking on a world tour of unlikely places like Cairo and Bombay. (Cynics said it was a tax dodge; they needed to spend time out of the UK to avoid being taxed there—as I later heard.)

The problem was that Miles had no idea how to organize a concert in Bombay. He had asked the hotel to send him to some 'local radio stations'. The bemused guy at reception at the Taj had sent him to Akashvani Bhavan.

This was not what he had expected at all and after realizing that nobody there had heard of The Police, he had asked if they at least knew any concert promoters. The babus at Akashvani consulted with their friends and told him that the Times and Talents Club organized Western music shows. But they didn't know how Miles could get in touch with the club.

Back at the hotel, he picked up some local magazines, saw my review in *Bombay* and realized with a start there was at least one person in Bombay who loved The Police. So he called *Bombay* magazine and here we were.

The problem was that I couldn't think of any rock concert promoters in Bombay in 1981 either. So I took him to the Times and Talents Club after all. This was an organization run by well-off and kind Parsi ladies (average age: sixty-five) who organized shows by Zubin Mehta and other classical artists.

Forget about The Police; I doubt if they knew who the Beatles were. But as I told Miles, they had experience of organizing shows, so they knew what official permissions were needed. They were also a charitable organization so they would put the profits to good use. (The Police were performing for free.) Miles said okay, and asked me to liaise with these nice old ladies.

The day after Miles left, I went for lunch at Victory Stall, the café the Time and Talent Club used to run by the Gateway of India. The ladies had invited Niranjan Jhaveri of Jazz India. Niranjan had been organizing the very successful Jazz India festivals every year at Rang Bhavan, a smallish open-air space near St. Xavier's College so he was less fazed than the ladies by the prospect of preparing for the show.

It will be loud, I told them. It's The Police after all.

Niranjan thought I was talking about the Bombay Police and the restrictions they placed on noise levels and promised to talk to them. 'I know the police,' he said.

Er, he didn't really, I pointed out.

After a lot of back and forth, I managed to explain to Niranjan that The Police was the name of a rock band and I was not referring to the local hawaldar.

The whole thing seemed jinxed but somehow between Niranjan and the Time and Talent ladies we managed to get the venue, get the permissions and then coordinate with The Police's advance team.

The Police flew in a few days before the show. Having done all the dirty work of helping organize the concert, I had no intention of not getting my money's worth. So I stuck to them like a leech, making myself comfortable in their large suite at the Taj and chatting with them.

By far the nicest of the lot was Stewart Copeland, Miles's brother and the founder of the band. Stewart had stories to tell about his Dad's CIA days and we chatted about music.

Andy Summers, the oldest member, was a jobbing guitarist who had struck it lucky with The Police. He was built like a little jockey and was nice enough but not very interesting.

Even in those days, the star was Sting. In later years, he became a frequent visitor to India, read widely about the country, did Yoga and (according to one, possibly jokey, interview he gave) took up Tantric sex.

On that trip, however, India seemed like a strange and unfamiliar place to him and on his second day in Bombay, he declared, 'India needs the British back.' He was being deliberately provocative but obviously I was not going to let him get away with that sort of remark.

'And what would you have been during the Raj, Sting?' I asked.

'There wasn't much call for working-class boys from up North in those days,' I said. 'You would have been as badly off as the rest of us while the toffs ruled India.'

He laughed that one off. But it seemed to me that he was both bright and opinionated.

At that stage, he sort of got along with the Copelands. But in later years he took to attacking Miles for his greed and his politics (which were very objectionable anyway) and relations between Stewart and him got so bad that The Police broke up.

One famous story about the band's later years had it that Stewart got so fed up of Sting prancing around the stage during shows that he had printed on his drums 'Fuck off, you c..t' to ensure that Sting stayed far away.

I have no idea if the story is true but there was no doubt that even then, Sting was deeply charismatic, massively talented and hugely annoying.

I have seen him live twice in the years that followed but nothing has ever topped the energy he brought to that little stage in Rang Bhavan when The Police played in Bombay.

Many other rock stars have come to Bombay in the years that followed (including the Stones) and now that India is part of the global touring circuit, the innocence and novelty of that first Police show has faded.

I can think of only one other show (I think it was in 1982) that matched the innocence of The Police concert. I was called by somebody to say that there was an English rock band called The Boom Rat Tails performing in Bombay that weekend. But they were stuck at the Sea Rock Hotel in Bandra and were bored out of their skulls. Would I like to show them a bit of Bombay?

I knew about the band, of course. They were called The Boomtown Rats (not Rat Tails or whatever) and had been part of the Irish New Wave that emerged along with the punks in England in 1976-77. They had a huge number one hit (I Don't Like Mondays) and were, as far as I knew, still relatively successful.

I called the hotel and asked for the lead singer, whose name I knew.

Bob Geldof answered in a strong Irish accent, was delighted that the phone had rung and asked if I could drop in and see him at once. I did and we had a long chat before he asked if I could take him to south Bombay the next day.

I did and we had a fun-filled day. He was accompanied by Johnnie Fingers, his keyboard player who came wearing his pyjamas.

I showed them the Gateway of India, built to welcome a British King ('focking English!' Bob spat out) the Royal Bombay Yacht Club ('focking British Empire') and then The Sea Lounge at the Taj ('focking English—' Er, no Bob, this was built by Indians . . .).

Fingers played the piano at both places. At the Sea Lounge, he played the famous intro to 'I Don't Like Mondays' and at The Yacht Club, he played, as a way of spitting on our common oppressors (or so I imagine), a version of 'Rule, Britannia!' ('focking song').

The concert was fun though nowhere in the league of The Police.

'Did we get a bigger crowd than them?' Bob asked.

I hummed and hawed. (Obviously they hadn't.)

'Focking c..ts' (I think he meant The Police not the audience.)

I never thought I would hear of him again but in 1984 he organized the Band Aid single ('Do They Know It's Christmas') and the following year's Live Aid concert.

In 2007, Bob returned to India to address the HT Summit. I reminded him of our encounter in Bombay. He remembered the show and his trip to the Gateway through regrettably I appeared to have faded out of his memory.

No matter.

At the dinner that ends the first day of the Summit, we found ourselves on the same table as Sonia Gandhi. Bob was determined to engage her in conversation. 'So Sonia,' he began, 'what are you stuffing your face with?'

Sonia Gandhi, who was not used to being spoken to like this, managed a polite smile.

But Bob was undeterred. 'So, which part of Italy are you from?' he asked. Relieved that the conversation had moved on from her 'stuffing her face', she responded with details. And the conversation continued happily till Sonia Gandhi asked me, sotto voce, in Hindi, 'Kaun hai yeh aadmi?'

She knew who Bob Geldof was, of course, but had not recognized him.

At that dinner I told him that I would be chairing his session the next day. Did he have any idea what he wanted to talk about?

'No', he said. 'I just make up this shit as I go along.'

In fact he was very good during his session and even told the audience that he remembered me dancing near the stage during the Rats concert. (I was dancing in the front but in truth he had no recollection of my being there at all. Still it was a nice gesture!)

If you had told me in 1980–81 that Sting and Bob would still be household names forty years later, I would never have believed you!

TWELVE

'DO YOU THINK I AM SHORT?'

Part of the *Bombay* magazine formula was a dose of politics. At first we tried to go hyper local and did a series called 'Know Your MLA' written in a droll, cynical style based, I think, on my years as a devotee of the British satirical magazine, *Private Eye*. The series was hugely enjoyable and popular but two of the MLAs (many of whom were worthless, crooked layabouts) sent us legal notices. This made us pause.

Should we write about more important state-wide issues? If nothing else, no one would sue us. We were a big deal for MLAs who were hardly ever written about but the chief minister did not care about a little magazine like *Bombay*.

That's how we started doing interviews with the likes of Sharad Pawar and Bal Thackeray both of whom were extremely accessible to us. When Bal Thackeray announced that he wanted Bombay to be renamed Mumbai, I phoned him. He had to make the request to the Centre, and was pretty sure that the chief minister (Pawar) would oppose it. It will never happen, he said.

I was sceptical. In covering politics I had discovered that the impossible soon becomes very possible. Bal Thackeray was leery. 'Even if it happens,' he laughed. 'You can still call your magazine *Bombay*.'

As relaxed as Thackeray could be, he also had an angry streak. Time-Life books, then a well-known publisher of coffee table books, published a book called *Bombay*. It had dull, not very attractive photos (odd because this was a photo book) and text allegedly written by Dom Moraes. Parts of the book did read like Moraes had written them: bits about his childhood, anecdotes about his friend J.R.D. Tata (described as having a face like a Kestrel), a bit about the Shiv Sena, etc.

Most of it, however, was written in a bland, info-packed but largely unreadable style. Moraes had already been paid (I suspect) so he did little to promote the book. Asked by the press about the text, he shrugged. 'It is a Time-Life book.' Asked about the photos, he was matter of fact. 'If you send a photographer here during the monsoon months, what do you expect?'

In private, he was more critical of the book. 'It was a nightmare,' he said. 'The worst experience of my life.'

When he handed in his text, Time-Life said that there wasn't enough about Bombay and too much about Dom. I was familiar with his writing during that period and despite his great talent, the average article went something like this: 'As I sat down in the barber's chair at the grand old Taj Mahal Hotel, the barber looked at me closely and said, 'How are you Dommie baba. You know I used to cut your father's hair. He was a real gentleman . . .' And so on.

This was good autobiographical stuff but hardly right for a book on a city. According to Dom, Time-Life called him to London where their researchers were at work, trying to make sense of the city of Bombay. 'They had a huge map of the city on the wall,' he complained, 'and they kept asking me about Malad and Versova, places I had never heard of.'

Eventually, various Time-Life writers rewrote the book, restricting Moraes's text to less than one-third of the final version. Dom needed the money, so he cashed the cheque but he did very little to promote the book.

It would have sunk without a trace had Bal Thackeray not suddenly launched an agitation against it. I could find nothing objectionable about the book so I questioned the Shiv Sena spokesmen closely about a) what they were complaining about and b) how they had managed to read this deathly dull book.

It turned out they hadn't read the book but they had looked at a few of the photos. One picture showed two labourers sleeping close together in a communal sleeping area.

'How they can show these two *bhaiyyas* as homos?' a Shiv Sena spokesman demanded. I responded that all over Bombay people often had to sleep in close proximity and it had nothing to do with sex. Besides, how could he tell from the photo that they were *bhaiyyas*?

The spokesman withdrew from the conversation but the agitation went on. Finally, one evening at Matoshree, Thackeray's home, I asked him why he was so angry about the book. He didn't say very much.

Then, he suddenly looked me in the eye and asked: 'Do you think I am short?'

He was around my height (that is, not very tall but average height for India). So I said that no, he was not short.

His face transformed with rage. His voice rose as he demanded: 'Then why this bloody Moraes has said in his book that I am short?'

So that was what it was about.

I went back home and picked out the book. In one of the few paras clearly written by Dom, Thackeray had been described as a caricature fascist: a little man with a complex.

Knowing Dom it was a safe assumption that the nearest he had got to Thackeray was to see a mug shot in some newspaper. Never overburdened by the need for research, he had decided to write up Thackeray as a shorty whose height made him feel inadequate.

The problem was that Thackeray was unwilling to say that the whole agitation against the book was about his height. And Time-Life, who had made many attempts to get through to him, were never told what the real issue was.

A few years later I ran into Dom at dinner at a mutual friend's home in Bandra. I told him the Thackeray story and he seemed totally uninterested. As far as he was concerned, the *Bombay* book was no longer on his mind. Still we had an enjoyable dinner, till he suddenly rounded on me.

'You were editor of *Bombay*?' he snarled. 'Weren't you?'

I admitted that this was indeed the case.

'Did you write the review of my book on Mrs Gandhi?'

Oh fuck, I thought to myself. Another of those bloody anonymous reviews at the front of the book!

'Did you think you were working for a good magazine?' he demanded.

I responded that it was okay enough, I thought.

'It was not! How could a fool like you dare to review my book?'

The review had been a hatchet job mainly because I suspected Dom had made up much of it, confining his research to as far as a bottle of Scotch could take him.

His wife, Leela Naidu, then rushed up to us. 'Oh Dommie,' she cajoled, 'Don't be like that. These people have to write these reviews you know!' (I thought this was actually more offensive than anything Dom had said but my hosts were looking alarmed so I let it go.)

'This is India,' Dom announced to the whole room. 'I have to live here and be thought foolish by fools.' The last bit was delivered while pointing directly to me.

I was more shocked by the outburst than angry and, in an effort to get our hosts to relax, moved to another side of the room and avoided Dom.

Half an hour later Dom came up to me. I steeled myself, wondering how I would respond to the next attack. But he was all sweetness and light.

'Do you live in town?' he asked.

'Yes,' I said.

'Where?'

'Carmichael Road.'

'Oh, can we hitch a ride with you? We live in Colaba so if he drops us off on Peddar Road, we will take a cab the rest of the way.'

I guess something of my nice middle-class upbringing kicked in and I said, 'Oh, not at all Dom! We'll drop you to Colaba. It's only slightly out of our way.' (It was actually twenty minutes, not exactly a short delay.)

'Thanks,' he said.

And so we drove to Colaba having a friendly conversation all along the way. It was as though the outburst had never happened.

Those were strange times. Though I shared an easy, jokey relationship with Bal Thackeray, whom my liberal friends regarded as the devil's ambassador on earth, I was also pals with Rajni Patel and knew Sharad Pawar well.

Then, Indira Gandhi won the election and installed A.R. Antulay as chief minster. This provoked angry reactions in Maharashtra mainly because he was the state's first Muslim chief minister. In those days, unlike today, people were not openly communal so the references to his religion were dog-whistled. (Sharad Pawar called him the new Aurangzeb, for instance.)

It also became clear that he was the choice of the thug-like Sanjay Gandhi, Indira Gandhi's second son. Despite the terrible rap he now gets in accounts of that period, I don't think he was that bad a chief minister.

Some of the things he did were reprehensible. Rajni Patel had devoted his entire life to creating a complex called the Nehru Centre dedicated to furthering Panditji's dream of developing a scientific temper in India. Sanjay told Antulay to have Patel thrown out of the Centre (Sanjay had nothing to gain; it was just that he enjoyed seeing those he hated parted from the things they loved). Various trustees of the Centre were called, threatened and cajoled till finally Rajni stepped down.

But equally, he was the first chief minister who seemed to really care about Bombay and tried to plan for the future of the city. One of these efforts led to his downfall. In those days, cement was a scarce commodity, allotted by the state government. Inevitably, this led to the growth of a black market and babus and politicians made lakhs allocating cement.

Antulay had a bright idea. He would end the black market. Anybody who wanted cement had to agree to make a charitable donation to trusts he had set up. There was an informal price list for what you donated in return for a bag of cement. There was never any suggestion that these were bogus trusts or that Antulay was pocketing the money. He could have just stuck to the old system and accepted payoffs in cash if he had been motivated by greed.

But there was now, as the Bombay High Court pointed out, a clear quid pro quo. The donations were made by cheque and there was a public record. If you matched the donations to the cement allocations, it was not difficult to work out what was going on.

The media went crazy. Antulay was cornered. Sanjay was dead and Mrs Gandhi did not want to protect him. He was forced out of office and a buffoon called Babasaheb Bhosale was installed in his place.

At the time, I went along with the media consensus. (In my next job we even printed documents that, we said, showed what a crook Antulay was.) But now I wonder, was Antulay really that guilty? Yes there was a quid pro quo. But wasn't it better to have scarce cement allotted on the basis of openly recorded charitable donations than through bribes?

Antulay would have survived if Sanjay had lived. But Sanjay's sudden death had changed everything.

What had happened was this. Mrs Gandhi's friend, Swraj Paul, had gifted Sanjay a two-seater stunt plane. Each morning, Sanjay would fly it over the heavily populated areas of Delhi. He always flew recklessly and one day, he crashed over Willingdon Crescent. He was killed instantly and so, unfortunately, was his co-pilot, a professional from the flying club.

Mrs Gandhi was heartbroken but much of India breathed a sigh of relief. Sanjay had become a power unto himself, a petty vindictive dictator with the intellectual sophistication of a very spoilt ten year old.

I had to make calls asking for quotes for the obituary. Antulay wept but other Congressmen were secretly delighted. By then, my best political friend (eventually our friendship would transcend politics and last till the end of his life) was Murli Deora, a Congressman who had stuck by Mrs Gandhi when she was down and out but whom Sanjay hated, presumably because Murli had once been close to Rajni Patel.

In those days, there was no news TV so for hours after Sanjay had crashed, even politicians did not know that he was dead. Many of the politicians I called heard the news from me for the first time.

I told Murli I needed a quote for the obituary. He was surprised to hear the news. '*Mar gaya saala*?' he asked. Yes, I said, he was dead.

'Ok,' he said, his voice growing solemn, 'Write down this. Shri Sanjay Gandhi was a dynamic youth leader who leaves a void . . .'

It was pretty much the same with everyone else I called.

THIRTEEN

THE ANGRY MIDDLE-AGED MAN

Within a few months of its launch, *Bombay* was a success. This was a heady feeling for nearly everyone involved though personally I wondered a little bit about my own future. Had I really gone to Oxford to study PPE to come back and run a glossy magazine?

This was, I told myself, a silly and snobbish view. I had become a journalist. This meant that I treated a story about Manmohan Desai with the same care and effort as a story about Morarji Desai.

But as these doubts came and went, I told Aroon that I wanted to do more writing for *India Today* even though the magazine now had a full-fledged Bombay bureau of its own.

He was kind enough to agree. I did a few stories, some of which still linger in my memory. The Janata Party, created to fight the Congress in 1977, had reacted to its electoral victory by collapsing messily while in office. The Charan Singh faction had left. So had the old socialists, most of them claiming that their departure was now inevitable because the Jan Sangh component owed loyalty to the RSS and not to the greater Janata Party.

This was partly true and in the 1980s, after Mrs Gandhi was back in office, the Jan Sangh component decided to hold a convention in Bombay to plan its future. It was clear what would happen: they would reunite the old Jan Sangh but would give it a new name with the blessings of the RSS.

I covered the convention and spent my time hanging out with as many top Jan Sanghis as I could. They were, it must be said, nothing like the poisonous RSS fascists that the Left warned us about. In many ways, they were no different from all the other cow-belt politicians I had met. Nobody said a word against Muslims. Instead they all cursed Charan Singh for betraying the spirit of the Janata Party.

The convention itself, held in a temporarily constructed shamiana-city in the Bombay suburbs, was well organized and good natured. There was free vegetarian food for all and the conventioneers were clean and disciplined, picking up their own litter and queuing up whenever they were asked to.

A few months later I would cover another convention in Bombay, one organized by H.N. Bahuguna who also used it to launch a new party. That was so chaotic and so disorganized, with Bahuguna trying—like some ineffectual Scoutmaster—to control his followers (in vain) that I came away with a new respect for the discipline of the Jan Sanghis.

Even before the new party was formally announced, it was clear that A.B. Vajpayee was a hero-figure to the Jan Sanghis. L.K. Advani deferred to him. Slogans of 'Pradhan Mantri agli bari, Atal Bihari' were regularly raised and, with the exception of the Rajmata of Gwalior, Vijayraje Scindia, who had financed the Jan Sangh in its early years and deferred to nobody, the party's leaders made it clear that their real mission was to coronate Vajpayee.

I was introduced to Advani who was polite but seemed, as Subramanian Swamy would say, like one of Vajpayee's sidekicks. Advani was soft-spoken and helpful, either because this was his nature or because the new party needed good press for its launch event. He said he would assign someone to show me around.

He beckoned to a rather vain and officious man in a bandi who came rushing up. 'Hello!' the man said cheerily. Then he announced grandly: 'I am Dr Murli Manohar Joshi.'

Dr Joshi turned out to be an articulate chap even if he seemed to be rather pleased with himself. He gave me the grand tour, speaking respectfully of Advani and throwing in more than a little bit about himself. (Years later, when I knew Dr Joshi well and discovered how much he resented Advani, I thought back to this encounter and how different things were in those early days.)

I did not meet Vajpayee during the convention but judging by his speeches, he wanted to continue the old Janata Party under his leadership. The name they chose for the new party had no Sanghi (as in Jan Sangh, Rashtriya Swayamsevak Sangh, etc.) influence but suggested that it was an offshoot of Janata: Bharatiya Janata Party.

But eventually, the gap between Vajpayee's vision and the heritage of the Sangh began to be revealed. The economic resolution spoke of the new party's commitment to 'Gandhian socialism'. It was the usual gobbledygook that political parties put into their public documents and manifestoes and so I thought nothing of it.

But at the end of the convention a revolt broke out. A faction, led by the Rajmata (who was the only person with the clout to question Vajpayee), objected to the phrase and demanded that it be removed. The old Jan Sanghis who had earlier seemed to be solidly behind Vajpayee took her side. Many of them, I guessed, came from small business families in the Hindi heartland and associated socialism with Indira while Gandhiji was a Congress figure. Even so, their vehemence was surprising.

As I wrote at the time, it was not clear what they hated more: socialism or Gandhian ideas. (Or Gandhiji himself.)

Vajpayee gave in. The party was formed. But I kept thinking back to the squabble over that resolution. It was clear that Vajpayee saw himself as a moderate leader who wanted to combine some of the Sangh's ideas with the liberal ideas of Indian politics. His followers, however, were not, at heart, moderates. Neither Gandhi nor socialism had any appeal for them.

The party could not survive successfully in this form, I concluded. Eventually it would have to choose between Vajpayee's view, the moderate way, and the Sangh's traditional approach. I did not realize it then but seeing the birth of the BJP gave me an opportunity to see history in the making.

Not all the stories I did for *India Today* were political. Aroon and I had been talking about doing another movie cover story. I suggested Amitabh Bachchan. He was the number one star in India. But, I said, he was more than a star. He dominated the film industry in a way that no other individual before him ever had. Moreover, he had stopped talking to the press. So, if we got access to Bachchan, it would be a real scoop.

We did get access (through Yash Chopra, another man that Aroon's father, V.V. Purie, had backed, if I remember correctly) and I went off to see Bachchan at a studio where he was shooting the climax for a forthcoming blockbuster.

In those days, many of his films would have a similar ending. Bachchan and his co-stars (usually two other guys and three girls) would gain access to the villain's lair by pretending to be part of a singing troupe. After they had finished their song and dance routine, they would be recognized by the villain and imprisoned. They would break free and defeat the villain and his little army of henchmen. (Later Bachchan would tell me, deadpan, 'It's sometimes hard to remember which film I am shooting for.')

He met me on the set wearing a curious costume that included short trousers that billowed out and were then tied together at his knee with ribbons and a ruffled shirt. His outfit was somewhat distracting but he kept the conversation focussed and polite.

After I had explained the story to him, he said he would do it. Then, I threw in the difficult part. I wanted access to his home, to his family (parents, wife, brother, etc.) and to him, all day, for at least a week.

I had thought about it. Every actor is always acting when he is in front of the media. Bachchan was sophisticated and well-read. He would work out what kind of actor would impress *India Today*'s readers: a fun guy, but focussed on work, reserved but not the snob portrayed by *Stardust*, a man who had respect for Hindi cinema but had a life outside it, etc.

He would keep this persona for two or three interviews and journalists would fall for it.

So, I decided, I would go to his studio early in the morning, spend all day with him, leave when he did, late at night, and watch him even when he thought I was not looking. (After the second day, subjects usually forget that a journalist is hanging around.) That way I would cut through the artifice.

To my surprise, he agreed.

And so I spent something like a week (or perhaps it was ten days), shadowing Amitabh Bachchan. He turned out to be one of the most fascinating people I had ever interviewed.

All of the clichés about him were true: he came early to the sets, he was disciplined, there were no tantrums, he was a vegetarian who liked simple home food and who did not drink, and he was devoted to his family: his father, the poet Harivansh Rai Bachchan, was his idol.

But there were things that were less obvious. He had a strong sense of propriety. His objection to the gossip magazines was not any specific article they had written about him but that they were cheap and vulgar. He had no interest in gossip himself. In the famously competitive film industry, he was one of the few who never ran down his rivals.

He had the best manners of anyone in the business. Everyone who came to see him was given a chair and a cold drink or a cup of tea. Often, he would walk visitors back to their cars. He had a deep and abiding contempt for co-stars who misbehaved, drank too much or threw starry tantrums—but he rarely let this contempt show.

He genuinely enjoyed being alone. Most of his thoughts were internalized and rarely expressed. He had lots of acquaintances but very few friends. When the Bachchans socialized, the friends were usually Jaya's. He was a music freak, obsessed with world music and though he had sung in his movies, he was dismissive of his own singing, saying, 'How can you call that singing? It's croaking.'

Because he was such a big star, he dominated every room he entered. Nearly everybody on the set would be eager to please him or terrified of incurring his displeasure. And yet, he would clown around and joke on the sets. I remember, one day, on the sets of *Namak Halal*, when he was not in a particularly sociable mood, we sat quietly in his dressing room at Seth studio for half an hour. When the shot was ready, he bounced on to the set, pretend-punched a spot-boy, laughed with the cameramen and did his takes for a song sequence.

We went back to the dressing room and he lapsed into silence again.

The next day, when he was more sociable, I asked him about his cheerfulness on the set and how it contrasted with his glumness in the dressing room.

'That's the real acting,' he said of his behaviour on the set.

Because he knew that his presence made people nervous, he went out of his way to play the cheerful star to put them at ease. It was, I thought, an extraordinary gesture that nobody gave him credit for.

He was also kind and generous. While we were waiting for a shot to be set up, a producer who had signed him up for a new film came to tell him about the arrangements for the shoot. 'We have got the biggest suite for you, sir,' etc.

Bachchan took the producer outside into the corridor but I could still hear them. 'Never mind the suite. I have some friends in the industry,' he said and then named three young actors. 'I would be grateful if you could find roles for them in the film . . .'

And unlike all the boastful stars, he was the sort of man who thought his world could end at any time. He was relentlessly pessimistic, believed every film would flop and thought that it was only a matter of time before the work dried up. (This was forty years ago!)

And, most important, he could laugh at himself. I asked if he saw himself still playing the angry young man in a few years' time. 'Good God no!' he replied. 'Then I would be the angry middle-aged man!'

The story appeared on the cover of *India Today* and created a storm and Bachchan shut down again for the next several years, refusing all interviews.

By 1981, I had come to the conclusion that my time at *Bombay* was at an end. I was offered an Assistant Editorship (which meant I would write ponderous editorials) by the *Times of India* but wasn't sure that the job was for me. Then I met Nicolo Sella of the Inlaks Foundation, which had just started sending Indian students to Oxford and Cambridge. I told him that while I had no interest in going back to university I would be grateful for a scholarship from the Foundation.

'What would you rather do?' he asked.

I said I would love to travel, to meet people and to maybe work on a project.

Did I have anything in mind?

As I turned out, I did. I was fascinated by the way in which Western media (mainly British and American) treated India. Mrs Gandhi often complained about it. But nobody had done a proper analysis of what was going on.

At the time, the controversy about the New Information Order and how the West dominated the flow of information in the world was very much in the news so Nicolo thought it was a good idea.

Inlaks would not give me a scholarship. But they would invent a new award called a Fellowship, he said. I could travel for a year at their expense. I accepted it gratefully on the spot.

I told Aroon and Mohini that I was quitting. I think Mohini was relieved to see me go. *Bombay* was a success and there was no room for two editors. After I left, I don't think the magazine ever had a proper editor. Mohini ran it herself till, a few years later, it closed down.

FOURTEEN

TAKING THE PLUNGE

I should have been sad to have left Bombay and to walk away from success but I felt strangely free and excited. It was nice to be able to travel again and I enjoyed the thought of hanging around newspaper offices in the West.

I knew nobody in the press in the UK, which was, as you might imagine, a handicap. So I decided to phone the offices of journos who had covered India on the grounds that they may be more inclined to see me. In those days there were no mobiles, only switchboards with operators which made it (oddly enough) a little easier. Instead of trying to find somebody's mobile phone number so that I could text them, I called newspaper switchboards and asked to speak to them. The phones rang on their desks and I was through.

I met Phillip Knightley at the *Sunday Times*, an Australian who had spent a year in India on his way to the UK. Ian Jack, also of the *Sunday Times*, was incredibly helpful, sending me off to meet Rosemary Righter, also at the paper, who had written a book on the New Information Order. I went from newspaper to newspaper and met two legends, Louis Heron of *The Times* and James Cameron, the ultimate India hand.

I went to Paris, spoke to people at UNESCO (United Nations Education, Scientific and Cultural Organization), which was spearheading the New Information Order campaign, to New York, Washington DC and a few other cities. It was nice to be on the road and to meet interesting people.

Slowly a broad consensus emerged. The UNESCO stuff about a New Information Order, I thought, was nonsense. UNESCO claimed that the flow of information was dominated by the West, which it certainly was. The solution, said UNESCO, was to set up a news service dominated by Third World countries (mostly tin-pot dictatorships) which could disseminate 'fairer' news. Obviously, this was a propaganda scam, conceived at a time when the Soviet Empire and the Warsaw Pact were both strong.

On India, there was a broad consensus: readers in Europe didn't really care. We were a country of no great consequence, worthy of coverage only when natural disasters occurred or when there was a light feature to be done. In America, they cared even less.

It shouldn't be so hard for Indians to understand, Dick Steele, who then edited the international edition of *Newsweek*, told me in New York. Did we care about South America in India? Well, that was how the West felt about Asia. They knew it was there but they didn't worry too much about it.

The break gave me a chance to think about what I would do when I went back. I had got into journalism by accident because I had been fortunate enough to be in the right place at the right time. But shouldn't I now consciously sit and re-examine that decision? There was no money in journalism. Did I still want to persist with it?

Was there anything else I could do? Should I talk to Bhaskar Menon again? I wrote to him. He said the offer was still open. But the record business in India was in trouble because EMI Records had stuck to vinyl for too long while a new cassette market—dominated by pirates and bootleggers—had developed. Any record business executive would have to know how to fight the pirates. That would be my top priority before they considered moving me to London or Los Angeles.

My old college at Oxford said they would be happy to have me back though, as one of the dons said to me, 'Nothing is as easy as it was in the old days now that Mrs Thatcher is here.' Funds to universities had been slashed and I was, effectively, asking the university to finance my second degree.

It was during this phase that I went to a Sichuan restaurant in London's West End with my father's old friend, R.V. Pandit.

Pandit was a mystery to most of us. He had been a friend of my father's and the rest of the 'Progressive' gang in Mumbai in the sixties but had never shared their political views and had been fiercely pro-American. In that era, this only meant one thing. He ended up being called a CIA agent by the lefties. (The Progressives were obsessed with the CIA.) My father had never subscribed to this view, and had stayed friends with Pandit who had even published a biography of John F Kennedy written by my father.

Then, Pandit vanished. We heard that he had gone to Hong Kong and was working there. One day, my father bumped into him in London and asked what he was doing now. It turned out that Pandit was publishing the *Asia Magazine*, a Sunday supplement that was distributed with the most important newspapers all over South East Asia.

Obviously Pandit had done well for himself. He was staying at the Savoy and clearly had a lot of money. He kept in touch with my father (though this was not always easy given that my father spent most of his time in London and Pandit was in Hong Kong).

I remember going out for dinner with him and my parents in London when he had told me about a magazine called *Imprint*, which published condensed reviews of American bestsellers. I remembered it from the early sixties, when it was owned by an American couple (who also brought Bullworker, the muscle development device, to India!) and my parents' friend, Annie aunty (Qurratulain Hyder), worked there.

Well, said Pandit, he now owned it along with several trade publications in Hong Kong. He also owned restaurants, he added. In the early seventies, before Indian food became a big deal, he bought restaurants in Hong Kong and Tokyo and gave them to the Taj group (which was not a big chain in those days) to run.

After my father died, Pandit was kind enough to keep in touch with my mother and in 1977 when Mrs Gandhi was defeated, he turned up in Delhi and Bombay as a super advisor to the new Janata government, living in style at Samudra Mahal in Worli in Mumbai.

When my mother told him I was in London in 1981, he got in touch and invited me to lunch. At lunch he asked me: did I know what I was going to do? I said I had no idea.

Well, he had a suggestion. He still owned *Imprint* where he used to write a regular editorial called 'On the Marquee'. This was always political and was usually critical of the Congress government. When the Emergency was declared and press censorship imposed, Pandit gave up the column and let Ruskin Bond run the magazine remotely from the hills by selecting unsolicited contributions from readers all over India. Pandit himself sold his Asian magazines and moved from Hong Kong to Tokyo.

But *Imprint*, said Pandit to me at our lunch, was the tip of the iceberg. The company (it was called Business Press) that owned *Imprint* made its money from many Indian trade publications including one called the *Industrial Products Finder*, which he said (probably accurately), was the single-most profitable magazine in India.

So, here was his proposal. When I came back to India, I would take over as editorial director of Business Press. I would learn the business side of the publishing industry and develop new (general interest) publications for Business Press. I would be my own boss, subject to his remote supervision, and he would pay me a little bit more than *India Today* had paid me.

That way, he said, I would learn a little bit about business and about developing new products. And if I ever wanted to move out of journalism, those business skills would stand me in good stead.

I thought about it. It was 1982. I was still only 25. What did I have to lose?

I took the job.

FIFTEEN

MORARJI DESAI AND HIS PAPERS

I liked the atmosphere at Business Press. It had a large, sunny open office near the sea at Cuffe Parade and the people were nice. Pandit had resumed writing On the Marquee but his new obsession was to convert a villa on the sea front in Nice to an Indian restaurant. He lived in France and hardly ever came to Bombay.

I took a look at the company and its publications, which were worthy (such as *The Indian Textile Journal*) and generally well-run. There was very little for me to do about any of them. The one exception was *Imprint* which neither sold many copies nor made any money. Ruskin Bond was still in the hills but there was a new editor called Arun Gandhi who happened to be Gandhiji's grandson. He was an exceptionally decent and upright person but he had no staff so he ran it just as Bond had done—on the basis of unsolicited contributions from readers.

There was only so far you could go with this approach, so I suggested to him that we ran it professionally, with an editorial staff, a proper cover story, etc. He saw the point but it was clear that the idea of running such a magazine did not appeal to him.

By then, anyway, he had received an offer to do something more interesting. He knew Morarji Desai. After resigning as prime minister, Morarji had returned to his flat in Marine Drive. Most days he sat cross legged on the floor, in a strange room mysteriously packed out with Air India attaché cases. (In the old days, if you travelled First Class, you got one free.) His controversial son, Kanti (who had starred in many corruption scandals, all of which involved leveraging his father's influence to make money for himself), would often be hanging around but father and son seemed to have stopped communicating cordially.

I had been to see him twice in the *Bombay* magazine days to get him to talk about his life. He had told candid stories (too candid; at one stage, he showed me the shingles on his scalp) about his time in Delhi with many scurrilous fantasies that even predated the Internet madness to come suggesting that, in this one respect alone, Morarji was ahead of his time.

But once you tried to get him on the record, he shut up and resumed his renowned stiff posture, his facial features set in a grim position that suggested a sanyasi who was suffering for the nation.

What none of us realized was that the sanyasi had gathered up every secret file he could get his hands on at the PMO before they booted him out. He had a treasure trove of confidential communications, government files and secret letters, all kept safely, perhaps in those Air India attaché cases.

He summoned Arun Gandhi one day in 1982 and showed him the files. He wanted Arun to write a book about Morarji's time as prime minister. The documentation was all there. Morarji would explain what was in the files to him and Arun would write the book.

In fact, Morarji had the theme of the book ready. A decent, honourable Gandhian called Morarji goes to Delhi to do his duty as prime minister. He is thwarted in this desire by such demons as Charan Singh and Indira Gandhi. Evil overpowers good. Our hero loses. But his has been a battle for the truth.

As a story it would have made a very poor Amar Chitra Katha comic book. There was clearly no real book there. But Arun was sharp enough to know that no journalist had ever seen so many secret prime ministerial papers before. He agreed to do the book.

After that, it was vintage Morarji. He would not go on the record. Not a single document could be quoted. (These were all serious violations of the Official Secrets Act anyway.) Arun would have to tell Morarji's story from the perspective of an all-seeing narrator who knows everything but will not let you see the evidence.

Arun was a nice man so he went along with this. He even chose a title, along with Morarji, that reflected our hero's view of himself. The book was to be called 'Morarji Betrayed'.

Each day Arun would come to the office with some secret file or the other and I would eagerly go through it. Some of it was sensational. There was a letter from Ram Jethmalani to Morarji saying that 'Charan Singh has lost his mental balance'. It was interesting because it provided an insight into the battles within the government. It is unusual for an MP to write to the prime minister to complain that the deputy prime minister is a lunatic. But it was topical, too, because even as Arun was researching the book Jethmalani went off to join Charan Singh. So was Charan Singh a nut case or was he Jethmalani's leader? Or both?

There was extensive correspondence between the prime minister and the president. Apparently, Kanti, Morarji's son, had asked for the Hinduja brothers to be invited to a Rashtrapati Bhavan banquet. The president believed that the Hindujas were not the sort of people who should be allowed into Rashtrapati Bhavan. Morarji defended his son but not (as far as I can remember) the Hindujas, saying that this was a minor matter.

When Janata had been in office we had speculated that there was tension between the prime minister and the president. Now, here I was, with the original letters in my hands.

There was more. I had always believed that, at some stage, the USSR decided to bring the Janata government down. Morarji hated communists (as I knew from my family's experience) and was consistently rude to the Russians to their faces.

At one of our meetings during the *Bombay* magazine days he had proudly told me the story of how India had either arrested Russian spies or thrown out Russian diplomats (I can no longer remember which one it was) when the Russian leader Alexei Kosygin was due to visit.

Kosygin had complained to Morarji that this had been done, and the story promptly leaked to the press, solely to embarrass him and ruin the visit.

Morarji proudly related his response to me. 'Look here,' I told him. 'In your country, you control what appears in your papers. In my country, we have a free press. I can't control what they write!'

According to Morarji, Kosygin was dumbstruck by the sharpness of the response.

For years and years, and especially during Indira Gandhi's time, India had been considered almost a part of the Soviet sphere of influence (even if it was non-aligned). Under Morarji that began changing. If the prime minister loathes the Soviets then how long can any understanding last?

I had always wondered about the timing of the revolt that brought down Morarji and the Janata government. It had started with Charan Singh's revolt which was regarded as no great threat because Charan Singh was not popular with his colleagues. Moreover, his ends were not ideological but personal: he wanted to be prime minister himself. And the only way he could do that was if Indira Gandhi backed him.

Given that the Janata Party had been created to oppose Indira Gandhi, it was thought unlikely that Charan Singh would ask her for support. When it became clear Singh's ambition vastly exceeded his scruples, his colleagues said that they were all shocked that Charan Singh would ask the woman who had jailed him to now assist him in his quest to become prime minister. But then, a strange thing happened: many politicians considered close to Moscow or hostile to Washington suddenly joined the revolt. This included those who had previously attacked Charan Singh and those who were bitterly opposed to Indira Gandhi.

Was this all spontaneous? How could so many politicians suddenly change their minds and back Charan Singh? Was I being paranoid or did the facts fit my theory that the Russians had worked to bring Morarji down? That they had used their agents of influence within the political system to wreck the Janata government?

Among the papers Morarji had stolen from the PMO was a handwritten letter from Nani Palkhivala who was India's ambassador to the US when Morarji was PM.

I don't remember the exact words so I will summarize what I do remember. Palkhivala began by saying that he was writing this letter by hand and sending it personally to Morarji by diplomatic bag because he did not want anyone else seeing it.

He had just been visited by a high official of the US government who had told him that US Intelligence had learned that the Soviets had taken a decision to topple Morarji's government. All their assets in India would be used to bring Morarji down.

For me, this was as close to a smoking gun as I had seen. Morarji's government had been relatively stable when Palkhivala had sent the note. And then, shortly afterwards, the upheavals had begun and the collapse had been startlingly quick.

Obviously, Arun was sitting on dynamite. Morarji's trove of secret files would benefit future historians.

It soon became clear that Arun could not edit *Imprint* and work on the book simultaneously. He went to see Pandit who said (correctly and generously) that the book was more important. Arun could stay on at full salary and write the book. All he needed to do in return was to give the first pre-publication extract to *Imprint* before the book hit the stands.

All of us were happy with the arrangement. Arun set about looking for a publisher. In those days Indian publishing was largely a small-time, fly-by-night business and there wasn't much choice. I don't remember who Arun finally settled on but he was a Delhi-based publisher who told Arun what we already knew. He could not write this book the way Morarji wanted. He had to include the documents and let them tell the story. Arun's tone could be sympathetic to Morarji but calling the book 'Morarji Betrayed' was out of the question. He should call it 'The Morarji Papers'.

Arun agreed (though I'm not sure that he told Morarji this) and started work on organizing the documents into a comprehensive narrative.

With Arun gone, *Imprint* needed a new editor. Pandit insisted I do it. ('You can leave in two years once the magazine is established.') We changed the format from the *Reader's Digest* size to the standard magazine size (easier for ads to fit too) and I set about creating a feature magazine for (let's be honest) the upper middle-class Indian. We ran articles on the secret networks that ran India (Doon School, St. Stephen's, etc.) on how the middle-class would soon want political clout of its own and the links between films and politics.

Our job was to spot trends and turn them into long-form stories (3000 to 4000 words). There were not many other people doing this so the magazine quickly gained a strong reader base among people who complained of the mindlessness of other magazines (that is, many of the people who had hated *Bombay*).

I kept asking Arun when the Morarji book was due so I could slot the cover story. He was uncharacteristically elusive and evasive. Eventually his publisher called me. Look, he said, we owe you an extract and we will give it to you. But you are a small magazine. So first we will go to *Sunday* and all the other big magazines to promote the book. Then, afterwards, we will definitely give you something.

This was not what we had agreed on so I called Pandit who pointed out the publisher was not doing us any favours. He had paid Arun's salary during the writing of the book. He spoke to Arun and told him that he had broken the terms of their understanding.

Arun, an essentially decent man, now decided to face up to the publisher and to assert that the first pre-publication extract had to go to *Imprint*. The publisher reluctantly agreed.

This was all very well but I was suddenly told that the book would be out soon so we had to put the extract in the first available issue. We were closing an issue on how India had gone all disco (this was during the 'Disco Deewane' madness of 1983) when I was informed that if we didn't put the extract in the issue, the publisher would take the line that we had lost our slot and give extracts to others. In those days it took ages to print and bind the magazine and last-minute cover photo changes were not possible.

So we pulled out some pages, remade them in a hurry and put in the chapter about the president's fight with Morarji over Kanti and the Hindujas. It was too late to change the cover photo so we had to content ourselves with listing the story on the cover and going with the disco photo.

The magazine appeared but not much happened. Then Harish Bhanot who was Bureau Chief of the *Hindustan Times* in Mumbai read it. He thought it was sensational and filed a story about it. The *HT* put the story on page one. Parliament was in session so MPs brought it up. A furore ensued. The issue sold out in Delhi by the end of the day. We retrieved copies from newsstands in Bombay and other cities and shipped them to Delhi where they sold out.

Suddenly the Morarji Papers became a big deal. The publisher sold extracts to *Sunday* (which put the Jethmalani letter about Charan Singh on its cover) and other publications.

As I had suspected, most of the questions that were raised were about how Morarji had been able to smuggle secret documents out of the PMO. Morarji was besieged by reporters. He was stoic about his theft of secret papers but made it clear that he had not authorized the publication of these documents. (Nobody believed him but I knew he was telling the truth.)

He never quite recovered from the controversy. He had hoped that the book, portraying him as a betrayed Titan, would redeem his reputation.

In fact, the uproar that followed polished it off.

(In case you are wondering, I never found out what happened to Morarji's trove of stolen documents. Did he have to give them back? I would hope so. As for Charan Singh, Mrs Gandhi played him for a fool. He toppled Morarji and became prime minister. But on the day he was to ask for a parliamentary vote of confidence, Mrs Gandhi withdrew support. Charan Singh had to resign. A new election was called. Mrs Gandhi won it and became PM again. It was vodka and blinis with caviar all around for her backers.)

SIXTEEN

'WHY DON'T YOU
ASK GIANIJI YOURSELF?'

A feature magazine in India has never been easy to run, mainly because nobody is ever sure what to put into it. We ransacked American publications for inspiration but as much as we tried to steal ideas from *Esquire* or *Vanity Fair*, it never worked out. So, we tried creating our own formula, which did not work either. Eventually, we ended up with a formula-less magazine that reflected—I am slightly ashamed to admit this—whatever I was interested in that month.

I knew enough about the film industry so that bit was easy. Maharashtra politics was also easy but boring. Mostly we just made instant judgments on what to write about depending on what was happening that month.

When Salman Rushdie came to India, post his Booker Prize for *Midnight's Children*, we took him back to the Warden Road bungalow where the early part of the book was set. The house was now occupied by the designer Sunita Pitamber who was happy to have Rushdie pottering around in her garden looking for childhood memories.

When Rajiv Gandhi was elected prime minister in 1984, everyone was obsessed with Arun Nehru, then regarded with the kind of awe that Amit Shah would later command. Nehru had no time to waste on us despite many requests for interviews so I settled on Finance Minister V.P. Singh as the guy to watch. I am still not sure how (perhaps it was easier to get to the finance minister in those days) but V.P. Singh met us several times and put time aside for a special photo session where he adopted suitably Gandhian poses to conform to his image as a simple man who had abandoned all worldly goods to fight for the poor.

The victory of R.K. Hegde in Bangalore had confirmed the popular view that a new kind of politics was here. We were told by pundits that the Karnataka assembly election, after which Hegde, a previously obscure figure, became chief minister showed how a new anti-Indira consensus was emerging. (This was a bogus view. Nothing emerged.)

I was fascinated by Bangalore which, though it was a relatively quiet place at the beginning of the 1980s, seemed set to become a boom town (with all the attendant infrastructural problems) so we wrote a lot about the city. It helped that we had an excellent correspondent in Rohini Nilekani, an old colleague from my *Bombay* magazine days, who had moved there because her husband Nandan had given up a secure job in Bombay to become one of the founders of a little technology company.

It was called Infosys.

We had more luck with Delhi stories than I had hoped. I got someone to introduce me to Tarlochan Singh, deputy press secretary to Giani Zail Singh, who was then the President of India. There had been rumblings of tension between Zail Singh and Rajiv Gandhi who was prime minister. I asked Tarlochan if the stories were true.

'Why don't you ask Gianiji yourself,' he said.

And so I found myself being led into the private quarters at Rashtrapati Bhavan into a modest (by the standards of what was built as the Viceroy's Palace) bedroom. Zail Singh sat on a bed. He had removed his turban and seemed weak and helpless, nothing like the president of the world's largest democracy is supposed to look.

I doubt if he knew anything about me. But because Tarlochan had vouched for me, he was willing to speak. He explained how he had sworn Rajiv in as prime minister. Mrs Gandhi, he said, had told him that if anything happened to her (and she knew that she was under threat), he was to swear Rajiv in before the Congress had a chance to react.

He talked about the terrible massacres on the streets of Delhi after Mrs Gandhi's assassination and complained that he had been prevented from going out on the streets and reassuring Sikhs.

I suggested (very hesitantly—I was not used to meeting the President of India) that perhaps they were worried about his safety were he to visit the riot-affected areas.

No, he said. They didn't want him to see what was happening. When his office got distress calls and asked the Home ministry to help Sikhs who were in danger, they were put off and no help was ever sent.

Yes, I said, again as tentatively as I could, but that was a general complaint during that period. The Janata politician, Chandra Shekhar, had told me that his son had a Sikh friend who was in danger. Like all decent people, Chandra Shekhar's son had asked this Sikh friend to bring his family over to their house where they would be safe.

He told his father and Chandra Shekhar immediately called Narasimha Rao (the Home Minister) and asked if he could arrange for a) police protection for the area where his son's friend said Sikhs were being murdered and b) a police escort for this family to come to Chandra Shekhar's house.

According to Chandra Shekhar, Rao responded, 'No, no. It is very dangerous, Chandra Shekharji. Tell your son not to allow any Sikhs into your house. Too dangerous.'

So Zail Singh's was not an isolated experience or necessarily part of any great conspiracy. The Home Minister had failed, the Delhi police had run away and the mob (led in many cases by Congressmen) had taken over.

But Zail Singh would not be convinced.

The government was scared, he said, that he would have come out in public and said that Sikhs were being butchered. 'If I had resigned then,' he said, 'how long would this government have lasted?'

'He would have become the greatest Sikh leader since Maharaja Ranjit Singh,' Tarlochan added.

Zail Singh had two basic grievances. One was that in the book *Amritsar: Mrs Gandhi's Last Battle*, by Satish Jacob and Mark Tully, he had been portrayed as the man who promoted Jarnail Singh Bhindranwale to fight the Akalis only to see Bhindranwale turn into a Frankenstein's monster. This was rubbish, he said, and had been fed to the authors by Darbara Singh, a former chief minister of Punjab and the Giani's great rival.

He may or may not have been right but that ship had sailed. The book was an international bestseller and nobody had mounted an effective challenge to its view of events.

Could the Giani talk about Rajiv instead?

He could. He would. And he did.

Rajiv had never liked him, he said. He had hated Pranab Mukherjee and R.K. Dhawan, too, because Mrs Gandhi trusted their judgment more than his. When the Giani became president, Rajiv should have let his personal prejudices lapse and taken a larger view and behaved as a prime minister should with a president.

Instead, Zail Singh was not accorded any respect. The prime minister never briefed him, as was the convention, about national affairs. When bills were sent to him, he was expected to sign on the dotted line. If he offered any advice, he was treated as an interfering buffoon who was not to be taken seriously. (My paraphrase; he actually said something that translated as 'given the respect I deserve'.)

I had heard that he was the canniest politician in India so perhaps Zail Singh was manipulating me. But at that moment, I was sold. I believed him. I felt bad for him. And I wrote a cover story for *Imprint* saying that.

You can't quote the President of India so I used the old journalistic code phrase 'friends of Zail Singh say' before each quote.

Zail Singh had been complaining to many journalists so if you were part of the Delhi circuit then nothing he said to me was very new or noteworthy. I knew that. And so I did not expect the article to have much impact.

Oddly enough, I was wrong. It had enormous impact. It was read by the prime minister's office (my friend Mani Shankar Aiyar called me to say how unfair the piece was), talked about in parliament and later Rajiv Gandhi told me that he had read it himself. (Only to say that I had got everything wrong!)

I was pleased that a little-known Bombay monthly was at least creating a ripple in Delhi where few people had read *Imprint* before. The foreign press began reading *Imprint*. We were quoted (as 'the respected *Imprint* magazine') in the *Washington Post* and foreign journalists (from the *New York Times, Time* magazine, the *Wall Street Journal*, etc.) would drop into our Bombay offices to get our perspective on what was happening in India. (We knew nothing!)

Imprint had a small team (five people) but we had stars. We had Amrita Shah who joined us when she was just twenty-two and went on to become one of the most respected journalists of her generation. And we had Shirin Mehta who actually ran *Imprint* as managing editor, designing and sub-editing every single thing in the magazine.

With these stars on board, I found I could travel as much as I wanted. I had the advantage of being backed by R.V. Pandit who had moved from his original position (RSS) to a more pro-Rajiv regime stance and did not want the ideology that his BJP friends espoused featured in the magazine. Even so, the likes of L.K. Advani, Dr J.K. Jain, Sardar Angre and Nanaji Deshmukh frequented our office. I grew to like Nanaji, Advani seemed well-meaning and harmless, and for a time J.K. Jain became my doctor.

When Pandit and I agreed, he was extraordinarily supportive. When Operation Bluestar happened, he was the only person I knew who agreed with me that the operation had been a military disaster and that we had now alienated even those moderate Sikhs who hated Bhindranwale.

When the Punjab Accord was signed I had the bright idea of going to Chandigarh to interview S.S. Barnala, the new chief minister and to check out the public mood. Pandit agreed and I made two trips. Looking back, I am sometimes astonished by the openness and hospitality of politicians in those days. Barnala had never heard of me but he gave me an interview on one trip and lunch at his house on the other.

On my second visit, we discussed his battle with the conservative faction of the Akali Dal and the Shiromani Gurdwara Parbandhak Committee (SGPC). He had been declared a '*tankhaiyya*' by the religious leaders of his community and ordered to sit outside the

Golden Temple and clean the shoes of devotees. As far as I knew, it was unprecedented for a sitting chief minister to be put in this position. But Barnala seemed unperturbed. 'It gave me a great deal of peace,' he said. And I got the feeling that he meant it.

Despite Barnala's willingness to do whatever it took to make peace within the Sikh community, I came back convinced that the Accord would not hold. Pakistan was training Khalistanis across the border just as it had in the pre-Accord days. Barnala was cornered in his own party and Parkash Singh Badal was openly opposed to him. And the scars of Bluestar and the Delhi massacres had not healed.

Sadly, I turned out to be right.

SEVENTEEN

MAIN HOON DON

In the early to mid-1980s, Bombay was dominated by criminals. We all knew the names of the leading dons of the underworld but we knew very little about the men themselves.

My one encounter with a don had come in 1979 when I went to see Bombay's most famous gangster Haji Mastaan for a quote for the cover story. (I have no recollection of what the quote was.) Mastaan lived in a bungalow on Sophia College Lane between Warden Road and Pedder Road. There was an old truck in the garden and the legend was that the old smuggler kept it as a memory of his first delivery of contraband. (I once asked Mastaan about this story and he denied it—but then, he would, wouldn't he?)

Mastaan liked fur hats and as he was an unimposing, dark man the hat sometimes made him look like a small furry creature in photos. But he had enormous confidence and showed no surprise to learn that a magazine wanted to put him on the cover. (He was one of six people representing various facets of Bombay: Parmeshwar Godrej, Amitabh Bachchan, the Doordarshan newsreader Nirmala Mathan, Viren Shah and Tina Munim, as she then was.) We chose them randomly not realizing that most of them would still be household names forty years later. He offered to give us a picture of himself. We said we would have him shot by our photographer.

Our interaction was brief but he bristled when he heard that we were planning to caption the photo 'former smuggler' or 'reformed smuggler'.

'Who says I am or was a smuggler?' he demanded.

I was startled.

'Er, you do,' I said. 'Isn't that why you and other smugglers took a vow in the presence of Jai Prakash Narain saying that you would give up smuggling?'

'No. That was not the vow. We only said we would work for the nation,' he said argumentatively. 'It is a good vow. You should take it yourself.'

I think we called him a former smuggler anyway. Then, in Rajni Patel's office, I bumped into Yusuf Patel, the only smuggler whose fame had rivalled Mastaan's. He was a cheerful, if slightly high strung, individual who kept shaking his leg compulsively. The vibrating leg revealed his ankle area and we discovered that he was wearing normal pyjamas under his trousers. I had heard of Y-fronts, boxer shorts and even long johns. But a pair of pyjamas?

I never wrote anything about Yusuf at that stage but as we looked for new areas to cover, it struck me that long-form crime writing, done in story-telling style (we were all reading books about New Journalism in those days) could interest people who read about gang wars every day.

I had to get the background right so I persuaded Yusuf to sit down and talk about the old days. He was not particularly forthcoming but he did tell me about the time he had been shot and left for dead.

According to Yusuf, Mastaan had put out a hit on him. The hit had been executed by a gang of Pathans run by Karim Lala, another well-known don. Yusuf was walking down the street when two gun men rushed up and pumped bullets into his body till they thought he was dead. Then they ran away.

But Yusuf was not dead. He was taken to hospital, made a full recovery and was now back in business.

It all seemed slightly fantastical to me. So I renewed my acquaintance with Mastaan, who invited me back to that strange bungalow between Pedder Road and Warden Road. The ground rules were that we would be off the record unless it was made clear to him that he was likely to be quoted.

I asked him about the Yusuf shooting. Yes, he said, it was true. Yusuf had double-crossed him on a deal. Nobody, he said dramatically, double-crosses Mastaan and gets away with it. So he organized the hit, was told that Yusuf was dead and felt a deep satisfaction.

Later, when he was told that Yusuf had survived, he took it as a divine signal. If Allah did not want Yusuf dead, then Mastaan would have to respect that. They became partners again.

I sensed that there were many stories waiting to be told so I took to dropping in on Mastaan every couple of months. He was now at the stage where he believed his own publicity. The Amitabh Bachchan character in *Deewar* had been pretty clearly based on him ('but my number was never 786,' he said) and Mastaan had even shot for a biopic made by the comedian Mukri, in which he played a glamourized version of himself complete with a full, black wig to cover his thinning locks. (As far as I know the film was never completed.)

He wore white clothes which his *chamcha*s told him added to the allure of sophistication he wanted to portray. He liked the dramatic gesture. The politician/social worker Rukhsana Sultan once told me a story about her first meeting with Mastaan.

She only used Camay soap, she said, which was not generally available in India in the 1970s. So she would buy it off smugglers. On one occasion, she parked her car on the road outside and went into a crowded market in Bombay to search for Camay. Nobody had it. They all said that the smugglers had not been supplying soap for a while now.

When she walked back to her car, she saw that there was a small crowd around it. Fearing that something had gone wrong, she rushed towards the vehicle. Except for the part of the back seat where she would sit (and presumably the driver's seat), the entire car was packed with hundreds of bars of Camay soap. Standing next to the car, watched by adoring locals, was a man in white clothes.

'I am Haji Mastaan,' he said and smiled grandly.

It is a great story and it says something about the way Mastaan liked to be portrayed. He was not a particularly impressive looking man but he had hypnotic eyes. I told him that the only other person

I had met with eyes like that was Rajneesh, the self-styled Bhagwan. (I had spent three days at the Poona ashram when I was at *Bombay* magazine but alas, nothing exciting happened which is why you won't find that story here!) Mastaan nodded politely but did not seem interested. I guessed that Rajneesh was not the parallel that he was looking for.

Only when I got to know him better, did he finally begin to open up. His smuggling days, he said, were not as glamorous as the movies made out. The racket involved smuggling gold from Dubai to Bombay in dhows. The kingpins were a (still) well-known Dubai family whom the laws of libel preclude me from naming. Mastaan's men would meet the boats, pick up the gold, which they would carry on their person in specially made jackets. This gold would be delivered to middlemen in Bombay who would supply it to jewellers. As Mastaan said, more than a little bitterly, 'They made most of the money. We went to jail.'

I believed him, especially when he said he was glad to be out of the business. He was making more money in real estate than he had ever made from crime, he said.

But the glamour came from the smuggling, didn't it, I persisted. Yes, it did, he conceded. If he had just been one of the men who sent the gold from Dubai, I pointed out, he would never have been such a well-known figure.

He accepted all that but he had begun to get a little tired of being portrayed as a roadside-thug-made-good. My guess was that somebody had lent him a video of *Godfather II* and had taken him through it, offering simultaneous translation because he referred to the film again and again. 'In my day, the underworld was like *Godfather II*,' he said, 'about honour and respect. It was nothing like *Deewar*.'

For all that, he never went so far as to pretend to be a law-abiding citizen. He still had friends in the underworld who were active. One of them was Karim Lala who he sent me to meet. The old man was hospitable but unforthcoming.

One of Mastaan's former sidekicks, a man called Varadarajan Mudaliar (or Vardhabhai) had taken over much of north Bombay which he ran with an iron fist. (Vardha is partly the inspiration for the Amitabh Bachchan character in *Agneepath*—Bachchan's voice in the movie is modelled on Vardha's—and for the villain in *Ardh Satya*.)

Mastaan liked Vardha because he was a Tamilian like him. Contrary to popular perception, the underworld was not divided on communal lines: often regional origin mattered more than religion. Hindus and Muslims smuggled side by side.

At the time a brave cop, Y.C. Pawar, was working to chase Vardha out of Bombay and the story fascinated me. I asked Amrita Shah if she could track Vardha down. It seemed like a tall order but I was travelling for a few days and I thought she might up come up with something while I was away. When I returned not only did she have an interview with Vardha ready but also a cover shoot with the old hoodlum posing piously for pictures.

Eventually Pawar won. Vardha moved to Madras and died there. (He spawned a whole genre of movies in his last days. *Dayavan*, *Nayakan*, etc. are all based on his purported life story.)

But even as Mastaan was pretending to be Robert De Niro or Al Pacino, the underworld that he lorded over (at least in his imagination) was coming apart.

It started out as a feud between two sets of brothers, one led by guys called Alamzeb and Amirzada and the other, by a family called the Ibrahims. Alamzeb and company killed Shabhir Ibrahim at point blank range at a petrol pump. His family, led by his brother Dawood, retaliated and the gang war spilled out into the streets. As the gunfights mounted, Mastaan called the warring factions to his bungalow.

He told them that the underworld had survived for so long because it had known how to operate under the radar. Once you began shooting people at traffic lights and assassinating witnesses in courtrooms, you attracted too much attention to the gangs. There would be a public uproar. Politicians would be forced to crack down on the underworld. And no amount of bribes could stop the authorities from responding to public pressure.

For the good of the entire underworld, the young hotheads had to put aside the violence and resolve their differences far out of public view.

Mastaan told me the story himself so he may have glammed up his own role slightly but other accounts say it is broadly correct. Dawood Ibrahim and Amirzada (or was it Alamzeb—I can't remember) put their hands on the Quran and told Mastaan that there would be no more violence.

Mastaan was reassured. He went to bed that night, he said, confident that the laws of the underworld (or of the *Godfather* movies, if you want to be cynical) would now be upheld.

The next day, both gangs were at it again, shooting each other in broad daylight. Nobody really gave a damn about Mastaan any longer. His time had gone. His legend had faded. Eventually Dawood (who was out on bail) skipped the country, set up shop in Dubai and well, you know the rest.

In movies made about the underworld, gangsters are always shown extorting money from builders. I am sure that happened but what that narrative misses is that, in many cases, the underworld dons were themselves the builders.

Yusuf and Mastaan were not joking when they said that real estate was easier than smuggling and much more profitable. It may be too complicated to explain in gangster movies but the dons made their money from construction in two ways.

First of all, there was the Bombay Rent Act, a socialistic measure that consigned central Mumbai to a slow death from the early 1970s onwards, when the Act was passed. The Act made a mockery of the principle of private property by putting the tenant and landlord on par.

Suppose you owned a flat. You gave it on rent. After a while you needed it for yourself. To ask the tenant to move out you had to prove in a court of law that your need was greater than the tenant's. The tenant would always claim he had nowhere else to go. If you had given the flat on rent, then presumably you had somewhere else to stay anyway. If you said your son had grown up and now needed to stay in the flat, the court would say that he could stay with you. Where would the poor tenant go?

Assuming you had a cast-iron case even with the law stacked against you, it would still take over a dozen years for the court proceedings to conclude.

In effect, therefore, you had to write off any property you had given on rent.

In central Bombay, this meant that the area never regenerated itself. Landlords had no incentive to look after their properties so they deteriorated. Wily tenants sub-let the apartments, often dividing them into two or three small flats.

And yet, the property that these tenants occupied was worth a fair sum as land values sky-rocketed in Mumbai.

So the underworld began buying up these buildings from landlords at distress prices. Then, they asked the tenants to leave. Those who refused would be kneecapped. Some were killed. As the fear spread, the tenants fled and the buildings emptied. The dons then demolished the buildings, built fancy new ones on the now-vacant lots, and made a killing.

If it seemed too tiresome to individually threaten each tenant, then it was easier to burn the buildings down. While it stood, the tenant had rights. Once it was rubble, ownership reverted to the landlord who promptly sold it to the underworld.

There was one other law that the underworld abused with impunity. All property in Mumbai had to conform to an FSI or Floor Space Index. The figure varied but it was around 1.75 or so. For every acre of space, you would build 1.75 times that (in terms of saleable or built-up area).

Except: who measured the built-up area when the construction was over? What happened if the builder/don had used an effective FSI of say 2.5?

Well, government officials were supposed to measure the FSI and it was easy enough to bribe them to look the other way. If they refused, the dons could always threaten to have their wives raped or to throw acid on the faces of their teenaged daughters. The cops were on the take so who were you going to complain to?

These building scams made more money for the underworld in a few years than they had made in decades of smuggling.

As for the gang wars? Well, the Mumbai police did the only thing they could. As public pressure grew (as Mastaan had predicted it would), they started bumping the criminals off. Once 'encounters' were normalized, most of the gangsters fled to Dubai or elsewhere. The building and other scams continued. But the roadside shoot-outs ended.

The gangsters, led by Dawood, decided that it was easy enough to run the Mumbai underworld from abroad. So many of them left the country and lived far from the reach of Indian authorities. And as technology advanced all it took to order a hit was a single WhatsApp call from anywhere in the world.

EIGHTEEN

'STILL A CIA OPERATION?'

Though I had started writing for *India Today* in 1976, I only felt that I had become a proper journalist by 1985. By then I had edited two magazines and got the measure of Bombay. I had also begun to venture out to other cities, talking to chief ministers, interviewing the home minister and the finance minister and doing interviews (not officially, as we have seen) with the president of India.

I was twenty-nine and all my early doubts about whether I really wanted to be a journalist were forgotten. I had zero interest in Business Press' other ventures but *Imprint* was going well enough for me to be relatively content. I enjoyed writing and liked putting a publication together.

But now, a new set of insecurities presented themselves. If I was going to be a journalist, did I want to be typed as a Bombay journalist all my life? Was Bombay really a reflection of India?

Pandit and I had often disagreed but he had always been supportive, taking my side no matter who complained. There was one time when I imagine it may have been difficult for him to back me.

It concerned Dhirubhai Ambani.

I had known Dhirubhai Ambani since my *Bombay* magazine days. He was not yet the Titan he was to become but I was a complete nobody, a twenty-three-year-old kid starting out in journalism. His office made the first call. Dhirubhai had noticed, the caller said, that Reliance did not appear on *India Today*'s list of active stocks. Could anything be done?

I responded, honestly, that I had no idea. The Active Stocks list was compiled in Delhi and nobody in the Bombay bureau had any input. The next day the same man called. He had explained it to Dhirubhai, he said, but as our offices were virtually next to each other in Nariman Point, would I like to drop in and have a coffee with him? (He was at Tulsiani Chambers in those days and we were at Jolly Maker II.)

I went to see him wondering what the agenda was only to discover that there wasn't any. My guess was that in 1979, when he was hardly at the pinnacle of his growth, he simply liked meeting different people and getting a sense of who was doing what.

At the time I had no real interest in business (not after that textile industry cover story for which, by the way, we had not even bothered to speak to Reliance!) But I liked Dhirubhai. I liked his earthiness, his humour and the total absence of pretence or pomp (we spoke in Gujarati and English).

I don't think I ever wrote about him for the first five years that I knew him. But I would drop in periodically for a coffee and he would keep me abreast of his adventures—at one stage it looked as if he might be toppled by claims that he had misused the NRI Investment scheme to recycle his own money back to India clandestinely through shell companies with such names as Crocodile and Fiasco.

Even when that campaign was at its height, he seemed on top of things and explained what was going on to me. A group of brokers backed by an established Marwari industrialist (whom I cannot name for reason of libel) had tried to drive down the price of his shares by short selling them. He had bought up every share they were selling short and then, by using the Crocodile-Fiasco money had bought enough Reliance stock to keep his share price soaring. Then he had demanded delivery from the short sellers. When they had been unable to deliver, he had forced them into bankruptcy.

I was no finance guy but I worked out that short selling meant that the brokers sold his shares at a price that was lower than the current list price. The brokers did not have to deliver the shares for a few weeks but they hoped that if enough of them sold then market sentiment would turn against Reliance. The share would crash and when it was time for them to deliver shares to the buyers they could simply pick them for a song in the market and still make a profit on the transaction.

Dhirubhai foiled them by buying every share offered for sale. So market sentiment did not turn against Reliance and the share price held firm. When it was time for delivery the brokers realized to their horror that the market price of Reliance was much higher than the price they had promised to sell at. When Dhirubhai demanded delivery the brokers were ruined because they had to buy high priced shares and sell them to him cheap.

On another occasion, we met on the day that a scandal about the import of beef tallow for use in soap was breaking.

'You understand what this means?' Dhirubhai asked.

I had no clue so I improvised. 'Ah, Mrs Gandhi will be in trouble . . .'

'No, no,' he said impatiently. 'Since nobody will trust imported tallow any longer, a huge opportunity has opened up for local manufacturing of tallow.'

He was right, of course, and every conversation had at least one or two such moments where I was impressed by the speed at which his brain moved and how good he was at smelling a business opportunity.

When we were thinking of cover subjects at our *Imprint* editorial meeting one day, I suggested putting Dhirubhai on the cover. He now ran the largest textile company in India, was the darling of the stock market and had been on the cover of many business magazines. It was a rags-to-riches story without any parallel in the history of Indian business and deserved to be told.

I wrote it myself and put a solo portrait of Dhirubhai on the cover. The issue sold well in Bombay on the very first day and I was quite pleased with myself till Mr Pai, Pandit's right hand man in the Bombay office came up to me, looking shaken. Mr Pai asked if he could see me privately.

We went to a cabin. Pai told me he had just received a call from Nusli Wadia who had begun by shouting at him. 'How much have you been paid, Pai?'

Poor old Mr Pai asked what this was about and Wadia shouted some more about how Ambani bought up everyone. Pai explained, shivering all the while, I imagine, that he had nothing to do with *Imprint*.

'How much has Vir been paid then?' Wadia shouted even before he could finish explaining.

Eventually as Mr. Pai strained and sweated, Nusli hung up on him and said he would call Pandit in Nice directly.

Pai was right to be shaken. Wadia was a shareholder in Business Press. Pandit was Godfather to his children. The two were best friends. Pandit would refer to Maureen, Nusli's wife, as 'my sister'.

Wadia and Ambani had been engaged in a titanic struggle. Wadia believed (with some justification, I imagine) that Dhirubhai was trying to damage his business. In his own eyes, he was an old-style straightforward Parsi industrialist. Dhirubhai was a shyster who manipulated the system.

I had no problem with Wadia's anger. He had a right to it. But as editor, I had a right to run *Imprint* as I pleased.

Pandit never called.

He told me later that Wadia had called him to rave and rant but to his credit, he had never once mentioned it to me at the time. He had read the story, he said, and it was fair.

There were several such instances and we followed a simple principle. Pandit wrote what he liked in his On the Marquee column at the front of the book and I looked after the rest of the magazine. By then, he had busied himself with his international investments. His Nice restaurant was a success and he was looking to sell it at a tidy profit. I don't think *Imprint* occupied much mind space. He had a daily call with Mr Pai to look at the figures for the whole company and I doubt if *Imprint* even came up in those chats.

So, from all perspectives, I had a dream job.

There was no real reason to look elsewhere though the offers did come streaming in.

I was friends with Samir Jain who was taking over the *Times of India* empire from his father and one day, he came to me with an idea. Why didn't I join the group which he was in the process of re-inventing?

I could start by being editor of the *Sunday Review*, the weighty supplement that went out free with the paper. Then, as he made other changes, he would put me somewhere else and we would see how it went.

It was a good offer. At that stage, newspapers were the one part of the media that still remained more or less as they had been a decade ago. The magazine boom made them seem tired, old and second rate. Samir argued that as bad as they were, the papers had power because we had grown up with them. The trick he said was to unlock the value of the brands by producing a paper that was worthy of the famous name it bore.

I had never heard anyone talk about newspapers like this before and I was convinced that Samir was on to something. In fact, I believed, if he could pull it off, he would end the magazine revolution or at least, shift the balance of power back to newspapers again.

The Jains occupied a special place in the Indian newspaper business. Not only did they own the largest newspaper group in India, their papers were also regarded as more authoritative than all the others. The Jains never interfered in editorial matters or pursued a political agenda. This gave their editors a sense of both responsibility and power. (A few years after Samir made his offer Dileep Padgaonkar who edited the *Times of India* told an interviewer that he had the second most important job in the country.)

I had breakfast with Samir's father, Ashok Jain, at their house on Carmichael Road and he seemed happy enough with the idea of my coming on board. I met his mother at their Delhi house and she, too, seemed to be pleased.

Samir had made it clear to me that it was an all-or-nothing choice. He was offering me the editorship of a single publication but he was also asking me to commit myself for several years to help him in his quest to re-invent the company. (As everybody now knows, he succeeded and transformed the newspaper industry.)

Samir had given me no deadline but I felt I had to discuss the idea with Pandit. Wouldn't I seem ungrateful after the way he had backed me?

In the end, Pandit solved the problem himself. He announced that he was buying a flat in Cuffe Parade and moving back to India full-time. He was going to immerse himself in the political scene and use *Imprint* as a vehicle to promote the values of what he regarded as a clean India. It was clear that there could be no room for the editor given his desire to run the magazine in pursuit of his own agenda so he didn't seem very surprised when I said I would move on within the next three months. It was 1986 and both he and I seemed ready for new beginnings.

Magazines had been fun, I told, myself, but I was now ready for newspapers—or at least for the newspapers of the 1990s by when I calculated Samir would have re-invented the industry.

I was wrong, of course. For the moment, at least, I would end up sticking with magazines.

There is a funny postscript to the *Imprint* story. Some years after I left *Imprint*, I had coffee with Phillip Knightley of the *Sunday Times* whom I had met in London when I was researching my Inlaks project.

Phillip asked what I had been doing and I mentioned *Imprint*.

'Ah,' he said, 'you know I worked there?'

I said I had no idea.

'Still a CIA operation?' he asked.

My jaw dropped.

He told me the story. In the year that he spent in India while travelling from Australia to England, he had worked with Gloria and Arthur Hale, the American couple who ran *Imprint*. At that time, the magazine consisted only of condensed versions of current American best-sellers so all Knightley had to do was to edit the text.

But Gloria and Arthur Hale were CIA agents? Really?

Yes, he responded. When he was writing a book about the Cold War, he interviewed Harry Rositzke, a retired CIA agent who had once been station chief in India. He told Rositzke that he knew India well, having spent a year in the country.

And what did you do in India, Rositzke asked.

Phillip told him he worked for a magazine called *Imprint*. Rositzke was delighted. 'One of my little operations,' he laughed.

He told Phillip the story. Apparently in the sixties, the Russians were flooding India with cheap fiction and comic books. The Cold War was on and the US feared that India would soon lose its cultural reference points, abandon Western popular culture and start reading Russian books. (Fat chance!)

So a plan was dreamt up to flood India with American popular culture. Imprint was one component. Making condensed versions of the latest American bestsellers available at very low prices might attract Indian readers. In any case, it was a relatively low-cost operation and provided perfect cover for Gloria and Arthur, who he described as his best agents.

At some stage, said Knightley, the Hales had moved on to a new assignment. Did I know who the CIA had then put on the project?

My face went pale but I put the idea out of my head. Then Knightley published a memoir in which he told the whole story.

I felt now, that I had to get to the bottom of the ownership issue. Pandit had always said vaguely that the Hales sold out to the Birlas who had no real interest in the publication, which enabled him to buy it cheap.

I asked a mutual friend to send him a message.

Which Birla was it?

He said it was K.K. Birla.

By some co-incidence, I knew K.K. Birla well. I asked K.K. Birla why he had bought *Imprint*.

'What is *Imprint*, Vir?' he asked in return.

He had never even heard of the damn thing.

I sent Pandit a message relaying what K.K. Birla had said.

He was agitated enough to dig up the original correspondence and sent it to me.

And there it was: a set of letters from K.K. Birla's office to Pandit and back confirming the sale of *Imprint*.

My guess is that it was too long ago and too insignificant a transaction for K.K. Birla to recall.

But how had the CIA managed to turn it around so that no trace remained of its original ownership?

I guess we'll never know.

NINETEEN

'WERE YOU PLANNING ON KISSING ME?'

Pandit had, quite reasonably, asked me to give him a little time to find a new editor. But, I suspected that I already knew whom he would settle on.

I have never been able to work out why Pandit was so smitten with Dom Moraes. Dom had worked for him at the *Asia Magazine* in Hong Kong, apparently with some measure of success. Dom already had the drinking problem which would later become more acute when he returned to India. But Pandit insisted that he could handle Dom. He told Khushwant Singh that he had thrown away the bottle of whisky that Dom kept by his side at the *Asia Magazine* (in another version, the bottle was locked inside Dom's desk), a story that enraged Dom who insisted it wasn't true and blamed Khushwant for putting it in his column without double-checking.

By the early 1980s, after Dom returned to India, the stories of his drinking were legendary in Bombay. Salman Rushdie told me that when he visited Bombay in the aftermath of the success of *Midnight's Children*, Dom phoned him and asked if they could have a drink. Rushdie, unaware of Dom's liquid reputation, invited him to the bar at his hotel where Dom drank solidly.

Then, Dom invited Rushdie to his home for a meal. Though Dom was clearly drunk, it would have been rude to refuse so Rushdie went along with him. When they reached the Moraes residence, Dom asked Rushdie to wait in the living room while he organized the food. As Rushdie sat alone, he could hear the sounds of an altercation from inside the house.

'No. I will not feed him,' a woman shouted.

Some indistinct mumbling from a male voice (presumably Dom) followed.

Then it was the woman again. 'You invited him. You fucking feed him.'

Nothing for a few minutes. Then, the sound of a loud crash, like someone falling.

As Rushdie wondered what to do, a servant arrived.

'Sorry sir,' he said. 'Sahib *to behosh ho gaye.*' (Sahib has passed out.)

There were many stories like this which Pandit knew. He must also have heard that Dom did not appear to have much affection for Pandit. Dom told me of one occasion when he returned to the office after lunch, more than a little merry.

Pandit saw him and said reproachfully, 'Dom, your mouth is smelling of alcohol.'

Dom was unfazed. 'Why RV?' he asked, 'Were you planning on kissing me?'

It did not augur well for *Imprint* but that was no longer my concern.

My real concerns were the other work I did when I was in Bombay. Because *Imprint* was a monthly, I often had a lot of time on my hands after the issue had closed and gone to press.

So I did quite a lot of freelance writing. I wrote extensively for the *Illustrated Weekly* which Pritish Nandy had revived and turned into the hottest magazine in India. I did the odd piece for *Movie*, edited by my friend Rauf Ahmed. I had a monthly column in *Debonair*, which the editor Anil Dharkar had very kindly given me. (That was the first signed column I ever wrote and I had to wean myself off *India Today*'s newsmagazine style and *Imprint*'s narrative tone to create a new voice for myself.)

And then, there were the food reviews. There were people who wrote about food in Bombay. The great Behram Contractor (Busybee) did a much better job than I ever could. But he was a nice man and never wrote anything bad. Since I had left *Bombay* magazine, the food writing genre had been ignored and I thought that there was a gap in the market. People wanted sharp, critical reviews of restaurants that they could trust.

I took the idea to Vinod Mehta whom I had known well and liked during his *Debonair* days. (He was Anil Dharker's predecessor.) Vinod was now editing the *Sunday Observer*, a feature-heavy broadsheet that was immensely popular with what might be called the chattering classes of Bombay. He had been pressing me to write for the *Sunday Observer* where he counted on a roster of writers who wrote more for the love of being read than for the money (Nirmal Goswami, Iqbal Masud, Dhiren Bhagat, etc.).

The *Observer* had no money, Vinod warned me, but he would love to have me on board. I gave him my restaurant review idea. He liked it but said that he foresaw one immediate problem. As the paper could only pay its writers a pittance, there was no way it could afford to reimburse restaurant bills.

I said that was fine. I would pay for the restaurants myself. I liked going out anyway and in those days, restaurants were not terribly expensive. But, I added, he couldn't tell anyone that I was doing the reviews. By the end of my time at *Bombay* magazine, I had become a marked man. Every time I entered a restaurant the kitchen was put on high alert.

I would sign the reviews Vikram Sinha and deal with only one or two people on his staff, who would know who Vikram Sinha really was. This sounded good in theory but in practice, it made no sense. The *Observer* office was one not very large room so everyone knew what everyone else was doing. Vinod himself was an open and expansive person, always ready to blab halfway through the first drink. So he never quite remembered that my identity was a secret.

Fortunately, he did not know too many people in the restaurant business so for over a year, I was able to conceal my identity from restaurants till people began putting two and two together.

I would have to give all that up once I joined *The Times* and disappeared into the embrace of India's largest media organization. It would be like working for *India Today* where the only writing I did was within the group. It would be a different feeling but if I was to remain a journalist then a large organization made more sense in the long run, than a benign but small proprietor like R.V. Pandit.

And yet, even as I prepared to move on, a single thought kept nagging away at me. It was that old doubt: did I want to spend my whole life being a Bombay journalist?

Almost on impulse I called Aveek Sarkar, proprietor of the Ananda Bazar Patrika (ABP) group. ABP was the go-ahead group in that era. It had made its reputation with *Sunday*, a weekly political newsmagazine (a sort of mass-market alternative to *India Today*) and had gone on to launch *Sportsworld* and *Businessworld* and then the *Telegraph*, the first really modern newspaper in India.

More important than that, Aveek Sarkar was known for being the kind of proprietor who pushed his editors forward, giving them complete freedom. It was said that when you saw Aveek and M.J. Akbar, the editor of the *Telegraph* together, Akbar seemed like the boss and Aveek like his sidekick.

I called the *Ananda Bazar* switchboard in Calcutta and asked to speak to Aveek. They connected me to his office, a secretary answered, asked me to hold on and then put me through in seconds.

Aveek Sarkar did not seem surprised to hear from me. I began to explain who I was but he interrupted to say that he already knew. I said I wanted to meet him and he responded by fixing a time for later in the week. He would be at his Bombay residence at Mafatlal Park on Warden Road, he said.

I turned up at the appointed time to discover a Bengali gentleman from the late nineteenth century sprawled out over a sofa. He wore a starched kurta of the thinnest, finest fabric with carefully arranged creases in the elbow area. His dhoti trailed the floor like an emperor's cloak and his kurta had diamond buttons.

Aveek himself looked as distinguished as his clothes. There was a barely tamed mop of salt and pepper hair which contrasted with the well-trimmed, mostly white beard on his chin. He had a languid air and only came to life when something gossipy or scurrilous was being discussed.

He showed no interest in why I wanted a job or what it was I intended to do. Instead, he questioned me closely about my background. What A Levels had I done? Had I gone to Cambridge or Oxford? I had the distinct sense that if I had said 'Birmingham', he would have terminated the interview.

Finally, after half an hour, accompanied by some newspaper gossip (most of which was wrong; Inder Malhota never became editor of the *Tribune* as Aveek assured me he would, Pritish Nandy was not begging ABP for a job, etc.) Aveek said I ought to come to Calcutta the following week.

Things were moving faster than I had anticipated but this was just as well; I had verbally accepted Samir Jain's offer and if I was going to backtrack, it had to be soon.

I turned up in Calcutta, a city I had never been to before, to be overwhelmed by the crowds and the sounds. I lived in Bombay so I was no stranger to big cities but Calcutta is such an assault on the senses (or at least it was in 1986, it has changed a lot since then) that it takes some getting used to.

I called Aveek once I had checked into the Oberoi Grand. He said to come and see him at the ABP office. Sure, I said, what was the address?

Aveek laughed at the naivety of the question. 'This is Calcutta,' he said. 'Ask anybody. ABP is the establishment.'

So, I found a taxi on Chowringhee and asked the driver to take me to ABP. He had no idea what I was talking about. The doorman from the hotel (in those days, the Grand only had a small doorway, almost hidden between rows of shops on Chowringhee) intervened. I said I was going to the famous newspaper office of ABP.

Yes, of course, he said and berated the driver in Bengali. 'He has newly arrived from Bihar,' the doorman told me. 'He can't even speak proper Bengali! I have told him where it is.'

And so we drove for a few minutes down Chowringee, turned right and came to an impressive old building that radiated Raj nostalgia.

My driver apologized for the mix up. I paid him, went into the newspaper office and asked for Aveek Sarkar.

They looked at me as though I was mad.

A peon led me back to the entrance and showed me the sign on the door. It said 'The Statesman'. I was at the office of ABP's great rival.

A very nice man who had observed all this, took pity on me, pointed me in the right direction and said that ABP was only a few minutes away. I walked till I reached what I assumed was the right street because it was named after Prafulla Sarkar, who I assumed was some relative of Aveek's. I walked further in, past something called Ananda Tailors (which Aveek later denied owning) and came to an ugly squat modern building with groups of men speaking loudly in Bengali in the driveway.

This was the right place because they took me up to Aveek Sarkar's office right away. I apologized for being late and explained that my taxi had taken me to the *Statesman* by mistake. Aveek showed no embarrassment at all. After all his bragging about how all of Calcutta knew ABP, he looked at me as though I was a congenital idiot with no sense of direction.

Then, he told me what the job was. *Sunday* had worked when it was a one-rupee publication, he said. But as costs rose, they had to increase the price and circulation fell. They had tried revamping it to make it more upmarket but for some reason that had not worked.

Akbar who had turned the original *Sunday* into such a success was now busy with the *Telegraph* (which he had founded) and had been persuaded to let the Sarkars find another editor for *Sunday*. Akbar had insisted that it had to be one of his deputies. So the choice was restricted to Shubhabrata Bhattacharya (Shubho) the head of the Delhi bureau or Tushar Pandit, a shambolic character who looked after the desk in Calcutta.

The Sarkars had picked Shubho. But within months, Akbar and Shubho had fallen out. Nor had the magazine done well under Shubho. So they were now looking for a new editor. Aveek had read *Imprint*, he said, and liked it. He had consulted with Akbar who had also spoken well of me. So would I be interested in taking over *Sunday*?

Except that it wasn't that simple. The Sarkars were old style feudal employers. They never sacked anyone. Tushar Pandit, once he was passed over for editor of *Sunday*, had refused to work under Shubho. So they had promised to send him to Washington as an ABP correspondent. That hadn't worked out. So Tushar hung around the ABP offices doing nothing at full salary.

As for Shubho, it would be too harsh to sack him. So they would demote him to political editor. He might be hurt if he was replaced at once by a thirty-year-old from Bombay. (The 'from Bombay' thing would come up again and again.) So Aveek would call himself editor. I would be called 'senior editor' which as Aveek explained, lying through his teeth, meant 'a person who is senior to the editor.'

This would be a temporary arrangement because he was sure, Aveek added, that Shubho would leave. But he wanted Shubho to leave on his own, with dignity.

How would all of us be described on the masthead?

'Oh, I will just kill the masthead.'

So, for all practical purposes, I was now editor of *Sunday* but for a few months at least, my official designation would be senior editor.

I pointed out that this seemed like an immensely complicated way of making an appointment. But Aveek had his arguments ready. What was Suman Dubey's designation at *India Today*? He was called, I said, as all editors in that group were, managing editor.

'But isn't he the editor?'

'Yes, he is.'

'What were you called at *Bombay*?'

'Managing editor. Aroon was called editor-in-chief.'

'There!' Aveek said with satisfaction. 'Point proven.'

Well no, not exactly.

At *India Today* you died as managing editor because that was the highest any journalist could go. Did Aveek intend senior editor to become a permanent designation?

'No, no,' he insisted. 'You will be editor in a few months.'

We discussed my salary. He was offering me less than the *Times* had ('*Arre baba*, this is Calcutta; our scales are lower') but he was throwing in a company house for free which Samir was not doing.

I pointed out that I didn't need a house in Bombay. And if he was making me shift to Calcutta and paying me less than the *Times*, he couldn't really expect me to pay my own rent.

And so it went, till finally it was time for me to take my return flight to Bombay.

I said I would call him.

TWENTY

'A MAN TRAPPED IN
THE WRONG CENTURY'

Why do we make the decisions we do? I often feel we make them purely on the basis of gut-feel or instinct and then look for justifications in retrospect.

On the face of it, there was no compelling argument for choosing ABP over the *Times*. Having got the measure of Samir Jain, I was convinced that he would revolutionize the newspaper business and turn the *Times of India* into one of the world's great media power houses. He was offering me an opportunity to be part of that journey.

Plus, he was offering me a solid, concrete job with more money than ABP could offer and access to millions of readers all over India. I would stay on in Bombay and even if the job at the *Times* did not work out, I would still be within my comfort zone and in a position to find a new job.

Aveek was offering me editor of *Sunday*, a magazine which was in trouble without actually offering me the real designation, at least for a few months. As smart as ABP was, I know it would never be in the *Times'* league because nobody there had Samir's vision or commercial brilliance. I was uprooting my life, going to a strange city and doing it all for less money.

I think Aveek sensed my hesitation. The following week when he was in Bombay again, he took me out to dinner at the Rotisserie, then billed as India's most expensive restaurant and advanced various claims on behalf of Calcutta. I could have a large house rather than a flat as I had in Bombay. It would be my own place as distinct from my Bombay flat which belonged to my mother. (He made it sound like I would own this accommodation which, in reality, ABP would rent in its own name.) Calcutta was the only city with club life. (When I said loathed Raj clubs and would never dream of joining one, he looked at me as though I was a bumpkin or a yokel.)

Eventually though, for reasons I still can't fully explain, I took the ABP job.

This was a breach of faith. I had verbally accepted the *Times* job, I told Pritish Nandy who was my friend and who, I thought, would be able to break the news more easily to Samir.

Pritish could not believe that I would pick ABP, a 'second-rate organization', over the *Times*. He had left Calcutta, a city he loved, and come to Bombay because he wanted to work for the best. Why would I make the reverse journey?

Besides, had I lived in Calcutta? Nobody who was from Bombay could ever live there. Our mutual friend Anupam Kher had gone briefly to Calcutta and had been so horrified that he kissed the tarmac at Bombay airport once he returned. I would be in the same position. (I never double-checked the story with Anupam so it is possible that Pritish may have rearranged the facts to dissuade me from going to Calcutta!)

Eventually Samir called. He was speaking as a friend, he said. He thought I was making a big mistake. He knew I would be back. So, here was his suggestion. The Jains had a large house in Calcutta. Why didn't I just move in there? The house was empty most of the time. I would not last long with ABP, so why bother to even rent a house?

Within six months to a year when I had accepted that the ABP job was a mistake, he explained, I could move back to Bombay without ever having shifted my residence or disrupted my life. There would still be room for me at the *Times*.

In the circumstances, it was an extraordinarily gracious and generous response. I thanked him and said, with more conviction than I really felt, that I was sure I would be okay with ABP. We kept in touch for the next few years (the *Times* made one more serious stab at hiring me in 1990) and he was always warm and friendly, never holding it against me that I had broken my word to him in 1986.

I hadn't argued too much with Aveek Sarkar about money because I had always had the sense that in the long run, I would have a much better standard of living at ABP than I would at other newspaper organizations. This was part instinct and partly observation. M.J. Akbar, the group's star editor, had a lifestyle that all other editors envied.

So I was not thrilled to discover on my first day at work in Calcutta that a) they had forgotten that I needed a residence in Calcutta and b) had booked me into a seedy hotel where cockroaches shared the room with me. In those days, Calcutta had only one good hotel: The Grand. The rest were all dumps. (The Taj Bengal opened years later.)

I asked Aveek about my house. He summoned a man from the Estate Department who said he would look for something. I complained about the seedy hotel which, of course, Aveek had never been inside. So, as if to make up he invited me home for dinner that night.

Aveek lived (still lives) in a beautiful bungalow decorated in a comfortable but distinctly Raj style. Presumably this was deliberate because, like the rest of us, he had bought his own furniture. On the walls were paintings by such contemporary masters as Bikash Bhattacharya and Ganesh Pyne as well as great works from the classical Bengali school.

I asked him about the house. 'I told the architect,' he said, 'that imagine if a Raj official in the nineteenth century had wanted to build a house in Calcutta. That is what I want, along with all mod-cons, of course.' He must have seen the look on my face because he added, by way of explanation, 'I am basically a man trapped in the wrong century.'

This was too much, even though it was my first day at work.

'Aveek,' I said, 'if you lived in this area during the Raj, you would have been a waiter. Life was not easy for Indians.'

He thought about this, shrugged his shoulders and we waited for the guest of honour to arrive.

It was Amartya Sen, whom I knew slightly from attending his seminars at Oxford. I discovered another Aveek Sarkar trait. He would invite the best economists, lawyers, historians and politicians home. But instead of trying to pump them for information as us ordinary journalists would do, Aveek would lecture them on their specialty.

So Amartya Sen was taught economics for two hours by Aveek Sarkar.

Over the years I would see Aveek do this to nearly everyone. (This extended to interviews. A few years later, we were interviewing Rajiv Gandhi and Aveek raised arcane points about the economy. Rajiv tried to explain what the government's position was when Aveek interrupted. 'I think I know what you are trying to say Prime Minister, but let me tell you why you are wrong.')

Because he had no malice and was personally likeable (even when he was wrong—and he often was) Aveek got away with it.

Even Sen treated him with indulgence and appeared to have a good time. The evening was powered along by the sound of Aveek's lecturebaazi and his elegant wife Rakhi's world-class cooking.

The next day, I woke up to a cockroach, packed my bag and checked into The Grand. In office, later in the day, I told Aveek what I had done. The Grand was double the price of the hotel they had booked me into but Aveek didn't bat an eyelid. 'If that's what you prefer,' he said.

Nobody had any clue what the house situation was so I asked Aveek if it was okay for me to go back to Bombay each weekend. In my mind, I had prepared a case for saying that the air ticket would cost as much as it would for ABP to feed and house me at the Grand.

I didn't need it. Aveek agreed at once, called his secretary in and told him to book me a business class return ticket to Bombay. Suddenly it didn't seem to matter that ABP was paying me a few thousand less than I could have earned elsewhere.

I was using beat-up Ambassador cars from the ABP car pool and each day a different little man in a dhoti would drive me around town, making sharp turns, forcing pedestrians to thank God they were still alive and cheerfully flouting every traffic regulation. On my second day, the driver deliberately drove into a street where it said 'No Entry'. A cop attempted to stop him. 'Ehh Ananda Bazar,' the driver shouted at him, pointing to the PRESS sticker on the car and kept driving.

It was a very different world from the one that I had left behind at *Imprint* and in the evenings, I would retire to the serenity of the Grand and find some peace.

Strangely enough, I never had a second thought about having taken the job, largely I think because, at some basic level, I liked and trusted Aveek, his Raj pretensions notwithstanding.

And then there was the challenge of the work. I had stopped reading *Sunday* after Akbar gave up on it so I hadn't realized how far it had sunk. I met the Calcutta staff. They seemed nice enough. But having spoken to them it was clear why they produced a magazine that was quite so terrible.

I had my work cut out for me.

TWENTY-ONE

'PONDIT HERE BUT CANNOT HEAR'

Though Aveek was (and still is) an optimist by nature, seemingly unperturbed by adversity, the situation at *Sunday* was grimmer than anyone at ABP was willing to state openly.

In many ways, the magazine was past its expiry date. Its glory years had been 1977–82 under Akbar who had used it, rather as Russi Karanjia had used *Blitz* in the 1960s and early 1970s, to raise matters of political concern forcefully. With a one-rupee cover price, it had become the overly political alternative to *India Today*, striving not for *Time* magazine–style neutrality but pursuing its own partisan positions aggressively.

To some extent, Akbar was still running the *Telegraph* in the same way (in 1986, he was a vocal supporter of Rajiv Gandhi) but it was clear that, at a national level, in a market dominated by *India Today*, no newsmagazine could get away with such an approach. In 1983, Pritish Nandy had revived the *Illustrated Weekly* but he had been careful not to inject his own opinions into the publication.

Aveek wanted an *India Today*-type publication with 'a little more flair and individuality' but ABP did not have the budget to create such a magazine. *Sunday* was still printed on cheap newsprint at newspaper presses, mostly in black and white and looked much the same as it had done in the one-rupee days. (The primary difference was an art paper cover page; the inside was unchanged.) In contrast, both the *Weekly* and especially, *India Today*, were superbly printed on high quality paper.

Why would anyone believe that a magazine that still looked like it cost one-rupee was worth five rupees?

Aveek accepted that this might be a problem in the short term. But, he said, he planned to buy high-quality paper and shift the printing to proper presses. So why didn't I use the period before that happened to get the editorial content in order?

This was easier said than done. At the time *Sunday*'s salaries were between a third to a fourth of *India Today*'s. (Admittedly, *India Today* paid the best salaries in the country.) There were good individual reporters on the staff but the bulk of the Calcutta office comprised mediocre and dispirited sub-editors who took little pride in their work or the publication that employed them. Nearly everyone spoke to everyone else in Bengali—even the few non-Bengalis in the office were Bengali speakers. I spoke no Bengali and was often at a loss to figure out what was going on.

Standards were low. On one occasion, a sub-editor was reprimanded by one of the senior-most people on my staff for 'misspelling', the word 'cudgels'. 'Don't you know that it is spelled cudgles?' the senior person shouted. Frequently there were English mistakes in the headlines, and often, even on the cover.

Aveek told me that Tushar Pandit, who had been passed over for the editorship when it went to Shubho, was a gifted journalist whom I should use more. Tushar was a stringer for the BBC and on most days, he would be shouting into the office phone, dictating an input to the BBC's London desk usually over a very scratchy line. (I will always associate him with the sentence, shouted very loudly into a receiver, in a pronounced Bengali accent, 'Pondit here but cannot hear!')

I didn't think he was a bad sort and when he suggested that he be allowed to go to Delhi to do a story on the rise of drug use among children, I readily agreed. He returned with a perfectly acceptable story which persuaded me that his written English was better than his spoken English. We ran the story—and ran into trouble.

Soon after the issue hit the stands, the acclaimed director Ramesh Sharma wrote to us to say that he had invited Tushar to a screening of his documentary film on—what else?—the rise of drug use among children. Tushar, he said, had tape recorded the commentary and reproduced large chunks of it as part of his own story. To prove his point, Sharma included entire passages of the documentary voice-over which had appeared, unchanged, in *Sunday*.

I asked Tushar. He did not deny that he had gone to see the documentary. (In fact I began to wonder if the trip to Delhi and the story suggestion had all been a response to an invitation to a preview of the documentary.)

So, I asked, how did entire chunks of the script turn up in his story?

He thought about it. 'I must have remembered them,' he said, ponderously.

The matter had already reached Aveek who seemed remarkably unperturbed. His view was that Tushar had clearly plagiarized his story from the film.

I said, with as much outrage as I could muster, that this was completely unacceptable. I would not be assigning any more stories to Tushar.

Okay, said Aveek and shrugged the matter off. So, the man who Aveek had said would be my number two in the Calcutta office did very little for *Sunday* for the rest of his tenure, choosing instead to loudly phone in his stories to the BBC while struggling with Calcutta's terrible phone system. ('Pondit here but cannot hear . . .')

In many ways, ABP was like no organization I had seen before. Every year when the city celebrated Durga Puja, a Bengali festival that lasted several days, the whole of ABP shut down. A single telephone operator would come in to work and if anyone called the switchboard, he would pick up the phone, bellow 'Poojo' into it and hang up immediately. For several days, there would be no papers and the magazines would miss that week's issue.

When I asked about this unusual practice, I was told it was a Bengali thing. 'We Bengalis,' I would be told, 'we are like the French. We are warm but we are passionate. We are quick to love but we are also quick to anger.'

Whenever I pointed out that this seemed more like the Irish than the French (The French are warm? Really?), I would get disapproving looks.

In the minds of many educated Bengalis of that era, Calcutta was Paris as it might have existed in another dimension. Jyoti Basu was Charles de Gaulle, Satyajit Ray was Godard and Truffaut rolled into one, and the *adda*s where Bengali intellectuals met each day were like the cafés of the Left Bank where Jean Paul Sartre held forth.

'We can be very quarrelsome, Vir,' one Bengali intellectual told me proudly.

'Yes,' I said, 'like the Irish.'

He changed the subject.

In retrospect, I was in Calcutta at a bad time. Rajiv Gandhi had called it a dying city in parliament. He had sneered that the only Marx the city's ruling communist elite had known was Groucho. (This caused more puzzlement than anger. I had to explain to various lefty intellectuals who the Marx Brothers were.)

Certainly, Calcutta could be depressing. Industry had been driven out by the communist trade union though the party itself was very close to the industrialists who had remained. We used to joke that the 'M' in CPI (M) stood for 'Marwari'.

Calcutta looked poor and dusty and traffic would often be stalled by demonstrations and *dharna*s. Bengal had invented the single-file demonstration. Even if fifty people gathered for a protest, they could halt traffic for half an hour or more because they walked very slowly, in single file, maintaining what we would now call 'social distancing' between each demonstrator.

Those of us who were new to Calcutta were fascinated by the level of pointless protest. Udayan Sharma, the editor of *Ravivar*, the group's Hindi weekly, once said to me, 'Have you noticed how they protest about everything in Calcutta? But not one *dharna* is ever about the lack of any basic civic amenities?'

And yes, it was true, the civic problems in Calcutta were enormous. The lights kept going off (Bengal had surplus power generating capacity on paper but the unions ensured that the power plants were inefficient.) The phone system was so bad that it took several minutes to make a successful call to Delhi (which is probably why Tushar Pandit spent his life trying to hear his BBC bosses in London) and even then, the voices were barely audible. The roads were a disgrace. I thought that there were fewer private cars in Calcutta than there were in Bombay, but the pot-holed streets were always jammed.

And yet, when people in Bombay asked me what it was like to live in Calcutta, I always said that the quality of life (for the middle class, at least) was much better. It was easier to rent a larger home than it would have been in Bombay. Shops and restaurants seemed cheaper. It was easy enough to find a driver or other kinds of help.

And I believed that Calcutta was actually turning a corner. The by-pass, linking the airport with the central Park Circus, had recently been opened. (A popular joke at the time was 'Calcutta may have been dying but now it has had a by-pass') and the metro had made it easier for people to get to work. Ferries were employed to allow people to travel on the river and the water ways.

In contrast, Bombay had nothing like the by-pass (the Sea link would not open for another three decades), it had no metro, only an overcrowded, ancient local train system and it refused to use the sea for transport.

Everybody in Bombay laughed at me when I said that but I believe it was true. Unfortunately, the world (and that includes Bengalis) had fallen for the Dominique Lapierre view of Calcutta as the City of Joy, full of cheerful paupers who rejoiced in their hunger and poverty.

That was not the Calcutta I found. And I soon fell in love with the real Calcutta.

TWENTY-TWO

'SOMEONE IS SHOOTING AT US'

One of Aveek's big concerns was that nobody at *Sunday* had any contacts. This was not strictly true. Many people in our Delhi bureau were well-connected. But I guess what Aveek meant was that we had no inroads into the prime minister's office (PMO), then seen as the source of all power. Shubho knew M.L. Fotedar well but he was not part of the PMO. I knew V.P. Singh from my *Imprint* days but though he was the finance minister, Aveek believed he was out of the loop. Even Amitabh Bachchan, who was Rajiv Gandhi's closest friend, was outside of the PMO circuit.

I knew Mani Shankar Aiyar from before he had joined the PMO. He was a very bright if somewhat indiscreet IFS officer who had made himself unpopular with journos by saying things like, 'The only reason we read the English media is because you people share a socio-economic background with us. Otherwise, you count for nothing.' Or even, 'Journalists are basically people who weren't bright enough to pass the IAS or IFS exams.'

The arrogance was, I thought, a deliberate strategy. The media would blame Mani for everything and absolve Rajiv of all responsibility. Because Mani served as a lightning rod, Rajiv remained popular with journos who scrambled to get an interview or even a brief meeting with him. Mani wanted Rajiv to be accessible and he broke through the ranks of Delhi-based reporters to provide access to regional journalists.

For instance, in that era, it was considered to be a big deal to travel on the prime minister's plane when Rajiv went abroad.

In Mrs Gandhi's day, access had largely been restricted to a small band of low-profile Delhi-based special correspondents. But such was Rajiv's glamour that editors and proprietors who normally travelled first class and business class squeezed themselves into economy class seats at the back of an Air-India 747, along with the attendants and the security men.

Journos rarely got to see the PM (at least not on a one-to-one basis) during these trips but the idea of sitting at the back of the PM's plane seemed irresistible to many proprietors.

Ananda Bazaar Patrika (ABP), the Bengali newspaper that the group was named after, did eventually get on the plane but legend had it that this was due to an error. When Rajiv looked at the press list for one of his trips, he pointed out to Mani that there were too few women in the press party. Mani looked through the Press Information Bureau's list of accredited journalists and discovered that ABP had a senior Delhi-based journalist called Sunit Ghosh. As Mani's wife was called Suneet Vir Singh, he assumed that Sunit was a girl's name and duly added Sunit Ghosh to the list.

He was most surprised when a distinguished Bengali gentleman turned up at the airport to take his seat on the plane. But by then it was too late.

(I am not sure if this story is true. Another ABP story had it that Aveek's father, who had run the group before Aveek, had a policy of not allowing either alcohol or women into the office. How then did one explain the hiring of Olga Tellis, the paper's star Bombay correspondent? Easy, or so the story had it. The senior Mr Sarkar had never heard the name Olga and approved the appointment thinking that Olga was a man. I find this story hard to believe so perhaps the one about the PM's plane is also made-up.)

But ABP was not a regular on the plane in the way that the *Telegraph* was. Akbar knew Rajiv well, had free run of the PMO and frequently went abroad with the PM's media party. The whole group envied his access, especially because access to Rajiv meant that other ministers also gave you access.

So naturally I asked Mani in January 1987, shortly after I had joined ABP, if he could arrange for me to meet Rajiv.

It took Mani only a month to deliver. Rajiv was travelling to Mizoram and Arunachal Pradesh, he said. Would I like a seat on the plane?

I explained that I was not keen on being stuck at the back of the aircraft with no access to the PM only to say that I had been on his plane.

No, said Mani. Domestic trips were different. When Rajiv went abroad, an Air India plane was reconfigured for him. But for domestic trips he used one of two Boeing 737s maintained by the Air Force for the use of the president, vice president and prime minister. These did not usually accommodate a press party and he could promise me half an hour with Rajiv on the Delhi–Aizawl sector.

I jumped at the opportunity.

In many ways, this was my first taste of the prime ministerial lifestyle. You drove to a separate terminal at Delhi airport (also managed by the IAF), were taken by the back door into a specially configured 737 that had a small area with normal seating, a larger area with eight seats that were laid out (like European train seats, I guess) facing each other with large tables.

The SPG and others sat in the normal seating area, ministers and senior members of the PMO sat in the comfortable area and there were three other areas at the front of the plane: a small space where V. George, Rajiv's personal secretary sat at his desk, a cabin that served as a sort of living room for the PM and a cabin beyond (which I did not see) which had a bed and more seating.

The attendants boarded first, then the ministers and officials (all from the back) and we pressed our noses against the plane's windows to see the prime minister's motorcade drive directly to the steps at the front of the aircraft. Rajiv, his wife, Sonia, and his young daughter, Priyanka, went up the stairs and then disappeared from our view.

As soon as the PM boarded, the doors closed, the plane began to move and we took off almost instantly. The seat belt sign went off in ten minutes and George came to tell Mani that Rajiv wanted him.

Mani vanished into what I assumed was the PM's cabin, returned a few minutes later and said that Rajiv would see me. At that stage,

I had been a journalist (in one form or another) for over a decade, much of that period as an editor and had never felt nervous or intimidated by the thought of meeting anyone.

But this time I was nervous. It wasn't just that I was meeting the prime minister of India one-on-one. It was also that the whole special plane–special terminal thing had, frankly, intimidated me.

As I was ushered into his cabin, I saw that Rajiv was taking photographs from the plane's window. I guess he must have noticed that I was nervous because he made a conscious effort to put me at ease. He asked if I had been to Arunachal before. I said I hadn't. He said that it was very beautiful and that he had tried to persuade his son Rahul to come along but that Rahul had backed out at the last moment saying that he needed to study.

As I had no small talk to offer, I asked if he was keen on photography. Yes, he said. But it often depended on the camera. He described his camera to me and then told an anecdote about his visit to Japan.

Apparently, the prime minister of Japan (I think it was Nakasone) had asked him about the latest Nikon camera and Rajiv had torn into it, saying that it was no improvement on its predecessor and that Nikon should have known better than to do such a shoddy job when expectations were so high.

'And you know,' Rajiv continued, 'I kept thinking that there was something wrong because his face kept getting smaller and smaller and then he stopped talking about cameras entirely. It was only after we boarded the plane and I opened the gift he had given me that I realized that it was exactly the same Nikon camera that I had been critical of!'

I have met nearly every prime minister since then but never have I met one who, realizing that a journo was overawed, made so much small talk to put him at ease.

The fun part of the conversation lasted ten minutes and, conscious that I was using up my time without getting anything of consequence out of the prime minister, I switched to politics.

Could Rajiv explain why the Congress was not doing as well in state by-elections given that only two years before he had won the largest mandate in Indian history?

He was frank. 'I have realized that crowds mean nothing. I campaigned in those states, and my rallies were so well-attended that we thought we would do well. But I think people only came to see me. They were curious and may be in some places I was personally popular. But at state elections, people vote on state issues. Just because they come to your rallies, it doesn't mean anything.'

We did ten minutes of this sort of stuff before I decided to push my luck. I told him that Giani Zail Singh felt that he was being denied the respect that should be accorded to the President of India. I expected Rajiv to give discreet denials and to move on.

But no, he went for it.

'Respect for the president? Hah, did you see the statements he made when he became president?'

I said I imagined he was talking about the Giani's famous remark that he had become president only because his leader had told him to take the job. 'If Indiraji had told me to take a *jhadhu* and sweep the floor, I would have done that too,' Zail Singh was quoted as saying.

'And he talks about respect for the office,' Rajiv said disgustedly. 'He wants only one thing. He wants a second term which we are not going to give him. He is creating all these problems so we will back down and give him another term.'

And why wouldn't the Congress give him another term?

'Do you know what kind of role he played during the Punjab crisis? We have documents, written in my mother's own handwriting, in which she recorded how much Zail Singh sabotaged any attempt at peace in Punjab. And he did this while sitting in Rashtrapati Bhavan. Punjab leaders would come to Delhi and we would work out a settlement. Then, when they went back, they would get a call from Zail Singh saying 'don't agree, the government will give you more'!' (This allegation had been leveled against Zail Singh before but never—as far as I knew—by the prime minister of India.)

'My mother stopped sending him any papers related to Punjab and we have also refused to send them to him. That's why he is so frustrated. He wants to sit in Rashtrapati Bhavan and play Punjab politics.'

I said that Zail Singh had pointed to specific slights. He had said that Rajiv had broken the convention that a prime minister discusses the outcomes of his foreign trips with the president.

'Foreign trips!' Rajiv was incredulous. 'The man is an embarrassment. Everywhere he goes, he creates chaos. He went to Bangladesh and told them that he would like to mediate between Khaleda Zia and Haseena. They were so startled that they called us to ask if we wanted to interfere in their internal affairs. We had to scramble and say things like "he is a well-meaning person who was only trying to help. This is not India's policy or intention". Nobody in the MEA sleeps at night when Gianiji is abroad because you don't know what he will say or do.'

There was much more in a similar vein. Yes, said Rajiv, he was stuck with Zail Singh because his mother made a mistake in appointing him. He had done his best, he added, to keep up a good relationship with him.

He spoke about an assassination attempt on Zail Singh and him at Rajghat, a couple of months before our conversation.

'We were walking out together when I realized that we were being shot at. Gianiji turned to me and said "what's that?" I told him "someone is shooting at us. That was the first shot." But the prime minister and President of India can't start running away during a formal function (it was Gandhi Jayanti) so just keep walking. Poor old Gianiji, he was so frightened. But he kept his nerve and neither of us ducked,' Rajiv laughed.

In his view, if Zail Singh served out the rest of his term peacefully, the government would give him even more respect than he deserved. 'But he just keeps playing politics. First Punjab politics and then national politics!'

Rajiv was still talking when the plan began to descend. I was sent back to my seat. 'I told you this was an off-the-record conversation,' Mani hissed at me.

I conceded that such an understanding had been reached. But, I said, nobody in the government of India had ever offered a complete refutation of Zail Singh's claims. If Rajiv was willing to talk this openly to a journalist he had never met before, then surely he wanted his version to get out.

Mani said he would check with Rajiv and went back into the PM's cabin. He came out and said I could use the conversation. 'But attribute it to sources,' he said.

We spent the day in the North East and when we returned to Delhi late that night, I knew that I had to get Zail Singh's responses.

I called Tarlochan the next morning. He was startled to hear that Rajiv Gandhi had finally responded to the many stories that Rashtrapati Bhavan had fed the media. He asked if I could come over right away.

I went to see him and K.C. Singh (a brilliant IFS officer who was part of the president's staff). They heard me out and said they would take it to the president.

By late afternoon, they had prepared a point-by-point response to all of Rajiv's charges. Some of it was convincing and much of it was not. But they (I think it was largely KC) had formulated the responses so cleverly that Rajiv's charges no longer seemed so devastating.

The story appeared a week later. There was a huge response. Nobody had managed to speak to both the key players in this emerging constitutional crisis in the same story before. And though I used the usual codes: 'friends of Rajiv' and 'friends of Zail Singh', everyone knew where it had come from.

Mani was not pleased. I don't think he had expected that I would get Zail Singh's version too. He was upset that I repaid his efforts to get me a meeting with Rajiv by doing a story he didn't like.

But Rajiv, I was later told, did not mind. And Mani later told me what had happened on the plane after I left the PM's cabin.

Apparently he had said to Rajiv: 'Sir, did you really intend to say all that about the president?'

'Yes', said Rajiv, 'Did I say anything very bad?'

'Well sir,' Mani responded, 'you revealed a lot about what he has being doing.'

'Oh really?' said Rajiv. 'But I didn't reveal any of the really bad stuff like his womanizing at Rashtrapati Bhavan.'

Mani had then come to my seat and said I could go ahead and use the information.

It was a great story. Good for me and good for *Sunday*.

But the constitutional crisis it foreshadowed was just about to explode.

TWENTY-THREE

'SO ALL THE ASTROLOGERS WERE WRONG'

The Zail Singh story caused enough of a splash for people to sit up and take notice of *Sunday* again. Aveek was pleased that we had been able to dent the perception that we had no access and because the story quoted both sides, we were able to assert that we were unbiased and objective, terms that were not usually associated with *Sunday*.

By then, events had begun to move at lightning speed and fortunately I actually knew many of the key participants. I went to see Amitabh Bachchan twice, first at his Bombay home and then at the bungalow on Motilal Nehru Marg in Delhi that he used as his office. (It had been Rajiv's office when Mrs Gandhi was alive.)

Bachchan was ill at ease in politics and argued that Rajiv did not realize that he was the victim of a conspiracy. According to Bachchan, this conspiracy centred around V.P. Singh who had linked up with Rajiv's estranged cousin Arun Nehru to run Rajiv out of office. They were using the finance ministry to launch investigations against Rajiv's associates and Sonia Gandhi's family.

I knew V.P. Singh a little so I went to see him. He laughed off the speculation and blamed it all on the Ambanis. In 1985-86, the finance ministry had launched a campaign against Dhirubhai. There were raids, criminal cases and leaks to the press about investigations. Dhirubhai was under so much stress that he had a stroke and went to San Diego for treatment.

The crisis management was taken over by his sons Mukesh and Anil. I knew both slightly but Anil was the one who interacted more often with the media. Anil told me that the campaign against Reliance was just one part of V.P. Singh's plan to oust Rajiv and to take over. Even the *Indian Express*, he said, was part of the campaign.

This seemed hard to believe. I had known Ram Nath Goenka in my Bombay days and he was a huge supporter of Rajiv Gandhi. No, said Anil, the RSS (which was now also part of this campaign, apparently) had appealed to Goenka to join the anti-Rajiv movement.

I had lunch with Goenka at his *Indian Express* building penthouse at Nariman Point. He was bitterly opposed to Dhirubhai, he said, but had nothing against Rajiv. As far as I knew, Goenka and Dhirubhai had been friends so I was a little intrigued.

Was it true, as the Ambanis suggested, that Goenka had turned against them only because of his friendship with Nusli Wadia? I asked him.

Goenka denied this. 'Nusli is an Englishman,' he said. 'He doesn't know how to fight these battles. I am the one teaching him.'

None of this augured well. Soon, it was revealed that V.P. Singh's finance ministry had hired a detective agency to investigate various foreign entities connected with the ruling establishment. Two letters—in my view, obvious forgeries—then made the rounds. Both suggested that V.P. Singh's men were investigating the Bachchans and Sonia Gandhi's family.

I asked V.P. Singh about the letters and he said that it was possible that his men had hired detective agencies to investigate the Ambani holdings abroad. But Bachchan and the Gandhis had nothing to do with it. I pointed out that Amitabh Bachchan was his political rival in Allahabad so he had reason to want to harm the Bachchans. He dismissed the idea.

While all this was going on, India and Pakistan nearly went to war. An Indian army exercise near the border so frightened Pakistan (which thought that it was the precursor to an invasion) that General Zia-ul-Haq, the Pakistani dictator, phoned Rajiv to ask what was going on. Rajiv denied that any attack was planned, invited Zia to

Delhi to watch a cricket match and the situation was defused even as both sides had massed their troops on the border.

A couple of years later, Rajiv told me his side of the story. He said that he had no idea that the exercise was going to involve such massive mobilization and go so near the border. His friend Arun Singh was the minister of state for defence and got along well with General K. Sundarji, the charismatic chief of the army.

Rajiv said he summoned them both to ask why they had gone so far without his authority. According to Rajiv, neither could provide a satisfactory answer and he got the distinct feeling that Sundarji wouldn't have minded going to war.

I have no idea whether it was a response to the forged letters suggesting that the Bachchans and Sonia Gandhi's relatives were being investigated or whether Rajiv really felt that the defence ministry needed a strong minister but V.P. Singh was shifted from finance to defence. His successor at the finance ministry put an end to the pursuit of the Ambanis.

But Singh had the last laugh. Shortly after he arrived at the defence ministry, he launched an enquiry into the Howaldtswerke-Deutsche Werft (HDW) submarine deal, claiming bribes had been paid. A section of Congressmen treated this as an attack on the Gandhis and denounced V.P. Singh. Then, as the fuss over kickbacks in defence deals was growing (the Bofors scandal is the subject of a later chapter), V.P. Singh resigned as defence minister. He was, once again, denounced by loyal Congressmen.

By now, the situation had taken a 180-degree turn. The Ambanis were once again very influential. The government's investigative agencies began to target the *Indian Express* group which turned viciously against Rajiv Gandhi. V.P. Singh, who had established himself as Mr Clean in his finance ministry days was projected by his followers as a shining alternative to Rajiv. He denied having any prime ministerial ambitions and according to Rajiv (I think this may even have been on the record in a later *Sunday* interview), the two men had a warm and emotional chat in which V.P. Singh assured him that the stories about investigations into Sonia's family were Ambani plants.

It was in this chaotic and confused environment that Giani Zail Singh decided to make his move.

The Giani had no hope of getting a second term without the government's support. But what if he exercised his powers as president and dismissed the Rajiv Gandhi government? Such a power existed on paper but it had never been tested and it was hard to see how Zail Singh could get away with exercising it against a popular prime minister.

Zail Singh was smart enough to understand that. But he also sensed that Rajiv was under pressure over Bofors. V.P. Singh's resignation had hurt him. There was a hostile Arun Nehru skulking in the wings. And he had been told, he said, that there was lot of 'masala' (his word, not mine) that was coming against Amitabh, Sonia and perhaps Rajiv himself.

If the Giani could threaten a weakened Rajiv with dismissal then wasn't it possible that the prime minister would make some kind of a deal that would guarantee him a second term out of his eternal gratitude for supporting him at this tough time?

It was a long shot. But what did the Giani have to lose? If the gambit failed, he would be no worse off than he already was as a one-term president in the last months of his term. And at least he would have got some measure of revenge on Rajiv by causing him grief and tension.

I don't think there will ever be a phase like that in Indian politics again. One of the Giani's primary advisors was a dodgy godman who called himself Chandraswami. He had hit the front pages of the British papers during a now-forgotten spat over the ownership of Harrods, the London department store. The fight was between Tiny Rowland (who ran a multinational called Lonrho as well as the *Observer* newspaper) and Mohamed Fayed (a mysterious—in those days—Egyptian businessman) who had emerged, seemingly out of nowhere, to buy Harrods.

Chandraswami was close to the Sultan of Brunei (then one of the world's richest men) and suggested that he could prove that the Sultan was the true owner of Harrods. Apparently, he couldn't. But the process made him rich and notorious and when Rowland and

Chandraswami fell out, Rowland kept urging Indian journalists to run stories against the Swami.

None of this mattered to Chandraswami. Like Amar Singh, a decade later, it made no difference what people said about him, he still found ways to make himself indispensable to politicians and rich and famous people.

I had first been taken to meet the Swami at his 'ashram' in Delhi by my friend Pammi Bakshi, a journalist who knew him. He struck me then as being an extremely sleazy character but he was in the news (on page one of the *Observer*, certainly) so I interviewed him. Throughout the interview, he dropped names. What was worrying was that despite being such an obvious charlatan he actually knew these people. He was, for instance, a friend of the Saudi arms dealer Adnan Khashoggi and showed me photos of himself posing with scores of global celebrities on Khashoggi's yacht.

To my surprise the Swami then became a regular fixture on the political scene and he turned up by Zail Singh's side during this crisis. I asked Tarlochan what the Giani saw in this humbug and he answered, accurately, that the Swami knew everyone in the opposition and could gather support for the president. Zail Singh himself revealed that Chandraswami had told him that he had friends who would provide damaging material against Rajiv.

It seems bizarre in retrospect but for at least two weeks it seemed possible that the government (elected with a two-thirds majority) would be dismissed at any time. Rajiv was tense and worried. He assigned Buta Singh, his Home minister, to negotiate with the Giani but Buta Singh had little to offer. At Rashtrapati Bhavan they claimed that the Intelligence Bureau had bugged every room. The president, I discovered, would only speak frankly after he had taken you to the garden.

Despite Zail Singh's best efforts, V.P. Singh and Arun Nehru (separately) refused to become part of the conspiracy and Chandraswami could not deliver any 'masala'. I doubt if the Giani had actually intended to dismiss the prime minister; it was an empty threat intended solely to intimidate. When he saw that the game was up, he conceded with bad grace.

Rajiv had been keen to make B. Shankaranand the next president but abandoned the idea as the crisis grew. He opted for the conservative choice of R. Venkataraman, the sitting vice president.

Zail Singh had been encouraged by various astrologers (including Chandraswami who was not above claiming psychic powers if the need arose) who assured him that a second term was in his destiny. And one of the last things he told his staff, just before he gave up the office, was, 'So, all the astrologers were wrong.'

They were. But even as that chapter ended, we knew that Rajiv, despite his massive majority, was in more trouble than he realized.

There was a cynical silver lining to this. It was boom time for journalists.

TWENTY-FOUR

'HE SAYS YOU CALLED
HIM A NONSENSE'

Thanks mainly to events that we had no control over but were lucky enough to be well-placed to cover, *Sunday* was doing okay. We were finally being taken seriously in Delhi, for the first time after the M.J. Akbar years. Shubho had moved on, as Aveek had intended him to, and I set about imposing some order on the office.

In Calcutta, we advertised for sub-editors and when the flood of applications came flowing in, Aveek asked me to employ two criteria. 'Look for people from Presidency College,' he said. 'And if two candidates seem hard to choose between, always hire the Brahmin candidate'.

I said I had no idea how to tell if a candidate was a Brahmin just by reading his application. '*Arre baba*, it is easy,' Aveek replied. 'If the surname is Mukherjee, Bannerjee, etc. then they are Brahmins. If you have any difficulty, just ask me.'

I was outraged but also a little mystified by this suggestion. Was Aveek, who seemed perfectly liberal in all other respects, a casteist? After thinking it over for a day, I finally decided I had to ask him.

'Aveek,' I began. 'I don't want to run a magazine where all you Brahmins dominate. I have never even noticed caste and I don't intend to start now.'

He laughed at my indignation. 'What do you mean "you Brahmins"? I am not a Brahmin. I am a Kayastha.'

I was mystified. 'Then why are you asking me to hire Brahmins?'

'I am not. They are usually the best candidates. I am only saying that if two candidates are equal in all other respects, the Bengali Brahmin is more likely to have come from a family background where they read books.'

I was not done. 'And as for your old college,' I continued. 'I don't think we should make this an old boys' club . . .'

He laughed again. 'I am not from Presidency. I am from St. Xavier's.'

I was once again mystified. 'Then why are you asking me to hire people from Presidency?'

'Oh, because they are better at writing.'

I ignored his advice, of course. And over the years, whenever I was to remind him of this absurd directive, he would defend it saying that he was only offering me a realistic guide to the Bengali middle class.

We tried hiring senior people in Calcutta with limited success. I had my eye on Chandan Mitra of the *Statesman* who turned us down saying that he had no interest in magazines. We couldn't think of very many others and decided we would promote from within. Rajiv Bagchi, who had already been at *Sunday* when I joined, emerged as a good leader and ran the Calcutta office when I was travelling.

That round of hiring led us also to hire the super confident Seema Goswami straight out of college, after a slightly bizarre interview where she treated both Aveek and myself as misguided elderly people whom she had to talk down to. (I was thirty-one and—for all her smugness, she didn't even know who I was—she went through the whole interview thinking I was Shubhabrata Bhattacharya, having been told by someone that this was the name of the editor of *Sunday*.)

I had no idea then that years later I would end up falling in love with—and later marrying—her.

I looked around the group for more talent. Rajiv Shukla was a correspondent for *Ravivar* but he was such a good reporter that we seduced him away from his original publication. Seema helped him write his stories (*Ravivar* was a Hindi publication) and they made an excellent team.

We also persuaded Alka Saxena (who later went on to find fame on TV) to moonlight from her *Ravivar* job and write for us. And Udayan Sharma, the editor of *Ravivar* became a frequent contributor and columnist. Aveek recommended R. Jagannathan who was the star of the *Business Standard* desk (he later went on edit almost every top business publication you can name) and we relied on him to do our economic cover stories. For a time, Akbar wrote a popular political column for us called 'Byline' before taking it back to his own *Telegraph*.

It took three months but ABP finally found me a house in New Alipore. No great search was required. They had simply forgotten that they had the lease on the house. It had been locked up and kept unoccupied for years while the accounts department kept paying the rent.

I was ready to move in immediately but was told that I could not buy any furniture. It would be made from scratch by Mr Tham, a largely silent gentleman from Calcutta's Chinese community. Mr Tham had made the furniture for Aveek's house, I was informed in tones of awe. So he must be the best.

He may or may not have been the best but he was certainly the slowest. The furniture took another three months to be made ('he makes it all with his own hands!' they told me) and it was hardly exceptional. Even the claim that Mr Tham had made Aveek's furniture turned out to be bogus. Aveek's wife strenuously denied that Mr Tham had anything to do with their furniture.

By now I had got used to the pace of life in Calcutta. Not only was it slow but if you tried to hurry things up, people treated you as the enemy. ABP itself was like one giant, slumbering pachyderm. It was badly managed and even the better people were soon seduced by the lazy energy of the place.

Lower down the ranks, there was a curious air of negativity. Any time you asked for something to be done, the answer would be '*hobay na*' which translated as 'can't be done'. (ABP joke. 'How many ABP employees does it take to change a light bulb? Ans: Seven. One to change the bulb and six to chant "hobay na".')

I was far less even-tempered than I am now and on one occasion I lost my temper with a clerical employee who had not bothered to perform the simple tasks assigned to him. 'I'm not going to stand for this nonsense,' I told him.

The next day, a delegation from something called the Jukto Committee came to see me. They were the bridge between the union and the management, they said. I offered them some tea and asked how I could help them.

They were here, they said, because a clerical employee (yes, the same guy) had complained that I had used foul language against him. The employee, they added reassuringly, did not deny that there may have been lapses in his performance but it was simply unacceptable for an editor to use foul language with clerical staff. It might be okay, they conceded, to talk to journalists this way. But never to clerical staff.

I racked my brains. What had I said in my anger? Try as I might, I couldn't think of any bad language I had used.

Yes, I had been angry. But that did not seem to be the problem. It was my foul language that had upset them.

Finally, I gave up. 'Look, I'm sorry,' I said. 'I was angry but, as you have admitted, he had failed to do what he was supposed to. So I had a right to be angry. But no bad language was used.'

Yes, it was, they insisted.

Okay, I asked, what exactly had I said?

'He says you called him a nonsense,' they said solemnly. 'It is not an abuse we would expect from a man in your position'.

'A nonsense?'

'Yes. He swears you said it.'

'I did say that I would not put up with this nonsense. But that was about the situation, not him personally. Besides how can you call an individual "a nonsense"?'

'It is a very bad word,' they concluded triumphantly. 'And now you have admitted you used it. We shall talk to the management and let them know that foul language has been used.'

And then they ceremonially trooped out.

I was stunned. I went to the newsroom. 'Is "nonsense" an abuse in Calcutta?' I asked.

I was told it was. It is one of the biggest insults you could give a Bengali.

I thought they were kidding.

They weren't.

I called Aveek. He wasn't interested in the circumstances, just outraged that the Jukto Committee had called on an editor without asking him.

'Forget about it,' he said.

So I did. And the matter was never followed up. But till I left ABP I never used the world 'nonsense' in office again.

Life in office was not entirely filled with this sort of nonsense (here I go again!). ABP was a big deal in Calcutta so lots of people dropped in. Mamata Banerjee was a regular visitor. She was then just a Calcutta figure, not having achieved any national prominence. But she impressed me with her passionate hatred of Jyoti Basu and the CPM. The state government had done everything possible to keep her down, even getting the police to assault her with lathis in public. (The injury was so severe that she was in and out of hospitals for months and would come to the office in bandages.) But nothing could stop Mamata except perhaps, Mamata herself.

On the Cal–Delhi flight, I frequently ran into Bengal politicians and got to know many of them (Priya Ranjan Das Munshi, for instance) quite well. On one occasion I was flying back to Calcutta after the budget had been presented, carrying a packet containing the budget papers (for *Business Standard*, our sister paper) and found myself sitting next to Pranab Mukherjee whom I did not know.

Pranab had been booted out of the Congress by Arun Nehru and was now trying to work his way back in. He was an engaging conversationalist and perhaps because he was totally out of the political scene, spoke candidly about the famous flight from Calcutta to Delhi in 1984, right after Mrs Gandhi's assassination when Rajiv Gandhi got the impression that he was trying to take over.

He spoke about being banished to Calcutta to take up a minor party post and about how it all ended when he received a call late one night from Arun Nehru who shouted at him and asked him to resign from every party post. He discussed the brief phase when he had left the Congress and tried to make it on his own. ('I found I am not that kind of mass politician.')

At the end, when I was struggling to balance my handbag and the big bundle of budget papers while negotiating the plane's staircase at Calcutta airport, he offered to help.

'Would you like me to carry the budget papers?' he asked. 'I have done it before.'

He was a nice man, with a droll sense of humour.

TWENTY-FIVE

THE CURIOUS CASE OF
THE COMMISSIONS

When the Bofors scandal broke, nobody had any idea that it would come to define the last years of the Rajiv Gandhi prime ministership.

The original story had very little to do with India. Bofors was a large Swedish arms manufacturer. The Swedish media went after Bofors in 1986-87, claiming that it had paid bribes to politicians around the world to secure contracts.

Among the allegations was the claim that it had paid Indians to secure a large contract for the supply of guns. This allegation, broadcast by Swedish radio in the spring of 1987 was only a part of a larger series of allegations about other countries.

One reason why the announcement attracted attention in India was because V.P. Singh had already turned defence deals into an issue by ordering an enquiry into the HDW submarine deal. So, as questions began to be asked, the government prepared its response.

It was this response that sunk the government even before the scandal really took off.

The sensible thing to have done would have been to have said something like, 'We have noted the allegations made by Swedish Radio. We are not aware of any bribe having been paid. But we will ask Swedish Radio to provide details and launch a thorough investigation.'

The government did not do this. Instead, it responded to a charge that had never been made.

It said that the Swedish Radio report was wrong and insisted that no commissions had been paid in connection with the deal.

Commissions?

Nobody had said anything about commissions. The government was responding to a charge that had never been made. Commissions are a normal business practice and unless it can be proved that the agents routed these commissions back to politicians or officials, there is no criminality.

But the government, with its strange response, had lowered the bar. Now, all its critics had to prove was that commissions had been paid. Once they did that, the government would be perceived as lying. Besides how did the government know that no commissions had been paid? It had no way of keeping track of Bofors accounts.

Several months later I asked Gopi Arora, who was then a key figure in Rajiv's PMO why the statement went out. He said that Rajiv and Arun Singh (who was at the PMO before he went to the defence ministry) had told Bofors to fire their agents in India and had gone so far as to ban all agents from entering the defence ministry. So they were outraged when the charge was made and issued a categorical denial. What they meant, apparently, was—forget about bribes; we didn't even let them pay commissions!

Nobody was thinking ahead.

The Bofors controversy erupted around the time Giani Zail Singh was planning his bid for a second term, when V.P. Singh was preparing to leave the Congress, when a dismissed Arun Nehru was looking for ways to bring Rajiv down, and when the opposition was demoralized and needed an issue to attack the government on. Bofors suited all of them.

Everyone tried to use Bofors for their own purposes. V.P. Singh let it be known that the Bofors payments had been made to Amitabh Bachchan. Was it not a fact that Bachchan's brother Ajitabh had moved to Switzerland? Surely he had moved there to receive the kickbacks! (It was never revealed that around this time, V.P. Singh's son was actually working—quite innocently and as a professional—for a Swiss bank. Nobody seemed to know this then.)

Any attack on Bachchan was guaranteed to ensure headlines because of the actor-MP's popularity so V.P. Singh made Bachchan the face of Bofors. There was no evidence against him, of course, and no link to Bofors, but when has that stopped the rumour mills from spinning?

Bofors might have ended with the fake charges against Bachchan but for the work of Chitra Subramaniam, the Geneva correspondent of *The Hindu*. She accessed internal Bofors documents that showed payments to a company owned by the Hinduja brothers, the wealthy Sindhi family, based partly in London and Geneva. The documents named G.P. Hinduja, one of the brothers, so even though nobody had heard of the companies that received these payoffs (obvious shells with names like Pitco and Moresco) it seemed fair to assume that they were connected to the Hindujas.

The documents showed no link to Rajiv or even to Amitabh. But they demonstrated that the government was lying. Commissions had indeed been paid. Rajiv was now hoist by his own petard. By making a claim about no commissions that he was not required to make, he had expanded the scope of the charges so much that any single payment from Bofors would blow his own position out of the water.

As Chitra kept publishing more documents, all proving that payments had been made, a Joint Parliamentary Commission (JPC) was set up under B. Shankaranand, the man who had so narrowly missed being president. The committee called several witnesses and established that even if bribes had been paid, the right gun had been selected. Bofors had emerged at the top in all of the army's trials and tests. It also discovered that the order for the guns had been placed within days of the army's recommendation.

So far, so good.

The problem came with the issue of commissions. Bofors sent executives to testify before the JPC and confirmed that it had paid three entities in connection with the India deal. One was Moresco (the company that *The Hindu* had linked to the Hindujas). Another was Svenska, a shell company with a Panamanian registration. It was the third company A.E. Services which was the most interesting because it was hired after the government had told Bofors that it had to sack its agents.

Why would the Bofors management go out and hire a new agent and risk losing the contract unless it knew the government would not mind if it hired A.E. Services? If there was a kickback, it was probably A.E. Services that got it.

The Bofors executives had no explanation for why A.E. Services had been hired. They tried to explain away the payments by claiming that they were 'winding up' charges given to the agents they were now obliged to sack but it seemed more likely that they were merely the first in a series of commissions that would be paid as the payments from the Indian government to Bofors arrived in tranches.

Though the JPC gave the government a clean chit (predictably) the Bofors executives' testimony blew a huge hole through the government's case. If Rajiv was innocent, and nobody had found anything to link him to the payments, then the right thing would have been to energetically pursue the trail wherever it led. But his government seemed keen to make the whole matter go away.

The official defence offered by the Congress party was the 'destabilization' theory favoured by Gopi Arora who was of a leftist bent of mind. Arora suggested that hostile foreign forces were eager to destabilize India and that Bofors was their way of doing it. This was a variation on the older version of the same theory offered up by Indira Gandhi. She used to say that the CIA liked to keep the Indian government unstable because of India's ties to the Soviet Union. (The Cold War only really ended after Rajiv left office.)

I have no doubt that there was something to this claim. We know enough about the CIA (and the KGB) now to recognize that foreign intelligence agencies did interfere in Indian politics. And yes, the CIA probably did try and make Mrs Gandhi uncomfortable. And it was never happy with Rajiv who was, at heart, a believer in his grandfather's policy of non-alignment.

But to blame every corruption charge on a plot to destabilize India simply made no sense. The government had to meet the charges head on, to question the alleged agents and to figure out what had happened.

It did no such thing.

The Hindujas actually grew closer to the government in the post-Bofors phase they were before. Win Chadha, who was Bofors' official representative in India, was brought back from Dubai to answer questions. It was widely believed that he was the beneficial owner of Svenska (and he did not bother to deny this too strongly when I asked him about it) but the government seemed eager to treat him gently.

On A.E. Services, the CBI acted as though it was a legitimate company based in Guildford in England. The CBI told the JPC that it had been set up by a retired military officer called (if I recall correctly) Major Bob Wilson under the name of Target Practice. It had changed its name after new shareholders came on board but Major Bob still ran it.

The government used this to suggest that perhaps Bofors had hired A.E. Services for 'industrial espionage' or some other form of legitimate activity. The official version was that while Pitco and Svenska were shrouded in secrecy, at least this company had a CEO, an office and a purpose.

This did not sound right to me. And there was only one way to find out.

So one day, I flew to London and drove to Guildford. I went to what the CBI and the JPC had both said was the address of A.E. Services. I drove past the street three times without seeing any sign for A.E. Services. So I got out of the car and walked along the street till I came to the building with what the CBI said was the number of A.E. Services.

It was the office of a firm of solicitors.

I walked into the office and asked at the reception if I could see someone from A.E. Services. Oh no, they told me, they were just a postal address. They accepted mail for A.E. Services and it was picked up every once in a while. They offered this service to other companies as well.

I asked if I could speak to Major Bob.

Who?

The lady at reception had no clue who he was.

I had procured what the government said was the Major's home address. I went there and rang the bell. Two large dogs came out and began sniffing me. Fortunately, they were soon followed by a friendly young woman who laughed and asked, 'Have you been eaten yet?'

She called the dogs off and listened while I explained that I was an Indian journalist and wanted to talk to the Major. She kept me waiting at the door while she disappeared inside. Finally, she came out and said, 'So sorry. But he's not talking to anyone.'

I drove back to London and sent in my story. A.E. Services was not a legitimate company at all, I wrote. It had no office and as far as I could tell, no staff either. It was a shell with a mailing address in a solicitor's firm. There was no way it could have done 'industrial espionage' on behalf of Bofors.

Presumably the CBI already knew this but had avoided telling the JPC.

It was hard to escape the sense that the government would not investigate Bofors sincerely and genuinely.

The Bofors saga went on for many years afterwards. When V.P. Singh was elected prime minister, his investigators found nothing new. Only much later did it emerge that the money from the A.E. Services account had been shifted to other accounts. Some of the Bofors money ended up in an account belonging to Ottavio Quattrochi.

I had met Quattrochi only once. It was in 1986 when I was still at *Imprint* and the Rajiv government was awarding the contract for the Hazira-Bijaypur-Jagdishpur (HBJ) gas pipeline. Quattrochi had spent many years in India representing Snamprogetti, the government-owned Italian multinational. He knew Rajiv and Sonia well (as he told me) and was not averse to throwing their names around. During Mrs Gandhi's time, Snamprogetti had won many government contracts and Quattrochi's influence was the subject of many discussions.

By the time I met him, however, he was a shadow of his former self. He had heard, he said, that his company would be denied the contract for the HBJ pipeline because 'there is a conspiracy against the prime minister'. The kingpin of this conspiracy, he insisted, was Arun Nehru. (This was before Rajiv sacked Nehru.) The conspirators had ensured that Snamprogetti would lose out.

I couldn't have been the only journalist Quattrochi spoke to. Clearly, he wanted us to write about how unfairly his company was being treated. I had no interest in the HBJ pipeline and had only agreed to visit him at his home because I was curious about the man I had heard so much about.

I asked Quattrochi the obvious question. If he was as close to Rajiv Gandhi as he kept telling me and there was actually a conspiracy against Rajiv then why didn't he simply alert the prime minister? Surely, as a close friend, it was his duty to do so, regardless of Snamprogetti's interests.

He offered some weak explanation along the lines of, 'We meet as friends so how can I talk about politics with him?' But he saw that he was wasting his time on me, and quickly lost interest.

Snamprogetti did not get the HBJ contract. And I never saw Quattrochi again.

And yet, clearly, there was a Bofors connection. Chitra had dug up the diary of Martin Ardbo, the head of Bofors when the deal was struck. In the diary Ardbo had written, 'Q's involvement may be a problem because of closeness to R.'

When it was revealed that one of Quattrochi's accounts was linked to the Bofors payments (possibly from A.E. Services), the entry made perfect sense.

But the questions remain?

Who got the Bofors money?

Here's my theory.

Svenska was Chadha. I spent quite a long time with him when he had come to India to testify and had discovered, to my surprise, that he had lived in the same building as me in Bombay when I was a child and he said he knew me.

Perhaps this made him more forthcoming but in the off-the-record, warm-up part of our chat before the tape recorder came on, he had bragged, 'I have made so much money that several generations of my family will never have to work again.' He was that kind of man, boastful one minute, angry the next and then sweet to anyone who could help him.

My question is: was Chadha worth so much money? One view is that Svenska was a slush fund from which Chadha/Bofors could pay off generals, officials, etc. Chaddha got to keep what he did not pay out. Another view is that Svenska included kickbacks to Bofors executives themselves.

Pitco/Moresco was clearly linked to the Hindujas. Later when investigations into the Swiss bank accounts were in progress, the Swiss leaked that the Hindujas (and a company called Jubilee Finance) had appealed against handing over details of the account to the Indian authorities.

But because Pitco/Moresco received funds from Bofors, it does not follow that any illegality occurred. It is normal for businessmen to receive commissions and no one has been able to show that the Hindujas passed on any of the money to any Indian official or politician.

That leaves us with the mystery of A.E. Services. Why would any middle man use a British registered firm? Anybody could have gone to its registered office and discovered that it was a front as I did.

I can't figure that out.

Why did Bofors pay Quattrochi?

There are two possibilities. The first is that he was a bumptious figure who roamed around Delhi boasting of his closeness to the Gandhis. Though Rajiv took care to distance himself from Quattrochi during his term as prime minister (which is why Quattrochi would complain to journalists about a conspiracy), sending out clear signals by giving the HBJ pipeline to a rival company, the impression persisted in Delhi that he was the go-to guy for the Gandhis.

So did Quattrochi muscle his way into the deal by claiming to be able to swing it for Bofors? If Bofors was willing to pay commissions to the Hindujas then Quattrochi seemed like a better bet.

And there is a second possibility. Quattrochi was given the money at Rajiv's urging and A.E. Services received the Gandhis' share.

Apart from the fact that there is not a shred of evidence linking Rajiv to the deal, there is also the question of logic. Of the three companies that received payments, A.E. Services got the smallest amount. If you were accepting a bribe and you were the prime minister of India would you be content with the smallest share?

And if this money was to be paid, wouldn't the Gandhis have simply taken it in a numbered account linked to say, a Panamanian or Liechtenstein shell company? Why would they need Quattrochi at all?

I guess we'll never know what the truth really was. Many of the principals in this story are dead. Martin Ardbo, Win Chadha, Ottavio Quattrochi and, of course, Rajiv himself.

But what is clear is that Rajiv's government handled the issue very badly. Right from the first statement about no commissions to the useless JPC to the whitewash investigations to the destabilization theory, all of it was ineptly managed.

Rajiv should have ordered a fair inquiry into the case and let the truth come out from his own investigators, not from journalists. You can say in his defence that he was badly advised.

But you can't deny the damage it did to his reputation and to the future of his government.

TWENTY-SIX

'IT'S A FUNNY VIEW OF THE WORLD TO THINK A BOOK CAN CAUSE RIOTS'

The conventional wisdom within the journalistic establishment is that the rise of the BJP began during the second half of Rajiv Gandhi's term because of Rajiv's acts—some intentional and some with unintended consequences. Further, this view states, the desire among the opposition parties to unseat Rajiv was so great that they joined hands with the BJP giving it a legitimacy it had previously lacked.

I am not sure how much of this is accurate. The rise of a Hindu vote began, I think, much earlier. I reckon it began in the early 1980s when the Punjab problem started. Till that point, Hindus had never dreamt that Sikhs could turn against them. But the thrust of Jarnail Singh Bhindranwale's campaign was that Sikhs had nothing in common with Hindus and that Hindus were, in fact, the enemy.

It has largely been airbrushed out of history now but the campaign for an independent state of Khalistan was often couched in anti-Hindu terms. Prominent Hindu leaders, newspaper owners and local notables were assassinated by Sikh militants. Buses were stopped, the Sikh and Hindu passengers separated and the Hindus shot. Bhindranwale would refer to Indira Gandhi as 'Bahman ke Beti' and the rhetoric was full of anti-Brahminism.

All of this was encouraged by Pakistan which trained Sikh militants, armed them and offered financial support. Some Sikhs began claiming that Sikhism had more in common with Islam because it was monotheistic unlike Hinduism with its multiplicity of gods. This made an alliance with Pakistani agencies seem more plausible.

The majority of the community did not support the extremists. In Punjab those Sikhs who would speak out against Bhindranwale's poisonous nonsense were killed. So this prevented the silent majority from being more vocal. No Sikh I knew supported the idea of Khalistan and most thought Bhindranwale was a dangerous lunatic.

Extremists know that this is true in most such situations. They can only win the support of the majority when the state retaliates. Usually such retaliation is disproportionate and indiscriminate and pushes the moderates into sympathizing with the extremists.

You can argue about the execution of Operation Bluestar, when the Indian army attacked the Golden Temple in Amritsar to take out Bhindranwale. The timing was a disaster. As a military operation it was deeply flawed. And through its ineptitude the Indian army managed to destroy one of the holiest sites in Sikhism (the Akal Takht) while damaging the Harmandir Sahib.

But there are two things you can't argue about. The first is that Mrs Gandhi had no choice but to send the forces in. Bhindranwale had to be taken out. And the other thing you can't argue about (though we gloss over it in retrospect) is that millions of Hindus (in Punjab and in the rest of India) were delighted by the army action.

Some of it was the normal nationalistic fervour ('it was a battle against the army of Khalistan,' a general told Doordarshan to explain why the Indian army had taken three days to defeat 500 sardarjis armed mostly with hand-held weapons) but there was always an unpleasant Hindus-strike-back element to it.

I opposed Bluestar and empathized with my moderate Sikh friends, some of whom had hated Bhindranwale in life but now saw him as a martyr, however illogical that shift in perception was. But I was roundly criticized by nearly everyone else for taking this stand. How dare I criticize the great Indian army? Was I on the side of Khalistanis? And so on.

The same Hindu anger erupted again following the assassination of Indira Gandhi later that year. It is foolish to deny that many

Sikhs were killed in Delhi as part of a pogrom organized by local Congress leaders. But it is as foolish to pretend that there was not a surge of anti-Sikh sentiment among Hindus in the aftermath of the assassination. Some of this was deliberately stoked by people who spread rumours that Sikhs were bursting firecrackers and offering sweets to celebrate Mrs Gandhi's assassination. But a lot of it was crude and spontaneous: 'You killed our leader; we will get you for this.'

We forget now how much this upsurge in Hindu sentiment contributed to the magnitude of the Congress victory in the winter of that year. Yes, some of it was a sympathy vote. And some of it was a vote for change with continuity. But some of it was also Hindus uniting behind the son of their slain leader. The Congress's election advertising campaign subliminally played on Hindu fears. 'Will the country's border be moved to your door?' And there were references to other communities who drove trucks.

I interviewed Arun Nanda of Rediffusion — the agency that had created the ad campaign — after Rajiv's victory, and asked if the appeal to Hindu sensibilities had been carefully calibrated. He denied it, of course.

He did not dispute that the campaign played on the fears of ordinary Indians. The references to communal tension and to the border being moved nearer your home were, he said, a way of addressing genuine fears (after a secessionist movement, the assassination of a prime minister and widespread rioting) that India might break up or that instability might set in.

It was a plausible enough explanation but it was hard to escape the fact that nearly every anti-minority riot is always followed by huge majority vote consolidation in the election that follows. (That is how the Shiv Sena came to power in Maharashtra in 1995 and how Narendra Modi won a landslide in Gujarat in 2002.)

When Rajiv Gandhi took office, he seemed unaware of the part that Hindu insecurity (and perhaps Hindu triumphalism) had played in his victory. He made no concessions to Hindu feeling and set about reaching out to the Sikhs, signing the Punjab Accord with Sant Longowal.

Even then, I heard whispers from Congressmen that Rajiv was losing out on an important constituency: Hindus who saw him as their hero. I didn't pay much attention to this but I do believe that a certain section of the Congress thought that the Hindu vote base had to be cultivated.

The argument was simple. The Congress usually counted on the votes of Muslims (around 12 per cent of the electorate). But if it could rely on a large chunk of the Hindu vote (around 84 per cent of the electorate) then it would be in power forever. There were more Hindus than Muslims and with the BJP wiped out in the 1984 elections there was no one to speak for the Hindu community.

I rejected this idea as I think did nearly every sensible person I spoke to. Yes, we conceded, minorities often voted as a bloc. But Hindus never voted as Hindus. They voted on a multiplicity of issues and though caste might be one of them, religion was never an electoral issue for a community that was in the overwhelming majority.

I don't know whether the whispers about appealing to the Hindu vote led anywhere. But many people now believe that they may have contributed to the rise of the Babri Masjid controversy.

The controversy was an old one but it had been purely localized for decades. A site in Ayodhya where a mosque (the Babri Masjid) stood was said to be the birthplace of Ram. The Mughal emperor Babur, a section of Ayodhya's Hindus argued, had destroyed the temple that stood on the site and constructed a mosque in its place.

The dispute had raged on for years without having had much impact on the rest of Uttar Pradesh let alone the rest of India. Most Hindus did not know that there was a specific geographical site assigned to the birth of Ram and in any case, there were other places that also claimed to be his birthplace. As the dispute had got more acrimonious, the gates of the mosque had been sealed so that no *namaz* could be said there and the site had been locked up. This had the effect of putting the dispute into cold storage.

Early in Rajiv's term, the gates were opened. The order came from a local official but it was rumoured in Delhi that the orders to open the gate had come from Arun Nehru, who looked after UP for the Congress and was Rajiv's primary political advisor.

It was later said that Rajiv had also given the go-ahead which is possible but unlikely given his subsequent behaviour. (Wajahat Habibullah, who was a civil servant in Rajiv's PMO, says in his memoir of that period, *My Years with Rajiv*, that Rajiv was not consulted.) Arun Nehru, it was said, had wanted to hand the site over to the Hindus, thus cementing the Congress's image as the avenger of the Hindus.

I asked Arun Nehru about this much later (in 1990) and he was evasive on the subject. Certainly, he did not say that the charge that he had anything to do with opening the gate was a foul calumny. Nor did he deny that during his term as minister for internal security, he had the headquarters of the Bible Society of India raided or that he worked for Hindu interests. (Arun Nehru later contested elections on a BJP ticket.)

In purely cynical, political terms, the decision to court the Hindu vote made a certain amount of sense. It was widely believed that the BJP was finished. Its leader and prime ministerial candidate, A.B. Vajpayee, had been defeated in Gwalior by Madhavrao Scindia and the party had won only two seats in the Lok Sabha election.

So if the Congress could annex the Hindu vote then it would have had the kind of electoral base that most parties can only dream of.

There was one major problem with this approach and that was Rajiv Gandhi himself.

Asked in 1985 by the *Sunday Times* (London) whether he believed in God, he chose not to give a vague response but answered in one word: no.

Nor did he have any time for a Hindu identity. He was half-Parsi, married to a (non-practising) Roman Catholic of European origin and was deeply committed to his grandfather's idea of secularism. His mother, Indira, who was also politically secular, had retained a special affection for some of Hinduism's less progressive aspects: she consulted astrologers and tantrics regularly, kept a yogi called Dhirendra Brahmachari in her court, believed in godmen and godwomen and wore a rudraksh mala around her neck.

Rajiv did none of these things and often appeared to sneer at them.

So he would have made an unlikely Hindu Hriday Samrat.

This was reinforced by the stands he took while in office. He first tried to broker peace between the Buddhist Sinhala majority in Sri Lanka and the Hindu Tamil minority. When that went wrong, the Indian army battled the Hindu Tamil minority's leading organization, the LTTE (eventually the LTTE assassinated Rajiv). He reached out to the Sikhs on an equal basis, not in the manner of a victor making peace with a vanquished enemy.

And then there was the Shahbano case. In India, even parties that profess to be secular (such as the Congress) believe it is right for different religious communities to have their own Personal Laws, governing such issues as marriage, inheritance, adoption, etc. The framers of the Constitution had wanted India to move towards a uniform civil code but successive governments had refused to do so claiming always that 'the time is not right'.

Whatever your views on religious personal laws (and I have always been opposed to them), there is no doubt that Muslim Personal Law can often be unfair to woman. A woman called Shahbano had been denied maintenance by her divorced husband and when the case came to the Supreme Court, the husband was asked to pay maintenance.

Though there were some doubts about the language the judge used, most people welcomed the judgment. Rajiv deputed one of his more articulate young Muslim ministers (and Arun Nehru-protégé) Arif Mohammad Khan to defend the judgement.

All seemed to be going well till Rajiv was besieged by representations from the Muslim community asking him to intervene and to find a way of changing the law so that the Shahbano judgement was rendered invalid. The representations all had the same theme: Muslim Personal Law is our Akal Takht. Do not damage it as the army damaged the real Akal Takht. Muslims must be made to feel that they are safe in India.

It was an appeal that Rajiv should have turned down. The protesting Muslims were on the wrong side of history and he should have seen that. Instead, some old-fashioned be-good-to-the-minorities instinct kicked in.

The conservative Muslims got their way. The law was changed. The Shahbano precedent was overturned. Arif resigned.

Three years later I asked Rajiv why he did it. He had no specific explanation except that it was an issue relating to the Muslim community and as Muslims felt so strongly, he thought it would be wrong to ignore their deeply felt sentiments.

He was more wrong than he was right. Yes, it was an issue relating to the Muslim community but only in a very limited sense. It was more an issue relating to the kind of India he wanted to create. Did he want to lead a nation where women were discriminated against only because of some medieval religious prejudice? And even within the Muslim community, should he not have listened to the progressive voices rather than the mullahs, maulvis and sarkari Mussalmans who had traditionally hung around the Congress claiming to speak for their community?

I don't know how deeply Rajiv thought about that decision but it changed many things. First of all, it knocked out any chance of his emerging as a hero for the Hindu community. (Which he might not have minded.)

Second, it showed him to be stuck in the shadows of the past, of his mother's legacy of pandering to the most reactionary elements in the Muslim community. And finally, it suggested that while he had thought deeply about the India he wanted to lead (in terms of military power, computers, panchayati raj, etc.), the massive mandate he had won across all communities had made him forget how fragile the communal balance was in India. This was something his experience with the Punjab issue should have brought home to him.

There was a second Muslim community issue that also showed that Rajiv did not think as deeply about community-related issues as he should have. And on this one, I had a ringside seat.

Aveek Sarkar was the Indian partner of Penguin books. Penguin was about to publish a book by Salman Rushdie called *The Satanic Verses*. The manuscript was sent to India because Penguin wanted to publish an Indian edition.

Penguin gave the manuscript to Khushwant Singh who was then its consulting editor. Khushwant read the manuscript and declared that it was deeply offensive to Muslims. Penguin, he said, should not even consider publishing it. Penguin's UK parent asked Aveek how he felt.

Aveek did not bother reading the manuscript. He took the traditional liberal line that even if a book by an author as eminent as Salman Rushdie offended people, it should still be published. Literature was not meant to find favour with everyone. Many great books had offended people before. Penguin India was in the publishing business, not in the censorship business.

It was very unusual for Aveek, who had a bewildering regard for Khushwant's critical and editorial faculties, to disregard his consulting editor's advice. But Aveek took the principled line that if the book was certain to be banned as Khushwant predicted, then Penguin India would bear the loss of pulping the copies.

This was an ethical decision which was his to make. If there were financial consequences, he was willing to bear them.

I don't think anybody outside of Penguin or ABP had any idea of the internal debate around publishing *The Satanic Verses* and Penguin UK started promotions as though it was just another book. *Sunday*'s London correspondent Shrabani Basu was invited by the publishers to interview Rushdie who wanted to promote the book.

Before she went for the interview, I briefed her, in confidence, about the internal debate to which I was a witness. Could she ask Rushdie about his views? Was he scared of offending Muslims? Did he fear that there would be a ban in some Muslim majority countries?

Shrabani quickly discovered that either Rushdie had no idea of the Indian view that the book was a ticking time bomb or that he had decided to ignore it. He was completely dismissive of suggestions that the book could cause any trouble. When Shrabani persisted, he retorted, in words that would come back to haunt him, 'It is a funny view of the world to think that a book could cause riots.'

When the interview came in, I was delighted but annoyed that *Sunday*'s antiquated technology meant that the Rushdie interview would not appear for another ten days or so. Meanwhile, the debate

within Penguin continued. I dropped in on Khushwant who told me
that the book should never be published and that Aveek was crazy
to go ahead.

When Shrabani's Rushdie interview appeared, one of the first
people to read it was Syed Shahabuddin. I knew Shahabuddin and
liked him. He was a former Indian diplomat who had joined politics
only, or so it seemed, to focus on Muslim issues.

There was no denying that these issues needed to be focused on
nor was there any doubt about Shahabuddin's patriotism (during
the 1971 conflict with Pakistan over what is now Bangladesh, he
had worked tirelessly as a diplomat to present the Indian case) but I
always felt that he was not so much a man who was offended by the
injustices meted out to India's Muslims as a man who was looking
for offence. None of this stopped us from getting along and he was a
regular reader of *Sunday*.

When the issue with the Rushdie interview appeared, he read
it and immediately called for a ban on the grounds that Muslim
sentiments would be hurt if the book was published. The following
day he read an extract from the book in *India Today* and redoubled
his efforts to get the book banned.

I called him after his demand had hit the news and asked him
whether, as one of the few opposition members in the Lok Sabha, he
should be advocating bans on books, especially books he had not read.

Shahabuddin said he did not need to read the book. He had read
Shrabani's interview.

I said that that was hardly the same thing.

Was it true, he asked, that Khushwant Singh had said that the
book was deeply offensive to Muslims?

I said it was.

Was Khushwant Singh a Muslim communalist? Was he even a
Muslim? Wasn't he a completely secular person?

I said yes, Shahabuddin was right on all counts.

Well then, how could I blame him from coming to the same
conclusion as a great author like Khushwant Singh?

There was a difference, I said. Khushwant had read the book. He
hadn't.

He had read the *India Today* extract, he said.

The extract was totally innocuous, I told him. There was nothing offensive in it.

Yes, perhaps, but how did I know that there was nothing offensive in the rest of the book? The whole premise sounded offensive.

And so, round and round we went till finally I gave up.

Shahabuddin's call for a ban was echoed by many mullahs and maulvis (including a famous Imam who thought the book had been written by Salman Khurshid!). Conservative Muslim organizations entered the fray. Mushirul Hasan, a distinguished professor, said that while he found the book offensive, he was against banning books on principle, and was beaten up by his own students. There were demonstrations and protests all over India.

The matter went to Rajiv Gandhi. Home Minister Buta Singh told him that his ministry apprehended widespread violence if the book was published. Rajiv agreed to ban the import of the hardcover edition on the home minister's recommendation. Penguin India was told that the cheaper paperback edition that it intended to publish would not be allowed.

At this stage, none of the people involved in the process, not Shahabuddin, not Rajiv Gandhi, not the mullahs or the maulvis or the protesters had read the book.

And soon there were threats of riots. The controversy even spread to Pakistan where mullahs encouraged protestors to riot.

It was a funnier world than Rushdie had suggested. *The Satanic Verses* had not just caused riots. It had caused riots before anyone who was protesting had ever seen the book, let alone read it.

Iran's Ayatollah Khomeini saw a demonstration outside a British Council office in Pakistan on TV. He asked what it was about and was told that it was about a book that insulted the Prophet. In that case, the old man said, the fellow who wrote it should be put to death. And the famous fatwa was issued.

It turned into a saga full of many 'what ifs'. Suppose Khushwant had not been given the manuscript to read and Penguin India had published it anyway. Would anyone have noticed?

Suppose Shahabuddin had not read Shrabani's interview and raised the alarm, would assorted mullahs and maulvis even have known that such a book existed?

In many ways, the internal Penguin India debate was the spark that lit the flame for a global conflagration.

And the final What If: suppose Rajiv had held firm. Suppose he had said that yes, there will be a few violent demonstrations but it will die down. So let's allow the book.

Or even if he had taken the more liberal position: that a free society does not ban books.

I argued with him about it later when Aveek and I went to interview him. He stuck to a simple law and order approach. No book, he said, was worth risking riots for. The world can do without another novel. But those who lose their lives and their livelihoods in riots will never get them back.

From his perspective I guess it made sense. From a deeper perspective, however, I thought it was a surrender to the forces of prejudice, illiberalism and fundamentalism.

More significantly, in terms of Indian politics, it put the final seal on any hopes that some Congressmen entertained of cultivating a Hindu vote bank.

There was now a vacuum in that space.

And somebody would fill it.

TWENTY-SEVEN

THE HOLIEST SPOT IN HINDUISM

One of the fringe benefits of working for *Imprint* was that I got to meet many of R.V. Pandit's RSS friends. I had been brought up in the kind of household where communalists were considered the scum of the earth and the RSS was beyond the pale. (For the first twenty years of my life I don't think I ever met anyone with an RSS background.)

So it was a surprise to me when Pandit told me he supported a lot of the work that the RSS was doing. They could be petty, he said. And some of them had, what he called, a frog-in-the-well attitude. But they were always the first people to reach the site of any disaster and worked tirelessly for the poor.

I did not necessarily dispute any of this. But I thought it was wrong to treat the RSS as no more than a Rotary Club where the members happened to wear Khakhi shorts. Could he really ignore the fascist roots, the anti-Muslim prejudice, etc.? That was all over-stated, he said. Look at people like him. He was a practising Roman Catholic. The RSS knew that. And it was never an issue.

Over the years I met many RSS functionaries with Pandit and I had to concede that they did not have horns on their heads. In fact, I quite liked some of them at a personal level.

Just before the 1984 general election, Pandit took Nanaji Deshmukh and me out to lunch at the Indian restaurant at the President Hotel near our office and I developed a certain admiration for the social work that Nanaji was doing and was impressed by his demeanour.

Nor were his political views quite what I had expected. He spoke openly in favour of Rajiv Gandhi, said there was no alternative to him and dissed A.B. Vajpayee. Nanaji said that he did not believe Vajpayee had it in him to gain mass support at an election. He had no doubt that the BJP would be wiped out at the polls as it deserved to be.

It turned out that he was right about the BJP's performance but his lack of respect for Vajpayee struck me as odd. Pandit, who knew the BJP leadership well and helped finance Nanaji's social work, explained that there were rivalries in every party. Nanaji had a personal problem with Vajpayee and this coloured his judgement.

Did this mean, I asked, that the RSS was not throwing its weight behind the BJP?

Pandit was ambivalent in his response. You can't draw conclusions about the RSS from what Nanaji says over lunch, he cautioned.

I have often thought back to that conversation. Of course Pandit was right about the danger of reading too much into Nanaji's words. But when Vajpayee later complained about having been let down by the RSS during the 1984 election I began to wonder if Nanaji was merely expressing an individual opinion.

It was through Pandit that I briefly met L.K. Advani (or 'Lalji' as Pandit called him). Anyone who has met Advani will tell you that, face-to-face, he is a polite, mild-mannered man who exudes no sense of self-importance or of power. (Mani Shankar Aiyar was later to describe him as looking like 'Uncle Walrus'. As mild-mannered as he was, Advani was not at all amused and let this be known.) It was hard to reconcile this gentle fellow with the Muslim-hating, communal RSS figure of legend.

By the time I became editor of *Sunday*, the BJP was going through a transformation. The moderate, vaguely secular line pushed by Vajpayee since the Bombay convention where the party had been formed was being quietly junked. The RSS began to play a more crucial role in the party's affairs. And Vajpayee himself receded to the background.

Instead, mild-mannered Advani suddenly became the face of the BJP. If you met him face to face, he was still the polite fellow I had encountered in the *Imprint* days. But he had found a way to turn that persona to his advantage. Many people said he looked like the 'common man', a character in R.K. Laxman's cartoons.

Advani liked the parallel. He was, he suggested, an ordinary Hindu, calm and mild-mannered in most circumstances, who had now been driven to anger by the injustices heaped on his community. Why, he asked, were Hindus treated as second-class citizens in their own country? He was as secular as the next man, he said, but he objected to the Congress's 'pseudo-secularism' which was not secularism at all but a way of 'appeasing' Muslims because they made up a convenient vote-bank.

All of it was quite ironic. The Congress was not appeasing a Muslim vote-bank to win elections. It had, more through instinct than design, kissed goodbye to the huge Hindu vote bank that it had acquired in 1984. Any fool could see that a vote bank consisting of the vast majority of the population was far more useful than the Muslim vote bank with its 12 per cent of the vote and the constant demands (for banning books, not paying maintenance to former wives, etc.) made by its (essentially primitive) religious leadership.

And it was as obvious that even as Advani attacked the Congress's vote bank politics, he was trying to create his own vote bank of disaffected Hindu voters.

Many of the Hindu voters who felt that Rajiv had let them down and were now political orphans, went with Advani. These were not RSS-types. They had no hatred of Muslims and had all voted for the Congress in 1984. They would never have voted for a firebrand Hindu leader. But mild-mannered Uncle Walrus seemed just fine. He was no fascist, just an ordinary guy motivated by his own frustration and the government's neglect of Hindus.

How do you make Hindus who dominate every aspect of Indian life, feel aggrieved in their own country?

Advani needed to find an issue to mobilize Hindu sentiments. He settled on the Babri Masjid/Ram Janmabhoomi dispute. Ever since the gates had been opened, groups of sadhus had restarted the campaign to reclaim the site. Some of these sadhus were, initially, pro-Congress but by 1987, felt abandoned by their original Congress patrons. (Some people separate Congress policy on Hindu issues like Ayodhya into two distinct phases: Arun Nehru and post-Arun Nehru.)

The Vishwa Hindu Parishad (VHP), a radical organization affiliated to the RSS, had taken over the movement, but its campaign had yet to gain much national prominence. The VHP's basic problem was that most Hindus had never heard of Ram Janmabhoomi. Even those who included Lord Ram in their prayers had no idea that his life had left physical manifestations such as an actual spot where he was born. The Ram of Hindu prayers was a God, not a chap who had lived and died in UP.

From a historical point of view, the claim that this was Ram's birthplace was impossible to sustain. We know so little about the historical Jesus who lived 2000 years ago that it is unreasonable to expect us to be more knowledgeable about Lord Ram who, if he was a historical figure, lived several thousand years before Jesus. Over the years, archeologists had argued about whether the Ayodhya of the Ramayan corresponded with modern Ayodhya and whether Ravan's Lanka was modern-day Sri Lanka. Were Hanuman and the monkeys who helped Ram actually tribals from the region or were they real monkeys?

But Advani knew he had a great advantage. The Rajiv Gandhi government had commissioned a TV serial based on the Ramayan that had gone on to become a national obsession. (In those days there was only Doordarshan, the state broadcaster.) Advani knew that any campaign predicated on Lord Ram would, therefore, have an immediate resonance with the public.

He began by raising the issue obliquely while claiming that it was the VHP's campaign, not the BJP's. When it seemed to him that the issue had enough traction, he took charge, turned it into a BJP issue and made himself the centre.

I remember going to see him just as the campaign was taking off. I asked him the obvious questions. How did he know that this was Lord Ram's birthplace? How did he even know that Lord Ram was a historical figure? Was there any proof that a temple dedicated to Ram had stood at the spot before being destroyed by Babur?

I was willing to concede, I said, that there may once have been a temple at the site. But was it a Ram Janmabhoomi temple? And what was the precedent? Would we now demand that Muslims handed over every mosque which may have been built on the ruins of a temple?

Advani seemed moderate and reasonable in his replies. Yes, he said, he could not prove that the historical Lord Ram existed. He could not prove that this was the Ram Janmabhoomi. And he could not prove that a temple marking Lord Ram's birth had existed on that spot.

But so what?

This was about faith, not about history. It did not matter whether Lord Ram had actually been born there. What mattered was that millions of Hindus believed that he had been born here. That made the site one of the holiest spots in Hinduism.

When I said that faith was no substitute for facts, he was ready for the question. Did I know when Jesus Christ was born? Was it not a fact that scholars disagreed about the exact date of his birth?

I said it was.

But did this mean that Christians did not celebrate Christmas?

Could anyone prove that Jesus had been crucified on Good Friday? The chances were that he hadn't. But so what? Faith made Easter a legitimate festival.

All religions were about faith, not about history.

It was a well-constructed argument and he paid no attention to my objections that 'millions of Hindus' only believed that this was Lord Ram's birthplace because he had told them that. They had never heard of the spot before his VHP pals began their campaign.

Advani was warming to his theme. Imagine, he said, that there was a spot that was as holy to Muslims where a Hindu temple now stood. He would lead a campaign for Hindus to honour that site and to vacate it for Muslims. That was true secularism.

Contrast that with the attitude of Muslim leaders, he said. The Babri Masjid (he called it the 'disputed structure') was not really a masjid at all. Namaz had not been read there for decades. It had no special religious significance for Muslims. And yet the Muslim leadership would not agree to move the structure so that Hindus could honour the great Lord Ram?

'Move the structure?' I asked.

Yes, said Advani. That was not a big deal. Mosques were moved all the time in Pakistan. Sometimes, they were moved even if they were in the way of highways that were being built near them. The technology existed. It was easy. The Muslims could move their structure to a site nearby and they could even run it as a proper mosque where namaz could actually be said. He would lead the Hindu community in helping Muslims build this mosque. That would be real secularism.

I left Advani's house more than little worried. I knew what was going on. I knew why he was trying to politicize Ram. But I had also underestimated him. Whatever the facts of the matter, he had built up a powerful case. It was intuitively appealing to many Hindus and his central argument that it was wrong that in so-called secular India, Hindus could not build a temple at one of their holiest spots only because Muslims wanted to hang on to a disused mosque (which was probably built by destroying a Hindu temple) had a powerful, emotive appeal.

At that time, the Ram Janmabhoomi movement was being opposed by a body called the Babri Masjid Action Committee. Syed Shahabuddin was one of the prime movers of the opposition to Advani's movement. I told Shahabuddin that while, of course, I did not agree with Advani, it would be a mistake to underestimate the emotional power of his position.

Shahabuddin was scoffing and dismissive. They would not move the Babri Masjid at all, he said. Not even an inch. What was Advani going to do? Tear down the masjid with his bare hands? (In fact, this is exactly what did happen in the following decades—though not at the hands of Advani himself.)

I said this sounded a lot like saying that possession is nine-tenths of the law. He continued to be adamant till the time I left his house.

My view at the time—rejected out of hand by every secular person I knew—was that Muslims needed to compromise. The Babri Masjid, as it existed, was of no use to them. It was not even, as Advani kept pointing out, a functioning mosque.

Suppose the community came up with a grand gesture. Suppose it said something like, 'While we do not recognize your claim to this site, we are willing to hand it over to you in the name of Indian secularism.' Advani would have no choice but to help them build a grand mosque a few miles away and the whole Ram Janmabhoomi issue would collapse.

Why were they so obsessed with this site? It meant nothing to them.

The first objection to my argument was that this would lead to a domino effect. Advani would start making similar claims about other mosques and demand that they also be handed over.

I conceded that this was a risk so Advani should be made to give a commitment that this was it. I believed that he would have made such a commitment if only to claim victory on the Ayodhya issue to his followers.

The second objection was that this would make Advani a hero to Hindus. I said there was already a danger that he would become that. But he would become a hero to a community in the grip of anti-Muslim feeling and full of a sense of victimhood. Far better that he become a hero only because Muslims agreed to be large hearted and generous.

In the short run, Advani would be a hero. But in the long-run his constant complaint that Muslims were being appeased in India would lose its power. The Muslim community would be seen as willing to help Hindus honour their gods.

I am still told that I was wrong; that I was asking India's Muslims to surrender their rightful heritage, etc.

I don't think I was. And in any case, how did the refusal to seem large-hearted and magnanimous work out for India's Muslims or for Indian secularism?

We know the rest of the story.

TWENTY-EIGHT

'MY BLUDDY SWIMMING POOL!'

By 1988, *Sunday* was once again a major player on the political scene. We were no *India Today* but we had the clout to be taken seriously by politicians and access was no longer a problem.

Our interview with Rajiv Gandhi, the first that *Sunday* had got since early 1985, and the first that Rajiv had given in a while to any publication, came about partly as a consequence of our enhanced stature and partly because of Aveek's relationship with G. Parthasarathy, who was now looking after media relations in the PMO.

Before we went, Aveek told me he wanted to make it hard-hitting. He was particularly interested in economic issues and wanted Rajiv to clarify whether he was a reformer at heart. I was more interested in the politics so this was fine with me.

Rajiv met us in the Cabinet Room at 7 Race Course Road, the official part of the prime minister's house. (The residence was at number 5.) He was friendly and welcoming and eager to explain himself. So he answered every single question candidly even when it might have served him better to be a little more circumspect. Early in the interview, I recognized that this was a key weakness in his style (from his perspective, not ours).

Most prime ministers speak from an elevated pedestal. Usually interviewers are too intimidated to ask awkward or rude questions. When they do cross some invisible line, the prime minister answers the question but you sense that he is not pleased. So, overall you can rarely squeeze more than two or three rude questions into an interview.

Rajiv, on the other hand, liked to banter. He treated interviewers as equals and enjoyed the back and forth of a lively conversation. This made him more likeable but it also made him more prone to gaffes.

This was particularly evident when we came to his friend and aide Satish Sharma. Satish had been a pilot at Indian Airlines and had flown with Rajiv. He had begun to get involved in Rajiv's politics even when Mrs Gandhi was alive but had only come into his own during the second half of Rajiv's prime ministership.

He was a shadowy figure and most people did not know that he even occupied a small hut in the Race Course Road complex that he used as an office. But among those in the know he was regarded as one of the country's most powerful people. Industrialists would line up in the waiting room of his hut and ministers would stand to attention when he called.

Sharma's importance stemmed from his closeness to Rajiv and while this should have made Rajiv hold him accountable it actually had the opposite effect. Rajiv took the line that Satish had given up so much to help him and was overly protective of him.

Sharma had hit the news after a paper reported that he had imported marble tiles for a swimming pool at his farmhouse in Mehrauli. I had gone to see him at his little hut shortly after the controversy broke and he offered an elaborate defence. His wife was Dutch, he said. Her father, who was well off, had gifted them the tiles. What was the big deal?

So when I started asking Rajiv about Satish Sharma and his marble tiles, I knew what the party line would be. Once Rajiv had finished telling us about Satish's father-in-law, I asked what I regarded as the key question.

Satish Sharma did not come from a rich family. He had never got much further than being a pilot in Indian Airlines. How did he have the money to afford a large farmhouse in Mehrauli with a huge swimming pool?

Rajiv was not expecting that one. And I guess, at some level, he had no answer. A politician would have said something like 'I don't know. You will have to ask Satish about his financial affairs. I can hardly speak for him.' That would have killed the conversation.

But Rajiv now felt obliged to defend Satish. And yet he did not want to deviate from the bantering tone of his interview. So he decided to take the question head on.

Well, look at us, he said. When I was a pilot, we saved and saved and built a small farmhouse in Mehrauli.

Yes, I said, but Satish Sharma's farmhouse was much larger than his. Could he think of many Indian Airlines pilots who had such luxurious farmhouses?

Rajiv said that, like him, pilots did indeed have farmhouses.

And did they, I continued, all have large swimming pools? Was this something all Indian Airlines pilots could afford?

Yes, said Rajiv stolidly. They have them.

This was demonstrably untrue and when the interview appeared, Indian Airlines pilot organizations, who were always asking for pay rises, put out statements saying how badly off they were. None of them could afford large farmhouses, let alone swimming pools.

Aveek then took over for the economic portion of the interview, a dangerous area for Rajiv because he had to defend the policies he had inherited from his mother while controlling his own more free-market instincts.

Still, he kept up the friendly tone. What he didn't realize was that when it came to subjects like free market economics, Aveek Sarkar did not banter with his friends. He lectured them.

So for about twenty minutes, while I watched in horrified fascination, the prime minister of India was Aveek Sarkared and could barely get a word in. At one stage, when poor Rajiv tried to expand on his position, Aveek interrupted magisterially to tell him why he was completely wrong.

I can't think of any other prime minister of India, before or after Rajiv, who would have tolerated this kind of behaviour from two journalists. But then, that was both Rajiv's strength and his weakness.

We went back to Calcutta to transcribe the interview only for Aveek to get a call from Parthasarthy, who had sat through the interview glumly. Could he come and see us in Calcutta?

Absolutely, said Aveek. He could even stay at his house.

So, Partha (as he is known) flew down, stayed with Aveek and then had dinner with Aveek and myself at Aveek's home.

There were one or two small things in the interview, he said, that the prime minister had said, that may have given the wrong impression. Could he amend the transcript a little?

I waited for him to mention the swimming pools. But no, he was concerned with one or two foreign and economic policy issues. Aveek listened patiently, offered him some very good wine and made it clear that he would not amend the transcript in any way.

It says something about those times that the conversation was conducted with no acrimony and with great cordiality. Partha was obviously disappointed that Aveek would not agree to any changes but he respected *Sunday*'s position. It made no difference to his relationship with Aveek.

The interview appeared. It was a big deal: the lead story in every newspaper. The swimming pool dominated political conversation for days and we were (justifiably, I think) very pleased with ourselves.

Rajiv never held it against us. When I interviewed him during his spell out of power, he even joked about it. ('You think you are going to get me to talk about swimming pools,' he laughed.) Satish Sharma was not pleased. I met him in Goa a few months later and he said: 'What kind of journalist are you? You go to meet the prime minister and all you can talk about is my bluddy swimming pool?'

By the time the interview appeared, it was clear that Rajiv was in trouble. Even his friends conceded that. Amitabh Bachchan (who had resigned from parliament by then but more about that in a later chapter) believed that the Congress would lose because it could only win in a wave-like situation. It was too lazy, badly organized and riddled with in-house rivalries to mount an effective election campaign. Nobody disputed that Rajiv was still the most popular leader in the country (as the opinion polls confirmed) but he had come up against many opposing forces.

The first were those like V.P. Singh who had left the Congress and linked up with Arun Nehru and Arif Mohammad Khan to form a new party dedicated to fighting corruption in public life. This group targeted Rajiv who was now vulnerable because of the mishandling of the Bofors scandal.

Singh had allies within the media including Ramnath Goenka of the *Indian Express* which had turned from being an anti-Ambani publication to becoming an anti-Rajiv paper. It did not help when Rajiv's government filed scores of bogus cases against the *Express* and raided its premises. That needlessly heavy-handed and vindictive response combined with a horrifically misguided attempt to introduce a harsh new anti-defamation bill (later withdrawn) convinced journalists that the government had no commitment to the freedom of the press.

Nor did it help that questions began to be asked about extra-constitutional authorities within the system. Who was Satish Sharma? Why did he deserve an office in the prime minister's house? What was his locus standi?

And there was the strange case of R.K. Dhawan. During Indira Gandhi's time, Dhawan had been the most powerful man in India. He ordered cabinet ministers around, and often played a key role in their appointment. Dhawan had been so powerful that even Arun Nehru and Rajiv found that Mrs Gandhi often preferred his advice to theirs.

Rajiv had removed Dhawan once he took office, which was fair enough. But then, totally unforgivably, a government-appointed commission of enquiry had declared that Dhawan had a role in assassinating Indira Gandhi. This was so preposterous that many journalists—myself included—who had attacked Dhawan's undeserved importance in the Indira Gandhi era, now wrote articles defending him as this frame-up unfolded.

With criminal charges hovering over his head, Dhawan had found himself isolated. When I met him later he was so grateful for the support he had received from the media ('but you didn't even like me') that he wept as he recounted the ordeal he had been put through. 'I used to go to the temple every day and I would ask God: who is stronger, you or Arun Nehru?'

Presumably God gave a convincing answer to his question because Nehru fell from favour and Dhawan fell off the government's radar. The witch-hunt ended.

Now, in his last year in office, before the general election, Rajiv recalled Dhawan and asked him to join his office, erasing the old hostility and the bogus allegations of involvement in the assassination. Rajiv even neutralized the opposition of his own wife Sonia who was not at all keen on Dhawan.

It was good that Dhawan had been exonerated of the fake charges. But what role was he going to play? Was it back to Indira-raj? What happened to the new style of governance that Rajiv had promised?

All this helped V.P. Singh claim that Rajiv was a lazy and corrupt throwback to the Congress of old and not—as he had first seemed—a new kind of leader.

The second kind of opposition came from the Hindu backlash. More people than Rajiv had expected bought the BJP line that Hindus were second-class citizens in their own country and that the government was 'appeasing' Muslims because they always voted as a block and you could count on their votes.

In Rajiv's view, much of this was related to the Ram Janmabhoomi/Babri Masjid dispute in Ayodhya (and perhaps some of it was) so he spent a long time with such ministers as Buta Singh trying to work out a way to satisfy Hindu aspirations (in fact, if there was any 'appeasement' going on, it was of fundamentalist Hindus) by allowing a *shilanyas* at a spot in Ayodhya that was not disputed. (Or was it? It later seemed that Rajiv had been misled.)

It was a hopeless endeavour. L.K. Advani's campaign had captured the Hindu imagination. Positions had hardened. The Muslim leadership would not yield an inch. And Hindus would not be satisfied till the Babri Masjid (a symbol of the way in which Muslim invaders had destroyed Hindu temples at the most sacred spots, or so the BJP claimed) was moved.

There was no middle ground to be found.

The election results had a personal significance for me. It was the first time I appeared on live television. Doordarshan was still the only network but it had allowed NDTV, a private company run by the husband and wife team of Prannoy and Radhika Roy, to handle the election results programming. Prannoy invited me to be on the panel and though I was nervous, I agreed.

In fact, it was not that difficult to be a guest on an election show. They only asked you for your opinion when no results were coming in to help fill the vacant time. I had decided on a position early on—that Rajiv would lose—and stuck to it.

What was more fun was sitting next to some of the principal political players in the studio and discussing what was really going on when the show was on a break. I met Yashwant Sinha for the first time there. And L.K. Advani gave me his own assessment of what the final results would reveal. ('We will do very well but not as well as Janata. But Janata will not be able to do anything without us.' He was right.)

The Congress spokesmen were told not to admit defeat and so they kept coming up with unlikely scenarios to explain how they would remain in power. Anand Sharma, a Youth Congress leader whom I knew a little from before, stuck to this line and Prannoy asked me what I thought of it.

I said this was nonsense. The BJP and Janata could not possibly align with the Congress. And as for the CPM, whom the Congress spokesmen were counting on, I lived in Bengal and I knew that their central message throughout the campaign was 'Rajiv Gandhi is a *chor*.' How could they possibly align with the Congress?

Anand looked like I had slapped him. Prannoy cleared his throat and went on to something else. Later, I was told that I was the first person in the history of Doordarshan to call the sitting prime minister of India 'a chor'. I explained that this was not my view. I was only summarizing the CPM campaign. But nobody was interested in the context.

There was a funny subtext. After the show was over for the day, Anand asked me home for a drink. His wife opened the door. Obviously, it had been a bad day for them watching the defeat of the Congress and they couldn't have been pleased with the dismissive way I had treated Anand's claims on camera. And yet there was Anand, accompanied by the man who had mugged him.

But the family was gracious and hospitable and Anand spoke honestly—off the record—about the future of the Congress.

By the next day (in those days, with manual counting, the results process took a few days) Rajiv had conceded defeat. Speculation focused on the next prime minister. The consensus around the panel was that it would be Chandra Shekhar, the Janata stalwart who had been prime minister-in-waiting for longer than Rajiv Gandhi had been in politics.

I said I disagreed with the panel. It would be V.P. Singh.

I knew him well enough to know that beneath that soft and gracious exterior he was not just shrewd and wily but that he had a stubborn streak. If he did not get the prime ministership then he would accept nothing else. And no one else would be allowed to get the job either.

TWENTY-NINE

'I WAS YOUNG. I MADE MISTAKES'

As Advani had predicted, the BJP did well but not as well as Janata. It got 85 seats while Janata got 143. (The Congress got 197, far more than any other party but around a hundred seats short of a majority.)

The BJP said it would support Janata but even together, the two parties did not have a majority. They needed another fifty seats and they got them when the Left parties agreed to support them from outside.

This three-cornered alliance was full of contradictions. The 1977–79 Janata government had fallen, at least partly, because Janata members objected to the Jan Sangh's communal roots. The BJP was even more of a Hindu party now than the Jan Sangh had been in 1977. Would this not be a problem? And what about the Left? Was it comfortable being part of a three-cornered arrangement with the BJP?

The only person for whom the alliance made sense was L.K. Advani. He would be remembered, he believed, as the man who had taken the BJP from a mere two seats in parliament to being the kingmaker at the next election.

There was yet another complication. Janata was not the old Janata Party any longer. It was now the Janata Dal, composed of some of the old Janata veterans but supplemented by a new party of Congress defectors led by V.P. Singh and Arun Nehru. The two sides did not get along. Chandra Shekhar, from the old Janata, for instance, had total contempt for V.P. Singh whom he viewed as a characterless opportunist.

How was this all going to work?

I was deeply sceptical about the prospects of any arrangement lasting. Till that point, India had mostly been run by governments with majorities in the Lok Sabha. Mrs Gandhi had briefly lost her majority after the Congress split in 1969 but even though she knew that she could count on the communists to back her, she had called a mid-term election (where she won a majority) as soon as she could.

Our sole experience with coalitions was the disastrous 1977 to 1979 period when politicians frittered away the goodwill that had got them elected and forced the electorate to recall Indira Gandhi, her transgressions during the Emergency forgiven.

I did not believe that this government would last even for a year. Apart from the contradictions between the BJP and the Left, there were too many differences within the Janata Dal itself.

I went to meet Chandra Shekhar at his 'ashram' (a large estate; 'ashram' sounded nicer than 'pleasure palace') in Bhondsi on the outskirts of Delhi. I had known Chandra Shekhar during my *Imprint* days because a friend of mine, Kamal Morarka, was a dedicated Chandra Shekhar supporter who boosted his prospects even when the Rajiv wave was at its height.

Chandra Shekhar believed he should be prime minister. He had opposed the Emergency and later had been the centre of all opposition to Indira Gandhi. He believed that with the Congress out of power his time had finally come.

I told him I didn't think he had the votes. Besides, V.P. Singh had led the campaign against Rajiv (Chandra Shekhar had refrained from personal attacks) so the media expected Singh to be the next prime minister. Chandra Shekhar did not agree with me but looked grim.

I have no idea what happened next but TV footage showed Chandra Shekar, Devi Lal (a Haryana leader) and others laughing delightedly before they went into the meeting of the Janata Dal parliamentary party. After the meeting was called to order, Chandra Shekhar was called on to speak. He said he proposed Devi Lal for prime minister.

Devi Lal was then asked to accept the nomination. He said that he was honoured to be nominated but felt that the position belonged to V.P. Singh.

V.P. Singh then got up. He did not nominate anyone else. He grabbed the job and ran with it.

Obviously some deal that excluded Chandra Shekhar had been struck. Devi Lal had agreed not only to accept V.P. Singh as prime minister, he had agreed to deceive Chandra Shekhar as well. They had made a fool of Chandra Shekhar in front of the parliamentary party and the TV cameras.

Afterwards, Chandra Shekhar told the press that he had been betrayed which may have been the understatement of the year. But even he did not realize how completely he had lost out. When the ministry was sworn in, Chandra Shekhar's supporters were sidelined or kept out. Yashwant Sinha, who was told he was only a minister of state, walked out of the swearing in and drove straight to Bhondsi to confer with Chandra Shekhar.

I met Chandra Shekhar a few days later at his MP's bungalow in Delhi. He was livid with V.P. Singh and with Arun Nehru who, he said, had plotted the deception. Oddly enough, he felt no rancour towards Devi Lal without whom none of this could have happened. The way Chandra Shekhar told it, V.P. Singh had publicly declared that he wanted no position. But his followers had made it clear that they would not accept Chandra Shekhar. So Devi Lal had been chosen as a compromise candidate.

Either, Arun Nehru took Devi Lal aside after the consensus was arranged and told him to give the job to V.P. Singh or the whole exercise was a con job from the very beginning, intended only to make a fool out of Chandra Shekhar. He preferred the first explanation. I thought the second was more likely.

The problem with V.P. Singh was that he was a little like Arvind Kejriwal is today. Financially upright, soft-spoken, competent and capable of evoking strong emotions among his supporters. But he was also a man without any core beliefs, without any long-term loyalty (except to one or two political friends) and without any transparency. Even Advani who was vilified by the secular media was a relatively straight person. If he said he was going to do something, he usually did it. V.P. Singh, on the other hand, was capable of such duplicity that if you asked him what day of the week it was and he said Tuesday, the chances were that it was really Friday.

But he was charming, intelligent and entirely plausible at first. I had admired him in my *Imprint* days and I could see why he was now such a hero to the media. But how long, I wondered, before the media discovered how hollow he was? How long before the early popularity faded?

As for Rajiv, the Congress united behind him, nobody blamed him (in public, at least) for the loss and he soon developed a core team of advisors including P. Chidambaram, Natwar Singh and strangely enough, Pranab Mukherjee. Rajiv was a great one for acronyms. So Arun Nehru was always AKN and Pranab Mukherjee was PKM. Years later, I asked Pranab why Rajiv chose to use a K in the middle of his initials. 'Because otherwise he would have had to call me PM,' Pranab Mukherjee explained. It was quite obvious, really. (How had Rajiv rediscovered Pranab? Perhaps it was R.K. Dhawan who helped bring his friend back. I never really found out.)

I got to know Rajiv a little better during this period because he had more time on his hands and was more accessible to journalists. He agreed that they had messed up the handling of Bofors (I think he blamed Gopi Arora which was a bit harsh) but insisted that neither the Congress nor he had gained personally. 'Let them investigate it,' he said. 'They will find nothing that links us to that deal. It was totally above board as far as we were concerned.'

He was unwilling to agree with me that the Congress had needlessly alienated its Hindu supporters with the foolish mixed messages over the Babri Masjid. He thought the collapse of the Soviet Union (happening as we spoke) was bad for India because it was difficult to be non-aligned in a unipolar world. And he was convinced that when he returned to power (it was always 'when', not 'if'; he was certain that the V.P. Singh government would not last), he would rectify the mistakes he had made while in office, including a reluctance to speedily liberalize the economy.

I pushed him on the mistakes, perhaps a bit too hard. 'Look Vir,' he finally said, 'if you become prime minister you would make the same mistakes.'

It wasn't easy being prime minister, he said, and few people understood how complex the job was or how many decisions a prime minister had to take in the space of a day usually on the basis of inadequate information.

I persuaded him to agree to another interview and Aveek and I went to 10 Janpath for a marathon interview that stretched over two sessions. He was still the bantering Rajiv of old but there was a new self-awareness. I took what I thought was the quote of the interview and put it on the cover: 'I was young. I made mistakes.'

Meanwhile, V.P. Singh decided to run his government on the basis of FIRs, investigations and Letter Rogatories to foreign governments. Having come to power on a plank that highlighted Rajiv's alleged corruption, he now had to make good on those claims. His investigators targeted Sonia Gandhi, even including the names of her sisters' husbands in the Letter Rogatory they sent the Swiss government. Of course this attracted a lot of media attention but there was an Inspector Clouseau-like ineptitude to his investigators. Many had little experience of global banking and bewildered the Swiss by asking about Credits Sweezy (Credit Suisse) and other entities whose names they could not pronounce.

In the end, they found not one thing that could link Rajiv or Sonia (or her distant relatives, even) to the charges that the prime minister had so cavalierly levelled when he was in opposition.

V.P. Singh had serious problems within his own government. As predicted, the shotgun marriage between the Congress defectors and the old Janata members did not go well. Devi Lal, who had played such a key role in making V.P. Singh prime minister, kept threatening to revolt. He gave interviews where he rubbished the government and abused its ministers. (The foreign minister was 'impotent' apparently.)

There were more serious and far-reaching problems. In those days the media always played down the separatist strand that had been a part of Kashmir politics from 1947 onwards. We were also largely ignorant of what was going on in Pakistan. Since 1972 when Indira Gandhi liberated East Pakistan which became Bangladesh, India had stopped worrying too much about our western neighbour.

Fortunately for Pakistan, it had been enlisted by the US as part of its jehad against the Soviet-backed regime in Afghanistan. This allowed it to distract its people from its failures against India. But when it could cause problems for India it did so, in a low cost, low key sort of way that stopped well short of military action. The Pakistani agency, Inter-Services Intelligence (ISI), had trained Sikh militants on the side while focusing mainly on sending fighters into Afghanistan to participate in the jehad.

In 1989 when the Afghan jehad ended, the ISI found it had resources and fighters and no battle to fight. It turned its attention to India, reaching out to separatists in Kashmir.

It's not clear to me if V.P. Singh realized how potentially dangerous the situation was. Or whether he was aware of the danger, but his ineptitude led him to mishandle the situation because he was simply out of his depth.

He first put his faith in Lt Governor Jagmohan who was appointed over the objections of Farooq Abdullah, the elected chief minister. The government resigned in protest, leaving Kashmiris with no elected government of their own but direct rule from Delhi through Jagmohan. This boosted separatist sentiment.

Nor did it help (as it should have) that India had a Kashmiri home minister in Mufti Mohammad Sayeed. Separatists kidnapped Mufti's daughter and the centre acceded to their demands to release militants from jail in order to secure her release. This destroyed Mufti's credibility in the rest of India.

Worse was to follow. Militants terrorized Hindus in the valley forcing them to abandon their homes and businesses and flee for their lives. This was ethnic cleansing but V.P. Singh's government did nothing to stop it. The Kashmir valley had always been a Muslim-majority area but now it also became largely Hindu-free.

V.P. Singh's solution was to create a central ministry of Kashmir affairs with George Fernandes at its head. Fernandes thought Jagmohan was a fool so the two disagreed routinely over policy.

I was editor of *Sunday* during this period and reckoned we were seeing the start of a problem that might never go away. We put Shiraz Sidhva, one of our best correspondents, on the beat and she made innumerable trips to Kashmir, spoke to all the major players and came back to Delhi less and less hopeful after each trip.

For anyone watching the deterioration of the situation and the skill with which Pakistan manipulated the separatists it was frustrating to see the mess that V.P. Singh was making of Kashmir. Had somebody more competent been in charge (say, A.B. Vajpayee) the problem could have been controlled at that early stage.

As the problems grew, V.P. Singh looked for a way out. On 15 August 1990, he announced from the ramparts of the Red Fort that his government would implement the long-forgotten recommendations of the Mandal Commission. These involved reserving government jobs for backward castes and were not as far-reaching in their import as V.P. Singh made out. But the prime minister acted as though he had rewired India's social structure, giving hope and opportunity to millions of backward castes.

Caste-based reservation had not been an election issue and V.P. Singh (an upper caste himself) had hardly mentioned it on the campaign trail. But now, with his government failing within less than a year of taking over, he needed to pull a rabbit out of his fur cap. His ministers were told that this would change politics forever. Their party would never lose an election again.

Nobody had expected what happened next. First came angry demonstrations from students protesting the extension of reservation. And then, in campus after campus, town after town, students began immolating themselves in public. If there had been news channels in those days, V.P. Singh would have been a goner by the end of the week. As it was, all of his middle class support vanished overnight. The people who had once hailed him for his financial integrity now began to regard him as the enemy.

V.P. Singh believed that his strategy would be vindicated at the next election. But that wasn't due for years. And his ministers and allies began to make their own plans.

I got a message from Arun Nehru asking if I would like to do an interview. I was a little surprised. I was hardly his kind of guy.

But of course, I went and met him at his office. We spent ten minutes meandering on about the commerce ministry (his portfolio) before getting to the point.

I asked him. 'Have you met Rajiv?'

Oh yes, he said, I met him just yesterday. We meet all the time.

I pushed him about the investigations his government had launched.

He was dismissive. Nobody can finish anybody in this country, he said. And they shouldn't try.

Naturally, the interview caused a sensation and worried the government. (Aveek had been told by the local Intelligence Bureau people in Calcutta that they had been asked to keep a watch on me.) Obviously Arun Nehru wanted to warn V.P. Singh that he was ready to go home to the Congress.

I asked Rajiv who said that while Nehru was telling the truth, he was presenting it in the best possible light. Yes, they ran into each other all the time but it was at banquets, government functions and the like. There had been no one-on-one meeting. But yes, Nehru had sent him messages saying that he wanted to come back.

If Arun Nehru reacted to Mandal by threatening to jump ship, L.K. Advani realized it was time for the BJP to strike out on its own. He conjured up the Ayodhya agitation. An aide from Maharashtra, a spiv-like politician called Pramod Mahajan, converted a Toyota van into a *rath* and Advani set off on a *rath yatra*, complete with actors dressed like Ram and Lakshman to stir up passions again.

The *rath yatra* was a clear violation of the spirit in which the Janata Dal and the BJP had come together. But Advani did not care. He had given up on this government. He was worried about the electoral impact of Mandal. And he needed to keep the Ayodhya fires burning.

What followed was inevitable. A Janata Dal chief minister, Laloo Yadav, stopped the *rath yatra* in Bihar and arrested Advani. The BJP withdrew support and V.P. Singh's government fell.

V.P. Singh had been in office for eleven months during which time Kashmir had exploded and a caste-war had been set in motion.

I was not sorry to see him go.

THIRTY

'IT'S NOT AN ASHRAM.
IT'S A COUNTRY CLUB'

With V.P. Singh gone, there were three possibilities. The first was for the Congress to break the Janata Dal. It needed around a hundred MPs to take office and with the support of the Left that number would come down to fifty. This was the easiest option. V.P. Singh was now so unpopular that there was nostalgia for the Rajiv raj.

The second was to hold a general election. This may have made sense (and in retrospect, it would have been politically advantageous for the Congress) but Rajiv took the line that with the riots provoked by L.K. Advani's *rath yatra* still raging in parts of India and the country divided over Mandal, this was not the right time to hold an election.

The third was for the Janata Dal to select a new leader who would be able to command a majority in the House, either by regaining the BJP's support or by getting the Congress to back him.

Chandra Shekhar, who had been cheated out of the prime ministership, was the obvious choice but he would not align with the BJP. That left only the Congress. Furious parleys began between the Congress and such Chandra Shekhar men as Subramanian Swamy. At the time, Swamy was close to Rajiv and able to persuade him that Chandra Shekhar would restore stability to the country.

Eventually Chandra Shekhar took office as prime minister with just sixty-five of the Janata Dal's MPs. His majority in parliament was guaranteed by support from outside—the Congress mainly.

Chandra Shekhar was under no illusions about the temporary nature of his prime ministership. He refused to shift to the prime minister's house and used the office at 7 Race Course Road only for official meetings.

But while it lasted, I thought (rather selfishly) to myself, *Sunday* had a unique opportunity in terms of access to the government. Many of us (myself, Rajiv Shukla and Seema Goswami) had direct access to the prime minister and he was surrounded by people we knew well. Kamal Morarka became minister of state in the PMO, my friend Gopi Manchanda became officer on special duty in the PMO. Swamy became commerce minister, Yashwant Sinha was finance minister and there were several others who knew us from what was considered Chandra Shekhar's dark period (that is, when V.P. Singh was prime minister).

We got most of the stories that mattered but, because of our deadlines, we could not run them first. Instead, we opted for a behind-the-scenes approach to the news, which worked well for us.

While we knew about the crises of Mandal and Masjid, few of us realized what bad shape the economy was in or that we had to borrow hundreds of millions just to survive. But lenders were not willing to offer favourable terms to India. At one stage, India was asked to deposit gold as collateral. Chandra Shekhar agreed but would only offer the gold that had been seized from smugglers over the years, not our original gold reserves.

All of this could have been managed but Chandra Shekhar did little to patch up the rivalries in his camp. The Janata loyalists were mistrustful of Swamy whom they saw as a recent entrant to the group. But Swamy had a direct line to Rajiv Gandhi so Chandra Shekhar needed him. Besides, Shekhar seemed to genuinely like Swamy.

The likes of Kamal Morarka and Gopi Manchanda glowered as Swamy began to become more and more influential. Swamy's own ire was reserved for Yashwant Sinha and he persuaded Rajiv that even though he was finance minister, Sinha could not be trusted to present a budget.

Somebody (perhaps Swamy again) also told Rajiv that Chandra Shekhar's old allies were crooks. I recall hearing Rajiv complain about corruption in the Chandra Shekhar government. When I said that he was exaggerating, Rajiv responded: 'What are you saying? They put all the files on one desk. And then Morarka says, "We'll charge five crores for this one." And somebody else says, "no, no, we can get ten for this". That is how the government works.'

I thought this was nonsense and told him so. He responded that he had heard this from someone who knew. I replied that I knew Kamal Morarka well, that he was independently wealthy and was not motivated by money. Rajiv looked at me pityingly. And we changed the subject.

I knew matters had passed the point of no return when we threw a *Sunday* magazine party at the Taj Man Singh hotel in Delhi. Rajiv and Chandra Shekhar were both invited and because it was a sit-down there was a scramble to get on to Rajiv and Sonia's table. I sat with Chandra Shekhar at his table but nobody paid us much attention.

Protocol dictates that the prime minister arrives last so Rajiv reached the drinks area (he drank soda water) a few minutes before Chandra Shekhar was due to arrive. But Shekhar was late and Rajiv began to look impatient. I said I would check to see if Chandra Shekhar was coming from his South Avenue Lane home or from the Bhondsi ashram.

'Ashram?' said Rajiv incredulously.

'Yes,' I said. 'Why?'

'It's not an ashram. It is a country club.' He was loud enough for anyone standing nearby to hear.

I mumbled something in Chandra Shekhar's defence.

'Have you heard the story about Brezhnev?' Rajiv asked. I said I thought I knew what he was referring to in the hope of heading him off but he told the joke anyway.

'Brezhnev's mother comes to visit him. He tells her she should be proud of him. He shows her his *dacha*. He shows her his many fancy cars. He shows her his luxurious living quarters. To his surprise, his mother starts to weep.

Brezhnev is surprised. 'Aren't you proud of me, mama?' he asks.

'Oh Leonid,' she says through her tears, 'What will happen to you if the communists come back?'

There were others in the group around Rajiv and they laughed.

'That's the kind of ashram he has,' Rajiv concluded.

I knew then that it was only a matter of months before the government fell. As much as I admired Chandra Shekhar, Rajiv thought he was a joke.

When the end came, it was over a silly and trivial issue. Two Haryana policemen were found to be keeping a watch on 10 Janpath. The Congress claimed that Chandra Shekhar had put Rajiv Gandhi under surveillance. It was time, Congressmen said, for the party to stop supporting this ingrate.

I found Chandra Shekhar at his office in Parliament House. He looked downcast and frustrated. He had been trying to get Rajiv on the phone, he said, but they wouldn't put him through. I told him that I had an appointment with Rajiv that evening and would ask him about it.

By the time I walked into Rajiv's office, it was clear to me that his mind was made up. I told him how upset Chandra Shekhar was.

'You can't refuse to accept calls from the prime minister of India,' I said.

Rajiv shrugged and told V. George, his PS, 'When Vir Sanghvi leaves, put me through to the PM.'

I left 10 Janpath convinced that it was all over. And indeed it was. By the time I had gone back to Calcutta, the Congress had withdrawn support and the government had fallen.

So, what happened next?

I asked George for time with Rajiv Gandhi, saying that I would fly back to Delhi if they gave me an appointment. They did and as I sat in the small waiting area at 10 Janpath, I could hear Kamal Nath and various other Congressmen discussing the formation of a new government. The Congress had the numbers. The Left would support it and most of Chandra Shekhar's supporters would vote for it. Arun Nehru would bring some of his flock for a homecoming.

When I went inside, however, I found that Rajiv was totally opposed to the idea of taking office. He wanted an election. He wanted a mandate.

I pointed out that while the Congress would probably improve on the 195 or so it had won at the last election, there was no guarantee it would win a majority. Mandal had changed the nature of caste-based voting patterns in north India. The BJP was now a factor to reckon with in the same region.

In 1989, the Congress had done well in the south and would probably hold on to those seats. But north India was a problem—perhaps a bigger one now in 1991 than it had been back in 1989.

He conceded all this but said that the Left had assured him of support. He just needed thirty or forty more seats than the Congress had won in 1989. And with no anti-incumbency and with the collapse of the Bofors issue after V.P. Singh had found nothing to link him to the matter, he was sure that he would do better.

And so an election was called and Rajiv began touring the country. I met him during the campaign in Calcutta. His throat was in bad shape. He drank warm water, spoke in a rasping whisper and was accompanied by his school friend, the journalist Suman Dubey, and just one security officer. We couldn't really talk so I wished him well and he took off on his travels on the campaign trail.

I was at a hotel in Bombay a week or so later when the phone rang, late one night. It was Anil Ambani. I knew Anil but not well enough to get late night calls from him. So I was a little surprised.

'What's the latest? Have you heard any more about Rajiv?' he asked breathlessly.

'Why? Has something happened?'

'You mean you don't know? A bomb exploded at a rally in Tamil Nadu. Rajiv, Mani Shankar Aiyar, Suman Dubey—they were all blown up in the blast.'

I said I would check. Anil hung up, disgusted (I suspect) that a journalist had no information at all to offer.

There were no national news channels so I switched on BBC and CNN. Both said that Rajiv had been killed in a blast at a campaign rally. They had no other information.

I woke the members of *Sunday*'s Delhi bureau. Our Madras correspondent already had the story. They checked and called back to say that yes, Rajiv had been killed in the blast but that Suman was okay. Mani had not even been at the rally. The early reports—which Anil had quoted—were wrong.

I left for the airport and took the first flight I could find to Delhi. We called a bureau meeting and began to plan the issue.

It took a couple of days for us to discover that an LTTE (Liberation Tigers of Tamil Eelam) hit squad was behind the assassination. Fortunately, there was no rioting or violence of the sort that had followed Mrs Gandhi's assassination.

All of India mourned and I kept thinking back to my last full conversation with Rajiv when he had turned down the easy option of taking office without a fresh election.

The journalistic consensus was that Rajiv would have been prime minister again after the election was concluded and it seemed particularly cruel that his life had been snatched away just as he was on the verge of coming back.

I went to the funeral and met Amitabh Bachchan who was helping Sonia through the trauma. He looked drawn and shattered. It had been a crazy roller coaster ride for him too.

I could only imagine what Sonia Gandhi was going through. From the day Rajiv had become PM she had been convinced it would end this way.

And it had.

THIRTY-ONE

THE RAJA AND HIS PARROT

Though I had met Amitabh Bachchan quite often during my *Imprint* days, I only got to know him well after I joined *Sunday*. Almost from the moment he became an MP, I could tell that something had changed.

He had been asked to contest from Allahabad by Arun Nehru, who was Rajiv's chief strategist as part of a grand master plan to defeat as many opposition heavyweights as possible. Nehru wanted H.N. Bahuguna out of the new Lok Sabha and was sure that Bachchan would be able to defeat him. In the event, Nehru needn't have tried so hard. So all-encompassing was the Rajiv Gandhi wave that Bahuguna would have lost anyway, regardless of who the Congress put up.

I am still not sure why Bachchan agreed to join politics, something he had often assured me he would never do. When he did become an MP he offered two reasons, both of which may have been part of the story.

The first was that not only was Rajiv his childhood friend but that the Bachchan and Gandhi families had always been close. For instance, when the young Sonia Maino came to India to marry Rajiv, she stayed in Delhi with the Bachchans. She continued to tie *rakhis* on the wrists of both Bachchan brothers.

When Mrs Gandhi was assassinated the Bachchan family was swept up in the wave of grief that followed. When Rajiv succeeded his mother he told Amitabh that he would only be able to do the job if his close friends helped him. So when Rajiv asked him to join politics during that emotionally charged period, he found it hard to refuse.

The second was what Bachchan called the '1982 episode'. That was the year when a fight scene in a movie went wrong and Amitabh was punched hard in the stomach. The blow caused internal ruptures and Bachchan remained in hospital for weeks, hovering between life and death.

Stars have been injured or fallen ill before but there was no precedent for the way in which India reacted. The whole country came to a standstill and millions prayed for his recovery. The prayers took the form of fasts, rituals and logic-defying stunts. One man kept front rolling (like multiple somersaults) for several miles from his home to a temple. He believed that God would reward this gymnastic display by restoring Amitabh's health.

Till that point, Bachchan had been famously professional saying that acting was just a job. But the public response to his injury stunned him and made him rethink his relationship with the Indian people.

Perhaps it wasn't just a job, after all. Perhaps he owed something to the people who had prayed for him. Perhaps he should look beyond acting.

And he did. He joined politics.

He found that something happened to him after the Allahabad campaign. Most MPs win their elections, periodically visit their constituencies and get involved only when there are major issues to be discussed. The rest of them depute MLAs and municipal representatives to handle the situation on the ground.

But Bachchan decided that he would adopt Allahabad. Every conversation I had with him in 1985 was about how hard it was for the poor in Allahabad or about how he would do something new each month to help his constituents.

Such attention to a constituency is unusual among MPs. And when the MP in question is not just India's most famous man, a hero to the masses, but also the prime minister's best friend, his interest in the city worries local politicians. In Bachchan's case it was V.P. Singh, Rajiv's finance minister, who was troubled by Bachchan's obsession with Allahabad, which he regarded as part of his own backyard.

Though V.P. Singh was now nationally famous, he never forgot that Allahabad was his base. No Congress leader of note was allowed to emerge in that city. And the local party unit acted as though the Congress in Allahabad was V.P. Singh's personal property. Everyone who tried to make an impression was doomed to fail.

Almost every initiative Bachchan launched in Allahabad unravelled and he could never figure out why, so subtle and skillful was the manipulation. To his face, V.P. Singh would be uniformly friendly and respectful and when Bachchan went to him to look for help with the initiatives that had unravelled, V.P. Singh would be sympathetic and say things like 'unfortunately, the toothpaste cannot be put back into the tube'.

I had known Bachchan as an actor who ruled the industry from a distance. He rarely socialized, had very few film friends and yet, because he was such a box office draw, the producers kept knocking at his door. He had faced his share of down moments but especially after his '1982 episode' there had never been any doubt that he had the love of the people of India.

Now, he seemed less sure. In Allahabad, they arranged stunt after stunt to shake his hold on the city. If he failed to visit the constituency for two weeks, they put up 'Missing' posters. Nor did he seem to have the kind of lofty power in Delhi that he had enjoyed in Bombay. In Rajiv's inner circle, Arun Nehru always treated him as a novice (which he was) with much to learn.

At first Bachchan seemed to get along with Arun Singh, another of Rajiv's close friends and his closest advisor, even renting a farmhouse on the outskirts of Delhi from him. But that relationship turned sour and Rajiv had to keep his two close friends apart.

I can't remember when the negative stories about Bachchan started but I think they began around the time that his brother Ajitabh moved with his family to Switzerland. In those days, even more than now, Switzerland was known for its numbered bank accounts and it was soon put about that Ajitabh (Bunty) had become a Swiss resident only so he could look after the Bachchan family's illegal money. (In some versions, Bunty was looking after Rajiv's money too.)

These rumours would have faded if they had been based on mere guesswork but they survived because V.P. Singh's finance ministry always suggested—off the record, of course—to journalists that officials were prevented from probing the financial affairs of the Bachchan brothers. Who knew what an independent probe might reveal?

Somehow, Bachchan managed to become a sideshow when V.P. Singh decided to go to war against the Ambanis of Reliance, claiming that they were crooks who had to be stopped. The rumour mill had it that Bachchan—who knew Anil Ambani socially—was the conduit for communications between Rajiv Gandhi and the Ambanis. When two obviously forged letters, purportedly from Michael Hershman, an American investigator, surfaced, suggesting that V.P. Singh's targets included Rajiv Gandhi's family, Singh's officials told journalists that Bachchan had carried the fake letters from the Ambanis to Rajiv.

Given that this whisper campaign was well underway before the Bofors scandal erupted, it was easy to work Bachchan's name into the story. Without any evidence at all, those claiming to be in the know in Delhi began to suggest that the Bachchans had accepted kickbacks on behalf of the Gandhis.

Even when *The Hindu* named others as Bofors agents, the rumour mongers found a way to drag the Bachchans into the story. Was it not a fact, they asked, that the Hindujas had financed producers who made movies starring Amitabh? And now that *The Hindu* had named the Hindujas, wasn't that conclusive proof that the Bachchans were involved?

It was during this period that I got to know Bachchan well. In private, he can often be a silent, brooding presence, quite unlike the characters he plays on the screen. But now, I thought, it had gone even further: he was becoming a depressive presence.

He had no idea where the rumours were coming from, no way of quashing them and feared that he was becoming an embarrassment to Rajiv. More than that, I thought, he didn't know how to cope with the absence of public affection. He had always been the idol of millions. Now the millions were beginning to have doubts about him.

One fine day, he suddenly resigned from parliament. He gave no interviews but only repeated what we already knew: he was not cut out for politics.

Rather than ending the campaign against him, it only fuelled it. Why had he resigned? Had Rajiv thrown him overboard? What was Amitabh scared of?

These questions were raised again and again when V.P. Singh decided to stand against the Congress candidate at the by-election necessitated by Amitabh's resignation from parliament. Glad to be back in Allahabad, V.P. Singh turned the entire campaign into a referendum on Rajiv's integrity. And Amitabh featured in every speech.

Rajiv was the raja, V.P. Singh would say in his folksy manner, but every raja had a parrot. The raja's soul lived inside that parrot. Catch the parrot and you have caught the raja. In India's case, V.P. Singh continued, Rajiv was the raja, Amitabh was the parrot. Catch Amitabh and you bring down the raja. (I always thought that this little folksy tale was a bit ironic with its talk of rajas, given that everyone on VP Singh's staff called him Rajasaab—he was, after all, the raja of Manda.)

V.P. Singh won the by-election easily and things began to look increasingly glum for Amitabh through no fault of his own. He was still close to the Gandhis: he was the man who finally persuaded Sonia Gandhi that Rajiv needed R.K. Dhawan (whose appointment she was resolutely opposed to) in his office. But in the eyes of the public, this closeness to the Gandhis made him took even guiltier.

I remember sitting with him in his attic/den on top of Pratiksha, his bungalow in Bombay's Juhu-Vile Parle scheme as he tidied his desk (he is a neatness freak) and worried what would happen if V.P. Singh became prime minister.

We agreed that V.P. Singh's ascent was inevitable but that, I said, was preferable to the current situation where Bachchan was fighting smoke and shadows. There were no charges against him and he was required to prove a negative. How can you prove that you didn't take a kickback? He would be better off fighting charges when they were actually levelled.

In the event, V.P. Singh did become prime minister and his investigators took off to Geneva to catch the parrot, as V.P. Singh would have put it. They were sure that with their Letters Rogatory, they would get the Swiss to reveal the names of the Bofors account-holders. They asked for five accounts to be frozen but were surprised when the Swiss told them that Bofors had also paid money into a sixth account.

The CBI officers were professional enough to wait to see who the sixth account belonged to but the political appointees among the investigators quickly leaked to the media that they had found Ajitabh Bachchan's account. It was the sixth account. 'Bachchan caught red-handed' became the headline all over India.

As we all subsequently discovered (and the Bachchans already knew), Ajitabh had nothing to do with the sixth account. But the certainty with which the press reported the story crucified Amitabh in the public eye.

A strange transformation took place. Whereas earlier Amitabh had been a brooding, non-drinking, vegetarian, he changed before our eyes. He was on a British Airways flight from Bombay to London and when the cabin attendant came over with a tray of champagne before take-off, he suddenly said to himself, 'Oh screw it!' and took a glass. He tuned partly non-vegetarian. And became an angry middle-aged man in real life too.

He read a letter to the editor in a newspaper denouncing him. He got into his car and drove from Juhu to the letter writer's home in south Bombay, rang the doorbell and when they opened the door, dumbfounded, said, 'Hello, I am Amitabh Bachchan. I believe you have some doubts about my integrity.'

He left only after he had convinced the surprised man that the charges against him were false.

He considered taking legal action against the Indian newspapers that had carried the sixth account stories and only held off when he was told that the cases would take years to come to court.

But, he discovered, the sixth account story had also been carried by *Dagens Nyheter*, a Swedish paper. He checked with Ajitabh who had moved to London by now and discovered that he could sue a

Swedish paper (which was also circulated in England) for libel in a British court. He asked Bunty to file a case immediately.

I was in the London court when the case was heard. Amitabh had been told that he would have to testify. Rather than make him nervous, the thought excited him. He wanted to get on the stand and declare his innocence.

It was not to be.

When the case began, the counsel for *Dagens Nyheter* got up and told the court that the paper had been misled by the investigators and was withdrawing the allegation which it found to be false. It would pay damages to Ajitabh.

This was a huge victory—the first that Bachchan had won in many years—but rather than exult in joy, Amitabh seemed frustrated. He went to his lawyer's chamber and took calls from a variety of journalists at Indian newspapers who had read about the case on the news ticker. His tone was combative. Asked how he felt, he said, 'I came here ready to fight but the fight was over even before the first round.'

He had strong words for V.P. Singh and for the Indian newspapers that had carried the story ('Because the truth exposes us all') and poured all his pent up aggression into those interviews.

He flew back to India the next day and was greeted at Bombay airport by cheering crowds. One consequence of the scandal had been that all his films were flopping. Now, as the verdict came in, ticket sales for his current release, *Aaj ka Arjun*, one of the worst films he had ever acted in, soared. It became his biggest hit in years.

And just like that, suddenly, it was over.

Or not quite. There was one bit of unfinished business. Ajitabh had bought (with bank finance) a flat in Switzerland. This had been revealed by the Indian press at a time when anti-Bachchan feeling was at its height. To demonstrate its fairness, the Rajiv Gandhi government had a filed a case against Ajitabh, though, given that he was a non-resident, it was hard to see how any prosecution could succeed. Even V.P. Singh's investigators had found nothing in the case and did not bother to follow it up.

But the case was still not closed and remained a source of annoyance and there was always the fear that a hostile regime might re-open it just to torment the Bachchans.

Enter Amar Singh.

I knew Amar Singh from Calcutta, where he was well known in Congress and business circles. He had visited the ABP offices and, as the rest of India would find out, in the years to come, he was a curious mixture of guile, deviousness and a desperate need for attention.

Amar Singh had helped Jaya Bachchan organize a film festival when she was head of the Children's Film Society during the Rajiv Gandhi era and when the Bachchans had come to Calcutta for the premiere of *Agneepath*, he had been a fixture by Jaya's side.

Amar Singh knew Chandra Shekhar and told the Bachchans that he could get the new prime minister to close the file. As there was nothing to the case, this involved no impropriety but officials and ministers were always reluctant to sign off on a high profile case for fear of blowback.

Chandra Shekhar, however, was fearless. Amar Singh took Amitabh to meet the new prime minister. Amitabh explained the genesis of the case. Chandra Shekhar saw that there was nothing in it and closed the case.

It was the last legacy of that terrible period and the Bachchans were now free of any encumbrance. Amitabh returned to normal, gave up non-vegetarian food and liquor and chugged along happily till the next crisis came.

It took the shape of ABCL (Amitabh Bachchan Corporation Ltd), a visionary company he had formed because he accurately foresaw the corporatization of the entertainment space. Sadly, he was not a good businessman, hired the wrong people and went on to lose crores in the venture. As this setback took hold, Amar Singh was constantly by his side and put together a financial package that saved the Bachchans and left them debt-free.

By then, Amitabh's entertainment career had also bounced back with the success of *Mohabattein* and the super success of *Kaun Banega Crorepati*, a show that everyone (from Amar Singh to Jaya Bachchan) had advised him not to do.

Curiously, he became more and more dependent on Amar Singh and often it was hard to say where Amar Singh's world ended and Amitabh's began. All of Amar Singh's friends: Subroto Roy, the promoters of Himachal Futuristic, Anil Ambani, Mulayam Singh Yadav, etc. became Amitabh's pals and the two men seemed inseparable even as Amitabh's other friends became more and more scarce.

Then, one fine day, it all ended. I still don't know what happened.

Amar Singh gave me a TV interview in which he was so critical (abusive even) of the Bachchans (especially of Jaya who was his original contact) that we had to leave most of it on the cutting room floor out of a sense of decency.

They never reconciled and when Amar Singh died in a Singapore hospital, Amitabh did not bother with a proper statement of condolence.

He had seen them all off, from V.P. Singh to Amar Singh.

And he was still standing.

THIRTY-TWO

'MY SON, I FEEL MUCH STRONGER NOW'

Some of the preceding chapters may have given the impression that I had moved to Delhi where the political action was. In fact, I continued to live in Calcutta but because *Sunday* was a national newsmagazine, I travelled a lot.

This didn't really work for my personal life. My then wife, Malavika, did not particularly like Calcutta. She missed her family and friends in Bombay and went back at every opportunity she got. She also complained that she felt unsafe living on the ground floor of a bungalow; she was used to living in an apartment building. In 1990, after our son Raaj was born, she more or less gave up on Calcutta and shifted to Bombay.

I travelled too much, she said, and she was not prepared to be alone in Calcutta. I spoke to Aveek who agreed to rent us a small flat in Gauri Apartments on Southend Lane in Delhi and Malavika and Raaj shifted there. This meant we saw more of each other than we had when I lived in Calcutta and she had lived in Bombay. But Calcutta was where *Sunday* was published from, and so two-thirds of my time was still spent in that city.

ABP took the line, reasonably enough, that I no longer needed the largeish home in New Alipore and offered me a smaller flat in Sunny Park in Ballygunge. I thought this was fair enough and did not object when my home was allotted to the ABP librarian.

But I had forgotten what it was like dealing with ABP on property matters. As I was preparing to move out, I was told that the new flat was not ready. Could I take a room at the Taj Bengal instead? I ended up living there for six months till ABP got the flat ready. Malavika and Raaj never came to visit even when the new flat was finally ready. Raaj was too young to notice and I think Malavika had had enough of Calcutta.

Which was not to say that we had never had a life in Calcutta. In our first year, we became friends with Naresh and Sunita Kumar, perhaps the most sophisticated and globally best-connected people in Calcutta. Nearly everyone of consequence from England who arrived in Calcutta came with a letter of introduction to them (from Stephen Spender to the photographer Derry Moore—later Lord Drogheda). My friend Nicholas Coleridge, editorial director of Condé Nast UK, was a frequent visitor to Calcutta. He had once pursued the gorgeous Georgia Metcalfe from England to Calcutta before persuading her to marry him.

Nick had once been editor of *Harper's Queen* (as it then was; it later became *Harper's Bazaar*, in keeping with the brand's titles all over the world) and his predecessor, Willie Landels, who had run the magazine for years, was at a post-retirement loose end. I arranged for him to come and spend a month in Calcutta advising local artisanal organizations, and he was great company.

Calcutta had its share of celebrity visitors—Simon Jenkins, the well-known British journalist who had been editor of *The Times* (London) came to dinner at Aveek's with his wife, the actress Gayle Hunnicutt. He had given up being editor of the paper, he said, but now wrote a column for the op-ed page thrice a week.

I said how much I admired him for that. I wrote a column only once a week and had to struggle to find a subject. 'I always think,' he said, 'that if you have trouble finding a subject, then you shouldn't be writing a column.'

I don't know if Jenkins was right but my struggle to find column-worthy subjects has continued in the decades that have passed since this conversation took place.

Hugh Grant was an unknown small-time actor when he came to Calcutta to star in a film called *La Nuit Bengali* and because Calcutta was a small town in those days, I kept bumping into him. Our budding acquaintance spluttered to a halt when an expatriate friend of his threw Hugh a birthday party. We had accepted the invite and then, on the day itself, Malavika, whose father had recently died, said she didn't feel like going to a party. I saw her point and we sent a note to our host apologizing.

The following morning we got two notes. One from Hugh Grant calling us 'common' for canceling. And another from our host who wrote, 'Don't mind Hugh. He is only upset because nobody turned up for the party.'

It's a cynical thing to say but I'm pretty sure that if Grant had come to Calcutta after *Four Weddings and a Funeral* had been released, every single person who had been invited would have turned up for the party.

Amitabh came to Calcutta twice in the time I was there. On the first occasion he came to speak at the *Telegraph* debate. The day before the debate, Aveek asked me to request him to come and meet ABP's editors. We didn't tell anyone he was coming, I picked him up from his hotel and we drove to the office in my car.

There were audible gasps as we walked through the reception lobby and within minutes of his entering Aveek's office, we heard a commotion outside. I tried opening the door only to discover that virtually all of ABP's employees had left their desks and were crowded outside Aveek's office, hoping to catch a glimpse of Bachchan. We cancelled the meeting with editors, the police were called and Amit was escorted down to my car.

I thought he might be upset but he was delighted. This happened during his low phase, when V.P. Singh was prime minister and it reassured him that no matter what the newspapers wrote, he was still the greatest star India had ever produced.

We had one more such incident. When Jaya and he were in Calcutta for the premier of *Agneepath*, they came to my house for dinner. There were only a few of us (mainly Aveek and Rakhi, his brother Arup and his wife, and a couple of friends) so I thought no one would notice. But somehow word leaked that Amitabh Bachchan was in the neighbourhood. A large crowd gathered outside our door, cheering and shouting Amit's name.

'Let me handle this,' he said and went out. He stood on the porch and waved to the crowd which cheered back. When he came back, he said, 'Now that they have seen me, they will disperse.' But they didn't. And eventually news of the disturbance reached the cops who arrived to break up the crowd.

Amitabh Bachchan was a national celebrity. But Calcutta had its own local heroes. They were, in no particular order: Jyoti Basu, Satyajit Ray and Mother Teresa.

I met Jyoti Basu but never on a one-to-one basis. My sole encounter with Satyajit Ray was slightly bizarre. Somebody had written something vaguely (if indirectly) unflattering about Sandip Ray, Satyajit Ray's film-director son in *Sunday*. Ray had called Arup Sarkar to complain.

Arup called me to his office and said that Ray was upset. 'As it is,' Arup said, 'it is wrong that though you have been in Calcutta for over a year, you have never met him. I have fixed up for you to call on him at 4 p.m. tomorrow at his home. Go and have a cup of tea with him. He is a very nice man. Once you say sorry, he will be very gracious. You will become friends.'

I have never been keen on apologizing to famous people about minor criticisms in the publications I edit unless it can be demonstrated that we made a mistake or got the facts wrong. In this case that was far from clear; the story seemed fair to me.

Even so, I said yes to Arup. He said he would call Ray and tell him to expect me.

The next day, I told Malavika I was going to have tea with Ray. 'I want to come,' she said. 'I want to meet Satyajit Ray.' Given that this was going to be a friendly tea and that perhaps, Sandip, Satyajit Ray's son and the offended party, would be there too, I agreed.

We arrived at Ray's building at the appointed hour. I said I was the editor of *Sunday* and was ushered into the great man's presence.

'Who are you?' he said in a booming voice with an accent that could only have been acquired at some imaginary Oxford-on-the-Hooghly.

'I am Vir Sanghvi.' I replied. 'This is my wife Malavika. Arup Sarkar must have spoken to you . . .'

'Oh yes,' he said. 'How can you print such rubbish? And it's just so unfair! What kind of magazine do you run?' He went on like this for another five minutes while we kept standing.

This was not what I had signed up for, so the colour drained from my face. Finally, when Ray had finished, I mumbled, 'Look I am very sorry . . .'

I got no further. 'That's all right,' said Roy and indicated that the audience was at an end. We were ushered out and left in silence.

Later, I told Arup how badly it had gone. 'Good,' he said cheerfully. 'At least you apologized.'

Mutual friends later told me that Ray had told them that the editor of *Sunday* had come to say sorry. 'Strange man,' he added. 'He brought his wife along for some reason.'

My experience with Mother Teresa was happier. I only met her twice and each time, before I went, everyone at ABP told me not to be taken in by her. 'The Ramakrishna Mission does much more work but you only hear of Mother Teresa because she fits the preconceptions of Western media,' Aveek told me. (He was right but that wasn't the old dear's fault.)

Then there was an old ABP story about how Mother Teresa only spoke to the foreign media. One of our senior colleagues was also the local stringer for *Time* magazine. According to the story, every time he called her for an interview for the *Telegraph*, she would say, 'Oh my son, what can I say? I have been so ill! I would have liked to talk to you but doing God's work has left me so weak and tired.'

'Okay, Mother,' he would say, 'I am so sorry to hear that because *Time* magazine has also been calling about an interview . . .'

'My son,' she would interrupt, 'You know, I feel much stronger now. When would you like do the *Time* interview?'

I am guessing that the story was an exaggeration but there was an element of truth to it. Mother Teresa had very little time for the Calcutta press. On the other hand, she needed the foreign press to raise funds so yes, she probably paid more attention to Western journalists than to the Indian press. I didn't think it was such an unreasonable or terrible thing to do.

I met her twice, both times at her ashram and she was just as you would expect: modest, kind and with a no-nonsense manner. I don't dispute that she had a shrewd streak to her or that she was a religious fundamentalist (she thought abortion was one of the greatest evils in the world) but so what? As long as she cared for the dying, I didn't really see how one could object.

The most interesting visitor I had during my Calcutta years was V.S. Naipaul. He was writing *A Million Mutinies Now*, his first book about India that would not be hostile or overly critical. He had changed his mind about India, he told me. It was now a country full of hope, being reshaped by a new generation of citizens.

I introduced him to some people whom he could interview and at least one of them turned up in the book. He came home for dinner. An English friend, visiting from London, who was also invited had thoughtfully brought along two bottles of good white wine. We had some champagne of our own and by the end of the evening, Naipaul was quite sozzled.

Some things then became clear as his tongue loosened. The defining influence in his life had been his experience of growing up as an Indian in Trinidad. He hated black people because of the ones he had met during that phase and stopped anyone from referring to them as 'black'. 'Call them negroes,' he would insist.

We know now, after the publication of Patrick French's biography, that Naipaul was racist but it was strange to have the great man sitting on a sofa in your house making fairly crude anti-black jokes.

I was taken aback. But, at some level, I was also satisfied. When I had read his withering critiques of India, I had always thought to myself, 'This is one screwed-up rootless guy.'

People had told me I was reacting emotionally, with illogical defensiveness. But now, as I saw him displaying his prejudices in my home, I felt a strange vindication.

THIRTY-THREE

'SMALL-TIME MANIPULATOR MASQUERADING AS A STATESMAN'

Back in Delhi, the assassination of Rajiv Gandhi had thrown India into turmoil. The remaining phases of the election were delayed and when they were finally held and the results declared, it looked as if Rajiv's calculation had been about right. The Congress won 244 seats, less than an overall majority but more than enough to take office with the support of the Left which had over fifty seats.

Except that Rajiv was not around to savour this victory. In the aftermath of his assassination, the Congress, in some Pavlovian reflex, offered the post of party president to Sonia Gandhi. She turned it down and Narasimha Rao was appointed as a sort of interim president.

After the election results were declared, Sharad Pawar, the powerful chief minister of Maharashtra, asked for a contest to choose the next prime minister and declared his own candidacy.

Rajiv had tried to get rid of Pawar during his time in office and the wily Maratha strongman had held on to his job only by the skin of his teeth. Now, Pawar saw a chance to alter the political balance. He would come to Delhi like Shivaji had once hoped to, and would overthrow the existing empire.

Obviously, the Congress establishment was not going to tolerate this. It believed that Pawar lacked national stature and it feared that if an election for prime minister were called, Pawar's financial resources were such that a majority of MPs could be swayed in his favour.

The panicky Congress leadership went to Sonia, who was still grieving. She had no clue what to do but said that P.N. Haksar, Indira Gandhi's old advisor, should be consulted. Haksar suggested Shankar Dayal Sharma who was then the vice president. He was a man of integrity and a non-controversial figure who would unite the party, Haksar said, if he was made prime minister.

Natwar Singh (and, I think but am not sure, Aruna Asaf Ali) went to see Shankar Dayal Sharma. He heard them out and then said that he had no interest in the job. He was not at an age where he could do justice to the job, he said. Besides he had never wanted to be prime minister.

The Congress was horrified. This was the first time in Indian history that two people had turned down the prime ministership in quick succession. But neither Sonia nor Sharma would be moved.

In desperation, they looked for a candidate who could stop Pawar. Narasimha Rao emerged as the obvious choice. If it was made clear that Sonia Gandhi backed Rao then Pawar would be forced to withdraw. And that is exactly what happened. Pawar walked away and Rao became the prime minister.

As one of Rao's own aides was to tell me a little later, his ascent to the highest political office in the land had less to do with his virtues than the 'absence of negatives'. He was an Andhra Pradesh politician (he had briefly been an unsuccessful chief minister of Andhra) with no great political base but he was essentially a creature of Indira Gandhi's making. She had promoted him in Delhi (where his lack of a political base made him perfect for Mrs Gandhi's purposes) and Rajiv had kept him on.

Except for the foreign ministry, where he had done a good job there was nothing memorable about his ministerial stints. (Except his role as home minister during the Delhi riots which was memorable but not in a good way.) He had made very few enemies and was in poor health. In 1991, he had refused to stand for election citing health concerns, had packed up his house and was ready to retire to Andhra.

Now, he found himself prime minister of India, a job he had never dreamt he would get. In fact, as he told me a little later, he had never even imagined that he would get as far as chief minister.

It is a measure of how much we journalists ignored Rao that in close to five years of covering the Delhi political scene, I had never once met him. Of course I knew who he was and I had been at functions where he was present but we had never had a single conversation.

Relatively early in his term, he granted *Sunday* an interview. It was actually one of the most enjoyable interviews I did, not because of Rao or anything he said, but because he kept me waiting and I spent the time chatting to his private secretary, Ramu Damodaran.

Ramu had been Rao's private secretary during his other ministerial posts but had gone off to New York to join the UN. I think I'm not giving away any secrets when I say that he was romantically involved with the pop singer Nazia Hassan in New York when Rao phoned and asked him to come back. Such was his loyalty to his old boss that he returned to Delhi and eventually, with Ramu in Delhi and Nazia in New York, the romance floundered.

I liked him instantly. We are the same age and he went on to become one of my closest friends. That, I guess, was Narasimha Rao's greatest contribution to my life.

The interview went nowhere. Rao had modelled himself on Morarji Desai and either gave cryptic answers or responded with a counter question. He treated all questions as a trick to try and trap him (perhaps he was still insecure about the job) and each time he managed to evade a question, his whole body relaxed as though he had dodged a bullet.

He said nothing of consequence except for one answer which gave me an insight into his personality. I asked him whether his government had the will to carry on with the economic reforms that it had launched. This was the time when Mikhail Gorbachev in Russia had been toppled briefly in a short-lived coup by old-style communists. So Rao pointed to the example of Gorbachev and warned of the danger of trying to reform a country that was not ready for such reforms.

I left thinking that the man had no real stomach for reform.

Rao owes his reputation to one decision: his choice of finance minister. When the Rao government took office, India was bankrupt.

We turned to the International Monetary Fund (IMF) for help. The IMF said it would help us but only if we abandoned our system of controls and licenses. No politician would have known how to do this so Rao turned to I.G. Patel, the distinguished governmental economist who had been governor of the Reserve Bank and director of the London School of Economics. Patel turned him down.

Rao then approached Patel's successor as RBI governor, Manmohan Singh, who took the job. (P.C. Alexander, Indira Gandhi's former principal secretary, played a large role in selecting Rao's first cabinet and he gave me the impression that the appointment of Manmohan Singh had been his idea.)

Manmohan Singh, assisted by a crack team of civil servants, did what the IMF wanted. They dismantled the license-quota-permit raj and created a system in which the market mattered more. Most obstacles to entry into business were removed for new players. It transformed India and finally unlocked the potential trapped within our economy.

For years, the debate about who gets the credit for economic liberalization has raged: Rao or Manmohan? In his book *Backstage: The Story behind India's High Growth Years*, Montek Singh Ahluwalia, who was there when it happened, offers the most balanced response. It was Manmohan Singh who opened up the economy but he was only able to do it because Rao pushed the political establishment into backing the endeavour.

I don't think Rao was, by nature, a reformer. I doubt very much, based on the conversations I had with him, that he had much interest in economics at all. He was at heart a pragmatist. He knew that we were sunk without the IMF's support and so, he got the reforms going. Later, when there was no external pressure, he lost interest in liberalization despite Manmohan Singh's desire to take the reforms process further.

Because Ramu and I saw each other so often and because he trusted me not to print anything I learned through our friendship, I got a pretty good idea of how Rao worked. Ramu sat in 7 Race Course Road, the traditional office of the prime minister. Till that point, 5 Race Course Road had been the residence. But Rao took over 3 Race Course Road and moved there. Number 5 Race Course Road was turned into a guest house, which meant that Rao's sons stayed there when they were in Delhi (which was quite often) and according to rumour (always denied by Ramu) this was where Chandra Swami (now more powerful than ever in the Rao regime) conducted *hawan*s to pray for the prime minister's success.

Another unusual regular at Rao's court was the astrologer N.K. Sharma, who was so powerful that ministers would plead with him to intercede with Narasimha Rao on their behalf. The media rarely wrote about the role of either man and when we ran a major story about N.K. Sharma in *Sunday*, Rao was not pleased.

My view of Rao never really changed in the five years he was in power. I think he was remarkably shrewd and extremely canny. Thrust into office as a sick man, he ingested the Viagra of power and turned into an extremely strong prime minister. His ministers were terrified of him and eventually he was powerful enough to take on Sonia Gandhi who had made him prime minister.

I don't believe he was personally dishonest—despite the allegations that later surfaced. I always saw him as an old-style politician who had contempt for money. That generation needed money for politics but never for themselves. They had no extravagant habits and no need for cash. Rao himself would take a personal cook with him when he travelled abroad but that was only because he needed to be sure that *upma* was always available.

He was never a reformer by nature; he was, essentially, a survivor. That was how he had gotten by for so many years. The only subject that interested him was foreign policy and he does not get the credit he deserves for working with distinguished diplomats (such as J.N. Dixit) to reinvent our foreign policy in the aftermath of the collapse of the Soviet Union.

He was, we knew, the sort of chap who operated better under cover of darkness than in the clear light of day. He was all set to test a nuclear device when the Americans found out and confronted him. He quickly dropped the plan. (In contrast I don't think either Chandra Shekhar or Vajpayee would have been so ready to bend to Washington's will.)

But those were my own views. After the reforms, the consensus among the intelligentsia was that Rao was a wise, old, Confucius-like figure. As for Manmohan Singh, Aveek Sarkar took to calling him the 'second Father of the Nation'. Sometimes he dropped the 'second'.

I knew Manmohan Singh a little from before. He was a very good friend of my uncle's and I admired him hugely. So while I thought this 'Father of the Nation' stuff was over the top, Aveek and I had no real disagreement about him.

Where we differed was on Narasimha Rao. Aveek thought that Rao was God's gift to India. Not only was he a wise, old genius, he was also a Machiavellian figure whom nobody could defeat.

I saw Rao at closer quarters than Aveek did and thought his views on the prime minister were nonsense. But Aveek was in love and would not be deterred.

He had sensed an opportunity for ABP in the liberalization process. The government of India had never explicitly banned foreign investment in newspapers but there was a cabinet resolution dating back to the 1950s on record that opposed it. Aveek believed that if that resolution could be ignored (and it had no legal force) then he could raise millions of dollars in funding abroad and turn ABP into a truly national group.

He had a scheme in mind. He hoped to get the *Financial Times* (from London) to invest 49 per cent in *Business Standard*, the group's financial daily, which was published from Calcutta.

With the *FT*'s money, the paper could open editions in Delhi, Bombay and other financial centres and battle the market leader, the *Times of India*'s the *Economic Times*.

Aveek's plan had three parts. One was to hire T. N. Ninan, probably the best newspaper editor in India, who had revamped the *Economic Times* but who had left the Times group. If he had Ninan on board, then good journalists would join and *Business Standard* could be turned into a great paper.

This, I thought, was the easy part. Ninan had worked with ABP before and would come back. I had no doubt that he would produce an excellent paper.

The second part was only slightly more difficult. Aveek had to get the *Financial Times* on board. I didn't think this was so tough. Post-liberalization India was seen by everyone as the next boom economy so why wouldn't a financial paper want a stake in India? Plus, the *Financial Times* was owned by Pearson, the same conglomerate that owned Penguin. As ABP already had a successful partnership with Penguin, this would work in its favour.

It was the third part that I thought was bonkers. Aveek was convinced that Narasimha Rao would help him in this venture. He was nuts to believe that.

Rao was nothing if not pragmatic. He knew that by allowing in foreign investment in the press, he would alienate nearly all of India's press barons, every single one of whom was frightened of foreign investment in the media. They were all terrified that someone like Rupert Murdoch would come in, start a paper and give it away for virtually nothing until he had forced everyone else out of business.

Murdoch had already turned up in India after bringing Star TV. Aveek and I had met him and Aveek had told him, rather grandly, that he was already 'spoken for' because of his association with the Pearson group. 'Ah Pearson,' Murdoch said. 'Nice people. They certainly have a lot of meetings,' and laughed.

I thought that with Murdoch on the prowl and every newspaper owner opposed to foreign investment, Aveek would have more luck in bringing *Dawn* to India than the *Financial Times*.

Naturally, he did not see it that way.

Wasn't allowing global media into India part of the logic of liberalization?

I said Narasimha Rao did not care about the logic of liberalization. He cared about the practical job of running his government.

I was wrong, said Aveek. He knew the prime minister well. He was sure the deal would go through.

I thought he was completely deluded.

But Aveek went ahead. He signed up with the *Financial Times*. He hired Ninan who in turn hired some excellent journalists. Plans were made to launch Delhi and Bombay editions. The size of *Business Standard* would get larger as more pages were added.

As the expenses mounted, Aveek grew increasingly perturbed. It marked the only occasion when he even made a gentle attempt to nudge me away from writing what I believed.

The first line of my Sunday column was (and I'm quoting from memory): 'The key to understanding Narasimha Rao lies in recognizing that he is a small-time manipulator who masquerades as a statesman.'

The column appeared. Nobody said anything.

Then Aveek went to meet Rao to push for his project. According to what Aveek later told me, Rao said to him as he entered, 'So Mr. Sarkar, why are you wasting your time on a small-time manipulator like me?'

Aveek came back to Calcutta, shaken, after that encounter. 'Look,' he said to me. 'I would never ask you to moderate your views on anything. But is it possible for you to be a little subtler when you write about Narasimha Rao for the next two months or so?'

This was so out-of-character and against the habits of a lifetime for Aveek that I realized how much pressure he must be under.

'How critical is this deal for ABP?' I asked him.

'Everything depends on it,' he said.

I knew then that all of us were in deep trouble. Unlike Aveek, I knew that Rao would never go for it.

But it was too late to stop now. The new *Business Standard* came out, with some kind of non-equity collaboration with the *Financial Times*. It was an excellent paper but it cost a fortune to produce. Aveek kept hoping that the *Financial Times* money would come.

I knew it wouldn't.

I asked Ramu if he thought his boss could be pushed. He responded tactfully that in his experience, either things happened quite soon or not at all.

We were now at the 'not at all' stage. ABP could not afford to produce *Business Standard*. Aveek had never counted on bearing all of the cost himself. He had been completely misled by his faith in Narasimha Rao.

Funds were diverted from the *Telegraph* and the Bengali publications to pay for *Business Standard*. ABP could no longer afford to keep the promises that had been made to me when I joined. There would be no proper presses for *Sunday*. And it would still be printed on cheap newsprint.

Eventually, when the costs of the *Business Standard* venture seemed set to topple the whole group, ABP sold (on the quiet—while denying it to all employees, myself included) *Business Standard* to Uday Kotak for one rupee.

Business Standard survived. It is still an excellent paper and I often write for it.

But the Sarkars have nothing to do with it.

THIRTY-FOUR

'THEY HAVE DESTROYED
MY MOVEMENT'

If you take away the reforms, there were, from my perspective at least, three defining moments in Narasimha Rao's prime ministership. The first was the Harshad Mehta scandal.

This was a time when the Indian middle class, encouraged by liberalization, had fallen in love with the stock market. At that time salaries were low and employees struggled while people in business made much more money.

When the market boomed the salaried middle class went a little crazy. At the *Sunday* office in Calcutta, small-time stockbrokers would come to see sub-editors to encourage them to apply for new issues or to trade in shares. All of the subs were poorly paid so even the opportunity to make a thousand rupees seemed immensely attractive.

How wonderful was it, they would say, that you can make money while doing nothing!

I was a bit of a spoilsport. I am the world's least entrepreneurial Gujarati, totally risk-averse, and have a strong middle-class streak that makes me believe that anything that offers you money for nothing is probably a scam.

But even as I warned against the cult of the stock market I seemed like a fool. The Sensex kept going up. All the sub-editors made money.

Inevitably small investors began to admire the new kings of the share bazaar. Harshad Mehta, who was one of the biggest players in the market was lionized by the media and nicknamed The Big Bull. Fawning newspaper profiles and magazine cover stories hailed him as a genius.

It was too good to last, of course. Soon evidence surfaced suggesting that he had defrauded banks and the market and, eventually, investigators and journalists proved that he was not the only one doing this. This came to be known as The Scam (always capitalized), the market crashed and the middle class lost what it had invested in the boom phase.

I had to stop myself from saying I told you so. People I worked with had lost money. And it was because they had not been adequately warned about the risks. I believe that the financial press failed. At a time when they should have sounded a note of caution, they became cheerleaders for the cult of the market.

When his legal troubles seemed to be at their height and the press had turned against him, Mehta let it be known that top ministers in the government had been aware of what he was up to. As cynics (like me) had always suspected that a boom of this magnitude could not have occurred without some level of governmental complicity, Mehta's remarks hit the headlines.

He did not say, however, who these top ministers were.

I knew Mehta's lawyer, Mahesh Jethmalani, from university and asked if he could set up an interview. He was kind enough to do so and also confirmed what I had suspected: the main minister in question was Narasimha Rao, the prime minister of the country.

Mehta would only announce Rao's name at a later stage, Jethmalani said. I explained that *Sunday* had terrible deadlines so could I speak to Mehta on the assumption that Rao had been named?

Mehta and Jethmalani both agreed and I went to Mehta's Bombay apartment where he filled me in on the details of his allegations. He had gone with an MP, Sat Pal Mittal, to Race Course Road with a crore of rupees in a suitcase. They had met Rao and handed over the suitcase.

I was familiar with Race Course Road so I questioned him closely. When he got every detail of the encounter and its setting right, and even produced the visitor's pass that had been issued to him by the reception at Race Course Road, I knew he was telling the truth to the extent that he had clearly been there and met Rao.

But had he handed over the money?

That depended on whether you believed Mehta. He had no proof at all and later when he went public with Rao's name, his claim was met with all kinds of objections including a practical one: could a crore of rupees fit into a suitcase? Mehta then arranged for another (similar) suitcase and a crore in cash and shot a video to demonstrate that it was indeed possible to carry all that money in a single suitcase.

Any other prime minister would have been severely weakened by such an allegation—most would have had to resign. But Rao went on as though nothing had happened. When his government faced a no-confidence motion in parliament, he relied on such operators as Chandra Swami who procured the MPs required to defeat the motion. (The manner in which some MPs were bought over became the subject of criminal proceedings later.)

Once he had won the confidence motion, Rao asked the central agencies to double their efforts at tormenting Harshad. The Big Bull had fired his one bullet and it had missed its target. Mehta died a few years later while the enquiries were still in progress but he was finished long before.

So what had really happened?

I felt Harshad was telling the truth but found it hard to believe that Rao, who had no personal interest in enriching himself, would actually accept a bribe in the prime minister's house.

I was told then by people close to the government—off the record—that Harshad had indeed a carried a suitcase with Rs 85 lakh (not the crore he claimed) and handed it over to Rao. The prime minister had forwarded the suitcase to Sitaram Kesri, the Congress treasurer, who had used it for a by-election in Punjab.

Was this what really happened? If it was, then it suggested that Rao did not trust his fund collectors and liked being physically present when the party accepted cash contributions. As far as I knew, no other prime minister had ever done this.

What I found odd was that far from embarrassing Rao, this episode actually made him stronger. He had always been handicapped by the

Congress's lack of a majority in parliament. Now, even that didn't seem to matter. He had proved that nothing, not even a corruption charge or a confidence vote, could dislodge him.

The second defining moment in Rao's tenure was the demolition of the Babri Masjid and the bloodshed that followed. L.K. Advani was scheduled to address kar sevaks near the masjid in Ayodhya. Everyone had warned of the risk of violence but Rao had taken the word of Kalyan Singh, the BJP chief minister of UP, that the day would pass off without incident.

In fact, according to some eyewitness accounts a well-organized strategy was executed. Kar sevaks assaulted journalists and photographers and drove them from the site. Then, as jubilant kar sevaks scaled the masjid, a highly trained group of men proceeded to demolish the structure. Once it had been razed to the ground, they levelled the earth and built a makeshift temple on the same spot.

This version of events remains controversial. The BJP still maintains that the demolition was spontaneous but what nobody can deny is that kar sevaks did demolish the temple and construct a makeshift structure at the spot. Spontaneous? Planned? Depending on which side you are on, the versions tend to vary.

I was in Delhi on that day and tried to get somebody in a position of authority in the prime minister's office to speak. Rao was unavailable. Various groups who had been in talks with him about the Ayodhya issue kept calling only to be told, 'PM is resting'. Eventually I was briefed by A.N. Verma, Rao's principal secretary, who pleaded helplessness. They had trusted the Kalyan Singh government. What could they do if Kalyan Singh had let them down?

It was clear that the UP government had never intended to honour promises made to the Centre and to the Courts to protect the masjid. The men who pulled down the mosque must have come with pickaxes and enough cement to construct a makeshift temple. Yet, Kalyan Singh had promised that no one with implements would be let on to the site.

The UP police had to have been in on the plan or at the very least sympathetic to the demolition men—we later carried photos in *Sunday* of UP policemen helping kar sevaks cross the barricades that had been erected near the masjid. Once the mosque was demolished, Kalyan Singh resigned.

If it was preplanned then who planned it? I have never accepted the claim that Advani knew what was going to happen. As the demolition unfolded, he burst into tears (he does that quite often) and was led away by Pramod Mahajan. According to Mahajan, Advani kept repeating, 'They have destroyed my movement.'

Later Advani called the demolition day, 'the saddest day' of my life in an article that was meant to express regret but only hammered home the point that he was upset because things had gone out of his hands and that the BJP's reputation for discipline had been damaged.

Did anyone at the top levels of the BJP know that the demolition was planned? I have seen no evidence to suggest that any top leader was aware. What is possible is that an RSS-affiliated organization (part of the so-called Sangh Parivar) planned and executed it with the tacit blessings of somebody at RSS headquarters in Nagpur.

Naturally India's Muslims were outraged. They rioted in many parts of the country and various state governments had to cope. Throughout it all, Rao slept. Mani Shankar Aiyar, by then a Congress MP, told me scathingly that Rao was not immobilized with fear, but 'rigor mortis had set in'.

The demolition of the Babri Masjid finished off whatever sentimental attachment India's Muslims had to the Congress. From that day on, the party lost a traditional support base in the north. (And in the next general election, Rao aligned with the BSP gifting away Dalit-dominated seats in north India which the Congress has never won back since then.)

When Bombay burned in a second wave of rioting, Rao slept through that too. I was angry enough to put a close up of Rao on the cover, in which he looked like a tranquilized bull frog with hair peering out of his nostrils. The caption read: 'Will this man please wake up'. It was much more direct than most *Sunday* covers but such was the mood that surrounded Rao's failures.

The third and most bewildering defining moment of Rao's prime ministership was his decision to pick a fight with Sonia Gandhi.

After her husband's assassination, Sonia went through what she herself has publicly described as 'a very bad phase'. She was upset and emotional and believed that Rajiv could have been saved if the V.P. Singh government had not removed his SPG cover. But when she calmed down, she had a single-minded focus. She wanted to find out who had killed her husband and why.

The woman who blew herself up was Dhanu, an LTTE operative. She was part of a team that had clearly been tasked with assassinating Rajiv. But why would the LTTE want to do that? Didn't it realize that such an action would make it impossible for any Indian politician to ever support the Lankan Tamil cause again?

This is exactly what happened. The Lankan army later swept through the north, destroying the LTTE and killing Prabhakaran, its leader. No national leader of consequence in India objected too strongly.

The government's working hypothesis for the investigation (which turned up in the chargesheet) was that the plot began when Rajiv told Aveek and me in our interview that Prabhakaran had been an obstacle to peace in Lanka. Prabhakaran read the issue (delivered to him in his hideout by jungle mail, presumably) and decided to assassinate Rajiv, who he thought was likely to return to power.

Prabhakaran denied this till the end. So clearly, there were questions to be asked and investigations to be conducted.

Except that Narasimha Rao was not particularly interested. Even if he believed that there was nothing to be gained in pursuing the investigation too deeply given that the actual murderers were clearly LTTE operatives, what did he have to lose in digging deeper given that Rajiv had been his leader and that this was Sonia's single obsession?

What's more, he began to get annoyed if he was asked about Sonia's desire to learn more about the investigation. 'Oh God! What more does this lady want? We have told her everything we know,' he once told me angrily during an informal chat.

The more he refused her information about the investigation, the more hostile Sonia turned. When it became clear that she was hostile, the PM's men began planting stories against her. And so the grief turned into anger.

The fourth and final defining moment of Rao's term was the Jain hawala scandal. A notebook belonging to a Madhya Pradesh businessman called Surendra Jain had been seized by the authorities during a raid. The notebook had a list of initials next to which were mentioned sums of money. The authorities took the position that these initials were not difficult to decipher: 'KN' was clearly Kamal Nath, 'YS' was Yashwant Sinha. And so on.

For many months, nothing happened. Then the Supreme Court begun monitoring the probe and pushing the CBI to interrogate those who had been (possibly) named. The CBI director at the time was an Andhra Pradesh cadre officer who was close to Rao and he was happy to take the probe further.

But for some reason, neither the Supreme Court nor the CBI ever launched a proper investigation.

The problems with the case were self-evident. For instance, I may say I have given a certain politician Rs 20 lakh. That, by itself, is not enough to make a case against the politician. The investigators must try and show when and how the money was paid. What the politician did in return.

They must examine the politician's accounts to see whether, during the period in question, the money inflow was reflected in any way or whether his spending pattern changed. For some reason, either this was not done or they did not find the evidence they needed.

The CBI director had kept Rao in the loop throughout and just before the 1996 election, the prime minister decided to go public and the CBI issued chargesheets. The list of those charged consisted mainly of Madhya Pradesh politicians but there were two surprises. One was L.K. Advani, charged on the basis of an entry which listed an LKA, and the other was Madhav Rao Scindia, based on a payment allegedly made to an MRS.

The inclusion of these so-called suspects would ultimately sink the whole Jain hawala case

At first, things seemed to be going well. The press swallowed the CBI's claims without question. 'A Nation Betrayed' it said on the cover of *Outlook* magazine. And Congressmen put it out that the chargesheets were a tribute to Rao's integrity. Which other prime minister would chargesheet his own ministers and party heavyweights? Rao was such an honest chap that he struck out at corruption wherever he found it.

Then, L.K. Advani began to get belligerent. He denounced the chargesheet as a frame up and said he would not stand for any electoral office till his name was cleared. Advani was not one of my favourite politicians because I believed he had begun the process of dividing the country. But I refused to believe that he was a crook.

So I wrote a signed piece saying that he had been framed. The BJP was surprised but pleased. At a press conference called to defend Advani, Sushma Swaraj held up the column as an example of how even people who disagreed with Advani's politics respected his integrity.

The case of Scindia was different. I had known him since 1977 when I was still at Oxford and he was an MP. We had become close friends and I had seen him enough to know that his integrity was spotless. It wasn't just that he was already very rich. It was more that he had contempt for businessmen who offered bribes and even more contempt for politicians who accepted bribes.

But even after Advani and Scindia went public with their declarations of innocence, causing people to question Rao's motives, many people believed that wily old Rao would triumph in the end.

Aveek and I went to see Scindia who was looking downcast and depressed. To my horror, Aveek told him, 'Unless you beg the old man for forgiveness, you are finished. He is the cleverest politician I have ever seen. You cannot hope to survive in politics if he is against you. Go and touch his feet.'

Clearly the fact that Narasimha Rao had led Aveek Sarkar on and fooled him into making investments he could not afford had reinforced Aveek's view that Rao was some kind of genius.

Poor Scindia looked even more downcast. I gave him my view, which had not really changed over five years.

Narasimha Rao was a small-time manipulator. And this time he had gone too far by including Advani and Scindia. He would be found out.

These were Rao's last weeks at Race Course Road. He was finished. Scindia should fight to establish his innocence.

He did. And he won.

THIRTY-FIVE

'I HAVE NOT YET TAKEN MY BATH'

The results of the 1996 Lok Sabha elections surprised nobody. The Congress lost over a hundred of the seats it had won in 1991. It was wiped out in Bihar and UP and I doubt if more than a handful of Muslims voted for it.

The BJP actually got more seats than the Congress, winning 161. The president, obliged to call the largest single party in the Lok Sabha, called the BJP, led now by A.B. Vajpayee.

Vajpayee was sworn in; he looked for allies to reach the majority figure, did not find them and resigned in thirteen days. This was what most people expected.

The objective for the non-BJP parties now became the formation of a 'secular' government. Those who believed that Narasimha Rao was a modern Chanakya waited for him to manoeuvre his way back to power.

I think Rao's fans had underestimated how much other politicians saw him as a nasty and untrustworthy character. The consensus within the non-Congress parties was that they would have nothing to do with Rao.

Instead, a Karnataka politician called H.D. Deve Gowda was chosen as the prime minister and the Congress agreed to support this government—a coalition of Janata-type forces and regional parties—from outside.

Narasimha Rao's troubles continued to mount. The courts threw out the Jain hawala chargesheets on the grounds that they

233

were not backed by any evidence other than the Jain diaries themselves. The lack of corroborative evidence had been clear from the start but Rao had thought it was worth going ahead with the chargesheets anyhow.

L.K. Advani said he would return to electoral politics now that he had been exonerated. Madhav Rao Scindia who had fought against the official Congress candidate in his constituency and defeated him made plans to return to his old party. And within the Congress, hatred of Rao grew to astounding proportions.

Then, Rao found his own tactics used against him. Having delighted in prosecuting his rivals, he was now the target of various criminal prosecutions. Chandra Swami was arrested and sent to jail.

Faced with this avalanche of ill-fortune, Rao resigned as Congress president. Though I had done nothing to lead him to believe that I had changed my opinion of him, he called me over to his new home and gave me an on-the-record interview for *Sunday* in which he said that he had resigned to protect the office of Congress president. It was not right, he said, for a Congress president to be the subject of criminal charges.

He chose, as his successor, the party's treasurer, Sitaram Kesri, the sort of oily, cringing politician familiar to viewers of Hindi movies. Rao's view was that Kesri would be his man. In fact, he told me, when we met for the interview, that Kesri had been so honoured by the appointment that he had taken his Gandhi cap off and placed it at Rao's feet.

That gesture seemed to me to sum up Kesri's style but Rao—the so-called modern Chanakya—was apparently so deluded that the *topi* stunt reassured him that he had made the right choice.

Then, there was the whole Jayalalitha factor. As the chief minister of Tamil Nadu, she had become famous for her dictatorial ways and her corruption. In 1996, Rao had mysteriously disregarded the advice of his party's Tamil Nadu unit and aligned with Jayalalitha. At this, every Congressmen of note had resigned from the Tamil Nadu Congress unit and formed a new party called the Tamil Maanila Congress (TMC). The TMC had tied up with the DMK, Jayalalitha's primary opposition and together the parties had swept the polls, wiping out the Congress and Jayalalitha. To make things worse, the DMK also won control of the state assembly by a landslide.

I went to Chennai to interview Jayalalitha who was down and out. She lived alone in a large house in a locality called Poes Garden. We spent most of the day together and the off-the-record bits were more interesting than any interview could have been. Legend had it that M.G. Ramachandran, the Tamil actor and former chief minister, had promoted Jayalalitha. She saw it differently and said that as she grew in prominence, he had grown increasingly jealous of her and resentful. Clearly, there was no love lost there.

Jayalalitha had just thrown out Sasikala, her closest confidant, after her critics and supporters suggested that she had misused her closeness to Jayalalitha. But when I asked about Sasikala, Jayalalitha grew tearful and said, her voice choking, 'Mr Sanghvi, I have never had a companion as wonderful as her.' ('Mr Sanghvi' was typical of her style; she spoke like the headmistress of a strict convent school.)

The on-the-record part of the conversation was also interesting. She attacked P. Chidambaram who she said had made a speech saying that she should be jailed and mosquitos introduced into her cell. (Chidambaram called me after the interview appeared to clarify that he had only said that she should face the mosquitos of the jail or words to that effect.) Chidambaram's hostility, she said, was motivated by her refusal to help him become chief minister of Tamil Nadu ('That was when I started laughing . . .' she said).

The meat of the interview lay in her version of the alliance with the Congress. According to her, it was Narasimha Rao who had approached her. And how, I asked, had he approached her?

'Though his astrologer,' she said.

She went on to paint a picture of an unsavoury style of working at the Centre where astrologers and swamis ran things.

After the issue hit the stands, Rao called. Jayalalitha was lying, he said. She was the one who had reached out to him. And so on. By then it was hard to know which liar to believe so I quoted his denial but decided to leave it at that.

Rao's fortunes continued to decline. Kesri now turned up at Sonia Gandhi's door, said what a terrible chap Rao was and tried to persuade her to join active politics. According to him (and he said this on TV) 'I have asked. But answer, I am not getting.' Sonia kept her own counsel.

But Kesri went on the offensive against Rao anyway. He directed him to step down as leader of the Congress party in parliament. This was a controversial move because the leader of the parliamentary party is elected. Rao could have simply ignored him and called for a vote. Instead, Rao quietly stepped down.

For all practical purposes his career was over.

I had known Deve Gowda from his Karnataka days. He was slightly in the Kesri mould. He would fight with R.K. Hegde, his chief minister, but bow down to touch his feet if this was to his advantage. As far as I could tell, there was no reason to believe that he even understood what the prime minister's job entailed.

For all that, I don't think he was a disastrous prime minister or anything. But he retained his comical side.

I was once invited to have breakfast with him at 7 Race Course Road. I am not a morning person and breakfast meetings are my least favourite kind of meetings but I turned up anyway only to be kept waiting for half an hour. ('PM is on his way from Number Three,' they kept telling me.)

Finally Deve Gowda arrived, looking unkempt and dishevelled, wearing bathroom chappals. He sank into his chair at the breakfast table and looked at me balefully. 'I have not yet taken my bath,' he announced.

As an appetite killer, this was powerful stuff. But Deve Gowda's real interest was in talking about his sleep pattern. 'Do you know that there is a tablet called Calmpose?' he asked.

I said I had heard of it. It was a tranquilizer.

'Do you know that I cannot sleep at night? Every night I lie awake worrying about the state of this country. It is very bad.'

I agreed that things did not look very good.

'Until I take this tablet, Calmpose, I cannot sleep. Sometimes even with Calmpose I cannot sleep,' he continued.

I nodded sympathetically.

'Every morning after taking Calmpose I have to sleep late because I have not slept all night.'

I assumed that this was by way of apology for being late for breakfast. I was wrong; it wasn't.

'This is why sometimes at meetings I become fast asleep. It is because the state of the nation keeps me awake at night. But what do newspapers do? They take photos of my sleeping and put them on page one. Is this fair?'

So that was what this was about.

Our breakfast ended inconclusively. Deva Gowda was upset but still tranquilized. I got nothing out of him and it seemed rude to eat the *dosa*s when he was clearly in such a grumpy mood and had pushed his plate away.

But when it came to political manoeuvering Deve Gowda was no fool. He knew that he had to control Kesri if he was to survive. So he asked the CBI to dig up dirt on the Congress president. Kesri saw this coming and told Deve Gowda's colleagues that the Congress would withdraw support from the government unless Deve Gowda was replaced.

They saw the point and eased him out, replacing him with I.K. Gujral. It was a wise decision. Gujral was the global intellectual of the Janata crowd. He had been V.P. Singh and Deve Gowda's foreign minister and was unwilling to play political games. He had no political base to speak of and that's what made his colleagues like him. He rarely raised his voice, was open and accessible to the media and if he had a problem, he called you himself.

I remember being at dinner with Aveek one night at a Delhi restaurant when my phone rang. It was the Race Course Road switchboard. They asked me to hold for the prime minister.

Gujral came on the line. He had just read my column, he said. He thought I had been unfair to his government and proceeded to explain why.

There was no rancour, no bitterness and no sense of reproach. It was as though he felt he should put his point of view across.

Aveek and I were both surprised. We agreed we had never seen another prime minister who felt he had a duty to explain rather than a right to complain.

THIRTY-SIX

FROM CONSULTING EDITOR TO INSULTING EDITOR

Though public interest in politics grew as governments came and went, it was clear to me that *Sunday* had a limited future. ABP no longer had the money to compete in the national market place no matter how much Aveek tried to pretend that the group was a national player. In the case of *Sunday*, it was the shoddy printing and the terrible paper quality but other publications within the group began to feel the pressure in other ways.

The *Telegraph*, which had finally turned profitable in 1992, saw cuts in its budget. After Akbar had left to join the Congress in 1989, Aveek had become editor himself and Delhi operations were overseen by Kewal Varma, a veteran journalist who had been with the group for years.

Kewal was deeply devoted to his staff and constantly complained that the group did not even have the money to fix the chairs in the Delhi office. They tried mollifying him with the title of consulting editor but Kewal would not be repressed. One day, he went to the head office in Calcutta and yelled at Aveek with such vigour that the joke in the office was that his title had been changed to insulting editor.

I was sympathetic to Aveek's plight. He had made a foolish business decision based on an overestimation of his relationship with an essentially devious prime minister. But there was no getting around the fact that while *Sunday* might remain essential reading in

Delhi political circles, it had no real hope of succeeding as a national newsmagazine.

I considered moving on. But I couldn't think of a job I wanted to do. The *Times* had last chased me in 1989-90 when it had sacked Vinod Mehta as editor of the *Independent* after he ran an unsubstantiated page-one story claiming that former defence minister Y.B. Chavan was a CIA agent who leaked secrets to the Americans during the 1971 war with Pakistan. The *Times*' Nandita Jain (Samir's sister) had been persuasive but I had told her that I was very happy at ABP.

I could go back there and tell Samir that I had made a mistake all those years ago but I was reluctant to eat humble pie. *India Today* was another option. I was pretty sure that Aroon would find something for me to do. But after having been editor of *Sunday*, it was hard to accept a lesser editorial position.

But I had to get out of *Sunday*. Aveek agreed to relieve me of the editorship and make me editorial director of the group. Then, he backed out. Finally he agreed that I could give up *Sunday* but was evasive about what group responsibilities I could have.

In any case, he had no money. So he was unwilling to hire a new editor for *Sunday*. Fortunately, Aditi Phadnis, who was already our political editor, was far better than any of the outside candidates we considered and so we gave her the job. To indicate that my role at *Sunday* had changed, I moved my Counterpoint column out of the magazine and into the *Telegraph*.

I was, frankly speaking, at a dead-end in my career. But somehow I was not that worried because by then, another medium had opened up.

Television was my way out.

Going on TV had not been my idea. There was only Doordarshan (DD) in those days and it only carried pro-government news. The news usually led with such headlines as 'The Prime Minister called on India to become self-reliant . . .' The scripts were written by faceless boffins under the watchful eye of the bureaucracy. Newsreaders were announcers. They read out the bland scripts with all the verve and flair of an Indian Airlines cabin crew making flight safety announcements. There was no TV journalism.

But under Bhaskar Ghose, who was the Information and Broadcasting Secretary, and Rathikant Basu, who was the director general of Doordarshan, the network was finally trying to find some credibility.

The drive towards credibility had been spurred on by Rajiv Gandhi's concern, when he was in opposition, that satellite TV would make Doordarshan irrelevant. He knew that technology would make DD's monopoly unsustainable and tried to think up solutions. One of Rajiv's ideas was to follow the British pattern and divide India into regions. Each region would have two independent, advertising-funded TV stations and the franchises would be auctioned by the government.

Narasimha Rao inherited this scheme and promised to implement it. But, of course, he did nothing. Ghose and Basu who felt the weight of impending irrelevance on their shoulders persuaded the government to approve the launch of a new channel to be called DD3, where the programming would be outsourced to private providers (Prannoy Roy's NDTV would handle the news, for instance) and propaganda would be absent.

The channel was aborted a few days before its much-trumpeted launch when a journalist close to Narasimha Rao attended a rehearsal and told Rao that panelists were actually criticizing the government on the government's own TV network! Rao cancelled the launch and eventually a low-budget version of DD3 went on the air a few months later.

But, even before the DD3 fiasco happened, Basu's team at DD was looking for new kinds of programming. One day, Urmila Gupta, whom I knew slightly from her work with the directorate of film festivals, called and said she was now with DD news. Could we have coffee?

Urmila wanted me to host a show roughly based on the BBC's *Question Time*. I said no, arguing that a) I had no experience of hosting TV shows and b) that I didn't think that *Question Time* would work in India. She asked me not to worry about the experience part, saying that they hoped to start a new chapter in Indian TV and they wanted outsiders, not DD's regular newsreaders. As for *Question Time*, why didn't I think it would work?

I said that *Question Time* worked because it moved from town to town and had a bright, engaged audience. Indian TV audiences were bussed into studios—as far as I had seen—and rarely seemed well-informed enough to ask intelligent questions on a range of subjects.

What would I suggest? She was insistent.

I said that it might work if we restricted the whole show to one subject a week and invited people who were interested in that subject to sit in the audience.

She agreed. And a month later I found myself at Doordarshan's fancy (but largely wasted) new studios at Siri Fort hosting the first episode of *Question Forum*.

Frankly, I remember more about my battles with the DD bureaucracy and the inept producer than I do about the show itself. I imagine I was pretty awful when we started but the thing about DD is that you are thrown into the deep end even before you know how to swim. So you have no choice: either you plunge to the bottom or you struggle to stay afloat.

By the time the show had completed several months, I received a new offer. My friend Malvika Singh (Mala) was part of BiTV (later called TVI) one of the first independent channels. Now that I had some TV experience, would I do a show for them?

I outlined the kind of show I wanted to do. I wanted two knowledgeable and articulate journalists to give a hard time to a political guest. We would shoot the programme on a living room–type set and would serve beer to the guests on camera. This would give it a relaxed Sunday brunch feel and would not only loosen up the guests but would also make tough questions easier to ask in an atmosphere of bonhomie.

Mala, who knew roughly as much about TV as I did, agreed. The show was outsourced to Kapil Batra and Himanshu Joshi, two producers I would work with again and again in the years to come and looked sleek and sophisticated.

BiTV paid well. I think I got Rs. 20,000 a week which was a lot of money in 1995 and the total remuneration easily exceeded my ABP salary. Sadly, BiTV then ran into financial problems, did not pay us our full dues (through no fault of Mala's, she lost what she was owed too) and collapsed just when it should have taken off.

But there was another opportunity. Rathikant Basu called me and said that DD had launched a satellite channel in collaboration with CNN (it was a short-lived venture called DD-CNN on which CNN used to show its own programming plus the odd Indian show, such as my programme) and there was a presenter's slot open on a show called Round Table. It paid Rs. 15,000 a week. Naturally, I grabbed it.

So, by the time I had worked out that the good years with ABP were over, I had also come to the conclusion that TV would be a useful second career to fall back on. So it didn't really matter that ABP had run out of money to put into *Sunday*.

I told Aveek that I would stay on as a columnist with unspecified other responsibilities as long as I could do as much TV as I wanted.

He agreed but obviously there were cuts to my remuneration. The Calcutta flat was taken back. By that time, Malavika and I had split up, our marriage a casualty of my frequent absences. Though both of us had tried to make a go of it for the sake of our son Raaj, we agreed that after a point, it made no sense to continue.

Malavika moved back to Mumbai where she went on to enjoy considerable journalistic success in her own right, first with the *Times of India* and then, with *DNA*. She is still one of the city's best-known journalists.

With her gone, ABP took back the Delhi flat as well. It also effectively stopped paying for my travel, hotels, etc. (There was now a complicated process to get any trips approved, we all travelled economy and the maximum you could spend on food, transport and hotel room—all included—in a city like Mumbai was Rs. 4000.) So I ended up spending the TV money on tickets to Mumbai to see Raaj.

For a while, I stayed rent-free in a small flat owned by my uncle, and as a paying guest in Anand Lok. Eventually, Seema Goswami, with whom I had become deeply involved, shifted to Delhi, rented a barsaati in Defence Colony and I moved in with her.

My life was in turmoil, I guess. But I reckoned that satellite TV would come to India and I would be okay in the medium term.

Fortunately, I was right.

THIRTY-SEVEN

'DON'T WASTE OUR TIME ON THESE FAILURES'

Events in the TV space moved much more quickly than I had expected. Rupert Murdoch had bought Star TV from Richard Li, the Hong Kong businessman who had set it up. Unlike Li who envisioned an all-Asia channel (Star stood for Satellite TV Asian Region), Murdoch knew that India needed a TV service of its own.

It was pretty much the scenario that Rajiv Gandhi had foreseen. Doordarshan was now set firmly on the road to irrelevance. What I had not expected was how much satellite television would change India. The English-speaking middle class suddenly felt plugged into the rest of the world. And Hindi-speaking viewers who had tired of the lowest-common-denominator approach of Hindi cinema now found entertainment that was designed to appeal to their sensibilities. I could tell that there would be many more channels and that the boom would spread to every corner of the country.

Murdoch raided Doordarshan for personnel. Rathikant Basu became the CEO of Star and brought his whole team (including Urmila Gupta) to Star. At first the idea was to treat Star Plus, the network's flagship channel, like Britain's BBC One with a mix of fiction, features and current affairs programming. Prannoy Roy was asked to handle the news, fiction programming was outsourced to production houses and the channel carried both Hindi and English programming.

Basu called and asked if I could do shows for Star Plus. Naturally,
I said yes. These took the form of special shows. I anchored a dual
language show with Rajat Sharma when the Deve Gowda government
fell. And I persuaded Inder Gujral to give us an interview right after he
became prime minister. We were the only game in town (excluding
DD) when it came to English-language Indian programming. These
shows had a huge impact on Star's audience.

Basu then asked if I could revive my old DD version of *Question
Time*, with all the changes I had introduced to the old BBC format.
Star found me Siddhartha Basu, and Synergy, the company
Siddhartha ran with his wife Anita, became my producer. The Basus
brought a gloss and sophistication to the show that had been missing
from anything I had done before.

Siddhartha also introduced a new innovation: a device on every
audience member's seat that let them vote. Usually we would poll
the audience before the discussion began and then once again, after
it ended, to see if people had changed their minds. Anita Kaul Basu
came up with the name *A Question of Answers* and we shot at Eagle
Studios, then Noida's best studio.

The show was an instant hit, largely thanks to the quality of
Siddhartha Basu's production. I saw an episode on YouTube the
other day and though it was shot in 1997, it had a freshness and gloss
that most shows do not have even today.

In those early days of television, guests had no trouble driving
to Noida to be part of a discussion programme. We got opposition
heavyweights (like Jaswant Singh) and even, then relatively
unknown, BJP figures like Narendra Modi. There is a clip of
the Modi episode floating around on YouTube, in which Modi
laughingly goads Jairam Ramesh and it always reminds me of the
Modi I used to know in those days; relaxed, jovial, approachable,
humble and unselfconscious.

He was fairly typical of the politicians of that era. I knew him
a little because he was often at the home of Arun Jaitley whom I
knew well. We were both Gujaratis in a non-Gujarati city (though
you would never guess from Modi's flawless Hindi that he had
grown up in Gujarat) and Modi was well travelled, happy to share

his experiences and seemingly reconciled to his status as a costar in the Arun Jaitley Show.

A Question of Answers even had a coup. One day Gujral asked me if I could interview him about his economic record. I said I would have loved to but the only show I had on the air at the moment was *A Question of Answers*, which required four guests.

Fine, said Gujral. I will be one of the guests.

Pushing my luck, I pointed out that if the subject of the discussion was economics, it would make sense if his finance minister also came. Ok, said Gujral, I will ask Chidambaram to come.

Terrific, I said, but he would have to come to Eagle Studios in Noida.

No problem, said Gujral, to my astonishment.

And so, the sitting prime minister of India and the finance minister both drove to Noida, sat in our studio and participated on equal terms in a discussion where opposition members and the audience asked sceptical questions to them.

It would never happen today.

As successful as *A Question of Answers* was I wanted to get away from discussions. I had done a lot of interviews for print, and was eager to see if I could do the same sort of thing on TV. I asked Rathikant Basu for an interview show and he agreed. But he turned down my suggestion that Siddhartha Basu should produce it. Star would produce it themselves he said, and would call it *Star Talk*.

It soon became clear why he had agreed. *A Question of Answers* was an expensive show to make whereas Star's vision of *Star Talk* was vaguely modeled on the BBC's *Hard Talk*.

All you needed were a small studio, two cameras, a round table and two chairs. This was not what I had in mind because *Hard Talk* was supposedly adversarial in tone whereas my style was much more to put the guest at ease and to then lull him into saying stuff he might not otherwise want to reveal. But it was cheap and Star liked it, even if I didn't.

For the first episode, we had Amitabh Bachchan who was then down and out after the failure of ABCL. He spoke movingly, I thought, about confronting adversity and about why he had failed to see that ABCL was heading for disaster. (Basically he trusted the wrong people, he said.)

I thought it was a very revealing and candid interview and viewer response was also positive. But not everyone liked it, of course. I can't bear to watch my own shows when they are telecast so Seema and I went out for dinner to avoid having to look at the TV. We were on dessert when the phone rang. It was Amita Malik, in her day the top TV critic (possibly because she was the only one) who was known as a dragon.

'Vir,' she said. 'I cannot begin to tell you how disappointed I am. Who cares about Amitabh Bachchan? He is finished. Why are you wasting our time interviewing that man?'

I said (accurately, as it turned out) that Bachchan had been written off before but had always bounced back.

'Don't waste our time on these failures,' she finished. 'Such a boring show!'

The call cast a pall over the evening though, as Seema pointed out, Malik was more interested in criticizing Amitabh than the show itself. But I began to wonder if I had done the right thing by giving up *A Question of Answers* for this show.

Fortunately, the response to *Star Talk* was uniformly good. Even Amita Malik changed her tone. We got good sponsors, very nice new sets and a gifted producer, Anju Juneja, who stayed with me for the duration of the show and ensured that the production quality was always first rate.

Once *Star Talk* had become one of the more popular shows on the channel, we had the budget to fly to other cities or to fly guests down to Delhi. We had started out in small studios which were often cramped though fortunately the guests didn't seem to mind. We shot with Pramod Mahajan at Jain Studios and when he asked to go to the loo, I directed him to the only one that was available. He got to the door, looked at the sign and said, 'But it is written ladies?'

He paused.

'Don't worry,' he decided. 'Even I am only for ladies!'

Shatrughan Sinha arrived late and I asked if he would like to get his make-up applied in the small area where our make-up artist had set up.

'Make-up?' he laughed. 'In my case, only plastic surgery will help.' (I mention this because Shatru is not known for his humility.)

But once our budgets were upped, we moved to Eagle and other large studios. Star was pleased that we were getting big names and Basu began to wonder if Star should plunge further into current affairs.

In 1998, after the Gujral government fell, a new general election was called. Basu had an idea. Suppose Star set up a new channel devoted only to news? ('Like CNN,' he said). It was an intriguing idea that had never been tried in India.

At the time, only NDTV had the studios required to make this happen and so Basu asked Prannoy if he would run Star News. Naturally, Prannoy said yes. He was less pleased when Basu said that he wanted to put Star Plus anchors on the channel along with the NDTV staff presenters. He had no objection to me, he said but he was not keen on letting Rajat Sharma into the NDTV offices. Neither was Rajat (then Star's biggest name) keen on using NDTV's facilities so it was agreed that Rajat would do his show from his own studio and send it to NDTV for telecast.

I was to do two shows a week on Saturday and Sunday night for a programme called *Weekend with Vir Sanghvi*. This sounded less grand than it actually was. The NDTV newscaster would finish and vacate his desk. In the ad break (about two minutes in those days), they would hastily add chairs for my guests and we would run in, take our seats, get miked and go on live, just as the titles began to flash on the screen.

I had never done live TV before so that was exhilarating. Nor had I anchored a TV show during an election campaign, so that added its own excitement. NDTV was a very professional operation with great anchors of its own so I leveraged the only advantage I had over them: much greater access to important guests.

For one show I got Narasimha Rao to come to the studio. Another was a face-off between Jaswant Singh and Pranab Mukherjee. This was good fun because Jaswant graciously deferred to Pranab while talking about the BJP's plans for the future. I wondered how Pranab would respond to Jaswant's old-world charm.

He responded with old fashioned Bengali aggression. 'Total bunkum,' he began. 'Joshwont Singh always talks bunkum.'

George Fernandes and Murli Manohar Joshi appeared together on another show to defend swadeshi economics. Eventually, I think people watched *Weekend with Vir Sanghvi* more for the guests then they did for the anchor. (But don't they always?)

News TV was new to India and everyone at NDTV was so rushed and tense that nobody there cared too much about the mechanics of *Weekend with Vir Sanghvi*. Fortunately, Star had hired me a very good producer, Shefali Bhushan, who put the show together, forcing her way into the NDTV control room.

NDTV wouldn't let her talk to me during the show even though she sat in the PCR but on one occasion, she seized control from the NDTV director. Because we had so little time before we went on, lapel mikes were hastily clipped on by NDTV's sound guys. This could have unfortunate consequences.

During one show, the NDTV director shouted into my ear 'Vir, don't say anything! Your mike has fallen off.'

Not say anything? How was I supposed to anchor the show?

Fortunately Shefali cut in. 'Lean towards the nearest guest!' she instructed. 'Let his mike pick up your audio. Now, ask a short question to the guest at the end of the table. As he is answering, lean down and find your mike.'

Which is what I did.

As the campaign progressed, Aroon Purie called me. Aaj Tak was, in that era, just another show on DD. But TV Today, the company that produced Aaj Tak, had been given the contract to produce the election results programming for DD. Would I like to be one of the anchors for the show?

My inclination was to say yes but I knew that I had a commitment to the newly launched Star News. I would check with Basu, I said, and let him know.

Basu wasn't having any of it. Star News was doing extremely well, he said. The original idea had been to run the channel only during the election campaign. But things were going so well that he was planning to make it a full-time channel. How could I even think of doing a show for TV Today?

I called Aroon and explained why I couldn't do it. He was understanding. (A little later when Aaj Tak became a full-fledged channel, he came on *Star Talk* to discuss the venture.)

As result day (actually, results days; manual counting usually took a few days) drew near, I waited to find out when Star News needed me. Basu called. He was sorry, he said, but NDTV had said that its own anchors would handle everything. There was no room for me.

Obviously I was disappointed and Basu was clearly feeling guilty. But it also raised all kinds of questions about the future. If Star News was going to be a regular channel, would I continue to appear on it? Or was it going to be all NDTV?

The elections threw up a BJP victory and there was lots of political excitement, enough at any rate, to ensure that Star News remained vibrant and alive. Basu decided that they would take current affairs programming off Star Plus, now that they had Star News.

But Star TV would continue to produce *Star Talk* though it would now be telecast on Star News, the only show on the channel not to be made by NDTV.

It was an unusual arrangement and I wondered how long the Star and NDTV alliance could last.

THIRTY-EIGHT

'WE LOST BY ONE VOTE!'

T he Vajpayee government was historic in more ways than one. It demonstrated that the BJP was no longer 'untouchable' in Indian politics and that other parties would align with it. But within the BJP, it also marked a return to an older order. Vajpayee was back in charge. L.K. Advani had conceded that only Vajpayee was acceptable to the BJP's allies. Vajpayee dragged the party back to the middle of the road. There would be no more emotive Hindu issues, no anti-Muslim sub-text to policies and no more talk of pseudo-secularism.

The RSS was not happy, either with Vajpayee or with the men he surrounded himself with. Vajpayee's choice for finance minister was Jaswant Singh. The night before the swearing in, K.S. Sudarshan, the head of the RSS, went to see Vajpayee and objected to Jaswant Singh's inclusion. I later asked Vajpayee what Sudarshan's objections were.

The ostensible grounds were reasonable enough. Jaswant had lost a Lok Sabha election from Rajasthan. It would not be right to reward this defeat with a ministership on the basis of a Rajya Sabha membership. But it was entirely possible that the RSS's real objection was to Jaswant Singh's liberal political views; I often heard Jaswant make disparaging references to the Sangh and its positions. (Years later, when Arun Jaitley was in a similar position, Narendra Modi had no hesitation in giving him not just the finance portfolio but also the defence ministry. The RSS did not object.)

I hardly knew Vajpayee but sometime during his first few months in office I became friends with Namita, his foster-daughter and her husband Ranjan Bhattacharya. As the weeks went on, our friendship had less and less to do with journalism or politics and became one which we believed would survive any political upheavals. (It did. We are still friends.) It could have been a minefield in terms of potential conflict of interest but it worked because the Bhattacharyas knew that I was an old-fashioned secularist who disapproved of much of what the BJP (even the Vajpayee version) stood for. They made many jokes about my political choices but never expected any kind of support from me.

It was Namita who introduced me properly to Vajpayee and though we had a few political conversations (that is, he asked me questions about what other politicians had said to the press but rarely gave anything away himself), Vajpayee treated me as he would treat any friend of his foster-daughter's.

What this meant, however, was that I was often at 3 Race Course Road and saw the family at close quarters. Most political households have a surprising similarity to them. There are aides rushing about and there are always favour-seekers, political contacts and *chamchas* floating around. The only conversations are about politics and there is virtually no sense of a personal life.

The Vajpayee–Bhattacharya home was refreshingly different. Vajpayee would come home in the evenings, change into a lungi, sit in the living room and have a mug of soup. His young grand-daughter Niharika (whom he doted on) would prance around the room and even at dinner, nobody would talk politics. Though, obviously, everybody in the house loved and revered him, they spoke to him as anyone would in any happy family. Namita stopped him if he tried to have an extra *kachori*. Ranjan insisted that he use the treadmill every day.

For something like three years in a row, Seema and I spent Diwali at 3 Race Course Road. It was always a completely non-political affair. They would light fireworks in the garden, there would be dinner afterwards and there was no sense that you were spending Diwali with the prime minister of India. At home, Vajpayee was just another doting grandfather who loved celebrating the festival with Niharika.

It did sound grand though, as we realized when Raaj went back to school one year after his Diwali break. The teacher asked the students how they had celebrated Diwali. When he answered truthfully she told him not to tell lies to try and show off. After that he always said 'with some friends of my father's . . .'

The Vajpayee PMO was run by Brajesh Mishra, a former diplomat whom most people had forgotten all about. I knew him because I had once invited him to my DD show. At the time, he worked in the BJP's foreign affairs cell and seemed like just another retired officer who couldn't bear to sit at home all day and so liked the sense of going to an office.

I was a little surprised though, by the confidence with which he spoke. When we discussed the nuances of nuclear policy, he stated categorically that the BJP was committed to a nuclear deterrent.

'Would you test a bomb the moment you got into power?' I challenged him. 'Yes, we would,' he said.

At the time I thought he was going beyond his brief. If the BJP did come to office, I doubted if nuclear policy would be handed over to this opinionated retired gentleman.

I was completely wrong, of course. The BJP did come to power and the first thing Vajpayee did was to order a nuclear test. I asked him about the decision and he said that even when he was the prime minister for thirteen days, he had tried to order a test. At that stage, Brajesh was not his principal secretary and Vajpayee had been told by the nuclear establishment that they needed more notice.

This time around, he was a full-fledged prime minister, not a thirteen-day wonder and he was determined to go ahead with the test. He put Brajesh in charge of planning the test and to avoid the information leaking out (as it had when Narasimha Rao had tried to order a test), they maintained absolute secrecy. Vajpayee did not inform, let alone consult, any of his cabinet colleagues and even Advani who was Home minister (he had returned to active politics after the Courts had quashed the hawala case) was kept out of the loop till much later.

Brajesh ran the PMO with absolute authority. In the early days, Pramod Mahajan (who had joined the Vajpayee camp after being evicted from Advani's circle) spoke for the PM. But Pramod was given a ministry of his own and in a matter of months, it was clear that Brajesh was the boss.

Not everyone in the BJP was pleased with Brajesh's ascent. His rise had taken many by surprise. From all accounts he had not been particularly close to Vajpayee when the BJP was in opposition and his appointment had not been predicted by any of the pundits.

I had my own theory. Every shy man needs a more forthright man to play bad guy and to say the things that sometimes need to be said. Had Vajpayee chosen a person who was very close to the BJP leadership then that person would always have been deferential to Advani and others.

That was not what Vajpayee wanted. He wanted his own man who would serve only him and would tell the party where to get off. Brajesh, with his arrogance and brusque manner, was perfect for this role.

So it was not surprising that Advani, in particular, resented Brajesh and when disaffected sangh parivar-types (led by Dr J.K. Jain) ran a campaign against Brajesh, this campaign was believed to have Advani's tacit support. But nobody could touch Brajesh. Not only did he have Vajpayee's full confidence, he was also very good at his job so it was hard to find fault with him.

But the government was on slippery ground. Sitaram Kesri had persuaded Sonia Gandhi to campaign for the Congress in the 1998 election. After the party went down to another defeat, Congressmen ousted Kesri and asked Sonia to take over as party president. Seven years after she had first been offered the job, Sonia finally said yes.

It sounded promising but Sonia really did not understand politics. I persuaded her to give an interview to Star Talk, her first to any TV show, and though she came off well, as a sincere and determined person who had joined politics only to prevent the Congress from disintegrating and her husband's legacy from fading away, the universal reaction was that she seemed too 'cultured' and 'nice' to be in politics.

I asked her, for instance about Bal Thackeray's joke that she was a 'reader' not a 'leader' because she read out all her speeches and she responded that she could see Thackeray's point. But, she added, her speeches were now more her own and less any speechwriter's and she was speaking extempore more and more.

Her primary aide during that period was a former civil servant called Ram Pradhan whom I got along with. But her political advisors included Subramaniam Swamy who had kept in touch with the Gandhis since the Chandra Shekhar days. Rajiv had liked Swamy, and for Sonia, who was still finding her way in politics, anyone who Rajiv had liked was to be trusted. Swamy often changed sides (as Sonia was to later discover). For instance, he had spent years opposing Jayalalitha, but was now suddenly the Tamil Nadu supremo's close confidant!

Swamy and Vajpayee had a long-standing antipathy dating back to the period when Swamy was a Jan Sanghi, which neither man was willing to let go. When Jayalalitha pledged her support to the BJP, thus helping the Vajpayee government reach the majority mark, she had suggested to Vajpayee that he make Swamy finance minister. Vajpayee had flatly refused.

Now, Swamy believed he could bring Vajpayee down if Jayalalitha and Sonia Gandhi aligned. This was more difficult than it seemed. While Jayalalitha had been keen on Rajiv, she was decidedly unkeen on his wife. But Swamy persuaded her that she needed Sonia.

Jayalalitha was so hostile to Sonia that when I interviewed her in 1996, she kept saying: 'Don't call her Sonia! Her name is Antonia!' I later discovered that while Sonia's family and everyone who knew her called her Sonia, she had, in fact, been baptized Antonia because Sonia is not a biblical name. For some reason Jayalalitha thought that by calling her Antonia she was putting Sonia down.

Yet so great was the lure of power that Jayalalitha agreed to call her Soniaji and to be sweet to her—at least to her face!

The plan was that Jayalalitha would withdraw support, causing the government to lose its majority. The Congress would then call for a vote of no-confidence. The Vajpayee government would fall and a Congress-led coalition would take office.

I asked Sonia why she was going along with this madcap scheme. To topple Vajpayee at Jayalalitha's behest would only win Vajpayee public support. Besides, could any coalition that included both Jayalalitha and her survive for longer than a few months?

She listened to me and politely disagreed. The Congress had been faring well in assembly elections. It had won in Delhi and Madhya Pradesh. There was a growing feeling in the party that if Vajpayee was allowed to remain in office, he would gain so much in stature that it would become impossible to dislodge him.

Then, there was the RSS factor. She believed that the RSS was inserting its men and women into key positions in the administration. They would rise through the ranks and poison the system. Meanwhile, under the two ministers at the HRD ministry (M.M. Joshi and Uma Bharti), textbooks were being rewritten and history was being distorted. If there was an opportunity to unseat Vajpayee it would be foolish not to seize it.

Though the loss of Jayalalitha's support was a blow, the Vajpayee government was still confident that it could gather the votes needed to survive. On the day of the vote, I spoke to Shakti Sinha, Vajpayee's private secretary, who seemed confident. He said that Mayawati had met the prime minister in the morning, had touched his feet and assured him of her support.

When the voting started, I called Shakti again and said that I had heard that Mayawati's MPs were voting against the government. We kept talking till the vote was over when Shakti finally said, 'Vir, we are out. We lost by one vote!'

There was jubilation in the Congress camp when it was assumed that Sonia Gandhi would be the latest member of the family to become prime minister. But it was not that simple. The Congress had to get everyone from the opposition to agree to back a Congress-led government. I didn't think that would happen.

Sure enough, Mulayam Singh Yadav was the first one to back out. All secular forces should come together, he said. But there was no need for them to come together under the leadership of the Congress. His key advisor, Amar Singh, put it more categorically, 'What does Sonia have that she should be prime minister? Mulayam Singh is much more qualified. If not Mulayam Singh, then there are so many others.'

Mulayam was vital to the new government because without his MPs, the Congress/Third Front government would have no majority. But Amar Singh also knew once Mulayam openly declared his own candidature, others would oppose it and put themselves forward. For instance, Jayalalitha would have loved to become prime minister and given her role in bringing Vajpayee down, why shouldn't she be the obvious candidate?

There was another problem. Ram Pradhan told me, in confidence, that Sonia did not want to become prime minister. She felt that she lacked the experience to handle the job. Her choice for prime minister was Manmohan Singh. But nobody in the Opposition would accept Manmohan Singh so the Congress was keeping quiet about this.

I believed him. After the Narasimha Rao government fell, I had interviewed Manmohan Singh and asked him straight out if he wanted to be prime minister. 'Who doesn't want to be prime minister?' he laughed. So I knew he would take the job. And from what I knew of Sonia, making him the prime minister sounded like the sort of thing she would do.

I don't think Mulayam knew any of this. But he bowled a googly. He would support Jyoti Basu as prime minister, he said. This was odd. It was well known that the CPM had no desire to take part in any government at the Centre, so how was Jyoti Basu even a candidate?

But, to everyone's surprise, Jyoti Basu was excited by the idea. Apparently he told Mulayam that he would take the job. Of course, the CPM Politburo said no, it would not join any government so there was no question of Jyoti Basu becoming prime minister.

This angered Jyoti Basu who had on a previous occasion, with uncharacteristic immodesty, referred to the decision not to let him lead the government as 'a historic blunder'. Amar Singh and the rest in turn went to Advani to see if some deal with the BJP was possible.

By now, the Congress was getting restless. 'We will not support any Third Front or Fourth Front,' Sonia told reporters. She had helped pull Vajpayee down on the specific understanding that the Congress would form the next government.

That left President K.R. Narayanan with no option. He called for fresh elections. This was in April 1998 and ideally the election should have been held immediately. But the Election Commission suggested a schedule beginning in September. For the next four months or so, Vajpayee would remain in office as caretaker.

There are many 'what ifs' surrounding this episode. What if the Congress had not toppled Vajpayee? Would he have gone on and on as Sonia feared?

Personally, I doubt it.

What if the Congress had formed the government? Would the coalition have lasted?

I don't see how it would have made it past eighteen months with Jayalalitha, Mulayam and the rest around.

Was Ram Pradhan right about Sonia wanting Manmohan Singh to be prime minister?

I asked Sonia who did not deny it but was unforthcoming. I asked Manmohan Singh who said that he had no idea what Sonia's plans were. Finally, I asked President Narayanan who confirmed that Sonia had told him that Manmohan Singh would be the Congress's prime ministerial candidate.

And the final 'what if'. What if the election had been held right after the Vajpayee government fell and not several months later— during which time many crucial events took place? Would the Congress have won enough seats to form the next government?

I think that could well have happened.

THIRTY-NINE

'THERE IS A BREAKING NEWS!'

The news trickled in slowly. At first the reports said that 'mujahideen' had crossed the border from Pakistan during the winter and occupied the Indian army bunkers.

Initially, like many others, I thought that this was just one more instance of Pakistan sending infiltrators across the border. Certainly, the army seemed keen to play down the intrusions. But as more details emerged I began to realize that what had happened was serious.

The Indian army traditionally abandoned its bunkers in an area called Kargil in Ladakh (part of Jammu and Kashmir) during the winter. When it warmed up and the snows began to melt our troops returned. Apparently this was well known to everyone.

According to the army, it received reports from local shepherds in early May that its bunkers had been occupied by armed men from the other side of the border while the Indian army's troops had gone off to warmer climes.

As army patrols went out to check, it became clear (by mid-May) that Pakistani forces dressed in mufti and pretending to be mujahideen had come across many points on the Kargil border. These were not isolated intrusions. They were part of a well-thought-out military campaign.

India's attempts to regain control of the situation were not very successful. Troops were sent to Kargil and the Air Force called in. But our planes were shot down and the bunkers remained under Pakistani control.

By June, when the Pakistani army began shelling National Highway number 1 in Kashmir, it was clear that we were at war—or pretty damn close to it.

As the chaos unfolded, the Vajpayee government went into damage-control mode. Only a few months earlier Vajpayee had travelled to Lahore, had met the Pakistani prime minister Nawaz Sharif and talked of peace. And yet, here we were, at war!

The government made it clear that it believed that the generals had launched this operation without telling Nawaz Sharif. The Research and Analysis Wing (RAW), India's external intelligence agency, had been tapping the phones of Pakistani generals. It made a tape available to its political masters that supported this hypothesis. To its horror, the government gave the tape to the media solely to prove that the Lahore trip had not been a mistake. This resulted in the Pakistanis changing their methods of communication so that RAW could not intercept their conversations any longer.

Eventually the tide turned. Young Indian army officers led from the front and won back the bunkers, many of them losing their lives in the process. It became a full-scale war and to the credit of the army, it drove the Pakistanis out. But it took time.

As the conflict escalated, the global community tried to force the two nuclear powers to pull back. For Vajpayee this was the gravest crisis of his political career. His peace initiative had collapsed and, for a bit, it looked as though he might be the only Indian prime minister since Jawaharlal Nehru to lose a war.

He became even more reticent and decided he would take all major decisions on his own. Afterwards, when we had won, he had a rare political conversation with me, telling me how great the pressure had been. He talked about receiving a call from US President Bill Clinton in the middle of the night. (The White House operates according to its own time zone.) Clinton asked if Vajpayee would come to Washington. He would invite Nawaz Sharif too and would help broker an end to the conflict.

Vajpayee had to think quickly. There was no Brajesh Mishra at that time of night and none of his senior advisors was around.

He went with his gut. No, he said, he would not go anywhere while India was at war. Washington should ask Pakistan to pull back.

Which is what happened. As the Indian army met with more and more success, Nawaz Sharif accepted Clinton's advice to lower the temperature and begun cutting off backing to the 'mujahideen'. But most of the 'mujahideen' were Pakistani army regulars in mufti and the army was reluctant to give in so easily. Eventually, Sharif went to Washington in early July and announced that the Pakistan forces would withdraw from the conflict. (In the months to come, the chief of the Pakistan army, General Pervez Musharraf, would stage a coup and take over from Sharif.)

The war was long (around six weeks) and bloody. For the first time in Indian history, we had a televised war as channels sent reporters to the front line. Fortunately for us, the Vajpayee government was willing to grant access to the media and even *Star Talk* focused on the war and its progress with many of those involved in the conflict (such as Defence Minister George Fernandes) agreeing to come to the studio and explain what was going on.

Questions were raised about intelligence failures. Some reports suggested that the 'mujahideen' had been in position from November–December 1998 but the army had only taken note of their presence six months later. The army blamed the intelligence agencies who responded that they had received reports from shepherds in the area and had relayed them to the army. Some army officers also claimed to have raised the alarm only to find their warnings ignored by the headquarters.

This led to a round of recriminations. An intelligence officer told me later that not only had the Intelligence Bureau (IB) written to the army, the agency had got so alarmed by the army's lack of action that the director of the Intelligence Bureau (DIB) had signed a letter to the army himself (apparently this was very unusual) to draw attention to the gravity of the situation.

But these recriminations did nothing to dampen the enthusiasm and patriotic fervour that spread through the country. Even the stock market began to boom once India had declared victory. Given the public mood, I found it hard to believe that anyone could defeat Vajpayee in the election that was due in a couple of months.

I think the BJP took the same view. I remember asking Namita Kaul Bhattacharya where the family would be over the New Year. 'Right here,' she said, 'at Race Course Road.' Given that Christmas and New Year came two months after the results were to be declared, there seemed no doubt that Vajpayee and his family were not worried by the prospect of any electoral reverse.

As the election drew near, Aroon Purie called once again. Aaj Tak had been asked to do the election programming for Doordarshan again. Would I anchor it?

I called Rathikant Basu who conceded that he had no moral right to hold me back this time. So I was delighted to say yes to Aroon.

The 1999 election was the last one before electronic voting machines took over completely from the ballot so our programme would be at least a three-day affair. Aaj Tak would use Doordarshan's facilities and its network of correspondents and the show would be billed as a coproduction.

There were some DD producers too, and we did a couple of dry runs with them. We were told that often news would break suddenly and we had to be prepared to stop what we were doing and tell our viewers what had happened immediately.

This was not news to us. My co-anchors, Karan Thapar and Tavleen Singh, were pros who had been doing this for a long time but we were not sure how to cope with the DD producers. At our rehearsal, a producer shouted into my ear, 'There is a Breaking News!' I waited for him to tell me what the news was. But all he would say again and again was 'the news is Breaking.' So I ignored him and continued with the show.

Later, in the break, he berated me for not flashing this news. I explained to him that he needed to tell me what this 'Breaking News' was if I was to interrupt the flow of the show. 'But this is only a rehearsal,' he objected. 'How can I invent news just like that?'

For the show itself, Aroon gave us Uday Shankar, an experienced producer who not only avoided the DD-type nonsense but also understood politics. Often when I was interviewing winners and losers live on the air, it was Uday who would feed me questions and information in my ear. (Uday had the most distinguished twenty-first-century career of all of us. He went on to head Aaj Tak, then moved to Star News before being asked to head all of Star and then becoming Asia head for Disney when it took over Star.)

I enjoyed the excitement of live TV enormously. I had done *Weekend with Vir Sanghvi* before but I had never done a show where I interviewed guests in remote areas on OB (Outside Broadcast) links live while keeping track of the results.

As I had expected, the BJP won easily. The Congress—at its first election under Sonia Gandhi's leadership—did badly. The BJP (without its allies) won 182 seats. The Congress only got 114. Some Congress leaders (Ghulam Nabi Azad, for instance) were philosophical but some were decidedly downcast. I had known Natwar Singh for years but he was too upset to be nice when his face showed up on our big screen (we had him on an OB).

'How do you explain the Congress's performance?' I asked.

'We have done badly,' he said shortly.

'What you think went wrong?' I asked.

'We have done badly. That's it,' he repeated.

'That's not very helpful,' I said smiling.

'I am not here to help you.'

End of interview.

We had guests in the studio too. Arun Jaitley, who had been largely unknown outside of Delhi when he started appearing on *A Question of Answers*, had risen so remarkably in the last three years that he was now considered one of the brightest members of the ministry. He gave us his perspective. And because in those days DD still had the reach, nobody turned down an invitation to appear on the show.

Not because of our competence or skill but because in that pre-satellite, minimal-cable era, only terrestrial TV reached every corner, we ended up being one of the most-viewed programmes of the year. The Star News election broadcast, Basu conceded, was a disaster. It was an NDTV staff meeting, and we beat them even within the cable and satellite universe.

Though *Sunday* had continued to cover the election, I had hardly any time left for print. Mentally, I had switched off and I recognized that with ABP's financial problems it was unfair to expect Aveek to do any more.

Was TV going to be my future? I wondered. I didn't see magazines surviving very long and the newsmagazine, as a species, was in its death throes all over the world.

There was one postscript to the whole Kargil business. A year or so later, Benazir Bhutto made a private trip to India to meet friends. She agreed to travel to Eagle Studios in Noida to shoot an episode of *Star Talk*.

It was a good interview, as I recall, because she confirmed what many of us had suspected, that Osama bin Laden had wanted to leave South Asia in 1989 after the fall of the Soviet-backed regime in Afghanistan but had been held back by the ISI which promised him men and money.

Further, she said, it was wrong to think of the ISI as a single organization. Many ex-generals had made millions and ran their own private armies (or terror outfits, depending on your perspective) which could easily be used to launch attacks on India.

General Musharraf had overthrown Nawaz Sharif and was the dictator of Pakistan when we spoke. Benazir said she had known Musharraf when she was the prime minister. He had tried to persuade her of the strategic value of an operation that would use bogus 'mujahideen' to take over Indian bunkers in the Kargil region during the winter. She had turned him down, she said. But as the Kargil conflict erupted, she recognized the plan as being the same one that she had rejected.

So had Nawaz Sharif accepted the plan she had rejected? Or was Kargil Musharraf's own little venture?

She said that either was possible. But India needed to remember that in Pakistan, it is always the army you have to look out for.

I only ever met Musharraf once—at the Agra summit a few years later—and I asked him about Kargil.

But more about that later.

FORTY

THE NEWSPAPER WARS

A t least in the 1980s (I don't know if this is still true), Calcutta was a city within a city. There was the Calcutta the world knew about, the so-called City of Joy of Dominique Lapierre and Mother Teresa. But there was also another Calcutta which remained hidden from public view: the Calcutta of the Marwaris.

The Marwaris have always been India's premier business community, laying the foundations of Indian industry. You hear much more about them now than you did then. In the 1980s and 1990s, they avoided publicity and quietly ran India's biggest corporations. The Birlas, then India's largest industrial group, were Calcutta-headquartered. R.P. Goenka, possibly one of the brightest businessmen of his generation, lived in Calcutta. So did dozens of other Marwari millionaires.

They did not socialize much except with each other and even then, they followed rituals. I was invited once to have dinner with B.K. Birla at his home. The Birlas were India's richest family and BK was the wealthiest member of the clan. But, despite the elegance of the home, there was no display of wealth, BK and his wife were courteous and humble and the conversation revolved around art and music.

After dinner, we adjourned to another room. A few minutes later, a server entered with a tray full of glasses of water. I had been told that this would be my cue to leave and indeed it was.

Many Marwaris had inherited the traditions of the British companies they took over. I once went to B.M. Khaitan's office for lunch and was surprised to see it served in a dining room straight out of a London club, with liveried staff serving sherry with the starter and wine afterwards. The old style Marwaris bought their spread collar shirts from London's Jermyn Street and some had their suits tailored on Savile Row.

Of all the Marwaris I met, nobody was quite as impressive as K.K. Birla (BK's brother). His father G.D. Birla had been a close friend of Gandhiji's and had helped finance the freedom struggle, even though this hurt his businesses during the Raj. K.K. Birla (or K.K. Babu as everyone in Calcutta called him), was the only one of G.D. Birla's sons to have inherited his father's commitment to public life.

He was a long-time member of parliament, had been a close friend of Indira Gandhi's and took an active interest in politics. His father had not given him any hugely profitable companies to run, arguing that as he only had three daughters and no sons, it was better to give the bigger companies to those in the family who had sons.

One of the companies he did get was the *Hindustan Times*, which was consistently unprofitable till he turned it into a hugely profitable enterprise in the 1980s and 1990s. He started Chambal Fertilizers on his own, creating a behemoth that kept spinning out money and ran his companies with such skill that it no longer mattered that he hadn't been given the biggies by his father.

Aveek was a friend of K.K.'s and first took me to have lunch with him at Birla headquarters in Calcutta. K.K. Babu was a formal man (always in a suit or a bandhgalla) and was obsessed with time. If he said he would meet you at five minutes past one and you arrived at one, he would keep you waiting till five minutes past one even if he was free. This was his way.

Lunch was a mix of cuisines. There would be soup (say asparagus), followed by vegetable cutlets and then rice and an Indian sabzi. The meal would end with an absurdly rich and sweet dessert. K.K. Babu would always have a pad in front of him in which he noted down the subjects he wanted to discuss with you.

In the twenty-plus years that I knew him, the pattern of our lunches never changed. Nor did the menu. We had roughly the same meal in Calcutta, Delhi and even London! (He got the kitchen at the three-Michelin-star Nico at Ninety to make the same menu for him.)

Originally, Aveek and I would go together but he soon began inviting us individually. And as I began spending more and more time in Delhi we normally met alone at Birla House (next to the garden where Gandhiji was assassinated).

When we first met I was not much more than thirty and he was the proprietor of the largest newspaper in Delhi and one of India's most famous and powerful industrialists. But he treated me with so much courtesy and regard that I never once felt intimidated.

This, I was later to learn, was his way. He was always curious about the world and eager to learn from everyone, no matter how old or young. As long as you kept him mentally challenged and engaged, he would call you back again and again.

As he got to know me better, we met for lunch at least once a month. I used to joke with him that I could read upside down so I always knew what the subjects he wanted to discuss with me were; I could read them from his pad.

But I was always on my guard. He would remember what position I had taken on a particular issue three years earlier and ask me to explain why I had now changed my mind.

He was an integral part of Delhi's permanent establishment by virtue of owning the city's top newspaper and had political connections across parties. So he had a great bullshit detector. He could tell when you really didn't know what was going on or were dissembling. Of course, he was too refined to point this out in so many words but you always knew that he knew that you were improvising.

A year before I moved to Calcutta, the Birlas had decided to split their assets so that they were no longer a monolith but were a group of several conglomerates, all independently managed. Till the split happened it had never been clear who would inherit K.K. Babu's companies. But he made it clear that he would depart from Marwari tradition and leave them to his daughters who, he said, were just as capable as men, when it came to managing companies.

When I first met him, K.K. Babu was hands-on at the *Hindustan Times* but he was in the process of inducting his youngest daughter, Shobhana Bhartia, into the running of the company. I met her for the first time in 1990 when K.K. Babu threw a tea party for Rajiv Gandhi (who was then out of office) at Birla House and Shobhana played hostess. We would later become close friends but that was my first encounter.

Though we talked about everything under the sun, K.K. Babu hardly ever mentioned the *Hindustan Times*. If Aveek asked what he thought of the current editor, K.K. Babu, who could be blunt, would turn uncharacteristically evasive. Clearly, he did not feel comfortable discussing the paper with other proprietors or journalists.

This began to change in 1997 when the *Hindustan Times* came under threat from the *Times of India*. For years, India's great cities had been divided between newspaper barons. The *HT* dominated Delhi. The *Times* dominated Mumbai. *The Hindu* was king of Chennai. The *Statesman* was the great Calcutta newspaper.

It changed in the 1980s when the *Telegraph* effectively challenged the *Statesman* in Calcutta and, ultimately, almost wiped it out. But now, there were indications that the *Times* would not accept supremacy in Mumbai alone. Samir Jain (who I was still in infrequent touch with) told me that he would take the *Times* to Chennai and Calcutta (which he later did) but that his immediate target was to overtake the *HT* in Delhi.

Samir's strategy was sound. He slashed the price of the *Times*. This made it more attractive to readers, which was the idea. Samir was convinced that once *HT* readers started getting the *Times* they would see how much better it was than the *HT*. (The economics of the post-Samir *Times of India* have always been advertising-driven, so subscription revenues did not matter much.)

The *HT* was stunned by the way in which the *Times of India*'s circulation surged. It responded by cutting its own cover price. This created a situation where you could now get both *Times* and the *HT* for the amount you used to pay for just the *HT*.

It stopped the *HT* from losing circulation but it did not have a significant impact on the *Times*' circulation surge. It looked as though Delhi would now become a market where two newspapers had equal sway. This suited Samir fine. For years, the *Times* had been trying to persuade advertisers that they could take advantage of a combined ad rate for both the Delhi and Mumbai editions. However, large advertisers believed that you still needed the *HT* in Delhi. Once Samir was able to show that the *Times* had nearly equalled the *HT*'s circulation in Delhi, there was no longer any reason not to take the combined *Times* rate for Delhi and Mumbai.

At our lunches K.K. Babu began mentioning his concern. Could it be possible, he asked, that the *Times* would overtake the *HT* one day?

I had to be honest. It would happen by the end of the decade, I told him.

I don't know what conversations he had with Shobhana but one day, she also came along for our lunch. He had a task for me, K.K. Babu said.

Would I look at the *HT* closely for a month or two and tell them what was wrong with the paper? They felt that they needed an outsider's opinion. 'Charge us anything you like,' K.K. Babu said. 'You can call it a consultancy fee.'

I said I was happy to do it but there were two conditions. The first was that nobody would know what I was doing or what my conclusions were.

This suited them fine. I don't think they were eager to tell their editors that they had asked an outsider to assess their work.

The one exception to this condition, I said, was Aveek. As long as I was an employee of ABP I could not, in all conscience, do anything for the *HT* without telling him.

They thought this was fair.

And the second was that I wouldn't take any money. It seemed wrong to hire myself out to the *HT* when I drew an ABP salary. K.K. Babu said he would clear it with Aveek but I was adamant. They agreed to discuss renumeration when I had finished my assessment.

So, for days on end, I looked at every line in the *HT*, read every story, compared it to the *Times* till I was sure that I had a fair idea of the problem.

I wrote out a report and, over lunch at Birla House, I told them what I thought. I said that I believed that the *HT* was not a bad paper. It often contained good stories that the Times had missed. So there was no problem there.

Then came the painful bit. For years the *HT* had been known as 'the only English language newspaper in the world to be written entirely in Punjabi'.

K.K. Birla winced. I don't think he was aware of the description though I remembered it from way back in the 1970s.

You couldn't write a paper in Punjabi any longer, I said. Readers had changed. The least they expected was correct English. Further, I added, the *Times* was written and edited by people who cared about the quality of writing. The *HT* did not seem as concerned.

This pointed to a deeper failing. In the glory years of the *HT*, Delhi had been a Punjabi-dominated city. It wasn't any longer. It was much more cosmopolitan. You couldn't get away with only catering to Punjabis. Moreover, even within the Punjabi community, a younger, more English-oriented generation was taking over. They didn't want to be seen with their parents' paper where sub-editors thought it was okay to put a 'the' before Delhi. (As in 'the monsoon will be reaching the Delhi next week' for instance.)

There were two other fundamental changes that the *HT* had ignored. The first was that Samir had changed the character and nature of newspaper management in India. In the old days, all newspapers (including the *Times*) had been run by bureaucracies. Samir brought in people from consumer products companies, began talking of the power of brands and redefined the way in which newspaper companies were managed. The *HT*, I said, struck me as still being a bureaucracy.

My final point was that India had been fundamentally altered by the 1991 reforms. We had become a consumer-oriented society where new goods were available in the shops, where movies were released at the same time as they were in America, where satellite TV had opened up the world to us and where a restaurant and hotel boom was underway.

The *Times* treated its readers as consumers and offered them a well-rounded package that reflected this new reality. The *HT*, on the other hand, still acted as though readers were stuck in some time warp where liberalization had never happened and no demographic changes had occurred.

It was not going to be as simple as changing the editor or re-designing the paper.

The problems were too serious for that.

They seemed a little taken aback and though K.K. Babu asked me a few questions I could see that he was convinced.

What I didn't know was that Shobhana and I would end up finding the solutions to the problems I had described ourselves.

FORTY-ONE

'YOU HAVE BECOME VERY FAT'

My TV career, meanwhile, continued on a parallel stream. *Star Talk* proved to be among the more successful programmes on Star News, at least partly thanks to the generosity of Star TV which never skimped on budgets, built a sleek set and hired the best studios.

It seems strange now to explain how we shot. Ideally we would try and shoot at least three interviews a day. We would rent somewhere like Eagle Studios in Noida for two days. One day would go in erecting the set and on the second day I would shoot the interviews at sixty-minute intervals. Because we were canning them, we would try and shoot one guest who was of topical interest (say, a politician) and two or three lighter guests whose shows could be held over.

Because not everyone agreed to turn up on the day we had booked the studio, we tried to fix four or five guests, knowing that only three would work out. Inevitably, there were times when all five said yes, so I sometimes would shoot five interviews back to back.

We liked to alternate our guests (a politician would be followed the next week by a movie star) which meant that we often shot in Mumbai. This was before PR companies took hold of stars and only allowed them to give interviews when they had a movie to promote. These days, the process is so tightly controlled that most stars give a dozen short interviews over two days to different channels and say the same things in each interview ('This is one of the most challenging roles I have attempted . . .')

On one day in Mumbai, we shot for *Star Talk* with Kajol, followed by Zeenat Aman followed by Anil Ambani followed by Madhuri Dixit. Kajol surprised us by coming early, fully made-up and asking to shoot immediately. Zeenat, on the other hand, came on time but spent so long inside her make-up van that her time slot came and went. We were still waiting for her when the next interviewee, Anil Ambani, turned up. Fortunately, he was a sport and said he would wait.

So when Zeenat did turn up (and gave us an excellent interview), Anil was already in the production control room, joking with the crew, who loved his easy informality.

We zipped through the Anil Ambani interview to be ready in time for Madhuri which, fortunately, we were. It was a slightly fraught and exhausting way of shooting a TV show but it had many compensations. I was well-paid by the standards of that era. If we shot four episodes in a day then I was free for the rest of the month. Because Anju Juneja was such a pro, I never worried about the editing. She cut and shaped the show herself, leaving me free to concentrate on my print career.

But Star was changing. One day, without warning, the Star management in Hong Kong announced that Rathikant Basu was being elevated to chairman, a largely meaningless post. The new CEO would be Peter Mukerjea, who had previously handled ad sales. Basu was an ex-bureaucrat but Peter was a consummate salesperson. He had worked in London and Hong Kong before coming back to India and was the sort of global corporate type whom Star's senior executives in Hong Kong loved.

He liked designer clothes, nice cars, and drinking and joshing with the boys. He had very little time for the ex-bureaucrats Basu had brought with him and was much more at ease with buddies from the corporate world.

This made no difference to *Star Talk*. But it did change Star. Peter turned Star Plus into an all-Hindi entertainment channel. His head of programming, Sameer Nair, persuaded Amitabh Bachchan to host a Hindi version of *Who Wants to be a Millionaire?* Rupert Murdoch, who happened to be visiting India, asked how much a million rupees was in dollars. When he was told, he said it was too little and forced Star to raise the prize money to a crore and thus *Kaun Banega Crorepati* was launched.

It became a national craze, totally resurrected Bachchan's career (then going through a slump) and had such a positive effect on the channel's fortunes that all its shows began to do well. We forget now that in that era, the cable and satellite TV universe was largely urban (it is much more pan-Indian now which is why the nature of programming has changed) and Sameer knew exactly how to cater to this audience with lush soap operas made by such producers as Ekta Kapoor. In no time at all, the new all-Hindi Star Plus was India's number one channel.

There was little impact on Star News or *Star Talk*. We kept doing our weekly show, still insisting that guests came to our studios. We made some exceptions, of course. Richard Gere asked if he could be interviewed at the Belvedere at the Delhi Oberoi and because the request came through our mutual friend Parmeshwar Godrej, I agreed.

Amitabh Bachchan said he was shooting at a Mumbai studio for a song sequence. He would have time between takes and would be happy to do the interview. But, as he pointed out, we would have to hire a studio anyway. So why didn't we hire a soundstage at the same studio where he was shooting? This made sense so we ended up on a soundstage next to his where he was shooting the 'Shaava Shaava' song for *Kabhi Khushi Kabhie Gham*.

We began the day by interviewing Raveena Tandon (I looked at a clip of that interview recently and was surprised by how candid she had been about her personal life). Then, we had a gap till the evening when we were to shoot with Bachchan. Amit asked me to join him on his set as the cast went through their dance moves. Joyeeta, a member of our crew, noticed that Shahrukh Khan had come out for a smoke and asked him if he would sit down for an interview sometime in the evening before Amit was due on our set. To her astonishment, he said yes.

I was a little surprised too. Were we really going to shoot Shahrukh Khan and Amitabh Bachchan back to back?

We were still discussing whether Shahrukh (who is notorious for being late) would actually turn up when somebody pointed out that he already had. He had slipped in and was sitting in the guest chair on the *Star Talk* desk. He was alone. There was no make-up person and there was no minder.

I rushed to my side of my chair and though we had never met before, he spoke with such breezy confidence that there was no sense in which meeting him for the first time was awkward. I pushed the envelope by asking if he was gay or bisexual as was rumoured in film circles. It was not a question anyone had asked him to his face before but he was unfazed, dismissed it with aplomb and we moved on to the next subject.

Though I thought the whole interview went very well, the only bit people remembered was the gay question. Shahrukh was asked about it for months afterwards, usually by film journalists who had never had the guts to confront him with the question before.

He was super cool. To one journalist who demanded to know why I had asked him if he was gay, Shahrukh responded: 'I don't know. May be if I had said yes, he would have asked me out to dinner.'

I suspect his wit eluded the journo.

Another person who refused to come to the studio was Bal Thackeray. I said I wouldn't do the interview at Matoshri, his bungalow. Finally, we agreed on a Bachchan-like compromise. A friend of Thackeray's had a studio that needed clients. If he could say that Bal Thackeray had shot there for *Star Talk*, it would advance his commercial prospects. Thackeray was eager to help him. Our producers checked out the studio, found it was modern and well designed and so I agreed to shoot there.

Thackeray came on time, was pleasant to everyone and said he was ready. I like chatting to important guests for a few minutes before a shoot so that the audio guys can be certain that the mikes are working, the camera guys can select their angles, etc.

I began by saying that though I had known him for over twenty years, he still looked the same. (This was not a lie.) 'Yes,' said Thackeray. 'But you have changed. You have become very fat.'

I ended the small talk and began the interview. The thing about Thackeray was that he never lied. No matter how outrageous his answer was, he gave it. He enjoyed shocking people. This never really came through in his later interviews because journalists were usually needlessly reverential and too scared to call him out on his behaviour.

I remember he had objected to the release of Mani Ratnam's film *Bombay* about the post-Babri riots. The film had a Thackeray-like character who, at the end of the riots, is so horrified by the death and destruction that he joins hands with his Muslim counterpart.

It was widely speculated that Thackeray was unhappy at being portrayed as a man who instigated violence. I had known him long enough to know that this could not be true: he had never shrunk away from violence. And yet that was how his objections to the movie were characterized in the press.

I went to interview him for *Sunday* and asked what his real objection to the movie was.

Well, he said, at the end of the film, the Thackeray character seemed to express regret for what had happened. This was far from the truth. He had no regrets at all about the violence. It had been necessary.

This time, too, sitting in the studio, I knew that he would be unapologetic and upfront (or brazen, depending on your perspective) about the things the Shiv Sena had done.

I asked him if it was true that his men had burnt down shops selling Valentine's Day cards. And was it also true that this was because his daughter-in-law had a commercial disagreement with the company that made the Valentine's Day cards?

He was calm. 'Not burnt,' he said. 'Destroyed. We destroyed them.'

Then, of course, he went on to defend his daughter in law. But he was not prepared to be in the slightest bit apologetic about the violence.

There were other memorable guests. We did what must have been one of the first full-length TV interviews with Infosys' Narayana Murthy, who was little known at the time. I interviewed Priyanka Chopra on the sets of her first film (no film of hers had been released so far) and told her that she would be a big star soon. Moon Moon Sen decided not to answer my questions but to embarrass me instead.

Kumar Birla asked, after we had shot the first segment, if we could shoot it again: 'I came across as very boring.' (He hadn't.) Kirron Kher insisted on swapping chairs with me and went and sat in the anchor's chair because she said that was a better profile for her.

Star Talk became part of a Hindi movie where I interviewed Abhishek Bachchan (or the character he was playing) as part of the plot.

We shot so many episodes and it was so much fun that I was sad when the inevitable happened: the NDTV-run Star News channel closed.

What happened was this. There were already tensions between Star and NDTV. When the contract to produce Star News ran out, NDTV was in a position to launch its own channel (which it did). Star, on the other hand, would have to start from scratch.

From what I heard at the time, Peter consulted Murdoch who said 'Our company is called News International. Can't we run our own news?'

So that was it for the old Star News. Peter decided that the new Star News would be all Hindi, seeing how successful the all-Hindi Star Plus had been.

That should have been it for me. The logical thing would have been to go to NDTV and ask to continue with *Star Talk* under a new name. But Ravina Raj Kohli who ran the Hindi Star News channel persuaded me that I could easily to do a Hindi show on the new Star News. They would call it *Vir Ke Teer*.

So I did the show. And it sucked. It did okay commercially but I was so uncomfortable in Hindi that I shudder each time I think of the experience.

Fortunately, Star World, the English entertainment channel, was doing an only-India beam. I went and saw Sameer Nair who ran Star's programming and asked if he would resurrect *Star Talk* for Star World.

He said he would. I was relieved. I gave up the Hindi show. And got set for more episodes of the new *Star Talk*, which I discovered, Sameer wanted to call *Cover Story*. In all other respects it would be the same show.

FORTY-TWO

'WITH WHAT FACE CAN I STOP YOU?'

Though neither Shobhana nor K.K. Babu said very much about their view of the *HT* at that meeting at Birla House, I soon learned that there was a back story to developments at the paper.

When Shobhana had taken over in the mid-1980s, K.K. Babu had not given her the full authority to change things. And at that stage, no change seemed to be required. The *HT* was Delhi's number one paper and the *Times* was a long way behind. Through the 1990s, it kept making large profits—higher than ever before in its history—so the status quo seemed acceptable.

Shobhana had instead focused her energies on new projects (a video magazine called *Eyewitness*, a partnership with global giants for the Home TV channel, and refinements to the editorial side of the operation).

Some of these moves bought her into conflict with one particular editor and this was resolved by also designating her as editorial director, which meant that editors reported to her and she reported to the board.

All this was good but it did not address the central issue. K.K. Babu's style of working was to put a manager in charge of each of his companies and, as long as the enterprise ran well, not to interfere too much in the operations. He expected his senior managers to be loyal to the group and he, in turn, was loyal to them.

In the case of *HT*, the company was run by a senior manager called Naresh Mohan who had K.K. Babu's support. From what I was to hear, Mohan ran the *HT* as absolute boss and resisted attempts by anyone else to suggest any changes or improvements. And to be fair to Mohan, he led the company through very profitable times.

The problem was that, by the end of 1990s, the market had changed, the readers had changed and the *Times* was a much more formidable threat. My guess is that the organization Naresh Mohan had constructed simply did not have the wherewithal to cope with this changed reality.

It was not his fault; it was the times that had changed, not him. But equally, as long as he maintained an absolute grip on the organization, there was no way that the *HT* was going to be able to cope with the changing market.

There were also editorial problems. K.K. Babu had chosen as editor, a soft-spoken man called V.N. Narayanan, who had previously been editor of Chandigarh's the *Tribune*. Narayanan was, frankly speaking, not the sort of man who should have edited a big city newspaper in the 1990s. He lacked the depth, the brains, the range or the imagination to cope with the market in post-liberalization India.

He was unwilling, however, to accept his shortcomings (which of us is?) and made life difficult for the executive editor, the man who looked after the news pages. But he usually won every minor confrontation because he had the backing of Naresh Mohan.

When I presented my assessment of the paper to K.K. Birla and Shobhana, both Narayanan and Naresh Mohan were firmly in place. In a few months, however, K.K. Babu realized that things were not going to get better as long as Mohan was in charge. He was allowed to retire and replaced by Deepak Shourie (brother of Arun). Unfortunately, Shourie left the *HT* in a few months to join Zee and the company scrambled to find a successor. In the interim Shobhana let Ashish Bagga (who later became business head at *India Today*) run the show.

I guess the paper would have had to confront the Narayanan problem at some stage. But nobody expected Narayanan to flame out so spectacularly. He had a column in the Sunday edition which (or so I was told) had a dedicated readership. One Sunday, he plagiarized an article by Bryan Appleyard from the *Sunday Times* (London) and printed it under his own name.

Psychiatrists could have a field day figuring out why a top editor, who had no difficulty in writing articles himself, would steal a piece from as popular a publication as the *Sunday Times*. Even in that pre-internet age, lots of Indian journalists read the *Sunday Times* so it was certain that he would be found out.

So why did he do it? Was it a cry for help? Did he want to be found out? Some suicidal urge to fall on his own sword?

For whatever reason, the *HT* had no choice but to sack Narayanan—especially after Bryan Appleyard himself wrote about the plagiarism in the *Sunday Times*.

I met Narayanan a year later. Though he had staged a vigorous battle to keep his job at the *HT* getting prominent people (including former prime ministers) to call the management to argue for his continuance, by the time we met, he was a sad and defeated figure. 'I have only myself to blame,' he said.

The *HT* was now without an editor or a CEO. I began to wonder if perhaps I should apply for the job. It would be nice to return to print and make TV a sideline. And though at forty-three, I was much younger than the *HT*'s recent editors, I reckoned that youth might not be a bad thing for the *HT*.

I asked our mutual friend, Raian Karanjawala, to tell Shobhana that I was interested in the job. She called back instantly and invited me home. We went over the salient features of my appointment. I would be a full-fledged editor not just editor of the editorial page. I would cut down on TV ('no more than one show a week', my contract letter read) and well, that was pretty much it.

Shobhana told K.K. Babu who called to say he was delighted, had thought of asking me himself but believed it would be ungentlemanly to try and poach me from Aveek as it was Aveek, after all, who had first introduced us.

Ah Aveek!

With a sense of dread I called Aveek and told him that the *HT* had offered me a job.

'Editor?' he asked.

I said that was the offer.

'I thought they would', he said.

So, was it okay with him?

'With what face can I stop you?' he laughed. 'You must take the job.'

It was a very classy attitude.

Being the editor of the *HT* was quite a big deal in journalistic circles so even before the appointment was announced, rumours circulated all around Delhi till we decided to announce the appointment immediately if only to quell the speculation. My old friend Behram 'Busybee' Contractor called from Mumbai to confirm the news and when I said yes, he put it on page one of his paper, *The Afternoon Despatch and Courier*.

The *Pioneer* ran a long profile of me drawing attention to my style (young, hip, TV-famous and other attributes it had clearly made up!) contrasting it with the *HT*'s old-fashioned image. And to my embarrassment, the *HT* also ran a long and laudatory story on page one about my appointment. (Those were different times. Who would care about the appointment of an editor now?)

It felt odd to be written about when I was used to writing about other people.

There was a tragic little postscript to my association with ABP. Shortly after I resigned, a fire engulfed ABP's headquarters in Calcutta. At least one person lost his life (fortunately the fire broke out early in the morning when the building was largely empty) and all the offices were completely destroyed.

How they managed to bring the *Telegraph* and *Ananda Bazaar Patrika* out the next day, I cannot imagine, but to their credit they did, in a truncated black and white form.

R.P. Goenka loaned them use of an empty space not far from the ABP office and the staff of all the magazines were shifted there. But it would take time to resume publication of the magazines, they were told. In the interim they could mark their attendance but not do very much.

I flew to Calcutta and met Aveek and Arup. They were mystified by the cause of the fire though some fire officials had told them that perhaps an accelerant had been used, which suggested arson. Nothing ever came of this theory and the fire remains a mystery.

I suggested to Aveek that he might want to look at this tragedy as an opportunity. Perhaps he could now prune the number of publications. If he was buying new presses perhaps he could invest in some high quality machines.

As for *Sunday*, I said, he had only two options. One was to improve the look of the magazine. The second was to sell it. The title still counted for something. Why not sell it to somebody who could afford to bring it out properly, something ABP had not been able to manage ever since the *Business Standard* debacle?

He insisted that, contrary to my pessimism (and to all the available evidence) ABP had more than enough money to resume all its operations and there was no reason for me to offer this advice. I thought he was blustering but I was slightly reassured by his confidence.

The staff of *Sunday* kept asking me when and if the magazine would resume. They had heard that ABP was planning to shut many of its magazines. Thanks to Aveek's claims, I was able to assure them that the rumours were wrong and that they were safe.

But, of course, the rumours were not wrong. ABP did close down the magazines making their journalists redundant. The staff of *Sunday* blamed me for offering reassurances that turned out to be wrong. They would have begun looking for other jobs had I not misled them.

I called Aveek and, for perhaps the first and only time in my life, lost my temper with him. He had made me lie to people who trusted me, I said.

He responded that at the time he had told me that the magazines would not be closed, no final decision had been taken. I said that if the subject was even being discussed, then he had lied to me by saying that there was no threat to the jobs of the journalists who worked at his magazines and by bragging about ABP's imaginary wealth.

Relations deteriorated even further when the *HT*'s Calcutta edition (the decision to launch in Calcutta had been taken before I joined and though I thought it was a mistake, I had to go ahead

and launch the edition anyway) was about to be established. The
Resident editor put the word out that the *HT* was looking for staff
and over half of ABP applied. I was reluctant to import an entire
team from a single organization so we turned most of them down.

But we did hire enough of them for Aveek to write a letter of
complaint to K.K. Birla, who replied to point out that many of ABP's
journalistic stars had also applied and we had decided not to hire
them out of consideration for Aveek. (In fact the only ABP star of
consequence who had not applied was Seema who had turned the
Telegraph's tedious Sunday supplement around and re-invented it as
Graphiti. In a few years' time, however, Aveek lost her too, through
his own stupidity; but that's another story!)

It got a little ugly and Aveek and I did not speak for at least a year
or more.

FORTY-THREE

THE (HINDUSTAN) TIMES,
IT IS A CHANGING . . .

Shortly before I joined the *HT*, Bharat Bhushan the executive editor, invited me to the office to meet the paper's editorial heads. I knew some of them and the others had bylines I was familiar with.

They were all aware that the *HT* was floundering commercially but they were of the view that this was a function of incompetent management. The *Times of India*, they said, was very well managed and therefore, was able to score over the *HT*, which was the much better paper.

Really, I asked. Did they think that the *HT* was the best paper in Delhi?

Oh no, said some of them. The best paper in Delhi was the *Indian Express*. So, I asked, would they want the *HT* to be more like the *Indian Express*? They said they would. In that case, I asked, what was stopping them? They gave vague excuses but clearly they had not given it much thought.

I said to Shobhana afterwards that I thought we had a problem on our hands. I loved the *Indian Express*. It was the first paper I read every morning. But it was a small-circulation, high-cover price paper, for people who were politically aware. The *HT*, on the other hand, sold over ten times as many copies and had, by definition, to appeal to a wider audience. Nor did I think that the smugness about the *Times of India* was warranted. There was a lot wrong with the *Times* but it was, certainly, a better paper than the *HT*.

Right after I joined, the *HT* hired a new CEO, Rajan Kohli. He came from outside the publishing business (fair enough, there were relatively few good managers in the newspaper business in that era) and, as far as I could tell, had no interest in newspapers or their content. I was not convinced he had ever read the *HT* or even, that he intended to. In any case, he had his work cut out for him because he said he wanted to hire a completely new team.

I knew that I would have to begin hiring too. But I adopted a slow-and-steady strategy on the grounds that the *HT* was like a giant ocean liner. You couldn't suddenly turn it around. You had to gently move direction. My idea was to begin the changes from the outside and work my way to the heart of the paper.

I had no choice but to look at the edit page immediately because that had been one of Narayanan's responsibilities. I thought that the quality of articles on the page was abysmally low and asked Amulya Ganguly, the very senior edit-page editor, how he thought we could attract a better quality or contributor.

Ganguly was frank. He had tried, he said. But too many of the people he had asked said that they did not read the *HT*. They thought of it, he said brutally, as a, 'West Delhi paper that people in South Delhi don't really bother with'. I said I thought this was unfair. Everybody who was anybody in political circles in Delhi read the *HT*.

But obviously there was something to what he said because he had tried hard to find better writers and had failed. So I began calling up people myself. Fortunately I was luckier than Ganguly had been and we soon managed to raise the level of the edit page pieces.

Generally, edit pages in India had three constituents. The primary components were the leaders, the actual edits that set out the paper's policy. The second was the middle, a sort of funny article that edit-page editors loved. I hated the middle which I thought was a tiresome waste of space and killed it at once to squeals of horror from all around. ('But even the *Times* has middles!') And then there were the articles, which people did read.

The edits/leaders themselves were different. I believed that less than 1 per cent of the paper's readers bothered with them and I could see why. In most papers, they were dull, statements of on-the-otherhandism, seeking to balance everything out and ending up saying nothing.

But they were regarded as the heart of each paper. At the *Times* and the *HT*, the chaps who actually brought out the paper sat in a grubby newsroom while the edit-page writers got cabins of their own. All they had to turn out were two or three 350-word edits a week, which they managed to do by tea time, after which they went home. They were paid well and at the *Times*, they preferred to hire Oxbridge graduates to perform this arduous task. It was the job the *Times* had first offered me when I was finishing at Oxford with a vague promise that I would rise up the ladder quickly. (This was long before I joined *Imprint* and met Samir Jain.)

I found the whole institution of the leader writer odd. First of all, there were the leaders themselves. Nobody wrote like that anywhere in the world, not even in England which had been the model for our edit pages. It was, as Ganguly conceded sadly, a dying art.

The leader writers rarely ventured out into the field or met anybody. They made it up as they went along. But they were possessive about their cabins. I tried once to get two of them to share a large cabin only to be told by one of them that this was out of the question. 'I have agoraphobia,' the man said.

'I am sorry,' I was puzzled. 'What do you mean?'

'Oh, I can't be in a place where there are people,' he responded.

Fighting back the unworthy urge to say, 'Well, you are in the wrong profession then, old boy,' I let him keep his cabin on medical grounds.

I was determined to change the style of the edits and since the whole edit-page institution seemed so Anglo-centric, I asked the leaders writers to read the *Guardian* and to model the edits on that style rather than the *Daily Telegraph* of the 1940s. This was more difficult than I thought it would be. So I wrote one or two edits a day myself and often rewrote the others. (It really wasn't that much work!) Bit by bit the old edit writers moved on and Indrajit Hazra, a gifted writer with a passion for rock music, took over the page and turned it around.

Next, I got to work on the supplements. The *Times* had started, largely by accident it seemed to me, a six-days-a-week supplement called *Delhi Times*. This was patterned on *Bombay Times* which had grown out of the ashes of a failed local newspaper called *The Metropolitan*.

Because the supplement grew out of a local paper, *Bombay Times* covered everything from the municipal corporation to crime to parties. *Delhi Times* followed that pattern.

At the *HT*, there had been a half-hearted attempt to respond with the creation of *HT City*, a *Delhi Times*–clone which came out three days a week. I recommended to Kohli that we make several changes to the format. First of all, the editor reported to the ad department, presumably on the grounds that the editor of *Delhi Times* was part of the ad department. I said that this was silly. The editor of *HT City* should be part of the *HT* editorial meeting, should report the Resident editor and should have the publication subject to the same standards of accountability as the rest of the paper.

Second, I said, three days a week made no sense. It had to be a daily publication. In fact, we had an opportunity because the *Times* did not produce *Delhi Times* on Sunday. We should make *HT City* seven-days-a-week.

Next, I suggested, we should throw out all the city reporting. There was already a lot of bad blood in the office because each time a local story broke, a reporter from the main paper (experienced, with contacts, etc.) would go to cover it only to find a person from *HT City* (just out of college; doing the job to kill time, etc.) was also covering the same story. The *HT City* person would file an inaccurate story and the reporters from the main paper would be blamed.

Why didn't we treat *HT City* as the second section of the paper, the one that had all the light stuff? Kohli agreed. And we were delighted when the *Times* followed our lead. Out went all the city news from *Delhi Times* and they began publishing it seven days a week.

I could have looked outside for an editor but I was quite determined not to hire too many people in the first few months to keep morale in the newsroom high. So I asked Sourish Bhattacharyya who edited the Sunday section if he would like to take over *HT City* and invent a new product. Sourish was excited by the idea and he proved to be a very good editor, creating the sort of publication that the *HT* had never seen before. Because he was already part of the editorial team, he fitted in easily at our editorial meetings and *HT City* was totally integrated with the rest of the paper.

I couldn't say this openly but I was trying to implement my own plan to completely transform the paper, step by step. I did not want it to be known as a Punjabi-paper (or 'West Delhi paper' to borrow Ganguly's damning phrase) that appealed to an older demographic.

The edit page was important because the writing needed to be crisp and energetic and contemporary. The edits were supposed to be the voice of the paper so they had to seem sophisticated and young. And *HT City* (which, throughout my time at the *HT* was vastly superior to *Delhi Times*—and still is, though I can't take any credit for that) appealed to a younger demographic and showed that we had made the shift to the new India of the twenty-first century.

None of this was enough. But it was a beginning.

FORTY-FOUR

ATLAS BIHAR VAMPIRE

Meanwhile, morale at the main paper continued to be low. The staff were politicized and divided into cliques and groups, each claiming that the editorial leadership played favourites. Most of the reporters were anti-BJP, which was fine. They had a right to their own political opinions. But when you have spent years cultivating contacts within the non-BJP establishment, imagining that the BJP will never come to power, it becomes harder to develop sources within the BJP. And yet, the BJP was now in power, so it was important to have an inside track.

That many of the reporters wrote badly was fine with me. Their job was primarily to get the stories. More worrying was that the desk, which was supposed to whip their copy into shape, either did not bother or did not know how to write English. Headlines were sloppily written, the articles were poorly put together and pages were made with no thought about the choice of photos or the placement of stories.

There were good people on the desk, headed by Ashok Kamath whom I had known from my ABP days. But Ashok lacked the staff to produce the paper he wanted and now he was being pushed to focus on the writing and the packaging.

The long-term solution was to hire better people. The short term solution was to rewrite. So I started rewriting much of page one myself and eventually we hired good people to take over the desk.

Ashok left us to join the *Times of India* and Avirook Sen (from *India Today*, but he had started his career at *Sunday*) took over.

After Bharat Bhushan left us for *Business Standard*, I stole Arun Roy Chowdhury who was the resident editor of the *Times of India*'s Delhi edition to perform the same job for us. (Shobhana and I agreed that since the editor's responsibilities now extended beyond the editorial page, the paper did not need an executive editor). Later, I hired V. Krishna (also from the *Times*) to look after design, forward planning and the out-of-town editions. This core team turned the paper around.

The out-of-town editors remained the subject of some internal debate. The *HT* had editions in Patna and Lucknow, neither of which did particularly well. Shobhana and I went and visited the Lucknow edition and decided to change editors, elevating Sunita Aaron, the paper's chief of reporting and news, to the job, which she then held for many years with great distinction. But while we tried our best, Patna was never the success we had hoped for.

Long before I joined, the *HT* management had planned a massive expansion. There would be new editions in Ranchi, Bhopal, Chandigarh, Calcutta and other cities. There were two arguments advanced for the expansion. The first made a certain amount of economic sense. Each time the company opened an edition of *Hindustan*, the group's Hindi daily, it cost only a little more to also open an *HT* edition in the same city. The second argument made no sense at all. Apparently, the *Times* would print copies of its Delhi edition in faraway cities and then claim that the Delhi edition sold massively, adding their non-Delhi sales to the tally. Now, *HT* wanted to do the same.

This plan had been in the works for several months and I thought it was a waste of money. There were no projections showing that any of these editions would make much money. I thought that the *HT* should save all this money and then launch a big bang entry into Mumbai with the money it had saved.

I discussed this with Rajan Kohli, believing that as these plans predated him, he might want to look at them again. Kohli asked if I thought any of the editions was worth launching. I said that I thought that Chandigarh would do well but that the others were bad ideas. Calcutta, in particular, would be difficult. The *Telegraph* was a strong number one and the *Times* had launched its own edition. Our only hope of fighting them both was to spend a lot of money— money that I thought we would be better off saving for a Mumbai edition.

Kohli said he would think about it but in the end he went along with the multi-edition plan. Either the process of launching the editions was too far gone for him to intervene or, like many managerial heads before him, he thought that a few small launches were easier to execute than the big one: the Mumbai edition.

We launched Chandigarh successfully with a good editor, Kanwar Sandhu, and an outstanding chief of bureau, Raveen Thukral. I was sure that the *HT* was set to eventually become the number one or number two paper in Chandigarh.

The other launches went okay but we realized that in smaller towns, technology could be a challenge. Shobhana and I were both in Bhopal when we noticed a headline on page one of the paper which read 'Atlas Bihar Vampire to visit Bhopal'. We read the story. It was about the prime minister. It turned out that the man who made the front page had decided to run a spell check programme on the page. So Atal Bihari Vajpayee became Atlas Bihar Vampire.

Sometimes, even the technology reflected the anti-BJP leanings of some of our staff!

Calcutta presented a particular challenge. Bharat Bhushan had already hired an experienced editor but I needed to hire the staff. All the old *Sunday* people wanted jobs. So, to my horror, did nearly the entire senior staff of the *Telegraph*. I was wary of importing wholesale the ABP culture with the organization's rivalries and prejudices into a newly launched venture so, to my regret, I had to turn down many talented people. But we built a good team headed by Rajiv Bagchi, my old deputy at *Sunday*, who eventually became editor of the edition.

Setting up the editions took up a lot of my time but, fortunately, the main edition was already showing signs of improvement. Thankfully, many people left so I did not have to sack anyone and we were able to hire first-rate replacements.

Morale improved too. In my first month at the *HT*, the editorial staff had been called to listen to an outside agency which had done extensive research into audience perceptions of the paper. The results were no surprise and by and large confirmed what I had already told K.K. Babu. The *Times* was seen as modern, sophisticated, pan-Indian, more comprehensive and better written while the *HT* was seen as old-fashioned, provincial, badly-written, etc.

The senior staff reacted with outrage, accused the agency of having got it totally wrong and the session quickly turned acrimonious. Afterwards they asked me what I thought. I answered with discretion and a certain economy of truth, that it was pointless getting agitated about surveys. They were just one measure of what a good paper was.

That still remained my view but surveys commissioned by the management some months after we started turning the paper around showed that perceptions were changing quicker than I had expected. We were no longer seen as the Punjabi alternative to the *Times*.

It helped that we had redesigned the paper so that it looked global and world class. Shobhana had long been a friend of Katharine Graham, owner of the *Washington Post*, and she asked Mrs Graham if the *Post* could help us with the design.

Mrs Graham sent over Michael Keegan, the *Post*'s design editor. He spent several weeks in Delhi with us, understood the needs of the paper and redesigned the *Hindustan Times* so that it still had enough of the *HT*'s character to look familiar but looked sleek enough to seem better designed than any Indian paper. (Later the *Times* also went in for a redesign.)

Our big gap remained political coverage. It helped, I think, that I knew many people in the government well. Apart from the PMO, I knew Jaswant Singh and Yashwant Sinha (both of whom alternated between the finance and foreign portfolios); George Fernandes was someone I knew and admired. I knew Advani, who was home minister, too but he already had contacts within our bureau; and everybody knew Arun Jaitley, a close friend of Shobhana's and a good friend of the paper.

Shobhana and I decided to promote Vinod Sharma, who had felt hard done by under the previous regime, to chief of the political

bureau. Pankaj Vohra, who was the best city editor in Delhi asked
to move to a national role and become political editor. All of them
worked hard to break stories.

But in 2000, I had a feeling that newspapers would have to do
more than just report news. Television was already a big part of our
lives and yet, many newspapers acted like it did not matter. I put
an editor from the desk in charge of monitoring the news channels
(there weren't many in those days) and asked him to brief us about
their headlines at the evening news meeting.

I told the staff that there was no point in just repeating what the
reader had already seen on the news. Our job was to provide context,
colour, commentary and analysis. Above all, we had to prove that
we knew more than the channels; that the *HT* always had the inside
track. We introduced new features like Behind the News, short six-
hundred-word stories, each with the reporter's picture and his byline
where we tried to explain what was really going on.

Before I joined the *HT*, well-wishers had called to warn that I
had no idea what I was getting into. The Birlas were different from
other employers, I was told. There would be constant interference in
news coverage.

I believed I knew K.K. Babu and Shobhana well enough to ignore
those warnings and I was right. I cannot recall a single instance
when Shobhana called me to kill a story or to carry something that
she wanted to promote. Both of us knew Sonia Gandhi and A.B.
Vajpayee so we were relatively neutral between parties and had no
agendas of our own. We both believed in a secular, liberal India. But
then, so did Vajpayee, so that was never a problem.

K.K. Babu was part of a generation that was used to political
interference in papers. He was persuaded to sack B.G. Verghese by
Indira Gandhi and wrote in his autobiography that he only hired
Khushwant Singh as editor because Sanjay Gandhi asked him to.

But not once did he interfere in the way I ran the paper. He
complained about stories but it was taken for granted that the
complaints were not commands. When politicians wrote him letters
of complaint about me, he sent them bland replies and forwarded
the correspondence to me. I always ignored them.

Even when what would now be called 'anti-national' stories appeared, my bosses stood by me. For instance, we covered a terrorist attack on a paramilitary camp in Kashmir that had resulted in civilian casualties. The late Jay Raina, himself a Kashmiri pandit and no friend of separatists, investigated the incident and discovered that many of the civilians had died in friendly fire, during the crossfire.

The story seemed sound so I put it on page one. All hell broke loose with people berating us for suggesting that civilians had died from bullets fired from the guns of paramilitary forces. I explained that it was not our position that the forces had fired on civilians but that the civilians had been caught in the crossfire.

Arun Jaitley told me the story was 'anti-national'. (I assume he said the same thing to Shobhana who was a much closer friend of his.) But neither K.K. Babu nor Shobhana stopped us from going ahead.

On another occasion we ran a campaign against the so-called Ansal Plaza encounter. The Delhi Police announced that they had foiled a terrorist attack on a shopping mall and had killed two terrorists. This was just before Diwali so L.K. Advani who, as home minister, was the ultimate boss of the Delhi police, took the credit and praised his men for protecting the citizens of Delhi from a bloody Diwali.

Except that we doubted that a terrorist attack had ever been planned. Witnesses said that the police brought two men who bore signs of injuries (as though they had been beaten up) to the parking lot of the mall and shot them.

We ran the developing story on page one for several days, pointing out inconsistencies in the police version and, in the process, turned Mr Advani's Diwali coup into a squalid little murder mystery.

Naturally, he complained. So did much of the government. Our police reporters were given a tough time by their contacts.

And yet, neither K.K. Babu nor Shobhana made any attempt to stop us.

With this kind of backing, I was able to hire good department heads for all of the paper. Pradeep Magazine, one of India's greatest and most honourable sportswriters, became sports editor.

Sandeep Bamzai revived our business section. Siddharth Zarabi introduced coverage of such sunrise sectors as telecom.

I noticed Yashwant Raj, who was then with the *Times*, when we were part of the PM's media party to Mauritius. He was easily the best reporter in the party and soon after, I stole him away to look after the Sunday paper, a job he performed with great distinction. Shobhana not only personally approved all the hiring but also approved competitive salaries which exceeded what the *Times* was offering.

K.K. Babu was intrigued by the new 'young people' (as he called them) I was hiring and at least twice, invited them to Birla House for tea. The meetings went well but there was a hiccup when Avirook Sen went to the wrong Birla House—the building where Gandhiji was shot, which is now a museum. He only realized that there might have been a mistake when they asked him to buy a ticket. He hastily retraced his steps and made it to our tea gathering a little late.

For most of us, I dare say, working at the *HT* in those days was pretty much the golden age of our careers. People still read newspapers. We had supportive employers. We were well paid. And we could write what we wanted.

FORTY-FIVE

'THE WRONG BALD OLD MAN'

For all of my time as the editor of the *Hindustan Times*, Atal Bihari Vajpayee was the prime minister. He was well-liked by the media though he rarely gave interviews. And while he often met journalists one-on-one, he remained enigmatic and Sphinx-like during these encounters, rarely divulging anything of note.

In contrast, L.K. Advani, who was home minister was far better organized. He gave interviews readily, was easily accessible to journalists, had his own media favourites who were guaranteed leaks from his office and could count on ministers in the government who kept referring journalists to him.

Vajpayee never said much about Advani (actually he never said much about anybody) but Advani was only too willing to talk about Vajpayee. He never once said anything remotely critical but he suggested that he was disturbed by what was going on in the PMO and his friends were only too ready to point fingers at Brajesh Mishra.

Advani's problem was that Mishra had emerged as the second most powerful man in the government, a role that Advani believed should be his. (As we joked at the time, the wrong bald old man got the job.)

Mishra's power derived only partly from Vajpayee. It had more to do with his own brilliance. Though he was a foreign service veteran, he soon worked out how the domestic administration worked. In the manner of Indira Gandhi's PMO, his officials gave orders to secretaries to the government directly, bypassing the ministers who were nominally in charge of the ministries. It was a risky gambit because Brajesh would have to accept responsibility if things went wrong but somehow they hardly ever did. Most ministers did not want to take tough decisions anyway and did not mind that their secretaries dealt directly with the PMO.

As national security advisor (a post he also held along with principal secretary), Mishra met with important officials in foreign governments and often undercut the authority of the foreign ministry. There was a clear clash and most foreign ministers (most notably Jaswant Singh) resented Mishra's role.

After the Kargil War, a report authored by the highly respected K Subrahmanyam made the reasonable recommendation that India deserved a national security advisor who was not also burdened with the responsibilities of a principal secretary. Mishra turned down the recommendation, referred snidely to Subrahmanyam's report as 'a job application' and continued to hold both jobs, with Vajpayee's backing.

Advani told me he had complained to Vajpayee about Brajesh's untrammelled exercise of power. And Brajesh, who presumably was aware of Advani's complaints about him, made no secret of his disdain for Advani.

In a way, this turf battle worked to keep the government free from RSS influences. Advani was the RSS's link with the government but as he had limited authority outside the home ministry, he was unable to saffronize the administration. Dr M.M. Joshi did some rewriting of history books but as Advani and Joshi were hardly on good terms, they could never unite.

In this way, Vajpayee managed to run a BJP government that kept the Hindutva ideology away from matters of policy and day to day administration. No one bothered too much about the Ram temple or about the Uniform Civil Code. And on Kashmir, Vajpayee actually reached out to Kashmiris and aligned with Farooq Abdullah whose son Omar became one of the brightest young ministers in the government.

Advani responded by making his own foreign trips and charting out his own agenda. According to Brajesh (who told me the story),

Advani was invited to the White House on a trip to the US. As he was not head of government, he could not call on President George W. Bush so the White House arranged a staged 'chance encounter' (common in the US), whereby Bush would walk into a meeting Advani was having with a high official.

Apparently, Bush asked Advani if India would send troops to join the US effort in Iraq and Advani, taken by surprise, and eager not to give offence, said of course we would.

When he returned to India, the US followed up on the request.

Vajpayee had no intention of sending troops but had to extricate the government from Advani's commitment. So Brajesh spoke to the Congress and asked if the party could write to the prime minister protesting the suggestion that India would participate in the US war effort.

Such a letter was duly sent. Vajpayee then asked for a meeting with Sonia to discuss her objections and the government then briefed the press about the lack of political consensus over the proposal. Next it used the meeting to explain to Washington that as much as it would like to help, there was too much domestic opposition to the idea.

I have never asked Advani for his version but if this story is true (and I think it probably is) it shows us how the opposition and the government worked together on foreign policy and national security issues. The usual channel was Natwar Singh whom Brajesh knew well and whom Sonia Gandhi trusted.

When Vajpayee wanted P.C. Alexander to be the consensus candidate for president, Sonia Gandhi objected. This came as a surprise to Vajpayee and nearly everyone else as Alexander had been Mrs Indira Gandhi's principal secretary (and for a while, Rajiv's too). But Sonia was unyielding (I have never figured out why) and so Natwar Singh and Brajesh agreed that Vice President Krishan Kant would be elevated instead. This news was conveyed to the vice president who was delighted. Except that Advani objected and his supporters within the government opposed the appointment.

Eventually Chandrababu Naidu suggested A.P.J. Kalam, a name that no one had any objection to and Kalam duly became the consensus candidate. But this was too much for poor Krishan Kant who had a heart attack and died, the only vice president of India to have died in office.

Was Advani's objection to Kant based on his antipathy to Brajesh and the fact that he had been kept out of the selection process? Or was he keen that the job should go to a BJP loyalist? (Though Kalam hardly fit that description.) Those were the questions that were keenly discussed during that period.

Advani asserted himself again over Narendra Modi. In 2001, the BJP leadership in Delhi felt that the chief minister of Gujarat, Keshubhai Patel, was performing poorly (especially in his handling of an earthquake in Bhuj) and decided to replace him. As the Gujarat BJP was faction-ridden it was decided to send someone from Delhi to replace Keshubhai.

Modi was not an obvious choice. He was a lifelong RSS worker who had been sent by the Sangh to the BJP in 1985 and became a well-liked party insider, rising to become general secretary. But he had no administrative experience and had not been included in the central government.

Vajpayee took a chance and agreed to send him to Gujarat. At first Modi performed extremely well, working hard to help Kutch recover from the earthquake. But when the riots broke out in 2002, it was widely alleged that the state administration and police failed to protect Muslims. There were two explanations. The first was that Modi was new to the job and was not able to impose his authority on the administration. The other was that he had not wanted to protect the Muslims.

Vajpayee, who had kept his government free of Hindu–Muslim politics, took the line that the experiment of sending the untested Modi to Gujarat had failed. He wanted Modi back in Delhi, either in the government or as general secretary.

In April 2002, the BJP held a meeting of its national executive in Goa by which time Vajpayee's mind was fully made up. He would ask Modi to accept some other responsibility and make the announcement at the meeting, allowing Modi to save face.

How Modi knew that this is what was planned is a subject of some dispute. It is possible he guessed after Vajpayee had been less than warm to him during a post-riots visit to Gujarat. Or it is possible that Advani told him.

Either way, he pre-empted Vajpayee by announcing his resignation at the start of the meeting. Various BJP ministers including Pramod Mahajan and Arun Jaitley urged Modi to reconsider. Others who knew that Vajpayee wanted him out of Gujarat hesitated till Advani threw his weight behind Modi. That tipped the scales and Vajpayee, who was not a confrontationist, retreated. Modi was 'persuaded' to withdraw his resignation and returned to Gujarat in triumph.

The incident caused a strain in the relationship between Vajpayee and Advani but Vajpayee had reconciled himself to the fact that the party was Advani's area. On one of the rare occasions when he spoke candidly about his feelings, he said to me that he was fed up and wanted to retire. 'Let Advani look after the party,' he said, with a trace of bitterness.

I never knew what had brought this on because Vajpayee rarely expanded on his pronouncements. But you could sometimes sense that the strain of managing the party, keeping the sangh at bay and handling the government were taking their toll.

Yet, for all this, Vajpayee and Advani had a close one-on-one relationship that nobody else seemed to understand. They had been friends for decades and had even shared a flat. My own sense was that Advani hero-worshipped Vajpayee to the extent that he was resentful of anyone else who came close to the old man. (Perhaps that included Vajpayee's foster family whom he never seemed keen on and whom journalists close to him would frequently attack.)

There was no doubt that Advani had been the junior partner in the relationship for most of their lives and I always suspected that Vajpayee resented him for that brief post–rath yatra period when Advani acted like he was number one. I guess that this was why Vajpayee never trusted him fully and relied on men like Brajesh.

And yet, Vajpayee also had to perform a balancing act. After I had once recorded a TV interview with Advani, Vajpayee asked me what Advani had said when the cameras were not rolling. I said he had spent his time complaining about Brajesh. Vajpayee was quiet for a while. Finally, he said, *'Is mein Brajesh ki bhi galti hain.'*

He did not expand on the pronouncement but I learned that day that it was a mistake to believe that Vajpayee necessarily endorsed everything Brajesh said or did. Vajpayee was his own man. Nobody spoke for him.

One fine day, to the consternation of many of those who were close to him, Vajpayee made Advani deputy prime minister. This was a courtesy title that conferred no authority on the holder but it held a special meaning for Advani because he wanted to model himself on Sardar Patel, and this had been Patel's title under Nehru.

Obviously, Vajpayee had told Advani he was giving him the job because an item speculating about Advani's promotion appeared in a newspaper, written by a journalist who was considered to have good sources in Advani's circle.

It was a measure of how Vajpayee operated that Brajesh laughed the item off. A journalist was briefed by Brajesh that this was mere kite flying and that no such proposal was in the works. The report, attributed to highly placed sources, led to no response from the Advani camp which led me to believe that it might be true. Perhaps Vajpayee had told Advani to keep quiet about it.

Sure enough when the announcement was made, many people who believed that they were close to Vajpayee were astonished. I was told later that Vajpayee had bypassed Brajesh and asked Ashok Saikia, an old friend of his, who also occupied a senior position in the PMO, to type out the letter to the President, not even going through his own private secretaries.

Why did he make Advani deputy prime minister?

I don't believe he was under pressure from anyone to give Advani the job. By now, Vajpayee was enough of a national figure to disregard what the RSS said.

I think he genuinely wanted to give Advani something he had always longed for. At the time, it was widely believed that the Congress was washed up and that the BJP would win the next election, due in 2004. So, I reckon, Vajpayee wanted to lead the party into the election, win it, return as prime minister and then give up the job in a year or so, letting Advani take over. The promotion to deputy prime minister was part of that grand plan.

Relations between the Vajpayee camp and the Advani camp did not significantly improve after Advani's promotion. Nor did Advani's elevation make any difference to Brajesh's position. He still ran the government in Vajpayee's name. By now, he had come to understand Vajpayee's mind so well that he could often guess what Vajpayee wanted him to do even without being told.

In 2001, when terrorists attacked parliament in Delhi, their original plan had been to take everyone inside the building hostage. This would have included Vajpayee, Advani and most of the cabinet.

Had the plan succeeded (it did not; they were all shot dead), many wondered, what would have happened? Who would have run the government of India?

Natwar Singh summed up the prevailing sentiment when he joked: 'Oh, it would have made no difference. Brajesh Mishra would have just continued running the government of India.'

Obviously, this was too vast an estimation of Brajesh's role in the government. But it does say something about the authority that Brajesh exercised and the awe his exercise of his powers inspired.

FORTY-SIX

THE MAN WHO FARTED AT A FUNERAL

I had always refused to travel abroad with the prime minister because I thought it was a mug's game. As I have explained earlier, the way it worked was that the prime minister and his family stayed in a private cabin that was created for them near the front of a specially reconfigured Air India 747 Jumbo Jet. This cabin, which included a bedroom, took up all of what was usually business class. There was a first class section at the front which was reserved for members of the delegation. The upper deck, configured with business class seats, was taken over by Air India officials.

The media, security, etc. all sat at the back in the economy class area which they were not allowed to leave. Though, theoretically, they were on the same aircraft as the prime minister, it was rare for the media to meet anybody of consequence let alone the PM himself.

Vajpayee changed all that. He kept the PM's cabin and the first class seating for the delegation but he had much of the plane reconfigured with business class seating for the media and a few other officials. Unlike other prime ministers, he would come to the media section at the start of each trip and say hello. There would nearly always be a press conference on board when we were returning to Delhi.

The real advantage for the media though was that Brajesh Mishra opened up the first class section. Journalists could come and go pretty much as they liked, could chat with the ministers and senior officials on board or even, have a relaxed drink or two with cabinet ministers.

Not only did this give journalists a chance to build relationships with sources but often we got stories out of the delegation. For instance, the bureau in Delhi had picked up whispers that Vajpayee was going to meet Naga rebel leaders in Osaka, Japan. We had no confirmation of this (so far) secret meeting so I told the desk that I would try and find out if any meeting was planned while I was on the plane. I got Brajesh to confirm it, phoned in the story when we landed and the bureau had a scoop.

On another occasion, on the flight to Mauritius, we waited for the result of a trust vote in Bihar to come in. Everyone in the PM's delegation looked anxious and we realized only later that Air India One, as the plane was styled, had no contact with anyone on the ground except for Air Traffic Control towers in the countries it flew over. There could have been a nuclear attack in Mumbai and the Prime Minister would not have known about it till the plane landed.

Yashwant Raj of the *Times of India*, picked up on this and filed a story as we landed and eventually, the government of India equipped the plane with satellite phones. (I hired Yashwant for the *HT* soon after!)

Once we got on the ground, the media's closeness to power usually evaporated a little. The delegation always stayed in a very nice hotel. The media were stuck in some Holiday Inn–style place, which may have been just as well as we had to pay for our own rooms and food and many newspaper proprietors complained about how expensive it was to send journalists on the PM's plane.

The advantage of staying in the media hotel was that it was equipped with a media centre, full of computers, free dedicated phone lines, etc. The man in charge of the media was the joint secretary, external publicity, usually abbreviated to JS (XP), who was also the official spokesman of the government of India. He kept us informed of what was going on and arranged interviews with senior officials. From time to time, ministers would drop in and brief us.

I enjoyed the trips and I began enjoying them even more when my friend Ramu Damodaran told me that I could ask Air India to change the date of my return ticket. When he was PS to PM (Narasimha Rao), Ramu had seen this done for officials. Instead of

taking say, the flight from New York to Delhi on the PM's plane, I
could stay on (at my own expense) for a couple of days, and file a
few feature or colour pieces. I soon made this a routine, staying on in
cities where Air India had flights and eventually, staying on anyway
and buying my own tickets back to Delhi.

This way, I got to see Moscow, Shanghai, Tokyo and many other
cities I had never been to before. If I was lucky, I would persuade the
media hotel to continue to give me the same discounted rate it had
given the Indian embassy and so, costs were not unmanageable.

That was one reason I enjoyed the trips. Staying on in Tokyo
meant I had an opportunity to discover Japan and to be able to come
back and write knowledgably about Japanese food. Touring Shanghai
on my own helped me realize how far ahead of us China really was.
And because most Indian prime ministers went to New York every
year for the United Nations General Assembly, this became an
annual pilgrimage for me. I kept going even after Manmohan Singh
became PM.

The advantage with Vajpayee was that he was willing to let his
hair down (to the extent that any prime minister can let his hair
down on an official trip) and enjoy the city he was in. The PM's
party usually included one or two senior chefs from the Taj group
(Satish Arora, Hemant Oberoi, Ananda Solomon, Julia DeSa, etc.)
who could rustle up great Indian food for any foreign visitor who
came to see Vajpayee. But the PM liked going out to restaurants and
moving out of his suite.

On many trips, he would take a few journalists with him and
go to a restaurant. (Usually, a Chinese restaurant.) It was a rare
opportunity to see Vajpayee in a relaxed setting and once or twice he
was less discreet than usual.

Some trips were truly memorable. I remember getting off the
plane in Jamaica, still slightly buzzed from the inflight bubbly, to
find that there was a red carpet on the tarmac, lined on both sides
with women jiggling their hips as a Bob Marley song played loudly
over loudspeakers. They had beer on the coach that took us to our
hotel and most of the media party cracked open a can, courtesy of
the Jamaican government.

The prime minister's party stayed at Half Moon Bay, one of the Caribbean's great resorts, but the media were put up in an all-inclusive three star beach resort. Obviously, nobody had told the hotel management that when Indian journalists see the phrase 'all inclusive', they check to see if this includes booze. And when they find it does, they forget all about the summit that Vajpayee was there to attend.

The delegation has to get on with its work of course, but on that trip, ministers were a little taken aback by the happy mood the media exhibited. When Jaswant Singh (who was then foreign minister) arrived to give a briefing, the JS (XP) thought it might be a good idea to hold it on the beach. By some coincidence, it was next to a Pina Colada bar ('all inclusive') and the journos were even happier than usual by the time Jaswant walked on to the beach.

The JS (XP) asked Singh if he would have a drink too. The foreign minister looked disdainfully at the Pina Colada bar and said 'I'll have some claret'. (Claret is the old English term for red wine from the French wine region of Bordeaux.) This threw the hotel into a tizzy but eventually a bottle of some cheap, third-rate plonk was produced.

Jaswant insisted on having a little poured into his glass so he could taste it. He had one lingering sip and then, with the air of a master sommelier tasting a Petrus, he declared, 'a bit young'.

To me, that encounter kind of summed up the two worlds—that of the media and that of the delegation.

There were other fun times too. One of Vajpayee's state visits to the US coincided with the end of Bill Clinton's term. Clinton threw a banquet for him but because it was the last big party the Clintons would ever throw in the White House, there was a huge clamour for tickets to the extent that the *Washington Post* even wrote an article about it.

I got an invitation as part of the Indian press party and was childishly excited to wander around the White House. Too many people had wanted to attend so the Clintons had put up a huge tent in the garden to host the party and we were driven there in shuttle buses, passing the windows of the Oval Office on our way there.

Every notable Indian who lived in the US had been invited. (Fareed Zakaria, Vijay Amritraj, etc.) and I shared a bench on the shuttle with Deepak Chopra, whom I knew. Deepak introduced me to the man sitting in front and said to me, 'Of course, you know him.'

Except that I didn't. So, in a little voice, I asked 'And you are . . .?'

'Night Shyamalan,' he said.

This was just after the Sixth Sense had been one of the biggest global hits!

The dinner was fine (the food was rubbish) but the real excitement came afterwards when guests were invited back to the White House for coffee. Most of the Indian delegation left but I hung around, discovering how different things were in America.

In India, at the end of every banquet, whether it is thrown by the president or the prime minister, the hosts leave and the guests make desultory conversation as they file out through an open door.

But here, the Clintons treated us as guests in their home. Bill Clinton came up to me and asked if I was enjoying myself. He introduced Hillary. I told her that I had just seen her debate her opponent in the New York senate race.

'Wasn't she great?' said Bill.

I said she was and we chatted for a few minutes before they moved on to their other guests. They had no clue who I was but felt, as hosts, that they had to put their guests at ease.

I noticed this in other countries too. While their banquets were much more egalitarian and gracious, ours tended to be hierarchical and stilted. At a party thrown for Manmohan Singh in London, the entire British Cabinet and lots of very famous Brits walked around and spoke to everyone. Everyone wore name tags, even Margaret Thatcher who said she had come because of 'my love for India'. At a banquet in Tokyo, I sat next to the chairman of Sony who told me how appalled he was that the prime minister of Japan was serving such bad food to the leader of a friendly country.

I did my share of Indian banquets under four or five prime ministers. They were nearly all held at Hyderabad House where the food was catered by the Indian Tourism Development Corporation

(ITDC) and was rarely better than mediocre. You got to meet the prime minister and his guest in the reception line but then they disappeared to a cordoned off area and you never had a chance to talk to them. Rashtrapati Bhavan was better because you had an opportunity to mingle at the start of the dinner before you moved into the main dining room. But journos came low down in the Rashtrapati Bhavan pecking order so we were always put at the end of the table with the president's staff.

The food and service were usually terrible. And when one of our presidents (I shall be discreet and not name him) announced that in future his kitchen would make one dish from the visiting head of state's country to make him feel at home, I groaned inwardly. Clearly, they were not satisfied with murdering our own cuisine and wanted to murder the cuisine of the poor chief guest's country as well.

Still, I was lucky to be invited. At a banquet for the Queen and Prince Philip (no, she did not ask me if I 'had come far' when I was presented to her!), I ended up next to the Buckingham Palace press secretary who (in the eyes of Rashtrapati Bhavan protocol officers) ranked low enough to sit with the journos. He had been on the Prince of Wales's staff during the publication of Andrew Morton's *Diana: Her True Story* and had wonderful tales to tell about Prince Diana. ('She could just sit there and lie and lie so convincingly . . .')

Vajpayee shifted the larger banquets to hotel ballrooms. I attended one for Clinton where George Fernandes motioned me over and said that one of the guests on their table had not turned up so would I mind filling the empty space. Brajesh Mishra was on the table along with Sandy Berger, Clinton's national security advisor, and it was fascinating to hear them chat informally.

The most significant event I attended however, was not in Delhi or London or Washington. It was breakfast in Agra as the guest of General Musharraf.

Unlike many north Indian (that is, Punjabi) journalists, I have no particular interest in Pakistan. Even Bangladesh seems more interesting to me. I can understand people who come from Partition families wanting to light candles at the Wagah border and say things like 'we are really the same people, yaar' but I don't think we are the same people—at least not any longer.

I liked Benazir and I have interviewed Imran Khan but they appealed to me as people, not as leaders of a country I was fascinated by. Besides, Pakistani presidents have a strange and annoying habit of arranging breakfast meetings with journalists and I am never at my best at breakfast.

I once went to a breakfast meeting with journos organized by the Pakistani embassy for President Leghari. The Indian journos treated him with so much warmth that Leghari felt obliged to tell us how Kashmir was really a part of Pakistan.

When it was my turn to ask a question, I asked Leghari if he did not think there was a contradiction between his talk of self-determination and his claim that Kashmir belonged to Pakistan. Surely, if the Kashmiris had the right to self-determination, then they could choose to stay with India or even opt for independence?

Leghari was firm. No independence, he said. We have a two-nation theory in the subcontinent. They can only come to Pakistan. All the other Indian journos were horrified by my impertinence and looked at me as though I had farted loudly at a funeral.

So I was not excited about the Agra Summit between Vajpayee and General Pervez Musharraf, Pakistan's dictator du jour. I thought the summit was a bad idea. It had been Advani's brainwave to invite Musharraf and everybody I knew in the foreign ministry was pretty sure that nothing would come of it. Usually, a lot of legwork (some of it Track II) goes into a summit before the leaders meet and officials have a pretty good idea of what the end result will be. This time, both sides were flying blind.

I attended Vajpayee's banquet for Musharraf which was notable only for a loud political argument between two Indian guests (Tavleen Singh and Renuka Choudhary) and for the tendency of Ardeshir Cowasjee, an elderly but extremely sprightly Pakistani columnist, to kiss all the women present on their cheeks. When he got to Sonia Gandhi, she refused flatly to be kissed saying, 'I am an Indian woman', and Cowasjee retreated, disappointed.

I was so convinced that the summit would be a waste of time that I asked the political bureau to cover it, saying that there was no need for editors to be present. But Vinod Sharma, the chief of bureau, and Pankaj Vohra, our political editor, were adamant. Every other editor was going, they said. How would it look if the *HT* was not represented at that level?

Grumbling all the way, I drove to Agra and discovered that Musharraf had invited Indian editors to breakfast. (Another bloody breakfast meeting!) I sat next to Prannoy Roy and we watched in horror as Musharraf went around the table asking editors if they had anything to ask him. One by one, the editors told him what a wonderful chap he was, how much they loved Pakistan and how thrilled they were to meet him.

My old friend Vinod Mehta, a dedicated Pakistan-loving Punjabi even said to Musharraf. 'Sir, I support you so much that in India they call me your man!'

As the president went around the room, I knew I would once again be the man-who-farted-at-a-funeral. When it was my turn, I said to Musharraf that we all knew that he was the architect of Kargil. Why on earth should we trust him now?

Musharraf bristled. 'Trust. Trust,' he said. 'This question should have been asked before you invited me here. Not after.'

Fair enough. But I was not the one who had invited him. When it was Prannoy's turn, he said that he found it odd that though Musharraf made so many references to the wishes of the people of Kashmir, he himself was an unelected leader. (He had seized power in a coup.) Didn't he see the contradiction?

Musharraf got even angrier and the breakfast ended on a sour note, which pleased me no end, because I was so annoyed by the sycophancy so many Indian editors had lavished on this devious dictator.

On my way out, my phone rang. It was Brajesh. Had Musharraf said anything offensive at the breakfast, he asked. Well, no more than usual, I said. Did he talk about peace, Brajesh continued. Not at all, I said. He restated Pakistan's position on every issue while the assembled journos looked on adoringly.

Earlier, at the breakfast, Prannoy had asked me if I noticed that a single TV camera in the centre was recording the breakfast. I said I had.

'What do you think they will do with the footage?' Prannoy asked. I said I thought they would put it on some Pakistani channel to show that Indian journalists loved Musharraf much more than Pakistani journalists did.

'Do you think they will give us a copy of the tape?' Prannoy wondered.

I said I did not see why not.

At the end of the breakfast, Prannoy went up to the Pakistani delegation and asked for the tape. Clearly they agreed to give it to him because in no time at all, NDTV was broadcasting the recording of the breakfast.

The summit failed, of course. That was always going to happen. The Indian side blamed it on Musharraf's attitude at the breakfast which I found odd. The general knew that the breakfast would be played on Pakistan TV. He was hardly going to sound soft and conciliatory in front of his domestic constituency.

The Pakistanis blamed Advani for the failure of the summit. Vajpayee, they said, was a peace-loving man but Advani was a hardliner.

This suited Advani perfectly. His camp portrayed him as the tough guy who was shocked by the proposed Joint Declaration because it made no reference to cross-border terrorism. Vajpayee, they suggested, was a peace-loving wimp.

In the confusion, people forgot that the summit had been Advani's idea. Musharraf cancelled a planned visit to Ajmer to visit the *dargah* and flew back immediately to Pakistan.

And I never ever agreed to attend another breakfast meeting with a Pakistani leader again.

FORTY-SEVEN

TONY NEVER FORGETS A FACE

The *Hindustan Times* Summit was Shobhana's idea. My sole contribution was to change the name, a couple of years down the line, to include the word Summit instead of the cumbersome 'Leadership Initiative' which had been the original name.

Shobhana had travelled to many conferences around the world and was determined to start similar ventures in India. The *International Herald Tribune*'s Luxury Conference inspired her to start the *HT* Luxury Conference, which did well as long as India was perceived as a luxury market.

But she also wanted to do something more weighty, a conference where India's leaders would face an invited audience. And we would also get top global leaders. This was harder to do because heads of government could only visit India as guests of the Indian government. So, we contented ourselves with seeking out people who had just stepped down from high office.

For the first Summit (though it wasn't called that then), we persuaded Vajpayee to give the inaugural address. More significantly, we also got Sonia Gandhi to come and answer questions from the audience. I anchored both sessions and though Vajpayee was the major figure whom people had lined up to see, the surprise was Sonia who came across as relaxed, smart and willing to answer questions about anything at all.

Shobhana had decided that we would tightly restrict entry so we refused to sell tickets and invited only those we felt would make the most of the opportunity. We persuaded the Tatas to sponsor the first Summit which meant we more or less broke even. And in future years, so many companies lined up to be associated with the Summit that eventually it even became a profit centre: all this without selling a single ticket.

In the years when I was associated with the *HT*, I anchored several sessions with prime ministers, party leaders (Sonia became a regular) and celebrities (Roger Moore, Shahrukh Khan, Sanjay Dutt, Ajay Devgan, etc.) and all of them were fun. But the ones that linger in my memory were the ones with world leaders, and former world leaders.

We had three former British prime ministers in a row. John Major was a very nice fellow, read out a very worthy speech and signed autographs. But sadly, he did live up to his reputation as being a bit of a grey man.

Tony Blair was one of the all-time hits of the Summit. I had met him before, when he was still prime minister and he had given me an interview. In the course of that interview, he said, 'We have met before, haven't we?'

I said we hadn't.

'No, I am sure we have,' he insisted.

I said that I had come to 10 Downing Street as part of Manmohan Singh's media party and had asked him a question but that hardly counted.

'Ah yes, I remember,' he said.

I found this a little incredible and put it down to good PR.

I told the story to one or two people who knew him (Jack Straw, who had been a member of his cabinet, and another former associate of Blair's) and to my surprise, both thought that Blair had been telling the truth. 'You don't know Tony,' they said. 'He never forgets a face.'

When Blair arrived at the Summit, he knew all about me and remembered our interview. Well, obviously, he has been briefed, I thought to myself.

That evening, the day before Blair was to speak, he came to the *HT* Summit party which was a large gathering (at least 200 people in the garden of the Taj Palace) and I took him around, introducing him to various guests. Later, Cherie and he hung around for ten minutes chatting to my son and to the senior staff of the *HT* (around twenty-five people).

Everyone thought he was bright, charming and witty (all true) while Cherie was the candid one. At one stage, Blair said, 'People don't realize this but I am also a foodie.'

'Really,' I said. 'I always thought of Gordon Brown as being the foodie in your cabinet'.

At which Cherie interrupted. 'Foodie? No. He just eats a lot.'

Blair shot her a warning look and said 'Cherie!' She stopped but it was clear she could have gone on. It was clear that the Blairs had no time for Tony's successor.

Blair made a terrific speech. Almost from the time he got up to speak, he had the audience eating out of the palm of his hand. (I asked him later about his technique. He said he had modelled it on stand-up comedians. 'They let the audience know who is boss in the first five minutes. Otherwise, it's over for them. It is the same with public speaking.')

Afterwards, we took audience questions and to my horror, I saw that my son Raaj, had put his hand up. Reluctantly, I asked Raaj what his question was (he had just gone up to University in Montreal that year) and to my relief, he asked a sensible and cogent question.

Neither Raaj nor I let on that we were related and tried to keep this as impersonal as ever but to my surprise, Blair had recognized him. 'That's a good question,' he said. 'Better than the ones your dad has been asking . . .'

Later, in the green room, Blair surprised me even more by recognizing the members of *HT* staff he had met the previous night. He recognized Pradeep Magazine at once and said, 'Ah, the sports editor,' before launching into small talk with him.

So maybe it was true. Tony Blair never forgets a face.

Often, when you meet leaders up close, you discover that you have to leave your political prejudices behind. I loathed George W. Bush's politics and when I anchored a session with him, I was not terribly impressed with his replies to my questions.

But, at a personal level, he was a perfect gentleman, courteous, gracious and humble. He went out of his way to make everyone

around him feel at ease. He joked easily with guests at the party and
after he had checked out of his suite, his butler gave us two letters, one
addressed to Shobhana and the other to me. Mine was handwritten
(as I imagine hers was too), thanked me for the *HT*'s hospitality,
praised Raaj whom he had met at the party, and said how much he
had enjoyed our session.

In all the years I anchored sessions at the Summit, not one other
world leader did anything like that.

Blair's successor, Gordon Brown, came to the Summit a few
months after he had lost the general election and I anchored his
session. He was bitter about his defeat, bitter about Nick Clegg, the
leader of the Liberals who had aligned with the Conservative party
and angry with Blair.

Blair's memoir, *A Journey: My Political Life*, of his years in office
had just come out and his portrayal of Brown clearly hurt. I asked
Brown how accurate the book was. Was he really a bruiser who made
life impossible for Blair?

Brown rubbished the book. It was gossip, he said. Prime
ministers shouldn't waste time on gossip. They should be concerned
with policy. He was working on a book of his own. It would be only
about policy, he declared loftily.

There was no doubt that he was a very intelligent man with a
great grasp of economic issues. But he was also deeply uncharismatic
and the session was a flop.

Sometimes there were funny moments in the green room. Kamal
Nath, who was India's commerce minister was late for a session with
Christine Lagarde, who was then a French minister. (This was before
she went off to head the International Monetary Fund.) I knew
Lagarde slightly from a previous encounter so I was not surprised
when she said, 'Let's give Kamal a good scare.' As soon as we were
told that Nath had entered the building, Lagarde went and locked
herself in the bathroom.

Kamal Nath bustled in, said hello to me and asked, 'Where's
Christine?'

I said, as Lagarde and I had agreed beforehand, 'I am very sorry
Kamal but she has left. She said she was not going to waste time

doing a session with a man who couldn't even be bothered to turn up on time.'

The colour drained from Nath's face. 'But, but,' he spluttered, 'it wasn't my fault. I got held up . . .' And on and on he went.

Eventually, once he had run out of steam, I knocked on the bathroom door and Lagarde appeared. 'Gave you a shock, didn't we?' she laughed.

And sometimes there were political ramifications that I wasn't fully aware of the time. When the Indo-US nuclear deal was the hot subject of the day (more about this later), I asked Sonia Gandhi the obvious questions about the deal.

The Left had said it would withdraw support to the government if the deal went through. Did she really think it was worth risking the future of the government over the deal?

We all knew the answer. Sonia had overcome her objections to the deal but she did not think it should be a make-or-break issue for a coalition that had been held together with such difficulty. And she said as much.

I learned many years later, from Sanjaya Baru's book, *The Accidental Prime Minister*, that Manmohan Singh was watching the session live on TV. According to Baru, he was disheartened and disappointed by her answer to this question.

If this is actually what happened, then I am surprised because by this time, Singh knew what Sonia's views were. Nor was my question 'pre-arranged' as Sanjaya claimed. It was the obvious question about the big political issue of the day. Anybody would have asked it and any politician would have expected the question.

Anyhow, according to *The Accidental Prime Minister*, my exchange with Sonia was enough for the prime minister of India to rethink what he had to say about the deal. When I asked him, during his session, about the nuclear deal, he said that even if it didn't go through, it was not the end of the world, which seemed like a reasonable enough response.

But Sanjaya may have a point. After that, Manmohan Singh never agreed to let a journalist anchor his session. He agreed to come if someone he could count on—in one year, Baru himself—would ask the questions.

FORTY-EIGHT

BEFORE 'EDITORITIS' SETS IN . . .

Though I had reviewed restaurants for *Bombay* magazine and then briefly for the *Sunday Observer*, my career as a food writer had ground to a halt by 1986. I was still interested in food, of course. A large part of my travel was prompted by food and, all too often, my memories of cities and countries were wrapped up with the food I had eaten.

But as the new century dawned, I had a sense that food was going to be big in India. The liberalization of 1991 had changed many things but the fruits of the new prosperity were only now reaching the middle class. I believed that as people began to earn more, they would spend their money on food and travel. There would, I predicted, be a boom in hotels. New restaurants would open. Private airlines would begin flying to foreign destinations bringing the real cost of air travel down. And the media's focus on a handful of (mostly Delhi-based) fashion designers would have to shift as the global luxury and fashion brands would enter the Indian market.

When we launched the new *HT City*, I said as much to Sourish Bhattacharya. He could find people to cover all the other areas that would boom but I wanted him to handle food himself because India was desperately short of good food and wine writers.

When we began to revamp the Sunday supplement, now edited by Poonam Saxena, whom I had pulled out of *HT City*, I suggested a two-pronged approach. There would be, I said, good columnists who covered food, drink, fashion, etc. at a slightly more elevated level than *HT City* was doing but the supplement would gain traction only if it had good feature stories that people enjoyed reading on a Sunday when they could spend more time on the paper. My advice to Poonam was: get good columnists so you don't have to worry about food, gadgets, fashion, etc. and spend your time planning and commissioning good feature stories.

I had been arguing, anyway, that we should introduce a Sunday magazine rather than a broadsheet supplement. The management countered by saying that advertising came in the broadsheet size. I responded that India had many magazines. Surely, they managed to get advertising in the right size.

While this debate was going on, two things happened. We launched a new broadsheet Sunday supplement which was a great hit and we did launch a magazine, called *Brunch*, to be distributed free with the Calcutta edition. My arguments won the day in Calcutta because we were up against *Graphiti*, the hugely popular Sunday magazine of the *Telegraph*. (The *Telegraph* had always published a Sunday magazine but this very successful *Graphiti* avatar had been conceived of and was edited by Seema Goswami, which led to some interesting moments at home.)

Once *Brunch* had taken off in Calcutta and our broadsheet supplement was a success in Delhi, it was easier to argue for *Brunch* in Delhi. But the management had a valid objection. The *HT* was now the top-selling newspaper in Delhi. Were we going to give away lakhs of free copies of *Brunch*? It was okay to do it in Calcutta but Delhi, with its huge circulation, was a different matter entirely.

Meanwhile, I had become a contributor to the broadsheet Sunday supplement. It had run into a pre-release problem. Poonam had found all her columnists except for one. Nobody seemed right for the food column. I asked her to go beyond journos and to find some arrogant bon vivant who would have no hesitation in rubbishing restaurants. I asked her to check out London's *Sunday Times* where the film director Michael Winner wrote such a column.

No luck. She still couldn't find anyone.

Finally, I agreed to do it myself. But, I said, I would only do it for the first few months to give her time to find somebody else.

I wouldn't sign it (I already had a political column in the main paper which appeared on Sundays.) We settled on the byline Grand Fromage, a sort of childish in-joke (it means Big Cheese) and called the column Rude Food, a silly name that I am always being asked to explain.

To everyone's surprise the column really took off. I maintained that this was not because of any special talent on my part. India was discovering food and the rest of the media had not worked this out yet.

With Shobhana's support and Rajan Kohli's grudging acceptance, we were finally able to start *Brunch* in Delhi. The Rude Food column was folded into a section in the magazine called Indulge and the emphasis overall was on good writing. The magazine did not look great because the paper and printing were not of high quality but it was always readable.

I thought it gave us an edge over the *Times of India* which fumbled through a series of mediocre Sunday supplements before more or less abandoning the idea. But how was one to judge the success of *Brunch*? The ad department, which knew nothing about selling magazines, had difficulty finding the ads and if you took the cost of producing the magazine and compared it to the ad revenues, *Brunch* lost money.

On the other hand, the *HT*'s circulation swelled on Sundays. We beat the *Times* every day but the margins were small. On Sunday, however, we were clear leaders. Plus, once *Brunch* became a success, we were able to charge more for the Sunday paper than we did for the weekday edition.

So how did you work out how much *Brunch* was earning? By looking at ad revenue alone? Or by looking at the additional subscription revenue that the *HT* earned on Sundays?

I sensed how much *Brunch* and Rude Food had taken off when, within a year of its publication, Diya Kar of Penguin books approached me to ask if they could publish a collection of my Rude Food pieces. I said I was fine with that.

But there was a condition. Penguin did not want to publish a book by man called Big Cheese. I would have to use my real name.

By then, many people had worked out that I wrote the column anyway so I agreed. And later Diya made sure that my cover was blown by putting a very flattering photo of me sucking my cheeks and my stomach in simultaneously on the cover.

As the column grew in popularity, I was bold enough to experiment with subjects. Rude Hotels was an obvious extension. So was Rude Drink. But I also sometimes did Rude Scent (on fragrance), Rude Music (on rock) and other variations.

Sometimes the columns were a little self-indulgent. One column discussed what you should drink with great rock songs. And I guess, in time, the column just began to reflect my interests. Fortunately, the readers did not seem to mind.

And there was one happy consequence. As more and more people in the food, hotel and travel business began to read the column, the ad department found it easier to find advertising from those sectors. For most of its existence, something like 50 to 60 per cent of *Brunch*'s advertising has come from the industries that Rude Food covers.

I wish I could say that this was because the column was so brilliant. Actually, we had just been lucky. We had accurately identified the boom areas of the early part of the twenty-first century. As those sectors grew, so did their ad budgets.

So now, I had three careers. I did *Cover Story*, a glossy interview show on Star World. I edited the *HT* and wrote a political column for it. And I was now a food writer.

It was inevitable that some of these careers would intersect but I was not sure how.

There was one thing I was clear about, though; I did not want to edit the *HT* forever.

There were many reasons for this but the most important one was that I had seen what being editor of the *HT* could do to you. In that era, newspapers were where the power was. If you edited a major newspaper, you were always at the centre of the action because of the job you held. And because people cared what your paper said, you became important to them.

The editor of the *HT* (anyone who was editor; not just me) could expect to be put through to anybody who mattered in Delhi, from the chief minister to the police commissioner. If the editor was coming back from abroad, customs officials at the airport would wave him through. Any Union minister would call back. The prime minister would give you an appointment. Even embassies would bend over backwards to accommodate you.

This was driven home to me when Seema and I were due to go to Singapore. The travel agent sent us the tickets in the afternoon. We were leaving on the night flight. I looked at the passports and discovered that he had got us Thai visas.

I called him. He admitted that he had screwed up. It would take another forty-eight hours to get a Singapore visa, he said. In any case the visa section of the Singapore embassy was now closed for the day. My secretary, the legendary Satish Kumar, who had worked with *HT* editors for decades, overheard the conversation.

Leave it to me, he said. I heard him calling the Singapore embassy. 'I am calling from editor's office, *Hindustan Times*,' he said into the phone. He hung up, took our passports, disappeared to the embassy, even though I warned him that the consular section was shut and that the rest of the embassy would also soon close.

He came back an hour later with the visas.

It was hard not to be seduced by the ease of doing things. Every week, some school would ask me to be chief guest at a function. When I wanted to refuse, Satish would tell me to leave it to him. He would tell the principal that I was unavailable. After much begging from the principal, he would finally agree to put it on my schedule.

There was a method to this. It was (and still is) difficult to get into most Delhi schools. But once I had done the school a favour, my recommendation counted for a lot. So members of the *HT* staff who had to get their kids into school would contact my office for a recommendation.

I am not going to pretend that I did not enjoy the perks of being the editor of the *HT*. The problem was that I feared that I might enjoy them too much.

Nobody stays an editor forever. And usually, when the end comes, editors are not prepared for it. They have got so used to being powerful that they can't face life as ordinary citizens. They try and cling on to power somehow. They join lesser publications. They ask their governmental contacts to make them ministers. They lobby for Rajya Sabha seats. They start their own publications. They may accept a certain amount of loss of power but they remain obsessed with being 'relevant', whatever that means.

I had a term for it: editoritis.

Delhi was full of former editors (though fortunately, not many from the *HT*) who still wanted to seem important. They wanted to be in the first row at any function. They wanted to never have to wait in line. They needed to have every minister on speed dial.

Early in my tenure at the *HT*, I had resolved that I would stay for no longer than three years and would leave before editoritis set in.

I had a chance to discuss this with—of all people—Aveek Sarkar. We had not spoken for a while after I left ABP but we came into contact again in strange circumstances.

I was an anchor (my terrible short-lived *Vir ke Teer* show) on the new Hindi Star News, which had been launched by Star with great fanfare. But the channel soon ran into trouble. The government said that no foreign entity could own more than 25 per cent of a news channel. Star complied with this regulation by divesting 75 per cent. The Tatas would take 25 per cent. Kumar Birla would take another 25 per cent. And 25 per cent would be divided among several 'friends of Star' who would buy 5 per cent each. I duly bought my 5 per cent but then, Star was hit by another shock.

The Tatas were partners with Star in a satellite service (later called Tata-Sky) and the government suggested both Star and the Tatas had to choose: either Star News or the satellite service. The Tatas stuck with the satellite service. Kumar Birla pulled out for reasons of his own. So Star decided to sell 75 per cent to a single Indian entity.

Various people met the Murdochs to negotiate buying the 75 per cent but ultimately ABP won the deal. (Star News lasted for a few years till Star sold ABP its 25 per cent and the channel is now called ABP News.) So Aveek bought my 5 per cent and we were suddenly in touch again.

When the deal was struck, Aveek suggested we go for a celebratory dinner with 'a very great chef' to which he would bring 'one of the world's greatest wines'.

The chef turned out to be Bill Marchetti of the ITC Maurya whom I knew anyway and the wine turned out to be Sassicaia, a very nice Italian 'Super Tuscan', but not, to my untrained palate, one of the world's greatest wines. And Marchetti destroyed the wine by serving it with fish when it was crying out for something redder and more substantial.

Anyhow, we were friends again and after we had cleared the air about *Sunday*, we got talking about my future. He had been the best kind of boss: helpful, thoughtful and generous.

I told Aveek I wanted to give up being an editor and explained why. It took him a while to see my point. He had lived that kind of life for years. But he was an owner, I said. He would always be powerful.

That wasn't true of professional editors who were employees and would have to move on eventually. I explained why I avoided doing many of the things that editors were expected to do. For instance, I didn't go to parties—because I knew that the day I ceased to be an editor, I would be dropped from the guest list. Far better, I said, to be known for yourself and not your job and to socialize with friends rather than contacts.

Aveek sipped his Sassicaia thoughtfully and seemed to see my point. Okay, he said, coming to a sudden decision, you will still need to earn some money. So you write for the *Telegraph*.

I thanked him but I said the *HT* still had first claim on my writing. And even as editor of the *HT*, I still earned more money from TV than I did from print.

In a way, that dinner sealed it for me. I had to get out. I was happy to be associated with the *HT*, I loved the people there, Shobhana was a dream boss and I wanted to continue writing.

But I had to go before editoritis became a permanent condition.

FORTY-NINE

FACING THE MUSIC

In the end, it did not work out that way mainly because Shobhana was so kind to me. I thought long and hard about what to say before asking to see her.

She was startled when I said I wanted to quit.

I explained my concept of editoritis to her and said that because she would always own the *Hindustan Times*, she would always be okay. But looking at the desperation of so many ex-editors in Delhi to remain connected, relevant or powerful, I was pretty clear that I didn't want to fall into the trap. Far better to quit now, when I was still in my forties and able to do television and travel than five years later when I would have no identity other than 'former editor of the *Hindustan Times*'.

She heard me out patiently and then, to my surprise, offered a solution I had not even considered. Yes, I could step down as editor. The *HT* would find my successor. But given that I would be writing, anchoring sessions at the HT Summit, etc., why didn't I maintain an official connection to the paper?

I said that yes, a title like consulting editor or contributing editor would be very welcome as would a guarantee of a salary (though, of course, suitably reduced) to anchor my income as I went from TV project to project.

But that wasn't what she had in mind.

'Why don't you stay on as editorial director?' she said.

Editorial director was her title. So to have two editorial directors would be to put me on par with her, I pointed out.

Yes, she said, she was fine with that.

The deal she offered me was so generous that I don't think that any Indian proprietor has ever been so large-hearted towards a journalist. I would stay on as editorial director. There would be no salary cut. I could keep my old office. We would hire a new editor. Did I want the new person to report to me?

I said no. That would amount to backseat driving. I believed that the editor should report directly to her. Fine, she said. She was sure that I would find plenty to do at the paper anyway.

I left her room shell-shocked and overwhelmed. This was an offer no sensible person could have dared hope for. And I would have been mad to have turned it down.

And so, the search for a new editor began. I told Shobhana that I had only one candidate in mind. I had known Shekhar Bhatia since 1986 when he had run the *Telegraph*. M.J. Akbar was the editor but given his frequent travels and interest in political activities, it was Shekhar who kept the show on the road. When Aveek took over from Akbar in 1989, Shekhar's role became even more important.

Shekhar had ended up in Delhi where he was executive editor of the *Times of India*. (For some reason, the *Times* did not like conferring the title of editor but that was what Shekhar was.) Apart from being an excellent editor, Shekhar also had great people skills, essential to running an operation the size of the *HT*.

Shekhar took a long time to say yes and even after he did, he seemed to have doubts about leaving the *Times* where the Jains had been nothing but nice to him. I remember getting an anxious call from him one cold night when I was in Moscow (as part of the prime minister's press party; my one and only visit to Russia) and spending a long time calming him down.

When he did join, however, he was a perfect fit. He got along well with everyone, and ran the paper superbly with the help of Arun Roy Chowdhary and V. Krishna. I stopped taking the edit meetings in the morning and when I opened my copy of the *HT* each morning, it was the first time I had seen the paper so I could judge it with a measure of detachment.

Cover Story was still running on Star World but I had a feeling that our days were limited. Karan Johar had just started Koffee with Karan on the same channel and it was clear that this was the future. Who would be interested in a standard, journalistic interview with a star when he could get a bunch of cool, Bollywood guys cracking in-jokes and laughing with each other?

I considered asking NDTV if I could do a more serious interview show when Aditya Tripathi came to see me. He worked for Discovery, he said, and was looking for Indian programming for Discovery Travel and Living, the group's lifestyle channel. He had been reading Rude Food for a while and wondered if I thought we could turn it into a TV show.

I said that the thought had occurred to me because I was getting very tired of wearing a suit and sitting behind a desk asking people questions in an air-conditioned studio. I longed to do something that took me on the road, let me wear jeans and tell the stories that I was interested in.

Aditya said that he had a school friend called Robin Roy who was a very talented film-maker. Would I like to talk to him? Or did I have a producer of my own in mind? Throughout my career I have always welcomed the opportunity to work with new people so I said I would be happy to talk to Robin.

It was a wise decision. Robin was bright, well-read and understood what kind of show I wanted to make. I said that I wanted do a show on India's obsession with milk. Another episode could be on the first masala dosa; the story of the Udupi restaurateurs who had so influenced the way Indians ate. Another could be the story of tandoori chicken which most Indians still believed was an ancient Afghan dish. And what about tea, one of the few world class food and drink products to come out of India? And wine? That was fast becoming a new interest for middle-class Indians.

Because nobody had done this kind of show before, we had to make up the format. And though I had made hundreds of episodes of TV shows before, I had never actually tried to tell stories through TV. Moreover, I was determined to get out of the big cities and to shoot all over India. To my surprise Discovery said they would pay.

It was hard work but we had a blast doing the show. We went to Banaras where I sat on a boat on the Ganga drinking *bhang thandai* with a man who kept shouting 'Bam Bam Bole!'. We traced the origins of Indian Chinese cuisine from Calcutta's Chinatown to the bylanes of Delhi's Lajpat Nagar. We looked for tea in the Nilgiris and ended up in Darjeeling where we met a tea garden owner who wore a hat and rode a horse; naturally we called him the Bengali cowboy. We traversed the length and breadth of Udupi and Mangalore; I ate at temple feasts and went out on fishing boats. I went back to Mayo College in Ajmer and discovered how so many of my classmates had converted their palaces and castles into hotels. My old history master now ran one of Rajasthan's highest regarded castle-hotels.

It took a while to shoot—and I was grateful that I had been freed from the day-to-day editing responsibilities at the *HT*—and it often got lonely on the road. (After that experience, I dragged Seema along on all my shoots!) And Robin took even longer to put it all together.

But when it was done, I was thrilled. Robin had taken a few vague ideas that I had tossed around and created a series that was truly world class. It was—as far as I know—the first show of its kind of Indian TV and because it was so expensive to do and such hard work, it was also the last. I did a global show for TLC (as Discovery Travel and Living had become) some years later with Robin again on a Discovery budget (always generous) but this remains the only show I ever did where I tried to put the spirit of Rude Food on TV.

After we wrapped up the show (which ended up being called *A Matter of Taste*), I got offered another TV gig. I knew Barkha Dutt, managing editor (as she was then) of NDTV, and she asked if I would like to do a show for the channel. I said truthfully that it had always been on my mind.

We did some brainstorming. I repeated my reluctance to do a straightforward interview show. And then Radhika Roy had an idea. Nobody in India had ever done, she said, a Parkinson-type show.

I knew what she was referring to. The British TV host Michael Parkinson would host a chat show with three guests and a musical artist. The guests would range from politicians to stars to authors and while Parkinson would have individual conversations with them, they would all chat with each other in the final segment.

The format had its origins in the US late night talk show (*The Tonight Show*, for instance) but while these were fronted by stand-up comedians (Johnny Carson, Jay Leno, etc.) the British tradition was to use journalists like Parkinson, to avoid the comedic monologue at the beginning and to make the conversations more substantial.

I said I would do it but only if we could shoot in front of a live audience as Parkinson did. A show with an audience always has a completely different energy. This was a vast enterprise but NDTV said they were willing to risk it. So we built a huge set, hired an in-house band, signed up guest singers for each episode and then had to persuade everyone we invited that it was worth driving out to Noida for about ten minutes of solo chat—we had at least three guests plus a musical guest each week.

God knows how, but we pulled it off. We called it *Face the Music* and gave it a slight rock and roll edge (I wore a T-shirt under my jacket!) which often shocked the political guests.

We ran into trouble for a reason we had least expected. When a guest walked on the set the band welcomed him or her with a short musical intro. This was usually a rock song and because it rarely exceeded fifteen seconds, we thought nothing of it.

But, as we were to discover, we were required to pay an international royalty to the people who wrote the song. So, if a guest was greeted with 'Money For Nothing', we had to pay a lot of money for something to Sting and Mark Knopfler. By the time NDTV did the math, we discovered that the show already owed large sums of money to various songwriters. And we had to pay a higher royalty to the authors of any song that was performed by the musical guests on our show. (And at least two were performed each week.)

In retrospect we should have thought of all this when we planned the show but news channels had no understanding of the realities of entertainment TV so this had never entered NDTV's calculations. There was a way out. We could do what many Indian companies do. Refuse to pay royalties and ask them to spend fifteen years in an Indian court trying to collect the money. But obviously, we were not going to do that. NDTV paid up and we decided that the format was even more expensive than we realized.

We decided to do a new show but while we were working that out, things were changing at the *HT*.

The company had a new CEO, Rajeev Verma, who shook up the management side and decided to put into motion two of the *HT*'s most cherished long-shelved plans. The *Times* had the *Economic Times*. The *Indian Express* had the *Financial Express*. So it had always made sense for the *HT* to start a business paper. But nobody had the guts to start one. Shobhana decided she would take the plunge.

The second plan was even more ambitious. The *HT* had talked about going to Mumbai since the 1960s. K.K. Babu had always thought that it was the obvious thing to do. But the managers and his editors had always funked it. They were nervous (with reason) about how a Punjabi-flavoured paper like the *HT* would fare in cosmopolitan Mumbai.

No professional manager had the courage to take the risk. But Shobhana decided that she would do it. She would challenge the *Times* in its own backyard.

From my perspective, that meant only one thing. A chance to go home to my city and to give it a paper it could be proud of.

FIFTY

I WALKED ON TIP TOES TO
KEEP MY NOSE ABOVE WATER

When I lived in Mumbai (then Bombay), the city supported many English newspapers. Of course, the *Times of India* was always the biggie but for many years, the far slicker Mumbai edition of the *Indian Express* was the paper of choice for many well-educated citizens. There was also the *Free Press Journal*, a paper that was taken seriously in the 1970s and later there was also a morning tabloid called *The Daily* launched by R.K. Karanjia of *Blitz*. The *Evening News* had led in the afternoon segment till a large chunk of its staff, led by Behram Contractor (Busybee), left to start *Mid-Day*. Later Contractor left *Mid-Day* too and launched the *Afternoon Despatch and Courier*.

By the time we were ready to take the *Hindustan Times* to Mumbai however, only the *Times* mattered. In the post-Samir Jain-era, it had emerged as the only paper of note. Some of the others were still around but not one was in remotely the same league as the *Times of India*.

But readers of the *Times* were grumbling. They believed the paper had dumbed down, that its feature pages were on sale (through a vehicle called Media Net) and that the paper was advertiser-led not reader-driven.

These concerns were strongest among readers in south Mumbai (defined roughly as south of Bandra) than those in the northern suburbs. So my strategy was to focus on those disgruntled readers and produce an upmarket, non-dumbed down paper targeted at this group. They were also, for better or worse, the most affluent segment among newspaper readers which meant that not only could they afford to take more than one paper (and therefore would be willing to try the *HT*) but they were also the segment that advertisers were most interested in.

The *Times* reacted to the news of our imminent arrival not just by improving their paper but by launching a new one. *Mumbai Mirror* was a mid- to down-market tabloid aimed at all of Mumbai (including the suburbs) that went out free (in most areas) with the *Times of India*. Order the *Times*, was their message, and we'll give you two papers for the price of one.

It was a shrewd (if expensive) strategy but it did not unduly worry me. I thought that the reader we were aiming for would still want the *HT* and would not be fobbed off with a free local tabloid.

Then, we had an unexpected development. Various *Times of India* employees left the company to start a new paper for Subhash Chandra of Zee and the owners of *Dainik Bhaskar*. The paper would be called *Daily News and Analysis* (*DNA*) and its purpose never seemed to me to be clear. Gautam Adhikari, its editor, was a friend and as speculation over media wars hotted up, we often sparred on TV. I took to referring to the paper as VRS (for Voluntary Retirement Scheme) rather than *DNA*, arguing that it was no more than a way for an older generation of *Times* employees to make a little money before they retired. (*DNA* paid better salaries than either the *Times* or the *HT*.)

I didn't take *DNA* seriously but the *HT* management did. They argued that the owners had lots of money (which they did) and feared that they would dump copies all over Mumbai at low prices to claim a larger circulation. I said that this did not matter. The *Times* was so far ahead that the important thing for a number two would not be total circulation but quality of readers. In any case, I said, the *Times* would probably claim that *Mumbai Mirror* was number two.

We went back and forth on this and given how worried (needlessly, in my view) the management was about *DNA*, we diverted slightly from my strategy, not in editorial terms but in terms of the larger print run which reflected a determined push for a suburban readership. I had said that we would go for the suburbs in Year Two but the threat from *DNA* meant that we went for all of Mumbai at once.

I still think that was a mistake but I understood what happened. Editors can be satisfied with the public response. Managers are judged on numbers. And none of them wanted it said that *DNA* sold more than the *HT*. So we spent crores printing more copies than we needed to and entering into circulation wars with *DNA*.

In any case, it all ended up much as I had expected. The VRS folks (the ex-*Times* employees) were soon evicted from *DNA*. Editors came and went. The paper never had much impact south of Bandra. (Its own staff called it the Borivali Times, after a Mumbai suburb.) And it bled crores and crores till finally, the print edition shut down. (Eventually, even the *Mumbai Mirror* shut down.)

The *HT*, on the other hand, grew steadily. We had a dream, big bang launch with a crime/film story on page one and terrific content inside (including a full-page profile of Ratan Tata) and the paper got most of Mumbai talking. I began to spend more and more time in the city, editing the paper though the crack team we had assembled (with Avirook Sen as resident editor) was more than capable of producing a great edition day after day.

We launched many initiatives with the Mumbai edition. With the economy soaring and luxury companies looking at India, we held our first Luxury Summit at the Taj in Mumbai. We also launched a monthly supplement to be called *Splurge* on luxury products and travel. The success of the full-page-interview-based profile of Ratan Tata led me to write a similar profile of a top businessman every Tuesday. (Eventually, the profiles were published as a book called *Men of Steel* which, years later, remains a steady seller.)

I enjoyed launching the Mumbai edition, though it was hard work and the risks were enormous, because Mumbai had a different editorial culture than Delhi. Nobody knew the name of any newspaper editor in Mumbai. We were all relatively anonymous. The people at the Mumbai *HT* who could get the chief minister on the phone were Sujata Anandan, our political editor, and Sailesh Gaekwad, our savvy political chief of bureau. There was no danger of editoritis and no danger of being hooked on the power and the access.

Of course, it helped that the edition was a huge success and finally provided a real alternative to the *Times of India*. Shobhana and I ran into Samir Jain at an event in Delhi. He was gracious enough to say that he thought that the Mumbai edition was a great success, but could not resist adding: 'much better than the Delhi edition . . .'

In fact, the Delhi edition was doing better than ever under the new editor and we continued to claim an edge in the everlasting circulation war with the *Times of India*. Shobhana had taken HT Media (which owned the papers but not the property) public and the stock was doing well. It seemed like a good time for the *HT*.

After about a year of running the Mumbai edition, I decided that it was time to walk away. Avirook left and we hired Samar Halarnkar to take his place. We gave Samar a paper that was running like a thoroughbred and I promised him that he could have a free hand in running it—which he did with great distinction.

Fortunately, he also kept up and increased our focus on Mumbai's collapsing infrastructure. This had been bought home to me when I nearly drowned in the floods of 26 July 2005.

I was in the *HT* office in Mahim when the rain started. As it began to get heavier, I decided to leave for my hotel, the Grand Hyatt in the BKC complex. The office had hired a car for me to use in Mumbai with an excellent driver and as we moved past Mahim sea-face, with the rain battering his car, he warned that this was going to be difficult.

He was right. By the time we got to the elevated road (the highway) that led to the airport (and my hotel), the water was already waist deep. We could go no further because all around us, cars had stalled or broken down and had been abandoned.

We left the car and began walking, even as the rain pelted down. It wasn't far from the Grand Hyatt. I estimated that it would take fifteen to twenty minutes. But I had not counted on the flooding. As the torrential rains continued, the water on the roads continued to rise. By the time I was halfway to the Hyatt, the water had reached so high that it was just below my chin. It is hard to walk in that kind of water especially as you can't see what you are walking on and I kept bumping into stalled cars and motorcycles or walking into ditches. Within minutes the level had reached my eyes. I walked on tiptoes to keep my nose above water. Fortunately, just as this seemed no longer possible, we came to the turn for the hotel where the water level was lower.

My opinion of the Hyatt, in those days a strangely anonymous and cold hotel at most times, shot up when I saw that it was offering food and shelter at no cost to anyone who was stranded in the flood. They found my driver a room and I returned to mine, determined to figure out why Mumbai had almost drowned.

The answer seemed to be that two things had gone wrong. The first was that the rains had been heavy. But the second was entirely man-made. To build BKC, the civic administration had ripped out the mangroves that acted as a natural barrier to flooding. Worse still, the Mithi River, normally a small stream, had been diverted to facilitate the expansion of the airport. In that season of heavy rains, the river had gone from being a small stream to becoming a full-fledged river again. And as the water level rose, it flooded its banks, seeking out its original course.

Around a thousand people died that day in Mumbai in the floods. I was lucky to not have been one of them.

We ran campaigns about the destruction of Mumbai's ecosystem. My story on the diversion of the Mithi River ran as the page one lead in the Delhi-edition, in the hope of attracting the attention of the central government.

I don't know if it made much of a difference. Each year, things just seem to get worse and worse.

FIFTY-ONE

'WHO DOESN'T WANT TO BE PRIME MINISTER?'

The year before I nearly drowned in Mumbai, momentous events had taken place in India. The 2004 election was supposed to be a sure thing for A.B. Vajpayee and the BJP. The fruits of liberalization had finally arrived and the middle class was more prosperous than it ever had been.

L.K. Advani set the tone for the BJP when he talked about the rise of India and the government commissioned an advertising campaign called India Shining to cash in on the middle-class euphoria. The BJP was so eager to capitalize on the feel-good mood that it even advanced the 2004 election by a few weeks.

At the time the popular view was that the Congress was finished, that Sonia Gandhi did not understand politics and that the BJP only had to go through the motions of fighting an election before returning to power. The opinion polls supported this view.

Halfway through the campaign, Sonia Gandhi gave me a print interview for the *HT*. Before we started, I asked her how the campaign was going. 'Not as badly as the BJP thinks it is for us,' she replied cheerily.

This made me sit up. Sonia Gandhi is a notorious pessimist. She is always prepared for the worst and never dares hope for the best. So, to hear her say that, made me feel that perhaps the BJP was being too smug.

But Vajpayee did not seem worried at all. Nor did anyone of consequence in the BJP. I spoke to reporters who had been touring the constituencies and they all agreed that the Congress stood no chance.

During the campaign the Congress hosted a dinner for editors and bureau chiefs at Sonia's bungalow at 10 Janpath. There must have been twenty-five or so of us and we sat at tables arranged in the garden. Sonia went from table to table chatting to journos, playing the perfect hostess.

The dinner was so successful that even journos who I knew were personally close to L.K. Advani and hostile to the Congress were swayed by her hospitality. One of them said to me: 'She is such a nice person. Why did she ever join politics which she knows nothing about? I feel bad for her because the Congress will be wiped out at this election. And she will be blamed.' His view reflected the prevailing consensus at the dinner which was that we were dining on the deck of the Titanic with the iceberg already looming ahead.

So why was Sonia sounding so cheery?

Perhaps she knew something that we did not.

In the final lap of campaigning, the polls began to predict a different outcome. The election was no longer a sure thing. In fact, it might even be a close-run thing. So, obviously, Sonia had correctly sensed the shift in public mood.

During the campaign I was doing a regular election program for Sab TV, where I would interview figures of note about the campaign. As the opinion polls began to change their predictions, I considered whether a Congress-led government was even a possibility. Eventually, I was forced to conclude that it was.

To me, this meant only one thing: Manmohan Singh would be prime minister.

I asked Singh to come on the show and he was kind enough to drag himself to Noida for an interview. He was expecting the standard campaign interview and was startled when I told him that I thought it entirely possible that he would be prime minister in a week or so.

He hummed and hawed till finally, in answer to a direct question, he said that yes, he would accept the prime ministership 'if the party wants me to'. He reminded me that way back, in the aftermath of the

Narasimha Rao era, I had asked him the same question and he had answered 'Who does not want to be prime minister?'

Oddly enough, nobody paid much attention to that interview or to Manmohan Singh's response. Partly this was because most people were not ready to believe that the Congress could form the next government. But mostly it was because everyone believed that if such a situation came to pass, Sonia Gandhi would be the prime minister.

I reckoned the Congress would form the next government. And that Manmohan Singh would be the next prime minister.

The day before the results were to be declared, I went to see Sonia Gandhi. I asked her if she was nervous and she answered candidly that she was. I said that it seemed likely to me that the Congress would form the next government. She was back to being the pessimistic Sonia of old. Well, she said, there was so much that could go wrong, and so on.

But, I persisted, if it did happen, was it still going to be Manmohan Singh? She clammed up and said she didn't want to talk about it, which I took as confirmation.

Seema had been present for the Manmohan Singh interview and shared my view that Sonia did not want to become prime minister. I told her about my conversation with Sonia Gandhi. She agreed with me that Sonia's refusal to discuss it meant that she had decided to try and make Manmohan Singh prime minister again. Seema's view was that Sonia did not lie. She just avoided answering awkward questions. But we decided to keep our speculation to ourselves and not to talk to anyone about it.

On election morning, we slept late. I was not going to be on TV and we both thought that a Congress-led coalition would win. By the time we woke up and switched on our TV sets, all the projections said that Vajpayee had lost. The only question that obsessed the anchors was: would India accept a foreign-born prime minister?

At first it seemed like I had got it wrong. The Congress Parliamentary Party met and elected Sonia as its leader. Sonia (aided by Ahmed Patel and Ambika Soni) set about pulling together a coalition which proved to be remarkably easy. Even Sharad Pawar who had walked out of the Congress a few years before saying that a foreigner could not lead the party now came scurrying back to join the coalition.

But I found one of Sonia's responses interesting. Asked by a journalist about whether the leader of the Parliamentary Party (that is, Sonia) would be prime minister, she responded, 'That is the normal practice.'

It was a classic Sonia response: it was true enough but it did not fully answer the question.

Then, with the coalition in place, she dropped her bombshell. It took the form of a personal statement saying that she had listened to her 'inner voice' (this was a phrase preferred by Gandhiji) and had decided not to accept the prime ministership.

There were the predictable pleas for her to reconsider. Congressmen wept. There were demonstrations outside her house. But she would not be moved.

I realized then why she had played it that way. If she had announced earlier that she would not be prime minister then many in her coalition (Laloo Yadav, Sharad Pawar, etc.) would have demanded the post for themselves. So, she waited till the coalition was in place before making the announcement. And now, she waited for the drama that followed her refusal to take the job to subside before announcing that Manmohan Singh would be prime minister.

Manmohan was not a popular choice within the Congress. He had no political base of his own. The one time he had fought a Lok Sabha election, he had lost. He had zero political instincts. He had a reputation for sulking and resigning when things did not go his way. He was the father of liberalization but the Congress had gone into the election with a vaguely lefty slogan ('Congress ka haath, aam admi ke saath') and had poured scorn on India Shining. How could the government now be led by a market-friendly figure?

But Sonia knew what she was doing. Too much of any prime minister's time goes in managing the party. (Vajpayee, for instance, rarely had problems with governance. All his headaches came from the Sangh Parivar.) She would look after the party and leave it to Manmohan Singh to focus on running the government.

She had some doubts about the market: she believed that it had failed to benefit the poorest Indians. But equally she was as sure that the old socialist way of doing things would not work. The choice of P. Chidambaram, an avid free marketer, as finance minister, confirmed that this would be a liberalizing government.

Why did the BJP lose? It is hard to say. There were some regional factors that benefitted the Congress: the parliamentary party was anchored by MPs from Andhra Pradesh where Rajshekhar Reddy had fought an excellent campaign. But mostly I suspect it was because Sonia had spotted a gap in the electorate and gone for it. The BJP seemed too obsessed with the middle class. It neglected those on the margins of society. The Congress spoke to the poor, the landless, the minorities, and the disadvantaged and promised them the share they had been denied of Shining India.

Vajpayee took the defeat badly, largely because he had not expected it. Shobhana and I went to see him at his new home and invited him to the HT Summit. 'Why do you want me, a defeated prime minister?' he said.

We tried to persuade him that we still thought he was India's greatest statesman but he wouldn't listen. In the end, I think we had to make do with L.K. Advani.

Manmohan Singh agreed readily to come to the Summit. He made a good speech, won the audience over and seemed very much like a man totally in control.

Sonia agreed to come, after some persuasion, and seemed to love the interaction once she was there. Speaking to the audience, she referred to some of the things she had said the previous year that the Congress would do if it came to power. 'And I am willing to bet,' she laughed, 'that not one of you thought that we would ever come to power.'

As always, Sonia was the hit of the Summit though one or two perceptive regulars pointed out that despite the change in her circumstances, she seemed no different from the previous year when the Congress had been down and out. Power really didn't seem to affect her much, which could be why she had no real desire for it.

I met Manmohan Singh at 7 Race Course Road shortly after he had moved in and asked him when Sonia Gandhi had told him that he would be prime minister. He was a little shifty but swore that he had no idea that this would happen when he had given me that 'who doesn't want to be prime minister' interview.

I believed him. I don't think Sonia Gandhi told him right till the end: either just before the result was declared or just after. She is always unwilling to jinx things by counting her chickens before they hatch so she would never have discussed the prime ministership too much in advance.

Was he the right choice for the job? I think he was. In the first term, he was an extraordinarily good prime minister. Sadly, he destroyed himself in his second term owing to a combination of factors, not all of which were his own fault.

But that came later.

FIFTY-TWO

'FIGHT SCENE!'

Once the Mumbai edition was up and running, I tried to forge a new post-editor life in Delhi. I had even more time on my hands because Shekhar Bhatia retired as editor and the *HT* hired Chaitanya Kalbag to be editor.

Kalbag had been one of three NRI journalists found for us by a head-hunter in keeping with Rajiv Verma's view that the best Indian journalists worked abroad. I thought one of the candidates was very impressive but he didn't get the job. Instead, the paper chose Kalbag who soon became deeply unpopular with the senior editorial staff, some of whom left. He hired unsuitable replacements and I saw no point in getting involved in this mess. I had chosen to give up the job and walk away. Now, it was up to the management to sort out the problems. (They did. Kalbag left in just a few months.)

I began writing more and Barkha Dutt at NDTV suggested that I went back to the kind of show I was most associated with: the interview.

I said yes because *Face the Music* no longer seemed to be workable and I was, in any case, talking to Discovery about a follow up to *A Matter of Taste*, which had been well-received. So a studio show seemed easy to do.

One on One, as the new show was called, interviewed all the big names of that era. We began with a one-hour special with L.N. Mittal, probably the most comprehensive and candid interview he had given till then. Then, over the next few weeks we did Ratan Tata, Sonia Gandhi and several others. Because of the calibre of the guests the show attracted even more attention than say, *Face the Music*. I was beginning to really get into it when a new job offer arrived.

This was a period of huge economic optimism. The stock market was booming (HT Media had just been listed) and the conventional wisdom was that media stocks were going to be The Next Big Thing. At NDTV, they were talking about launching an entertainment channel called Imagine. Raghav Bahl of TV 18 whose stock had risen so much that many of his employees (including journalists) were millionaires, was planning his own entertainment channel, to be called Colors. With foreign institutional investors pumping money into the market and private equity fascinated by media, TV and newspapers were hotter than they had ever been.

It was during this boom that Peter Mukerjea asked to have lunch with me. Though I was no longer shooting *Cover Story* for Star World, I had a rough idea of what was going on at Star. I knew that Peter had been kicked upstairs (in much the same way as Rathikant Basu had been when Peter took over from him) and that the network was really run by Sameer Nair.

Peter confirmed all this to me at our lunch and said that he had been approached by various equity funds and bankers (he mentioned Uday Kotak in this regard) about starting a new network. The centerpiece of this network would be an entertainment channel but he wanted to create a bouquet of all kinds of other channels: music, regional language, city specific, and yes, news.

He did not see the news channel as a money maker, he said. He wanted it to be a high-quality, upmarket, sophisticated channel that would impress foreign equity investors and others and serve as a calling card for the network. Money would not be a problem. People were lining up to invest in the venture.

I was tempted but cautious. I had been lucky to find some success as a TV presenter. But I knew nothing about running a channel. On the other hand, I had given up being editor of the *HT* to focus on TV. So when an opportunity like this came along, could I afford to turn it down?

And then, there was the money. Peter offered me a tiny piece of sweat equity in the entertainment channel (which I would have nothing to do with), but even that tiny amount he said, would net me crores in a few years. At the news channel, I could have up to 7 per cent (we would negotiate the exact proportion later), he said. We had both turned fifty, he added. We could do this for five years, cash out and live off the money we made for the rest of our lives.

I am always sceptical when people talk about equity and future earnings but Peter was willing to offer money upfront too. My salary would be three times what I was earning at the *HT* with an option (guaranteed, he said) of a 50 per cent bonus at the end of each year.

In the end, I decided to take the job. A large part of my decision had to do with the money. The way I saw it, the worst thing that could happen was that the channel would fail. In that case, the investors would probably force me out and install a new editor. But by then I would have made enough money to have made the job worthwhile.

Plus, there was also the excitement of launching a new channel. Peter had offered me a dream ticket: a high-cost, upmarket operation that didn't have to worry about ratings or revenues but had only to be of sufficiently high quality to serve as an ambassador for the network. I was reasonably confident that I could manage that— especially if we hired the right people.

I went and saw Shobhana who said that the offer was too good to turn down. But I should not sever my connection with the *HT*. The columns should continue and I should have an advisory designation. K.K. Babu was even more generous. I should keep my office, he said. And I should keep my old salary.

I thought he was kind to offer to give me my full salary but there was no need. At that stage, money was the least of my worries. And so, when I sat down with Rajiv Verma to work out a new contract, we negotiated a reduced salary but agreed that I would try to come to the *HT* office as often as I could. My secretary, Mukesh Rawat, would keep his office and I should keep the office car. (I didn't keep the car but the *HT*'s generosity was overwhelming.)

At first, the news channel project seemed fun. Peter was used to the global News Corp (Star's parent) way of doing things so he insisted that we used as much foreign talent as possible. I said I knew nothing about TV technology (cameras, editing suites, etc.) and he said I didn't need to. Had I ever understood printing presses when I edited newspapers and magazines? (I hadn't.) He had hired his old team from Star and they would buy the equipment, plan the distribution, etc.

We went to London to get someone to design the channel, interviewed several companies and then finally settled on different people to do the sets and the graphics. Peter had called the entertainment channel 9X so X was going to be our brand and the news channel would be NewsX. Designers were asked to submit prospective logos. A British set designer told us that we needed a revolving desk, which sounded like a good idea, so he was duly commissioned.

At the entertainment channel, however, things were not going so well. The key person is the one who commissions the programming. With a budget of roughly one crore a day to spend on commissioning shows, this has to be a person who knows the mood of his viewers inside out.

Peter first chose a person who, some believed, lacked the experience needed to make programming decisions, and then fell out with him. When he left, Peter did not hire another programmer but gave the job to his wife, Indrani, who had no programming experience at all. Indrani was also made the chairperson of the news channel on the grounds that Peter, as a British citizen, could not take the job, and she soon became the final managerial authority on everything. Needless to say, she had no TV experience.

I was always nervous about my own lack of experience at running a channel and kept looking for someone who could show me the ropes. We were very lucky that Nick Pollard who had made Sky News the best news TV channel in the UK had just left Sky. We persuaded him to come to India and set up the channel for us. Once Nick was on board, I began at last, to feel confident about what we were doing.

By then, however, a new set of problems had emerged. A news channel takes time to launch because you have to hire the staff, build the studios, etc. But an entertainment channel takes no time at all. You only need to commission shows from independent production houses and put them on the air once they come in. So it was always envisaged that 9X would go on the air first and would, or so Peter and Indrani predicted, wipe the floor with Star Plus, Zee and the competition.

Except that it did not work out that way. Nobody in the TV business was very surprised when 9X did not live up to those expectations. Most of the programming was terrible and it never got the ratings that it had been expected to. The private equity investors were not TV pros so it was possible, in the short run, to befuddle them with combined ratings for 9X and 9XM, the music channel. But, at some stage, I was sure, the truth would dawn on the money men.

From around the time that 9X flopped, Peter's attitude to the news channel began to change. Suddenly, the plans for the studio seemed too extravagant. Did we really need to spend money on distribution? Couldn't our distribution budget just be transferred to 9X?

All of us sensed the tension but nobody was sure what to do. We had come too far to turn back now. And I had an additional responsibility. I had persuaded people to leave good jobs to join NewsX, telling them what Peter had told me: 'upmarket channel . . . no TRP pressure . . . large budgets . . . international quality', etc. Was I now going to say to them that I had hired them under false pretenses? And if I left, where would they go? What would happen to the channel?

In the end, the decision was taken out of my hands. Peter and I had a huge blow-up over distribution budgets in our basement conference room and things get so heated that when it was over, I wondered how we could ever work together.

The meeting had been planned as a routine 'catch-up' with the senior staff and one of our camera operators was even asked to shoot it as part of a making-of-NewsX documentary that we were planning. We knew that things would not go well when Peter began by blaming us for what he claimed was a delay in the launch of the channel.

We responded that as journalists we could only start work once the sets were ready, the cameras had arrived, etc. All of this was handled by Peter's trusted lieutenants from the Star days who chose the technology and ordered it. If the equipment they had ordered had been delayed (and the studios were still not ready) then this would affect any launch schedule he had devised.

Peter tried a new tack. He had wanted an upmarket channel, he said. We agreed that he had and said that we were executing that brief.

Well then, he said triumphantly, why did we need distribution?

We were startled. All TV channels reached the public through cable networks. And cable TV operators charged money to carry each channel on their networks. So, though we bitterly resented it, we spent a large part of our budget on distribution. All channels did. If we did not then nobody would be able to watch us.

What about Tata Sky, asked Peter.

I explained that Direct to Home (DTH) distribution (like Tata Sky) was still a fledgling operation in India and reached only a tiny proportion of the audience. Surely, he knew this? He also knew that our revenue estimates had been based on advertising money that no DTH channel could expect. And in any case the financial plan for NewsX had included a budget for distribution. What would happen to that money if we gave up on distribution?

Peter had no answers to these questions. So he got angry instead. I got as angry. An alert senior member of our staff shooed the camera guy away ('fight scene!' he told him, half ironically) and the meeting ended in a stand-off.

Peter went back to Mumbai. He did not take my calls. Then one day, I got a call from a reporter asking whether I had any plans now that I was leaving NewsX. I was startled. I was sitting in the office, I said, with no plans to leave.

Peter continued to refuse to take my calls but various small-time TV news sites that survived on advertising from TV channels (and 9X was a big advertiser) were fed stories to the effect that Peter had sacked me.

I called one of the investors, a man who worked for a sovereign wealth fund who, in turn, called Peter about the leaks to TV websites about my departure. According to him, Peter said there was no truth to the stories and he had no idea where they were coming from.

The stand-off continued for over a week till the investors forced Peter to fly out to Delhi and talk to me. By now, my mind was made up. There was no way I was going to stay. The investors had told Peter as much. So, when we met, he raised the subject of my contract, which like his was valid for three years with no exit clause. If the investors had wanted to sack either of us, they had to buy us out. (How the investors had agreed to this kind of contract, I have never understood.)

Peter said that while I had a legal right to be paid for the full three years, he was sure the investors would fight this in court. So could we just agree to a compromise? I had only worked for ten months. So, if they paid me for another 12 months (including my bonus), would I agree to leave 'on good terms'? I looked at the figures. They were offering me a sum that was large enough to buy a flat in south Delhi.

I took the deal.

I went to Mumbai and we signed the papers in my lawyer's office. I went then to the Oberoi where I was to meet Peter and Indrani. Only Indrani showed up and said how much she regretted what had happened. I said that I was sorry that things had turned out this way. I then showed her the letter I intended to send to the staff to say that I was leaving and to wish the channel well. Best, I said, to leave with some grace.

She agreed. We shook hands. We said we would keep in touch, a promise that, I imagine, neither of us intended to keep, but which sounded gracious enough. I got into my car and drove off to the airport.

By the time I had reached Chowpatty, they had disconnected my email account and told the IT guys to block any mail I might try to send to the staff.

The following day, they began sacking staff. Many resigned. There was a fracas. Security was called. It got very ugly. And by the end of the week, something like 134 people (that is, most of the editorial employees) had been sacked or had resigned.

Why they needed to behave so badly was never clear to me. The staff then went to the I&B minister to complain. They also raised questions in writing about the way in which NewsX funds were being diverted. I had already been to see Priya Ranjan Dasmushi, the I&B Minister, to warn him that something was very wrong at NewsX so he was not surprised to hear the sacked staff members.

Dasmunshi wrote to the finance minister asking for an enquiry. I then went and saw P. Chidambaram myself and told him that there was a definite case for an enquiry. He said he had received the letter from the I&B minister and would order an investigation.

I met the investors too who were apologetic about how things had turned out but still unaware of the disaster that was 9X. When I told them how badly the channel was doing, they seemed incredulous. They represented international funds from America and Singapore and had never invested in TV before. They had been swayed by Peter's reputation at Star and still believed him when he said that 9X was doing fabulously.

Nothing much happened to Peter and Indrani. They continued to run their empire without seeming concerned about any investigation. They hired a low-cost new team to launch the news channel and, when the launch was a disaster, sold off NewsX. Eventually, when the network had run through all the money that had been raised, and the investors refused to put in any more, they walked out and went to live abroad in luxury, in their homes in the UK and in Spain.

I went to see Chidambaram again who assured me that the investigation was in progress. But nothing seemed to happen to the Mukerjeas. Various employees who had sued NewsX for wrongful dismissal were eventually paid off; one of them got a settlement of Rs 2 crore. This was just before the sale of NewsX so I imagine that the buyer had asked them to settle all cases before the transaction went through.

There are, of course, a few postscripts to the story.

The Mukerjeas' life of globe-trotting luxury would have continued if Indrani had not been arrested in 2015, over seven years after the events described here. She and Peter were charged with the murder in 2012 of Sheena Bora, whom Indrani had introduced to all of us as her sister but was actually her daughter from a previous husband. That trial is still on as I write this.

In the aftermath of the murder case, a new enquiry was launched into how the Mukerjeas got away even though the finance ministry's investigations (launched after NewsX employees wrote to the I&B minister and after I met P. Chidambaram) had raised serious questions about their handling of NewsX funds. That case is still making its way through the legal system as I write.

The people the Mukerjeas sold NewsX to sold it again to Kartikeya Sharma who asked me to do some programming for him. And so in 2014, I made a documentary series for NewsX called *Mandate With Destiny* which later became a book called *Mandate*.

When I was back in the NewsX office, I thought back to the days when we had launched the channel. Could it ever have worked out? If 9X had been a success, and if Peter's empire had not begun collapsing, would he have given NewsX a chance to succeed? Or had the whole thing been no more than an exercise in raising hundreds of crores from investors before settling down to live in luxury abroad?

I guess we'll never know.

But I have one final doubt and that's about my vision for the channel. Nick had wanted crack teams of reporters. He had wanted us to be the first channel that everyone turned to whenever a big story broke because we would have the best reporting and the best analysis. He gave us the example of Sky. In every newspaper office in Britain, he said, the newsroom TV was always tuned to Sky because journalists knew that it would be first.

I agreed with all this. But I was also taken with the expansive look of the Sky newsroom. I wanted the channel to look grand and well-produced and often gave the example of the sets for the BBC's Newsnight programme.

There is a chance that if the problems with Peter had not erupted, we could have pulled it off. We may not necessarily have had the best reporting but we would certainly have created a channel that looked bigger and grander than anything else on Indian TV.

But—and here's where I have the most doubts—would that have done us any good even if we had pulled it off perfectly?

We were scheduled to launch in 2008, in an era of hope and prosperity. Middle-class Indians still watched the BBC and CNN and NDTV was considered the model for all TV.

But within three or four years, this model had collapsed. Suddenly nobody cared about the look of the programmes. Channels filled their screens with small windows from which shouting heads flung abuse at each other. Anchors became participants in the mayhem. Nobody cared what the studio was like. And as for reporting, forget it. TV was not about covering the news. It was about strong opinions, loudly expressed.

So here's the doubt that niggles away at me. Suppose we had produced a beautiful-looking channel with elegant graphics, state-of-the-art studios and an emphasis on reporting and analysis, would we have been doomed to failure in a few years anyway?

My guess is that we would have. TV would change. And the kind of channel I had in mind would have been out of tune with the times.

FIFTY-THREE

'MUSHARRAF IS A MAN
WE CAN DO BUSINESS WITH'

Though this is not how we remember it, the truth is that nobody thought that the UPA I government would last. Later, Manmohan Singh would tell me, 'I thought it would last for six months.' The problem was that it was a coalition and no coalition had survived a full term in Indian politics.

The list of prime ministers whose coalition governments fell is long: Morarji Desai, Charan Singh, V.P. Singh, Chandra Shekhar, H.D. Deve Gowda and Inder Gujral. Even A.B. Vajpayee's first coalition fell after Jayalalitha withdrew support and only stabilized in his second term. (Narasimha Rao did not really lead a coalition.)

Plus, there was the additional factor of shared/divided responsibilities. Manmohan Singh had no mandate. Hardly anyone who voted for one of the UPA partners in the general elections believed that this was a vote for Manmohan Singh. Manmohan Singh's cabinet knew that. There were many ministers who were sceptical of his authority. Arjun Singh, the veteran Congress leader whom Rajiv Gandhi had made vice president of the party way back in 1986, never really accepted it. ('I don't know what he is thinking,' Manmohan Singh once told me. 'He never says anything at cabinet meetings.') But Arjun Singh was kept in line by Sonia Gandhi who would not tolerate the slightest sign of disrespect towards the prime minister.

Pranab Mukherjee had fallen from favour once and was too smart to make the same mistake twice so he rarely asserted himself in that first term. I once found myself on a flight to New York with him and asked if he did not find it odd to work under Manmohan Singh? After all, when he had been finance minister and number two in Indira Gandhi's cabinet, Manmohan Singh had reported to him as the governor of the Reserve Bank of India.

Pranab had obviously thought through a reply because he said immediately. 'It would have been a problem if it was not for Manmohan Singh. He must know it is a little awkward so he goes out of his way to show me respect and courtesy.' And Manmohan Singh confirmed that he had never had any problems with Pranab: 'He gives me full cooperation.'

But there were areas where Manmohan Singh lacked the requisite experience. One of them was foreign policy. I was part of the press party that went with the prime minister on his first trip to New York to address the UN General Assembly. On our way to New York, he called two or three of us into the cabin to discuss his meetings.

Only one of the meetings really mattered. He was meeting General Musharraf and was nervous about how it would go. Why, he asked us, had we not been able to solve the Kashmir problem? I imagined that this was a rhetorical question—whole books have been written on the subject—and did not bother to respond. But one of our number did and Manmohan found his answer disappointing. 'We have solved Mizoram! We have solved Nagaland! Why should Kashmir be different?' he demanded.

I suddenly realized that this was not a rhetorical question at all. So we told him the usual stuff about how the Nagas and the Mizos did not have an option but that Kashmiris had a clear alternative. The separatists regarded Kashmir as the unfinished agenda of Partition and so it was impossible for us to offer them a Mizoram-type solution. This was much more complicated than Mizoram had been. He remained unconvinced and gave us the impression that his meeting with Musharraf would be all about solving the Kashmir problem with Pakistan's help.

I met him again (this time alone) on his way back to Delhi from New York and asked how the meeting had gone. 'Very well,' he said and candidly admitted that at the start of the meeting, his hands were shaking because he was so nervous that it would go badly. But Musharraf had been warm and though it was too much to expect progress at the first meeting, he was convinced he could strike a peace deal with the general. To the press he said: 'General Musharraf is a man we can do business with.'

In fact, Musharraf was much shrewder than Manmohan Singh who while brilliant, was not cunning. Musharraf knew how to encourage him just a little and then bring him down to earth with a thud. On a later trip, by which time Manmohan Singh had become confident of his relationship with the general, Musharraf threw the Indian side into disarray by making an aggressive speech at the UN and taking a hardline on Kashmir.

Musharraf was to have dinner with Manmohan Singh that night and we waited to see if the two men would sort out this unexpected development. In fact, rumour had it that the dinner was a disaster with Manmohan Singh being taken aback by Musharraf's belligerence.

The Indian side refused to brief the media that night so the Pakistanis gave their account of what had happened—an account in which Musharraf, naturally enough, came across as the hero.

I was woken up early the next morning by the Delhi office who had read accounts of the Pakistani briefing and wanted an analysis piece 'about the under-currents at the dinner'. I had no idea what had transpired and nor did anyone else in our media party. I went looking for Natwar Singh who was foreign minister but his staff said that they had no clue where he was. When he turned up a few hours later, we discovered that he had sneaked off to the Barnes and Noble bookshop to escape from his entourage and spent his time browsing the shelves. This was not how a foreign minister was supposed to behave so the Indian delegation was perplexed.

Natwar Singh, who had been present at the dinner, gave me a blow-by-blow account which seemed to confirm my original fear that Musharraf was too slippery for Manmohan to handle. I filed my story (shorn of all my own theories, of course) and Manmohan was not happy. He still believed that he could solve the Kashmir issue.

In those days, he would frequently meet journalists informally at Race Course Road to get a sense of the public mood. Perhaps, because he had known my family for a long time, he was indulgent to me at those meetings.

On one occasion he talked about the US sub-prime crisis and I said, honestly, that I did not understand it. He then reverted to being an economics professor and explained to me how the American housing market worked, how the rush to push people into acquiring homes they could not afford threatened the banks and how this could lead to a crash.

He was completely right, of course, and it was hard not to think of the fictional President Josiah Bartlet (also an economist) from *The West Wing*, the American TV show. I can't think of many top-flight economists, let alone a prime minister, who would spend so long taking a complex issue and breaking it down so that civilians like myself could understand it.

While he is not, by nature, an indiscreet man, he was always candid and never hid his frustrations with the way the Congress system worked. In those days, there was always an understanding that nothing said in those off-the-record chats could be attributed to the prime minister but it could be used on a background basis to explain a decision. Often such meetings are set up by the PMO's press machinery but Manmohan Singh, like Vajpayee, had excellent private secretaries who understood his mind and would readily provide access to many journalists.

In every one of our meetings he always came across as a decent, well-intentioned man though, after a year or so, he began to sound a little petulant or angry. He loathed the Left, which kept the government in power by providing support from outside, and had a particular antipathy towards lefty economists whose economic credentials he did not take seriously.

He could be sensitive about articles too. I was used to prime ministers and other senior politicians complaining how news had been reported but few of them bothered to read the opinion pieces that appeared on the editorial page. But Manmohan Singh read every opinion piece. And if it was critical of his policies, he took it to heart.

At one of our meetings, he complained about Cho Ramaswamy. At another one he asked why I bothered to give space to a BJP-type writer. I explained that it was our job to offer space to all points of view. He said he realized that but this particular writer never made any sense. And so on. It was never a serious complaint. I think he just needed to get his irritation with articles he did not like off his chest.

By the second half of his first term, a new urgency entered his tone. He talked about how India had only a tiny window to get its economic reforms right and how that window was now closing. But people did not seem to realize this, he would say, sounding very annoyed.

I am sure he meant what he said. But the cynic in me believed that he had a deeper motive. He was the most brilliant man since Jawaharlal Nehru to become prime minister of India. And yet, he was unable to do anything that would leave a legacy of any lasting value. Was some of his frustration, I wondered, caused by his inability to leave a legacy?

He would be remembered forever as the finance minister who liberalized the economy and put India on a high-growth path. But how would he be remembered as prime minister?

I suspect that he began to look for a legacy to leave behind, something that made history. His desire to strike a deal on Kashmir with Musharraf emerged from his desire to leave India a little better than when he had taken office.

The deal he wanted emerged from his view that the concept of borders had changed in the twenty-first century. We lived, he told me, in an era of soft borders. People could travel across Europe without ever having to show their passports. Asean (Association of Southeast Asian Nations) was working towards a similar understanding. This change in how nations were defined (not as states with hard borders) could work to our advantage.

Supposing, he said, that India and Pakistan softened the Kashmir border. Citizens could come and go as could goods. Kashmir would still be a part of India (there would be no redrawing of borders) but the border would be irrelevant because people could come and go as they pleased. Both India and Pakistan would reduce their military presence in their respective parts of Kashmir. Both countries would give Kashmir autonomy and because India and Pakistan were united in this, there would be nothing to fight about.

This took me back to our first if-we-can-settle-Mizoram-why-not-Kashmir conversation. I told him that I saw what he was getting at and while I was no foreign policy expert, I did not think it would work. I said that the BJP would call the proposal a sell-out and would make it appear that we had given up Kashmir. Besides what about the Kashmiris themselves? What about the people who had argued for independence or union with Pakistan? Would they just abandon those demands?

Manmohan Singh said times had changed. People only cared about economic progress and prosperity these days. The era of aggressive nationalism was drawing to a close. The world was becoming one.

I was unconvinced. In any case, I said, how could any Pakistani leader agree to this deal? They had spent decades telling their people that they would 'win' Kashmir 'back'; what would they say now if Indian sovereignty over our Kashmir was to be maintained.

He said that the Pakistanis were more forward-looking than I realized. They were also coming around to his view.

The so-called Musharraf–Manmohan deal, which never went through (at least partly because Musharraf was ousted) included many of these elements. I don't believe it would ever have worked. ('Era of aggressive nationalism is ending . . .' Ha!) But Manmohan Singh clearly believed that it could be his legacy.

For nearly all of the second part of UPA I, the only other issue Manmohan Singh would get animated about was the Indo-US nuclear deal. There is no doubt that the deal was a good one, that it ended nuclear apartheid and that Manmohan Singh had done very well to secure it.

The basic problem was that the CPM (Communist Party of India [Marxist]), with its mindless anti-Americanism, was determined to oppose the deal. Despite efforts by nearly everyone with any influence, including Sonia Gandhi, to persuade the Left of the obvious—that the deal was in India's interests—Prakash Karat and his party remained stuck in a Cold War mindset. The deal would draw India too close to the US seemed to be the crux of the Left's objections.

The more stubborn the Left got, the more passionate Manmohan Singh became. In his mind, it went from being a simple deal about nuclear materials to the dawn of a new Golden Age. 'Our window is closing,' he said, yet again. 'If this deal goes through, billions of dollars of American investment will come to India. It will enrich our country and spread wealth. Those who oppose this deal are opposing India's poor. This is our chance to lift them out of poverty.'

Personally, I thought he was now overselling it. Yes, it was a good deal but it would not transform India and lift the so-called starving millions into an era of prosperity. But with each passing week, he spoke of the deal less in nuclear terms and more in terms of helping the poor.

And the more he acted like it was a fundamental change, the more intransigent the Left got. With each outburst, he made the passage of the bill less and less likely.

Sonia Gandhi took a pragmatic attitude. She was for the deal. But she did not believe it was worth sacrificing the government for. And if the Left withdrew support, then that was that.

But Manmohan Singh began to get more and more obsessed with the deal. 'What is the point of our being in office if we cannot do the things that need to be done for our country?' he once asked me in a state of exasperation.

Finally, he presented Sonia Gandhi with a fait accompli. Either India signed the deal or he would resign. Sonia now had two choices. The easy one was to let him resign and to appoint say, Pranab Mukherjee (whom the Left liked) in his place. The other was to let him stay and to sign the deal.

Most people advised her to take the first option. There was no mandate for a nuclear deal. The Congress had not included it in its manifesto. When the original negotiations for getting the Left to support the government had been conducted, nobody had mentioned the deal. So why make it a breaking point now?

Somehow, I was not surprised by the decision she took: she would back Manmohan Singh and the deal.

I was not surprised because, contrary to the public perception that she was the boss and Manmohan Singh was the underling, their relationship was very different. She was very protective of him, had genuine admiration for his intellect and his integrity and believed that if he felt so strongly about something well, then, as the prime minister of India, he deserved to be taken seriously and listened to.

The problem was that without the Left, the government did not have a majority in the Lok Sabha. Manmohan Singh could deliver the Samajwadi party through his new pal Amar Singh (they had entered into a bizarre alliance that never really made sense to me) but that still left the Congress short of the required numbers.

The only way out was for the Congress to persuade MPs to vote for it by winning them over: either by making promises to them about posts, appointments, etc. or simply by buying them off.

There is no doubt that Manmohan Singh knew that. What he was really saying was: my moral position in favour of the nuclear deal is so strong that all of you will have to do immoral things and buy MPs to get a majority in the House.

In the end, he got his way. The MPs were procured. The government survived. The nuclear deal went through. The Left went away.

But nothing really changed. The great transformation he had told us about never really arrived. The struggling millions still live in poverty. Billions of dollars did not flow into India from America.

And though the Congress won the next election, I was of the view that it would struggle through that term.

This was the beginning of the end.

FIFTY-FOUR

A PATSY IN A CORPORATE WAR

With the NewsX phase over I was ready to resume my own TV career. Going back to *One on One* was the easiest thing to do but I was reluctant to go back to a suit-and-tie-interview format. My old producer at NDTV, Monica Narula, had now joined a new channel called NDTV Good Times dedicated to lifestyle programming. She wanted me to do a show.

So did Discovery. Their old Travel and Living channel was now called TLC and encouraged by the success of A Matter of Taste, they wanted to do a global show called *Vir Sanghvi's Asian Diary*. Beyond wanting it to look slick and international, they had no specific brief in mind.

The NDTV Good Times' show was more difficult to conceive of because I wanted there to be a distinction between the shows I did for Discovery/TLC and the ones for Good Times.

Finally, I found two completely different formats. I wanted the Good Times show to be completely Indian. It was predicated on my conviction that the flood of factory-made international 'luxury' products that were flowing into India would kill off our local artisanal traditions. Indian craftsmen, I believed, were capable of true luxury at a fraction of the cost of what the so-called designer brands were charging.

So why not do a show called Made To Order and get somebody to make a piece of artisanal luggage, to design an *attar*-type personalized fragrance, to make me a bandhgala in a traditional Rajput court style (we went to a tailor whose family had made formal clothes for the Udaipur court for generations), to create a Tanjore painting for me? And so on.

As we thought about it, the idea expanded to include India-specific experiences: a ride on a royal barge, a night in a tree house in the hills, and more.

Monica and her co-producer, Tanu Ganguly Yadava, planned the shoots and because they worked quickly (coming from a news-channel background) we were able to wrap the show up in no time though we travelled all over India, from Calicut to Rajasthan to the foothills of the Himalayas.

In the end, this show was not called Made To Order. They changed the title to *Custom Made for Vir Sanghvi* which gave me rather more importance than the concept itself. But it worked. They ran versions in Indian languages and kept repeating it for years. It is still the one TV show that most people mention when they meet me. Perhaps that's because we did Indian language versions or because Good Times repeated the episodes so often. Or maybe people just liked the idea of the show. For whatever reason, *Custom Made* has become a sort of calling card.

The TLC show was different. Robin Roy was producing again and he and I sat down to work out themes for the episodes. Because TLC wanted glamour, we planned an episode on how Asia pioneered the modern luxury resort. We did one on Asia's creation of spa culture. Another on Asia's grand hotels. And so on.

We travelled widely: Kuala Lumpur, Penang, Singapore, Hong Kong, Chiang Mai, Bangkok, Bali, and many other places. We even tagged on an episode on biryani which did not really fit but which we enjoyed. Besides, as Robin pointed out, as the show was called *Vir Sanghvi's Asian Diary*, I could do whatever I liked.

The show did well in India (though *Custom Made* was the bigger hit) but what surprised me was how well it did in the rest of Asia. For a couple of years afterwards, I would be stopped in the street in various Asian capitals and asked if I was the guy who made the show. (It didn't last; TV fame is ephemeral.)

But while I was leading this packed life, travelling the world for TV and writing about politics in the *HT*, an unexpected problem cropped up.

Most journalists who wrote about the corporate world knew Niira Radia. She ran Vaishnavi, by far India's largest PR agency and handled PR for many of the big names of Indian industry including the Tatas and Mukesh Ambani. She had been the person I went through to get my interviews with Ratan Tata and she was the one who agreed, in a matter of seconds, on the phone, that the Tatas would pick up the tab as primary sponsors for the first *HT* Summit when it was still in the planning stages.

Sometime in the summer of 2010, stories started appearing in the papers, claiming that the authorities had proof of her interference in government affairs and there was a long list of things she was alleged to have done. One of them was that she had got Barkha Dutt and myself to lobby for A. Raja, the telecom minister. I had never met or spoken to Raja so I was a little taken aback by the suggestion that I had lobbied for him. Barkha was as astonished.

The leaks said that the investigation had been conducted by the finance ministry so we went and saw Pranab Mukherjee who was then finance minister. Mukherjee told us that the Income Tax department had been tapping Radia's phones. He was not clear why they were tapping her phones. It had all happened before he was finance minister, he said.

But, he said, from what he could gather, officers in the ministry and the department had made off with copies of the tapes and were leaking these stories. Worse still, he had been told, they would leak the actual tapes next.

But why would they do that?

Well, there were corporate interests at play, he said.

This was pretty disgraceful but what did it have to do with us? We had never lobbied for Raja. Pranab agreed that we seemed to have been dragged into it unnecessarily.

The stories died down and then, a month later, when I went to see Sonia Gandhi she showed me a transcript of a call between Niira and myself. I explained the context to her.

During the 2009 election when UPA II was being formed, allies were being considered and discarded. I was writing a daily column for the *HT* (and appearing on the NDTV election show) so I was constantly in touch with people to find out what was going on behind the scenes. Niira kept calling to get a sense of the machinations. I knew that she was a friend of Kanimozhi, the daughter of M. Karunanidhi, and a member of parliament, so she had access to the DMK's thinking. So we traded information as journalists and sources often do.

Sonia looked at the transcript with me, agreed that there was no question of my lobbying for Raja and we guessed that the stories were coming from people who wanted to destroy Niira. There was no shortage of such people: the Tatas were a frequent target of corporate dirty tricks and the war between Anil and Mukesh Ambani was at its height.

I thought nothing of the tapes till later that year, on the eve of the HT Summit, *Open* magazine carried what purported to be transcripts of some of Niira's calls. Among the conversations were some of mine. The problem was that these conversations did not accord with my recollections of the calls. Had the transcripts been tampered with? I wrote a statement explaining the context and stating that the published conversations did not seem to be accurate.

That should have been that. Except that even though Barkha and I were both on it, neither one of us really understood how Twitter worked. We were shocked to find that the Radia Tapes became a trending subject, hundreds of tweets abusing us were posted every hour and the spin—on Twitter—became that we had been fixing cabinet berths in the new government.

At that stage, we had not heard of trolls, bot-farms, control rooms, the IT cell, paid tweeters and all the things we now know to be a feature of Twitter. We were surprised by the ferocity of the tweets and the lies about what had actually been said on those tapes (though they had clearly been doctored).

Even then, I suspect the fuss would have died down. People would have asked for both sides of the story. Questions would have been asked about the source of the tapes. But then, transcripts of some of the conversations were delivered anonymously to many newspaper offices along with audio files containing recordings. Many newspapers chose to wait till the source and authenticity of the tapes had been verified.

But *Outlook* did not wait. The newsmagazine tried to link the tapes to the 2G spectrum scandal, which was then current and put photos of Raja, Niira, Ratan Tata, myself, Barkha, the journalist M.K. Venu and others on the cover with the headline, The 2G Scam Tapes.

I was horrified when I saw the cover. *Outlook* had used the same transcripts that been delivered to newspapers but had chosen to give a false and sensationalist spin to the story, linking the conversations to the 2G Scam which actually happened much before the taped conversations were recorded.

I went and saw Vinod Mehta, the editor of *Outlook* who had been my friend for years. He was sorry, he said, that it had come to this. *Outlook* had been given the tapes early on but he had hesitated about carrying them. But now that they were in the public domain, his staff believed he had waited too long. *Outlook*'s finances were in the red, circulation was falling and the paper could not afford to ignore any scoop.

I told him that at least the tapes featuring me had clearly been doctored so did he not think it was worthwhile getting an independent expert to verify the tapes? And in any case, given that he was going to make the absurd claim that I was involved in the 2G Scam, did not he feel obliged to at least ask me for a comment before putting me on the cover?

Vinod said that he would be happy to carry anything I wanted to write in my defence. He took my point about the authenticity of the tapes but pointed out that even as it published the transcripts, he had made them write that *Outlook* could not confirm the authenticity of the tapes.

He asked what I intended to do now. I said that the *HT* had been very supportive. But I intended to give up writing my political column for a bit because, as the 2G Scam was the big news of the day, it would seem odd for me, a man who Vinod had told the world was somehow involved with that scam, to write political commentary about it. He agreed but said that once I started writing again, he would be happy if I also did a column for *Outlook*.

It was a sweet gesture and he later wrote a column about how the whole affair had saddened him and how I had given him a weekly column in *Sunday* when he was unemployed. In his autobiography, published a little later, he said very nice things about me and my conduct during that difficult phase.

Meanwhile under pressure from social media and the opposition, the government was forced to come clean on the tapping. It had been ordered, it said, by the finance ministry because somebody had written them an anonymous letter asking how Niira had built such a large empire in such a short time. That, apparently, was all it took for various branches of the UPA government to tap phones.

Further, the government also admitted that there were thousands of conversations of which only a hundred or so had been leaked. It was not able to say who had leaked them and why or how. The Supreme Court asked the CBI to check if the tapes contained evidence of criminality. The CBI then interrogated several people (including prominent journalists whose conversations had not been among those leaked to the press; but not Barkha or me) before concluding that there was no criminality.

The CBI also informed the court that the tapes published in the media had been doctored. The judge acknowledged the doctoring in open court and this was widely reported in the following day's papers.

Meanwhile *Outlook* had apologized to M.K. Venu, one of the journalists whose picture had been on the cover with the rest of us. Venu's conversations with Niira were about gas allocations so it made no sense for *Outlook* to put him on the cover for a story claiming to relate to 2G and telecom.

I asked Vinod why Venu got an apology while the rest of us did not. He refused to consider any kind of clarifications about us but repeated that I was free to write a rebuttal which he would carry.

I decided to go one better. I got in touch with forensic labs used by the FBI and Scotland Yard in the US and the UK and asked them to examine the tapes for signs of tampering. I would not send them the tapes, I said, they could simply download them from the Outlook website. There was one tape relating to the Ambani dispute that I found particularly suspicious. So I sent along a voice sample and asked them to check if it really was my voice.

The results were categorical. All of the audio tapes featuring me had been manipulated or doctored. As for the Ambani tape the audio had been so manipulated that it was not even recognizable as my voice.

I called Vinod. I now had proof, I said, from unbiased and unimpeachable sources that the tapes had been doctored. Would he now concede that *Outlook* had been tricked into being part of a corporate war and that he had needlessly slandered innocent people?

He hummed and hawed. But if I had actual forensic evidence then he was happy to carry the results of the tests, he said. And so, I wrote a column including the test results. Outlook ran it but neglected to say whether they agreed with the test results or whether they stood by their story. If they did not accept those results—and they had a right to challenge them—then the thing to do would be to conduct their own tests to prove that the tapes had not been doctored.

But Vinod was not willing to risk that.

I called Venu and asked how he had got *Outlook* to apologise. He said he had sued and gave me the number of his lawyer, the legendary Nitya Ramakrishnan, famous as a gutsy human rights lawyer and Rahul Kripalani, a sharp, young lawyer. They knew the facts of the case, having handled Venu's matter, and thought that I had an open and shut case.

They sent a letter to *Outlook* asking them to withdraw their allegations. *Outlook* refused saying that it already carried the results of the tests on the tapes.

So we sued. The case was heard at the Saket court in Delhi where a smart, young lady magistrate seemed ready to proceed with the case. Alas, she was transferred and the case went to another lady magistrate who seemed less enthusiastic. She kept asking us to settle, which I was ready to but *Outlook* refused point-blank.

By this time poor old Vinod had been kicked upstairs to a largely titular position and the new editor was determined to hold firm.

Eventually, the *Outlook* lawyer, sensing the magistrate's hesitation said that *Outlook* could not prove that the tapes were genuine unless the government gave the magazine the original tapes. As the 2G Scam was being prosecuted and those tapes were not available, it was not in a position to mount a defence.

To my incredulity, a relieved judge accepted the argument and put the entire matter in cold storage.

Nitya and Rahul went to the High Court. The case did not come up for a while and nearly everyone told me to forget about it. The Radia tapes story had passed from public memory. I was discussing politics on TV every day, there had been no long-term damage to my career, etc. Why remind people of an unhappy episode?

I am not normally a stubborn man but my outrage over being collateral damage in a corporate war and a victim of editorial laziness and sloppiness was such that I refused to let it go. Fortunately, Nitya and Rahul agreed with me.

One day, the matter came up in the High Court. The judge seemed surprised by the magistrate's decision, ordered that the case be heard again and to make up for the delays instructed that the new magistrate settle the matter in a year.

By now, Vinod had died, the man who succeeded him had parted ways with *Outlook* and it all seemed like water under the bridge. I asked *Outlook* if they would settle: all I wanted was a Venu-type withdrawal of all the allegations. Bizarrely, they refused.

And so we went back to court, me against *Outlook* and assorted ex-employees of *Outlook* whose legal fees the magazine was still responsible for. Fortunately, we had a smart and efficient young magistrate who proceeded quickly with the matter. When it became clear that *Outlook* had no defence, he suggested to them that they might want to settle through a court-appointed mediator.

Which is what we did. I got my Venu-style clarification. Outlook expressed its regret, withdrew the allegations (about helping Raja, being somehow involved in the 2G Scam, etc.) which apparently it now claimed it had never intended to make!

So nine years after I had been defamed, I had squeezed some regret out of the magazine that had relied on fake tapes and made outrageous charges.

Who had given *Outlook* the tapes? Who had paid off people in the finance ministry to tap Niira Radia's phones?

Who had then organized the audio files and transcripts to send to newspapers and magazines? Which industrialist had a well-oiled PR machine and stood to gain from finishing off Mukesh Ambani's PR person and damaging Ratan Tata in the bargain?

I have no proof so I will not take names.

But can it be that difficult to guess?

Poor old Vinod, old friend and decent man. He was just a patsy in a corporate war.

FIFTY-FIVE

'HISTORY WILL BE KINDER TO ME'

The first thing we need to remember about UPA II is that it was by no means clear that Manmohan Singh would be prime minister. It wasn't even clear that UPA would get a second term.

I was on NDTV on results day and the general view elucidated by Prannoy was that 2009 would be a close-run thing. My own guess was that the UPA would get roughly the same number of seats it had won in 2004. But not everyone agreed with me.

The BJP was certain of victory. The vote over the nuclear deal had been accompanied by an unseemly scandal over the bribing of MPs and Advani went into the election claiming the high moral ground. I didn't think it would work because basically, Advani lacked the charisma to sway an electorate. He was good when he was sitting in a *rath*, stirring up communal passions. But take away the chariot and there was no real reason to vote for Advani. Besides, even in his *rath yatra* days, the BJP had never won enough seats to come close to forming the government.

Obviously, Advani did not agree. A friend of mine, who was optimistic about the BJP's prospects, flew in from Mumbai on results day and went to Advani's house for lunch. A room had been specially decked out with multiple flat screen TVs and a huge buffet had been laid on. By the time my friend got there, however, the results were more or less in and it was clear that the BJP had lost.

There was hardly anyone in the room, the plates lay unused and the food was rapidly congealing. Obviously, things had not worked out as planned but even on the morning that the results were to be declared, Advani still expected to win. On our show, when it was clear that the BJP had lost once again, a grim faced Balbir Punj appeared via a link to concede defeat in what Prannoy (on the air) called the 'most graceless concession speech ever'.

I thought the Congress would win because Sonia had delivered on her promises to the poor and those on the margins of society with such schemes as the Mahatma Gandhi National Rural Employment Guarantee Act (MGNREGA) which guaranteed incomes and employment. Plus, I believed that the urban middle classes had done well under Manmohan Singh. They had no reason to vote against him and besides, compared to Advani, he cut a more impressive figure.

There was just one problem, the traditional one: the Left. If the UPA got as many seats as it had in 2004, it would still need the Left to secure the majority required to form the government. And after the fracas over the nuclear deal, it was not clear what the Left's attitude would be. Even if it accepted the nuclear deal, it would certainly refuse to back Manmohan Singh as prime minister.

The Congress had factored this in. The back-up plan was for Pranab Mukherjee to take over. Perhaps Manmohan Singh could be made the rashtrapati when the presidential election came around. (As it turned out, Manmohan became prime minister and Pranab became president.)

But then, the unthinkable happened. The Congress won many more seats than it had in 2004. It had 145 seats in 2004 but the 2009 election gave it 206. (The BJP, in contrast only won 116 in 2009.) It no longer needed the Left. Not only did this mean that Manmohan Singh would be prime minister again but it also meant that he could govern without having to worry about the prejudices of the Left.

Elections are tricky things to interpret. Many people said that the real winner was Rahul Gandhi who had spent the last five years devoting time to UP where the Congress was struggling. In 2009 the Congress won twenty-one seats in UP, many more than it was expected to. Others said (correctly, I think) that the mixture of Manmohan Singh's sound economic management along with Sonia Gandhi's social outreach proved unbeatable.

But somehow, I think Manmohan Singh thought that he had won the election largely by himself. It was not an unreasonable view. The last big issue before the election had been the nuclear deal, which he had staked his prime ministership on. Not only had he won the vote in parliament, he now had an endorsement from the people of India. All around him, people were saying things like 'Singh is King' and telling him that he was the first prime minister in decades to have served a full term and then won election to a second one.

Even so, he told Rahul and Sonia Gandhi that he would take the job again only if he was guaranteed that he would serve his full term. (He may have been worried by rumours that he would be eased out after a couple of years so that Rahul could take over.) Rahul assured him that he did not want to be prime minister and the prime ministership was Manmohan's for as long as he wanted it.

To go from believing that you might not be prime minister again to coming around to the view that it was a job you had now earned for yourself thanks to the support of the people of India can be a heady feeling. And I believe that the way in which Manmohan Singh approached his job changed after that victory.

He became more assertive at Cabinet meetings, more sure of himself now that Sonia had let him drop the likes of Arjun Singh. He also allowed, for the first time, the emergence of a group that owed personal loyalty to him, that met at 3 Race Course Road (the residential part of the complex) and assured him that he was now the unchallenged master of India. (Within the Congress it was punningly referred to as the Kaur group.)

There was nothing wrong with that; he was not expected to spend his life looking for Sonia's approval on every issue. But the dynamic at the centre of power now shifted ever so slightly. There were Manmohan people and Sonia people. In particular, there was a huge gulf between the party in general and his PMO. Nobody in the party had any respect for T.K.A. Nair, the PM's principal secretary. Nair was a Malayali and a frequent complaint was that the top echelons of the administration were packed out with his fellow Malayalis.

Much of this was uncharitable and unfair but the feeling grew that the PMO was incompetent and arrogant and Manmohan

Singh's own private secretary, a harmless little man called Jaideep Sarkar, was termed foolish, arrogant and rude by the party and blamed for isolating the prime minister. (In fact, no PS can isolate a Prime Minister unless he wants to be isolated and Sarkar, who, admittedly, may have let the power go to his head a little, was still essentially, only following orders.)

This tension might have passed if a series of events had not taken place and caught the government unawares.

The first of these was the unilateral decision by Vinod Rai, the Comptroller and Auditor General (CAG) (appointed by the Manmohan Singh government) to go rogue. Governments have had problems with CAGs before. During Rajiv Gandhi's time, T.N. Chaturvedi, the CAG wrote an unfavourable report on the purchase of the Bofors gun which was leaked before its release. Chaturvedi then joined the grateful BJP which made him a Rajya Sabha member.

Vinod Rai never did join the BJP or politics, but like Chaturvedi's Bofors reports, his reports were leaked to the media or released in a way designed to attract maximum publicity. Moreover, Rai used intriguing methods of calculating a loss. On the 2G Spectrum allocation, he claimed that if it had been done by auction, the government would have earned Rs. 1.76 lakh crore. So there was a presumptive loss of Rs. 1.76 lakh crore.

The media seized on this figure to claim that this was India's biggest ever scam and the public was led to believe that somebody in the UPA government had made Rs. 1.76 lakh crore. This was nonsense but who understood what a presumptive loss was? (And in any case, even this figure has now been shown to be bogus, designed perhaps to attract the most attention.)

The truth was that there probably was a scam in the allocation of 2G Spectrum. A. Raja, the telecom minister changed dates, rules, etc. to help his favourites. But this was not what Rai was talking about. And even when Raja and the beneficiaries of his largesse were tried in Court, the government (by then, the Modi government) failed to make the charges stick and everyone was acquitted.

Manmohan Singh had been unable to rein in Raja but, at least partly, this was because of a curious dichotomy in the way that

Sonia and Manmohan treated corruption. Unless it stared her in the face or became a huge embarrassment for the government, Sonia allowed the allies a great deal of leeway in how they ran their ministries. Allegations of corruption were often ignored on the basis, presumably, that this was the price to be paid for keeping a coalition alive.

On the other hand, when it came to Congress ministers, Sonia adopted a self-righteous off-with-their-heads approach. Her old friend Natwar Singh was the first to go when it was suggested that his son had profited from a scam in Iraq. Then Shashi Tharoor was sacked because he might have been connected to a group that wanted an IPL franchise. Ashok Chavan was sacked over suggestions that his relatives had got flats in a high-rise he authorized. P.K. Bansal was sacked as railway minister over his nephew's behaviour. Ashwini Kumar, who was close to Manmohan Singh, was sacked over another scandal.

Nobody doubted Sonia Gandhi's motives in sacking all these people. She genuinely believed that she was keeping the Congress clean. The problem was that it reached a stage where the media had to merely sniff a scandal for Sonia to sack the minister concerned.

This encouraged the media so much that they believed that they had the government on the run. A few days of prime-time programming was all it took to get the government to start sacking ministers and go scurrying for cover. (Narendra Modi, on the other hand, ignores demands for resignations no matter what the media says. As a consequence, the media has given up.)

Not only did Sonia's behaviour give the media too much power over the government, it also gave the impression that the government was full of crooks who had to be forced out under public pressure. Otherwise, why would so many ministers have been sacked?

Sonia had intended the sackings to show that the government had zero-tolerance for corruption. What they suggested, instead, was that the Congress ran a very corrupt, scam-ridden government.

Aided by the CAG's reports, by judges' comments in court and a hostile media, UPA II lost itself in a welter of scams, some of which, it turned out, were not really scams at all. In the process, the Congress lost control of the narrative. Even now if you ask most people about UPA II, all they will talk about are the scams.

Worse was to follow. In 2011 not even two years after the UPA had taken office, Sonia Gandhi fell ill. She was flown to an undisclosed destination abroad for surgery and was away for a considerable length of time. This would become the pattern with her travelling abroad for frequent check-ups and follow-up treatment.

The delicate balance between Sonia and Manmohan, that had kept the UPA II afloat, was now broken. The party looked for leadership. Manmohan Singh could offer none. The bureaucracy was demoralized. Corruption investigations were so all-pervasive that civil servants thought it was better not to take a decision rather than be accused of taking one on the basis of corrupt considerations. The PMO, run by incompetents, had no real hold on the administration and so governance ground to a halt.

Manmohan Singh who had begun his second term so full of self-assurance, retreated into a shell. Always overly sensitive, he now began to resent those who disagreed with him more and more. He believed (and was encouraged to believe by those around him) that the Congress party was working against him.

Alternative mechanisms were created to keep the government going. Ahmed Patel and Pranab Mukherjee began to meet nearly every night to make the governmental decisions that Manmohan Singh was now unwilling to make. The government began to be run by Groups of Ministers (GoMs in babuspeak), set up to look at key decisions. Many of the more important GoMs were headed by Pranab Mukherjee.

One of the most pervasive myths about the UPA was that it was finished off by Narendra Modi.

This is not true.

It was finished off by Arvind Kejriwal.

Kejriwal was a Revenue Service officer who had managed to remain posted in Delhi long enough to acquire a considerable reputation for his work with NGOs. I met him when the *HT* partnered in the campaign for a Freedom of Information Act (which was eventually passed) and, though my colleague and old friend

Namita Bhandare handled the campaign, I remember Kejriwal as being sincere and well-liked.

But in 2011, he came to public attention in a new avatar. He turned up on TV every day as the brains behind what was then called the Anna Hazare movement. Any journalist who had worked in Maharashtra had heard of Anna Hazare who was a well-known social worker.

But now Hazare was presented in a fresh incarnation. He was, we were told, the new Mahatma Gandhi, a selfless leader who had come to Delhi to fight the corrupt political system. Added by such well-known figures as Prashant Bhushan, a public interest lawyer, and Kiran Bedi, a former policewoman and of course, Kejriwal, Hazare demanded the appointment of a Lok Pal or an ombudsman.

This was not such a big deal but the Lok Pal was only a symbol of a more generalized anger over corruption. The movement had a magnetic effect on sections of the urban middle class and especially the media. It was the first headline on prime time news every day and debates were conducted over the Lok Pal proposal where Bhushan and Kejriwal were accorded the respect due to heads of states.

A more confident government would have ignored the demonstrations after offering to accept a memorandum or something similar. Indeed, within the government, there was a divergence of views. P. Chidambaram, for instance, argued that it would be a mistake to give a media-hyped movement too much credence. But the Manmohan Singh government, weak and worried, caved in and treated Kejriwal, Bhushan and Bedi with deference and agreed to take their draft Lok Pal bill seriously.

We know now what happened later. The movement first tossed Hazare, who had only been a mere figurehead, aside and was soon divided to the extent that eventually only Kejriwal and his faction were left. (They formed the Aam Aadmi Party.)

Were the crowds they generated in Delhi packed out by RSS volunteers? It is hard to be sure but when I interviewed Yogendra Yadav, one of the movement's early leaders, years later, he conceded that he had been concerned about the RSS influence. And Prashant

Bhushan has since said that the movement was propped up by the RSS.

The so-called Anna movement shook the government so badly that when Baba Ramdev announced that he would come to Delhi to stage his own protest, several ministers went to the airport to receive him and to plead with him to go easy on the government. Ramdev was so chuffed by this show of servility that he went ahead anyway. At this, the government changed tack and ordered the police to lathi charge Ramdev's audience.

Who was making these polices? Who was responsible for these idiotic U-turns?

It was widely believed that Sonia Gandhi, who regarded the Anna movement as an RSS operation, was bitterly opposed to giving it much importance. She remonstrated with the prime minister about the reception accorded to Ramdev. (Which might explain why the government suddenly changed its mind and resorted to lathis instead.)

Was Manmohan Singh actually the decision-maker? Who were his advisers? Nobody was sure. The balance between Sonia and Manmohan had broken (at least partly because she was in and out of India because of her health) and the Manmohan who had once believed the toadies when they told him that Singh is king had vanished. Now, he was a frightened but embittered figure, who was convinced that an injustice was being done to him but was too weak to do anything about it.

The final blow came when the government passed an ordinance allowing politicians with criminal convictions to contest elections. The ordinance (intended probably to help UPA member Laloo Yadav) was controversial but, even so, people were surprised when Rahul Gandhi ceremonially tore it up at a press conference.

Rahul, who had always opposed the ordinance and had been expected to speak out against it (but not to tear it up), later conceded that the public display of contempt for the government's decisions was unnecessary and apologized to the prime minister.

But when the ordinance was duly withdrawn, the UPA had no answers to the questions that were raised. Who exactly was Rahul

Gandhi to overturn a cabinet decision? If any other Congressman had behaved in the same manner, wouldn't he have faced disciplinary action? Was Rahul an extraconstitutional authority who was above party discipline?

As the election neared, Manmohan Singh who had once been so keen to leave a legacy had become the butt of jokes focussing on his silence and his weakness. He told a press conference sadly, 'History will be kinder to me.'

But will it?

I am not so sure.

He may well be remembered as the prime minister who created the leadership vacuum that Narendra Modi filled.

FIFTY-SIX

'A WONDERFULLY RUSTIC DISH'

While the Manmohan Singh government was fighting with itself, I was snowed under with television work, most of which was either very strenuous or which required me to travel out of Delhi and sometimes, out of India.

The first of these seemed the most prestigious at the time: a twelve-episode series called Achiever's Club on Star World. It consisted of twelve one-hour programmes profiling Indians who had made it big.

We shot the episode about self-made telecom millionaire and politician Rajeev Chandrasekhar in Bangalore and Kerala and on his private plane. (It was that kind of show.) We went to Dubai first to shoot with Naresh Goyal of Jet Airways (he was an NRI and didn't want to spend too many days in India) and then again to shoot with Sania Mirza. We shot with Amjad Ali Khan in Delhi, with Javed Akhtar and his family in Mumbai, with Vidya Balan, in a single shoot at a hotel suite (it was the one episode that was just a long interview but it worked because Vidya was so good.) Shankar, Ehsaan and Loy, whose music I loved, may have been the most fun to shoot with. And we flew to New York to shoot with Deepak Chopra, who spoke brilliantly.

The show did well but it was never as good as I had hoped it would be largely because Miditech, the production company, was on its last legs and outsourced the production duties to a not-very-talented producer. In the end, it just rested on my shoulders. I had to make it interesting through my conversations which had never been the original intention.

What made the shoots so exhausting was that they ran over schedule and we were still shooting Achiever's Club when I began shooting for *Foodistan*.

This was hard work made enjoyable by the combination of two sets of people I had always liked. It was an NDTV Good Times production (with Monica, Tanu, and all my favourite people) but the show was actually made by Siddhartha Basu, the first time I had worked with him since *A Question of Answers*.

In the interim, Siddhartha had produced *Kaun Banega Crorepati* with Amitabh Bachchan, the most successful non-fiction show in the history of Indian television and had got even better at this craft.

Foodistan was a hugely ambitious project. It pitted a team of Indian chefs against a team from Pakistan. Each episode was a contest and the judges would decide who had won. I was one judge, the British food personality, Merrilees Parker, was another. And the third was supposed to be a Pakistani food writer who dropped out a few days before the shoot was due to start. Fortunately, Good Times found Soniya Jehan, a French Pakistani actress who had married and settled in India. Then, at the last moment, one of the Pakistani chefs did not board his flight. So, a diplomat at the Pakistani embassy entered his young cook instead.

The format was new to me. (I have never been a great fan of shows where people cook under pressure. But these were professionals so they should be used to it. Or so I told myself.) As Merrilees was unwilling to be bad to chefs in a foreign country and Soniya was too nice, it fell to me to be the Simon Cowell figure, a role that never really sat easily with me.

As tiring as it was, the shoot was fun. Siddhartha ran everything with precision timing and I discovered some interesting things about India and Pakistan.

We keep being told that we are really the same people who eat the same food. Well, actually, we are not. Yes, there are similarities between Punjabis on both sides of the border. But that's about it.

The Pakistani chefs, nearly all of whom had never been to India before, had no idea what south Indian food was, no familiarity with say, a dosa, and no sense of the range of flavours that India offered. They were all familiar with the intricacies of Avadhi cooking but couldn't really make great Lucknow-style dishes without adding a Punjabi touch.

The Indian chefs, many of whom worked for deluxe hotels, had a much more sophisticated approach, in terms of technique and presentation, to their food. The Pakistanis cooked pretty much as they must have at the time their country was created. It was the sort of food that you would expect at Moti Mahal or Sher-e-Punjab. That doesn't get you very far in a competition when the Indian team includes a chef of the calibre of Manish Mehrotra of Indian Accent.

Given all this, it was hard to always say something nice about the Pakistani food ('a wonderfully rustic dish, there' was the sort of comment I ended up making). And yet, as the 'Indian' judge I bent over backward to be nice to them and tough on the Indians. But the Pakistanis knew they were losing. They were even more annoyed that the judges thought that the best chef on their team was a woman called Poppy Agha, who many of the more old-fashioned Pakistani chefs were dismissive of.

Just as we were coming up to the semi-finals, one of the senior Pakistani chefs walked out and flew back to Pakistan. Once he was home, he appeared on various TV shows rubbishing the competition. The producers were appalled but I thought it was good publicity for the show. *Foodistan* had already featured extensively in global media and a little Indo-Pak conflict could not hurt.

I watched one of the shows where the Pakistani chef tore into *Foodistan*. He was upset about the calibre of the judging, he said. 'Merrilees is British. What does she know? Soniya Jehan may have grown up in Pakistan but now she is married to a Hindu!' And on and on he went. I got off lightly. 'Yes, he may understand food. But I find that he has never been to Pakistan in his life. How will he understand Pakistani food?'

It was the kind of publicity that money couldn't buy and, eventually, when a Dubai channel bought the show, Pakistanis could see it for themselves. While the show did very well in India, it was thought to be too expensive to do a second season.

By global standards, of course, our budgets were very low. Some years later I was asked to be a judge on an episode of an American streaming show called *The Final Table*. (I had to turn it down because of a scheduling conflict.) When I finally saw the finished version (which must have cost one hundred times as much as *Foodistan*), I marvelled at the sleek look Siddhartha had given *Foodistan* on an NDTV Good Times budget.

When I try and think back to that period, it seemed like I was rarely off television. We did a second season of *Custom Made* which was even better received than the first and expanded our horizons beyond India to take in the Maldives only because I loved the islands so much. I had first gone there in the early 1990s when it was a budget destination for Eastern European tourists and I had quickly worked out that it was cheaper to go there than it was to go to Goa—and the Maldives is far more spectacular.

We went back to shoot *Custom Made* and, I am told, encouraged waves of Indian tourists to visit though most of us were unable to go there as much as we liked because hotel rates kept rising till it became one of the world's most expensive destinations with prices exceeding the south of France.

I made a foray into business television, shooting a series of weekly interviews for CNBC for a show called *Tycoons*. The brief was simple enough. I talked to the country's top businessmen. Some of the interviews were fun. It was good to be able to ask Vijay Mallya how he hoped to survive given the massive debt he had taken on. And it was fun to get Nusli Wadia talking about M.A. Jinnah who, most people did not know, was his grandfather.

But by the end, I was flagging. I didn't find businessmen that interesting. And though I tried to include business-related guests (such as P. Chidambaram who was the finance minister then) along with the pure tycoons, I soon tired of trying to make businessmen sound interesting—which could often be really hard work. We tried briefly to expand the show beyond business, interviewing other guests but my heart was not in it.

I began to wonder too if I was repeating myself. The world was changing and yet, here I was, interviewing people and writing columns, the same things I had done for over a decade.

That was when Kapil Chopra approached me with a proposal. All around us, internet-based start-ups were booming. Why didn't we do something with food?

Kapil's idea was to run a restaurant reservation service which charged diners nothing but which guaranteed them tables at restaurants along with a deal of some kind (a free cocktail, a free dessert, a discount, etc.). The economics were based on the willingness of restaurants to offer these freebies (and to pay us a fee) and to treat the expenditure as part of their marketing budgets.

The idea of an internet-based restaurant booking service was not new. It had worked everywhere else in the world. What Kapil added to it was the concept of 'no meal without a deal' because we believed Indian diners rarely bothered to book tables when they went out. This way they had an incentive to use us.

We called the service Eazydiner and Kapil ran it, retaining the majority of the shares but I took a minority stake. We both said we would not take salaries from the company and worked on the assumption that one day the company would be worth enough for us to be assured of a nice little nest egg when we retired.

A start-up is always hard work and because we were determined not to load Eazydiner with high overheads, we did as much as we could ourselves. This was not easy because Kapil continued (at the start) to work for the Oberois while I still did TV, wrote and remained an advisor to the *HT*.

It was fun, though, and the company grew into an all-India operation with our own awards and our own reviews of every restaurant on our platform. As I write, we have over 250 employees throughout the country and the brand is well-known enough to get people to book through us.

Perhaps one day, when we are ready to retire, we will make some money because the value of the company has risen considerably since those days when we founded it.

Among the other things I did during this phase was to serve for four years on the Broadcast Content Complaints Council. This was an unusual body set up by the TV business with the full cooperation of the government. Till that point, complaints about TV content were addressed to the information and broadcasting ministry where a minister or even a junior bureaucrat would take decisions about what was considered acceptable to show on TV.

I had long lamented the arbitrariness of the process. In fact, one of my first column in the *HT* had been about 'The Nipple Police' (the headline raised more eyebrows at the *HT* than it did with readers) when Sushma Swaraj was I&B minister. The ministry's censors watched every TV show for an offending flash of nudity and arbitrarily took channels off the air.

One of the few sensible decisions taken by UPA II was that this ad hoc system could not be allowed to continue. Instead, the TV industry should create a body with representatives of the channels, officials nominated by the government and four so-called 'civil society' representatives. I was one of these civil society representatives (along with Shabana Azmi, Bhaskar Ghose and others) and served two terms under two excellent chairmen, both retired High Court judges, A.P. Shah and Mukul Mudgal.

One of the first initiatives we took was to insist that after a certain hour (10 p.m.) when children should be in bed, different standards would apply to nudity, sexually suggestive material, etc. In effect, we eliminated most of the I&B Ministry's objections to the odd flash of nipple.

We argued that the internet was already a dominant medium and that streaming services would soon draw viewers away from TV. So it made no sense to impose one set of standards on TV, while viewers could switch channels and see total nudity on, say, Netflix.

Our real concern, we said, was not with the odd French kiss but with the regressive values that many TV shows promoted. For instance, when the villain had to assault a woman (sexually or otherwise), TV serials lingered on the scenes of violence and the woman's humiliation. We said this was not acceptable. Use an assault if you have to advance the plot but don't linger on the scene or wallow in the degradation of women on the screen.

We took other decisions that slightly worried me but which, I eventually felt, were justified.

There was a time when nearly every serial showed men hurling acid on the faces on women who had spurned them. This was accompanied by a rise in acid attacks all over India. We did not ban shots of acid attacks but we urged TV producers to move away from them and to be a little more creative. We were also worried by the spurt in supernatural shows which advanced superstition. We told producers we would take a long hard look at such shows.

I felt very strongly about the sexualization of young children on TV talent shows. Little girls would appear, heavily made up, to dance to suggestive songs, complete with hip thrusts and seductive gestures. I wrote the advisory myself telling channels that we would not tolerate this appeal to the paedophiles in the TV audience.

Nearly all of this was alien to my nature. I am not a regulator or a censor by temperament. But even the few boundaries we set fell far short of what the ministry expected of us. Though we were meant to examine viewer's complaints, by the end of my time, too many of the complaints we were examining came from the ministry's own 'monitoring division'. They were not pleased when we dismissed nearly all of them.

The Broadcast Content Complaints Council was significant because it marked one of the few instances in India where the government let an industry regulate itself. It was very unusual for an independent body to tell the bureaucrats and politicians to go to hell—but, in effect, that is exactly what we did a lot of the time.

Other such bodies have not been as successful. The body to regulate news channels has been much less effective. Some of the credit must go to UPA II which launched and backed the principle of arm's length regulation of content.

Everything does not have to be done by babus. In fact, the less power they have, the better it is for the world.

FIFTY-SEVEN

A CAR CRASH IN SLOW MOTION

During the 2014 election, I spent most evenings in the studios of India Today TV where I was on the so-called 'expert' panel. Nobody had any doubt about what the result would be. Narendra Modi would wipe the floor with UPA II. But equally, few of us expected (at least till the exit polls were published) the Congress to be virtually wiped out.

I believed that the perception that the UPA was scam-ridden was now too deeply rooted for anyone to vote for the Congress. I believed also that Manmohan Singh's refusal to assert himself or to take any decision once things went wrong for him, had made India long for a real prime minister again. Narendra Modi was a controversial figure but he exuded confidence and leadership. Put him next to Manmohan Singh and it was as though you had a lion standing next to a mouse.

There were a couple of other factors. After the whole fabricated tapes incident, I had first gone off Twitter and then, realizing that this was just foolishness and cowardice, begun looking at social media more closely. The closer I looked, the clearer it became to me that the BJP had mastered social media and was using it to influence public opinion. My original focus was just Twitter where organized campaigns, paid tweets, troll-farms, control rooms and glove puppets were all operating.

But I also suspected that Facebook, which I was not on, was being put to similar uses. Later, after the election, when I interviewed

Arvind Gupta who had handled social media for the BJP, he told me that Twitter was only a lot of noise for English-speakers. Facebook—and Facebook in Indian languages in particular—was really the key to changing minds and convincing people.

In 2012, the Congress caricature of the BJP was that it was a party of bumpkins. The Congress, on the other hand, had Rahul Gandhi and his smart young men (most of them, children of older Congressmen) who had been to American universities, used gadgets and said they were tech-savvy.

Yet, strangely enough, none of them seemed to understand the importance of social media. I remember asking Sonia Gandhi why the Congress was ignoring social media. I bored her with my pet theory: as smart phones became cheaper and more ubiquitous, so would social media. Once the BJP had a direct connect with the phone in every voter's pocket, the Congress would not be able to get its message across.

Because we now live in the age of ubiquitous smart phones, we forget how recent the phenomenon is. When the Congress took office in 2004, there were no smart phones. In 2007 Apple introduced the first iPhone. It took a couple of years but soon other companies were offering cheaper knock-offs of the same kind of phones. Once you had an internet-enabled phone, one you could watch video on, there was no way you could ever go back to a normal mobile phone.

In 2009 when the UPA won its second term, smart phone penetration in India was still negligible. But in the years that followed this, things began to change at a rapid pace. By 2014, there were enough smart phones for a social media campaign to be much more potent than ever before.

When I told Sonia Gandhi that the Congress was making a mistake by ignoring social media, she denied that the party was ignoring it. They had a whole social media wing, she said. I told her that this division was largely ineffectual and suggested, as politely as I could, that once leaders came to power, they sometimes neglected to see how much the world around them was changing.

I told her about Tony Blair. At the *HT* Summit, Blair had told a funny story about how out of touch he had got while he was at

Downing Street. When he was elected prime minister, mobile phones were around but neither he nor his colleagues used them because they were not so popular. By the time he stepped down however, they were ubiquitous.

So Blair got himself one and was startled to learn that if you sent a text to someone or phoned them, your name would automatically flash on their phones so they would know it was you who was calling or texting. Nobody told him that for this to work, they had to have first entered your number into their phone directories.

So, shortly after he returned to civilian life, Blair sent one of his old colleagues a text from his new mobile. Because he had been told that recognition was automatic, he did not bother to sign his name.

Five minutes later, he got a reply. 'Who is this?' it read.

Telling the story at the *HT* Summit, Blair paused and then said, with perfect timing, 'I thought: it has only been two weeks since I left Downing Street!'

He brought the house down but the story indicated how out of touch powerful people get from normal life when they are in office. Could it be, I asked Sonia Gandhi, that something like that had happened to the Congress? That the party was blind to the way the dissemination of information was being transformed?

She did not agree. And so the Congress did nothing as the BJP took the 'party of scams' narrative that was already being telecast night after night (especially after the Anna movement had become a mainstay of prime time news), and moved it a step forward on social media. The Congress was not just the party of scams, the social media messaging said, but the Gandhis were profiting personally from these scams. On websites, blogs and on Facebook, the Gandhis were portrayed like the Marcoses. They were a family that had robbed India blind for generations, the BJP's surrogates claimed.

At first, a second campaign, directed at making Rahul Gandhi out to be an entitled idiot, a buffoon or a 'Pappu' did not really take off. I had met Rahul and he was both well-read and thoughtful. You could accuse him (as some did) of lecturing people but it was clear that he knew what he was talking about. During his early days in politics, he called on scholars, academics and experts, asked them insightful questions and then took notes. At times he seemed less like a politician than a graduate student.

Given this background, I doubted if any campaign aimed at portraying him as a fool could ever succeed. Then Rahul scored an own goal.

Anybody who understands media will tell you that there are only two approaches that politicians can take. Either they are accessible or they are not. They cannot refuse to give interviews and then finally agree to give just one. That makes the one interview too important and if that is all that people see of a politician, then the slightest mistake can badly damage his image.

But that is exactly the approach Rahul chose. His people promised the first interview to NDTV's Barkha Dutt and then suddenly postponed. While she was dealing with rude and haughty Congress intermediaries, Arnab Goswami who ran Times Now asked to see Rahul. He explained that Times Now had higher ratings than NDTV (which it did) and that Rahul should talk to him instead.

Ignoring the promise to Barkha, Rahul suddenly decided he would talk to Arnab instead. The interview was an unmitigated disaster.

TV is a funny medium. Shy people can sometimes come off well in interviews. Sonia is a classic example. Despite her shyness, she always comes off as natural and guileless on TV, Rahul is very well-read and bright but something went wrong that day. Watching the interview was like watching a car crash in slow motion. Arnab has a naturally aggressive inquisitorial style (which perhaps Rahul did not know, never having watched much news TV) and as he flung questions at him, Rahul visibly wilted. He gave very few coherent answers and insisted on repeating, like a schoolboy who had been sent to an elocution contest with only a single poem to recite, how much the Congress had done for women.

I didn't know if Rahul realized this but the interview was the spark that finally lit the BJP's campaign to brand him as an idiot who was not up to the job. The thing about TV is that because it creates a sense of false intimacy with the viewer, people believe what they see with their own eyes. And if you have come across as a fool the first time they have seen you in an interview, well then, that image sticks.

And so, from that point on, the real Rahul Gandhi has never got through to people. Every time I say that he is very well-read and thoughtful, people either look at me incredulously or just laugh.

Given the success of the BJP in painting the Congress as a party run by a greedy dynasty and the contributions of Manmohan Singh (who, rather than owning up to his own shameful inaction in office, was content to be portrayed as a victim of the Gandhis) and Rahul (that interview and some other misjudged gestures and comments), there was no way the Congress stood any chance in the election.

It had all gone badly wrong. Five years earlier when I had been on the election results programmes on NDTV, Prannoy had asked me what I thought the next election would be like. I had stuck my neck out and said that Narendra Modi would lead the BJP's campaign. The only way for the Congress to shrug off anti-incumbency after two terms would be for the party to project Rahul who would be relatively untainted by the failures of the incumbent government (and all incumbents have failures) and who would appeal to the youth of India.

It is a measure of how badly things went that in reality, it was Narendra Modi who won the youth vote, not Rahul. In fact, Rahul made such a mess of the campaign that even if UPA II had not been a disaster, the Congress would have found it hard to win.

The Modi victory marked a turning point for India. Almost everything that had been the norm till then was now turned around on its head. The victory had been made possible—at least in part—by the role of the media. Social media damaged the Gandhis and built up Modi. And TV destroyed Manmohan Singh's government by slavishly covering the Anna Hazare movement and according undue importance to the allegations it made.

But what we did not fully realize then was that the media itself was about to undergo a huge change.

And forget success, even its survival would be called into question.

FIFTY-EIGHT

THE TWILIGHT ZONE

One of the strange and contradictory aspects of my personality is that while in some ways, I am a Luddite (I still write in longhand for instance) I am also quick to embrace new technology—at least in my chosen profession.

I was among the first journalists to make the switch to TV. I launched my own website in 2008, long before most other journalists did. I accumulated lakhs of followers in the early days of Twitter.

Not all of it worked out. I probably started my own YouTube channel too early: certainly, it never took off as I had hoped.

So when the internet became a big deal, I looked closely at how it would affect print media. Though I was right to be sceptical of the dot.com boom in 1999/2000 (the bubble soon burst), I was convinced that newspapers were an endangered species as the web caught on. And when smartphones became the norm, I realized that the way in which we consumed information would change forever.

In 2008 I was invited to speak at a global media conference in Amsterdam. My session was about television and I was asked to explain the news channel boom in India. News channels all over the world were in retreat, the rest of the panel said. So how, asked Ray Snoddy of the BBC who was moderating the discussion, did new news channels manage to launch in India every month?

I said that there were two reasons. Firstly, many of the regional news channels were only interested in wielding influence or power and were owned by dodgy businessmen or politicians. They were not making money and were not expected to.

The second reason, I said, was more worrying. Regional news channels (and some in Hindi) no longer defined news in the old ways. A story about aliens having left their mark on earth could count as a first headline. So could a story about a woman who turned into a snake.

Our news channels were often like the worst reality shows. They didn't use actors and focused on real people but the content was fictional. They were not so much news channels as a sub-genre in the general entertainment category. Compared to the real GEC's (general entertainment channels) they got low ratings. But they still managed higher ratings than news channels that actually reported the news.

This astonished the panel and ruined the one 'good news' story at the conference: that the news genre was supposed to be alive and kicking in India.

Later, I explained that a similar misconception about newspapers should also be put to rest. Many Europeans and Americans at the conference believed that India was the one country where newspaper circulations were increasing.

This fact (and it was undeniably true) had given rise to a whole mythology. Could it be, people suggested, that when countries became more prosperous and more people joined the middle class, the newly prosperous families would all want to read newspapers?

This was a popular belief at the time and many foreign groups were considering investing in the Indian newspaper market believing that this was where the future lay. (Some, like the *Independent* and the publishers of the *Daily Mail* did invest. I believe Rupert Murdoch would have invested if the Indian government had let him have majority control of a newspaper).

I said that the mythology was based on a dangerous fallacy: that people were voluntarily buying newspapers. In fact, I said, since the 1990s, the model for newspaper economics had changed. I didn't name Samir Jain or the *Times of India* as the creators of new model but I explained it as succinctly as I could.

In essence, the new model said that a newspaper was created for advertisers. The circulation only mattered so that you could tell the advertisers that they were reaching more people. To boost your circulation numbers, you charged everyone a ridiculously low price for the paper. And if that didn't work then you gave the paper away (bulk sales, free sampling, two-for-one offers, etc.).

So circulation figures were meaningless. I had seen that myself in Delhi where the *HT* had to fight the *Times*'s willingness to give the paper away. In Mumbai, we believed that *DNA* was dumping thousands of copies. And the *Times* was giving *Mumbai Mirror* free with copies of the main paper.

There were, I continued, two huge dangers with this model. The first was that when you moved from the traditional economics of the newspaper in which the reader was your consumer and the advertiser subsidized the product, to one where the advertiser was your primary (or only) customer then you often put advertiser interests before the truth.

At many papers in India (though I had refused to allow it while I was at the *HT*) advertisers were now being allowed to buy editorial space.

But there was a second, more profound danger. The newspaper proprietors were creating an environment in which nobody was willing to pay for news. They expected it for free. This was a crazy thing to do because newsgathering is an expensive, labour-intensive process.

And as new technologies caught on (they were already beginning to in India, I said) readers would see no reason to start paying for newspapers while advertisers would defect to new media. That would leave newspapers with no source of revenue—neither subscription nor advertising.

Worse still, the expectation that news had to be free would finish off any attempts by newsgatherers to charge for news across all media, including the internet.

I had been saying this for a long time in India but nobody had paid much attention. But in Amsterdam, they seemed interested. And they had their own tales of woe: they thought all newspapers in the West would be in deep trouble over the next ten years. And most would shut down in the decade after that.

I came back from Amsterdam profoundly disturbed about the future of the news business. I spoke to Shobhana and told her what the consensus at the conference was. She seemed to agree and said that she had been worried about the future of the newspaper industry for a long time herself.

I told her how everyone said that the internet seemed to be the future and that everyone at the conference believed that sooner or later, people would agree to pay for news. I said that I wasn't sure that this was true and anyway, I found it hard to believe that Indians, used to getting news for free in our current newspaper model ('free' was an exaggeration but it was true that we gave away our papers at joke prices), would now be willing to pay for it, especially on the internet with its multiplicity of options.

My view was that older people would keep ordering newspapers for a while but as long as we kept delivering the papers to them at joke prices, we could not be sure that they were actually reading them. Younger people, moving into homes of their own, would not order newspapers.

So where would people get their news from?

My view was controversial then but I suspect that it has been borne out by later developments. I pointed out that between 60 to 70 per cent of the content of a newspaper consisted of stuff very few readers actually bothered to read: an increase in railway capacity, a new plan for India's rivers, our policy towards SAARC nations, etc. But people bought a newspaper for the overall package so if they saw a story on say, SAARC, they might skim-read it anyway.

In the future, I suggested, people would care less about the overall package that newspapers provided and more about individual stories.

In my mind, the parallel was with music. I had given up buying albums on which only four songs were any good. Thanks to file-sharing, MP3 players, etc. it was possible to pick individual songs and cut out all the faff. (This was before Spotify, etc.) The same thing would happen with news stories. As for the edit pages, people would read columns by writers they liked. They would not waste time on an academic piece about India–Burma relations on a mainstream platform.

Not everything I predicted has come to pass. But enough has. We know that newspaper circulations are collapsing (though we may disguise the true extent of the decline by dumping papers). Advertisers are moving away from newspapers. And even people who do read newspapers, spend much less time on them than they used to.

The newspaper's place in society has slipped too. There was a time when the names of editors were known to readers. That's no longer true. (Perhaps that is a good thing; I'm not sure.) And while we used to once brag that no matter how many people watched TV, it was newspapers that set the agenda, that boast is no longer true. Newspapers have lost their old importance.

As a journalist, it is the economics of the profession that have always worried me. Even when I was making little-watched shows for DD–CNN, I was making more money from TV than I was from print. When I shifted to the *HT*, thanks to Star's budgets, I made as much money from TV for relatively little work as I did from print which consumed my waking hours.

But now both newspapers and TV channels have much less money than they used to. And neither can afford to pay very well.

In 2012 or so, I came to a worrying conclusion. I decided that it would be hard for journalists to make a good living only from news and current affairs. Fortunately, I had other side careers: in food, travel and features. So I made a conscious decision to focus more on the lifestyle stuff on the grounds that it was a more reliable way of earning a living.

My heart is still in the news but I need the lifestyle journalism to keep body and soul together. I imagine many other journalists of my vintage are in the same situation. Those of us who rely on the old ways, on political columns and discussions may enjoy a degree of fame. But with each passing month, it gets more and more difficult to survive on hard journalism.

My view (and I guess you would expect me to say that) is that society is the loser. We now live in a twilight zone where nobody knows what is really happening, where facts count for nothing, where spin is everything, where opinion masquerades as analysis and where the big global tech companies (Facebook, Google) control a large chunk of public opinion.

It is a terrible way for democracy to function and it can be no surprise that leaders, all over the world, get by, not on the basis of performance, but on the basis of their ability to twist the truth out of shape.

FIFTY-NINE

THE LAST DALAI LAMA

Just as I had decided that I wasn't going to do any more interview shows, I got a call from Rahul Joshi asking if we could meet. Rahul was well known as the top editor at the *Economic Times* but he had recently taken over News 18, the network set up by Raghav Bahl and then sold to the Ambanis.

The sale had clearly not been smooth and there seemed to be hard feelings on both sides. The Ambanis themselves had made a mess of some of the channels by hiring the wrong people and sending out mixed signals. Obviously, Mukesh Ambani had realized this because Rahul had been brought in as overall boss with the brief of turning the network around. The Ambanis, it turned out, also had shares in various regional language channels and the idea was to combine it all into one network, which would be, when completed, India's largest news TV operation.

As far as I could tell (and this turned out to be accurate) Rahul had been given a free hand to do what he liked with the network. His immediate priority was a channel then called CNN-IBN. It had been set up by Rajdeep Sardesai for Raghav's TV 18 and Rajdeep had stayed on after the sale. But he appeared to have been driven out by the attitude of some of the managers the new owners had installed.

Ever since he left, the channel had floundered and when the agreement with CNN had come up for renewal, the American network had pulled out. This made no real difference to the day-to-day running of the channel (CNN had no executive involvement) but it dealt a blow to its prestige.

Rahul had managed to get CNN back on board and wanted to rename the channel CNN-News18 (which did happen). He also wanted to run it as a serious channel, not unlike CNN. For instance, he wanted the channel to have its own in-house experts (as CNN did) who could be counted on for a knowledgeable take on any developing story. He wanted me to be one of those experts and he also wanted me to do a weekly show.

I was happy to be a commentator but the thought of a weekly show worried me. I had been approached, as I have said in an earlier chapter, by the new owners of NewsX (oh happy irony!), to do a show and I had agreed on the condition that they would let me do a show of my choice. They were kind enough to agree.

I loved *Mandate*, the show I did for them, and it got a much higher viewership than anyone expected. I put the scripts together for a book called *Mandate* and this sold well too.

Mandate was a show with a limited season. Twelve episodes and it was over. That left me free until I thought of another idea and planned another show (also ten or twelve episodes) around it.

There was a problem with the format, of course. It was hard work and it was an expensive kind of show to make. NewsX was willing to spend the money to establish itself in its new avatar with its new owner. But once *Mandate* had done the trick, they didn't really need a 'different' show with an experienced anchor. Rolling news would be their bread and butter.

So, I suggested to Rahul, that we could do something similar for News 18. In my experience, proprietors always gave the top managers they had hired, lots of money for the first year or two till the realities of the TV business sunk in and budgets were slashed. But, in that time, I could probably do two *Mandate*-type series.

But that wasn't what Rahul wanted. He was keen on a regular show, telecast first on Saturday and then repeated on Sunday. I said I would do it if he let me vary the format. One week, I would do something like *Mandate*, where I would tell a story, using footage and interviews. Another week I would do an interview. And on a third week I would host a discussion. He agreed and we decided we would start the show in a couple of months. Till then, I would join the panel of experts (which at that stage included Swapan Dasgupta and Ajoy Bose).

In real terms, this meant that I appeared on the news nearly every night. And because I was not used to talking from home on an Outside Broadcast (OB) link, I went to the studio most evenings. It was a long drive but I was glad I did it because it gave me a sense of the channel and how it worked. Nobody liked the term 'expert' so I invented the term resident commentator for myself which soon became the official title for all of us.

The regular use of resident commentators made us seem different from other channels where random guests from a pool of around thirty people would go from network to network, saying the same things on every channel and fighting with each other with a predictable regularity.

A little later, Anuradha Sengupta, a well-known anchor came on board as senior editor and wanted to call my proposed show 'The Virtuoso'.

This was kind of her but embarrassing for me so we finally settled on *Virtuosity*. We began with an episode on Vijay Mallya who had just fled to London and I told the story of how he had landed in so much debt. My director Ninay Desai did an outstanding job of pulling it all together though I was told that I seemed too 'low energy'. (TV had changed.)

For the second episode, we did one hour-long interview with Smriti Irani who was then a controversial Human Resource Development minister. I had known Smriti from before she joined politics. Hers was the very first interview I had shot for *Cover Story*. And now, she was the first *Virtuosity* interview. She was brilliant and when the episode rated at number two in the Top 200 shows that week, we breathed a sigh of relief.

Virtuosity was hard work especially when we were not doing full-length interviews (and most of the time we were not). The average episode had at least four separate short interviews, all of which had to be shot (we then plundered them for bites that advanced our story), hours of editing and a long painful shoot when I read my script from a teleprompter (which I hate).

Ninay, who was the channel's leading studio director (she did the main news), simply did not have the time to spare for all this and with great reluctance we agreed to let her go back to prime time. We got lucky though because in her place came Chetan Dhalla from NDTV who took over the show and soon became its life and soul. (When *Virtuosity* won an award, I insisted that Chetan accept it: by then, it was more his success than it was mine.)

We did *Virtuosity* for over three years—our season ended a few months after Narendra Modi won his second term—and during that period, CNN-News18 became my professional home. I enjoyed every minute of it—if you like the news, then there is no substitute for being closely associated with a news channel.

We did big interviews (the Dalai Lama, Hamid Karzai, etc.), we did fun interviews (Vidya Balan, and a rare interview with Sridevi, which, sadly, was the last interview she ever gave), thoughtful interviews (Nandan Nilekani during the phase when the Aadhaar controversy was raging; Omar Abdullah when the future of Kashmir was up for grabs) and topical interviews (Narayana Murthy when he came out against the current management of Infosys, for instance) and many other kinds.

As budgets tightened (as I had expected), we were less and less able to do the big, story-telling *Virtuosities* and focused on interviews (which seems to be my destiny) and discussions.

Sometimes the budget constraints were frustrating. When Hillary Clinton released her memoir of her failed presidential race, *What Happened*, she chose just one Indian show: it was *Virtuosity*. Sadly, the channel did not have the money required to fly me to New York and NDTV, the second choice, got the interview. (They found the money to go to New York.)

I have many happy memories of the interviews we did. Chetan pushed and pushed till the Dalai Lama agreed to give us a full-length interview. I had interviewed him for the *Hindustan Times* before and had marvelled at his candour. This was at a time when Hollywood was obsessed with making films about him. Martin Scorsese had

just released *Kundun* about the Dalai Lama's youth and he had
been a central character in *Seven years in Tibet*, based on a memoir
by Heinrich Harrer. That film, starring Brad Pitt, had become the
subject of controversy when it was revealed that Harrer had been a
secret Nazi.

I asked the Dalai Lama about both movies. He said *Kundun*
was full of inaccuracies and as for Harrer, he had never made a
secret of his Nazi past when he was in Tibet. So the controversy
was pointless.

He was as candid about sex. I asked him about the Buddhist
injunctions against homosexuality which, I expected, he would have
to uphold. To my surprise, he said that he paid no attention to them
at all. If two people consented to any kind of sex and it was done with
compassion, then nobody should object, he said.

When he went to Los Angeles, he said, people always asked
what kind of sex was allowed: 'with the hand, with the mouth.' He
always told them that between consenting adults, there could be no
restrictions.

Obviously, I had been fortunate enough to have caught him in
a candid mood. A little later I ran into Richard Gere at our mutual
friend Parmeshwar Godrej's home. I told him about the interview
and while he knew what the Dalai Lama thought of the Martin
Scorsese film and was aware of his liberal attitude to sexual matters,
he was startled that he had said all this to an interviewer.

'Did he know it was for publication?' he asked.

I said he did. He was meeting me for the first time so he couldn't
have thought he was gossiping with a pal.

The interview appeared and caused a mild stir. But the Dalai
Lama stood by it.

When I went to Dharamshala to interview him for *Virtuosity*,
the focus was more on the political status of Tibet and the Dalai
Lama's views on China. He was as forthright. We shot for over an
hour because he was in such good form. This made Seema, who used
to accompany me on shoots as de facto location director, a little
nervous because the length of our interview made it impossible for
us to catch our flight back to Delhi.

The problem was that the interview had started late. We had set up on time and the Dalai Lama had started to come directly to the room where we were to shoot but he had been waylaid by scores of visitors (most of them Hindus from the rest of India) who begged for *darshan* and some of whom wept when they saw him. Unlike Indian gurus, the Dalai Lama is not big on darshan and foot-touching so he tried to be as warm and affectionate as possible to the visitors while discouraging genuflecting.

Seema was getting more and more anxious and perhaps the Dalai Lama sensed this somehow because he looked at her through the window of the room where we were waiting and made a funny face. She laughed and relaxed immediately. When he did arrive, he first went up to her and pulled her cheeks!

After our interview when the crew crowded around him, he was the same mixture of deep thought and child-like exuberance. When I introduced him to our cameraman, he laughed delightedly, 'Hello sardarji,' he said and stroked his beard. Stroking a Sikh's beard can easily be misconstrued but the Dalai Lama was so full of affection and laughter that our cameraman laughed along.

As for the flight, we needn't have worried. It was late and we made it to the airport well in time.

What will happen to the movement for a free Tibet after the Dalai Lama goes? He told us that day in Dharamshala that he thought he might die soon. In which case, he might well be the last Dalai Lama. (Presumably, this is meant to forestall the possibility of the Chinese 'finding' their own Dalai Lama.)

I hope he stays around for many, many years. He is a truly remarkable man.

The interviews were always fun but even the studio gigs as a resident commentator were enjoyable.

The one thing we learned very quickly was that in the reign of Narendra Modi, nobody knew anything. We would have discussions about cabinet reshuffles and the experts who said they knew how the government worked would make their predictions. Either the reshuffle would never happen or if it did, the experts would have made the wrong predictions.

But then, I have come to the conclusion that most predictions about politics are nearly always wrong. On the US election night of 2016, when the results of the presidential election were expected, we settled down in the studio to deliver our assessment of what a Hillary Clinton victory would mean for India.

And yes, there was no doubt that it would be a Hillary victory. We were coordinating with CNN headquarters in Atlanta and they had told us that not only would Clinton win, the scale of her victory would be such that we would know the results of the election within half an hour of the start of counting. So we prepared for a short programme.

We hadn't even got into the US election results when we were told that Narendra Modi would address the nation shortly. Our Modi experts had not expected this so they struggled to come up with theories about what he would say. One view was that, as he had met the defence chiefs that day (Had he? We never really confirmed this bit of speculation.), there was an important announcement about Pakistan coming up.

When Modi did come on and announce demonetization, everyone in the studio was gobsmacked. We forgot about the US election and quickly tried to put together informed analysis about demonetization. This was hard to do because we knew very little about how such a measure worked. We phoned economists. They had no clue either.

Finally we went home, saying that we would phone in our analysis when the picture was clearer. But it never really cleared up, millions of people were inconvenienced, and the move made no real dent in the stock of black money.

And as for the US election, which we promptly forgot about, we would have been wrong about that too.

Hillary lost. Trump won.

SIXTY

FOOD FOR THOUGHT

Meru Gokhale and Tarini Uppal had approached me about a follow-up to the first *Rude Food* book. Penguin had done the first collection and had been pleased when it won the global Cointreau Award for the Best Food Literature Book in the world, a first for an Indian publication.

That book had been put together by Diya Kar who had spent months going through old copies of *Brunch*. It was easier now because everything was on the net. My own website had been up and running since 2008 and contained nearly every article I wrote. All an editor or compiler had to do was to scour the net and choose pieces.

Meru and Tarini wanted to move away from the 'More Rude Food' format which would have been the obvious follow-up and to publish a book called *The Indian Pantry* which used only the pieces about Indian food. It seemed like an interesting idea and though Tarini took a while to put the book together it was ultimately published to considerable acclaim.

As it turned out, *The Indian Pantry* was released at roughly the same time as *The Game Changers*, a new book full of original (in the sense that it was not previously published) material. The idea had been floating around in my head ever since *Men of Steel* had done well. When I was doing the *Tycoons* show on CNBC, publishers had approached me about doing a follow-up to *Men of Steel*. It sounded easy enough to do but somehow the idea never really came together.

Then, after the publication of *Mandate*, Sudha Sadanand, my editor at Amazon, suggested that this might be a good time to revive the project. I said that I did not want to write about industrialists again. India was changing so quickly that at least some of the people who I had written about in *Men of Steel* no longer deserved to be in a book of that nature.

What if I did a book about self-made people who had changed the paradigm in their chosen fields?

Sudha liked the idea and I wrote the first two profiles relatively quickly. I believed that Arnab Goswami was the most significant figure in the history of Indian news TV because he had transformed the way in which news was covered on television.

Obviously, not everything he did met with everyone's approval but it was hard to deny his impact. Besides there was a lot that people did not know about Arnab: he had been to both Oxford and Cambridge and, when he was off-camera, was thoughtful and cerebral.

Arnab had just left *Times Now* to start his own channel and I was willing to bet that he would beat *Times Now* (which he had made number one) and change the rules of the game all over again. Sudha, who had worked at *Times Now*, was not as enthusiastic as I was and my friends all had strong negative views about Arnab's influence on journalism.

I argued that this did not matter. This was going to be a book about people who made a difference, not people whom my friends liked. Arnab proved hard to pin down and by the time I went to see him at Republic TV, the channel had already been launched. I wrote the chapter immediately after that meeting and Amazon published it on the net as a standalone chapter, a taste of what *The Game Changers* would be like.

The second chapter I wrote was about Sameer Sain, I had heard of Sameer before—he was well-known as the co-founder of Everstone Capital. But it wasn't till Deepak Shahdadpuri, one of the first private equity investors in EazyDiner, arranged for us to have lunch that I became fascinated by Sameer's story.

He was a guy from a middle-class family in Mumbai who had talked his way into Cornell, into Goldman Sachs and had eventually partnered with his friend, Atul Kapur, to set up a multi-billion-dollar conglomerate while he was still in his forties.

He seemed to me to be an obvious choice for the book. When we met, I was impressed by his grasp of food, wine, philosophy and nearly every subject we discussed. His father had been a professional so there was no *bania*-business gene lurking somewhere in his make-up. He epitomized, I thought, the rise of the global Indian, the sort of Bombay boy who could take on the world and combine an ability to make money with an interest in the arts, philosophy and the finer aspects of life.

We had dinner at Masala Library in Delhi (which Everstone part-owned) and talked and talked. The chapter more or less wrote itself.

Other chapters proved to be more difficult to write. I interviewed Karan Johar, whom I had known for years, for *Virtuosity* and was impressed by his willingness to go beyond movies and to talk about sexuality, about society and about freedom of expression.

I turned that conversation into a chapter but was conscious while I was writing it of how difficult it was to say anything new or different about Karan Johar. That probably explains why the chapter took so long to write.

Nandan Nilekani was a very old friend from the days when he had been a young engineer in Mumbai. His wife Rohini was my colleague, first at *Bombay* and then, at *Imprint* and *Sunday* so we had seen a lot of each other over the years.

Nandan had been in *Men of Steel* when he was rich and successful but not necessarily easily recognized. We had done one of the interviews at the Emperor Lounge at the Taj in Delhi and we had got through it without strangers coming up to him to bother him.

By the time we were ready to do the interview for *The Game Changers* however, he was so famous that we had to retire to his suite at the Oberoi to chat in peace. I put Nandan in both books because, unlike most of us, he had a second act to his life. And that second act may end up being even more significant than the first.

Every time you use your Aadhar card, you do something that would have been impossible without Nandan's vision and drive. That counts for much more than anything he achieved at Infosys.

Even when Nandan was at Infosys, I remember him being more interested in using technology to find solutions to India's problems than in business. He was a billionaire but the money didn't seem to matter. Rohini and he gave so much of it away that my jaw would drop when I would hear of their philanthropic work.

When he stepped back from a management role at Infosys, he sent me the manuscript of a book he had written about the ideas that had shaped India. It was a masterwork and I told him so.

But Nandan was not done. He then accepted an invitation from Manmohan Singh to come to Delhi and help the government. He was offered a political job but said he wanted to set up a Unique Identity Programme for India. It was a massive enterprise which Nandan executed in record time.

By the time I was doing *Virtuosity*, the identity project was called Aadhaar and had become a huge controversy and we did several interviews about it. Nandan launched an effective defence (calling me a 'Khan Market Liberal' on air in one of our interviewers) and it was clear that he had gone from being a successful businessman to becoming one of India's leading intellectuals.

For all that, the Nandan chapter took weeks to write. And I found I was slowing down on *The Game Changers*. This had happened to me before—when I was writing a biography of Madhav Rao Scindia—and I have never been sure quite how to overcome it.

Eventually, I did some interviews and wrote more chapters but the book was couple of years behind schedule and the quality was, I thought, somewhat mixed. But even as *The Game Changers* went to press, my life took a new turn, influenced at least partly by *The Game Changers* experience.

I bumped into Sameer Sain at the newly renovated Oberoi Hotel in Delhi. We had a drink and he told me about a dream he had. He believed that Indian chefs were never given the recognition they deserved. He would like to set up a body that rewarded Indian chefs and gave them the opportunity to interact with the world's best chefs. His concern extended to street-food cooks and those at humbler establishments. In those cases, he said, he would just like to give them cash.

We talked about it again and eventually we agreed to set up Culinary Culture, a body that would do all of the above and more to promote good food in India and reward the people who cooked it.

The obvious problem with such an idea was that it had relatively few opportunities for making money. But Sameer was willing to put his own money into the project and to look for nothing in return. He wanted to run it as a non-profit.

Eventually, we came up with the idea of rating restaurants. We would not follow the Michelin model but would create something that was uniquely Indian. And because neither Sameer nor I had any interest in making money from the restaurants and the chefs, this would be—we hoped—a completely credible and unbiased way of rating India's best restaurants.

We started first with the street-food guys. We worked with the National Association of Street Vendors to co-sponsor their annual street-food mela and gave awards for the best street-food vendors in each region.

I am not a stranger to restaurant awards. We used to organize them at *HT City* and EazyDiner also rewards the best restaurants in each city. But this was very different. Nobody had ever given awards to these street-food vendors before. When they came on stage to accept their awards, they wept and were overcome with emotion. It was the sort of recognition they had never dreamt they would ever receive. For me, personally, giving those awards was one of the most fulfilling things I have done in the food space.

To rate the restaurants, we chose an academy of over fifty food writers all over India (nobody from the food business who might have an interest was allowed to join) and all of us met every five or six weeks to listen to top chefs and to ask them questions. My close friend Gaggan Anand, who had mentored the project along with Sameer and me, did the first conversation. Since then, we have had some of the world's greatest three-star chefs as well as the top Indian chefs (Vineet Bhatia, Manish Mehrotra, Asma Khan, etc.).

My son Raaj had gone into another aspect of the food business after coming back to India once he had acquired his degree at McGill

University in Montreal. Raaj ran a company that brought great chefs to Mumbai and Delhi and organized pop-ups by them.

Sameer thought that there was a synergy between what he was doing and persuaded him to join Culinary Culture. He would organize pop-ups under the Culinary Culture umbrella for such Michelin three-stars chefs as Spain's Dani Garcia and France's Mauro Colagreco (whose restaurant was rated as the world's best).

Gradually, Raaj's role at Culinary Culture has expanded and he handles the project on a day to day basis. Though I had tried very hard to persuade Sameer not to include Raaj in the venture (I didn't want Culinary Culture to seem like the Congress party or some other Indian family-run political outfit), so far, at least, the arrangement has worked well.

As I write, our restaurant ratings are ready. Though Covid has pushed everything back, with a bit of luck, we will be steaming ahead by the time this book hits the stands.

SIXTY-ONE

'VIR IS A LITTLE BETTER NOW.'

On 20 February 2017, my mother died. She was ninety-seven years old. She had outlived my father by forty-six years and had outlived nearly everyone else in her generation in her family. She had outlasted all her friends and when the end came, there was only my son Raaj with her. I was in Mumbai, fortunately, but was hosting an EazyDiner event at the JW Marriott in Juhu.

Halfway through the event, Raaj phoned. 'I think you should come home now', he said. 'There isn't very long to go.'

I left the event, jumped into a car and rushed to Carmichael Road. She died while I was still on the road but Raaj did not tell me even though I kept calling.

When he opened the door to our flat, and I saw his face, I realized immediately what had happened.

A part of me took the sensible approach. She had been severely unwell for many years. In 2014, she went to the Intensive Care Unit of Breach Candy Hospital, was put on a ventilator and we were almost sure that we had lost her. But my mother had cheated death before (most, memorably in 1965/6 when the doctors had nearly given up and I had been sent to boarding school) and she did it again.

But—and this seems a terrible thing to say, but there it is—I often wonder if she may not have been happier going while she was on the ventilator. Till that point, she had been in poor health (at one stage, in 2007, I had admitted her to Bombay Hospital and they discovered that her brain carried the imprint of multiple minor strokes which

407

had gone undetected), but still largely lucid for the most part and able to move around the house.

But when she returned from the ICU, she was never herself again. She was confined to bed, could not go to the loo and was fed through a tube in her nose. She required round-the-clock medical care (nurses, attendants, etc.) and bit by bit, she lost her mind till she got to the stage where not only did she stop recognizing people but was barely conscious of her surroundings.

When she died, I thought she had gone to a better place. We considered organizing a funeral. We spoke to Seema who was still in Delhi (she got the early morning flight out the next day) and decided that as nearly everyone who cared for her had already passed, we would cremate her ourselves, quietly that night.

So we took her in an ambulance to an electrical crematorium, her tiny body (she had always been short and delicate) now shrivelled up like a sad, dead sparrow and watched her being consigned to the electric fire.

It took half an hour. And when we returned home, it sunk in that she had gone, after spending nearly a century on earth.

It was a strange moment for me because it marked the passing of a generation. Raaj organized the cremation and handled the arrangements (with the help of our family friend Milind Deora who I had known since he was a child) while I stumbled around helplessly. I had expected to be upset – isn't everybody in such a situation? – but there was a deep sadness inside me that just wouldn't come out.

I guess it had to do with the complicated relationship I had with my mother. As time went on, and especially after my father died, she transformed from the smart young woman who had organized their elopement to Paris and held jobs in London to becoming an increasingly helpless, emotionally needy person.

When we came back to India in 1971 after my father died she was, not unnaturally, distraught and unable to do very much on her own. There were crying jags, mood-swings and periods of unreasonable behaviour. When you are an only child, you rise almost unconsciously, to fill the emotional voids in your mother's life. So by the time I was sixteen, I had begun to look after her, rather than the other way around. She looked to me for emotional support. And I looked inside myself to find what I needed to carry on.

Fortunately I was extraordinarily lucky (and I guess, privileged). I had family abroad. I was able to go to school in England and get a generous grant to go to university. I had the *Bombay* magazine job waiting for me when I came back from Oxford.

Some of it was due to the kind of India we lived in then. *India Today* found me because of my school-friend Nikoo, the Business Press job was facilitated by the fact that RV Pandit had known my father.

So I did okay. I found a measure of professional success and I was able to look after my own emotional requirements while attending to my lonely mother's need to have me to depend on.

But both of us changed after I moved out of her house in 1986 (when I was thirty) and shifted to Calcutta. Looking back, one reason why something within me may have led me to turn down the very good job that Samir Jain had offered me was a desire to get away from my parents' home, from people that I had been to school with, from friends of my father.

There is no other reason I can think of for opting out of an important job with India's largest newspaper group and cold-calling Aveek Sarkar who I had never met to ask for employment.

In fact, I sometimes feel that I really came into my own only after I moved into the unfamiliar environments of Delhi and Calcutta. It is not just that I found the greatest professional success there. It was also, I think, that, at some primal level, I could finally become my own man.

My son Raaj was born while I was in Calcutta. (Though his mother had her delivery at Mumbai's Breach Candy Hospital.) My first marriage broke up while I was in Calcutta. I met Seema who gave me an emotional completeness and strength that I had never known before. And though Seema took her time about making an honest man out of me I think it is safe to say that once we fell in love, long before we married, I never again felt alone.

Happy marriages are primarily partnerships and it may have helped that we were both in the media. To this day, Seema edits every single thing I write and comes along on every shoot to act as a director, often to the annoyance of the nominal directors who only back down when they realize she knows her stuff.

She gave up editing magazines some years ago and switched to writing columns but Seema being Seema, she made a huge success of that too. Her column has a massive following and her books always sell well. (She took time off from writing the follow up to her bestselling political thriller *Race Course Road* to copy edit this memoir. But she still managed to hand in her complete manuscript before I did!)

After I moved to Calcutta, I never really stayed at my house in Mumbai again and my mother always acted as though it would be a bit of an imposition. ('Who will iron your clothes?' 'Will you need the car?' And so on.) It didn't matter because I worked for companies that paid for hotel rooms.

When my marriage broke up and my mother said she didn't want to get involved, that worked too. I had mined my own inner emotional resources by then.

As time went on, though I kept in regular touch with my mother and paid all her bills, she became less of what I remembered of her as a child and more and more like another person entirely. She had never entirely bought into my father's lefty agnosticism but now she went several steps further, becoming a member of an obscure (at least in India) sect called the Christian Scientists. She would go to their church, read their texts and refuse medical treatment (apparently Christian Scientists believe prayer is stronger than medicine) which may be one reason why her minor strokes went undetected for so long.

As she grew older and her friends died, she fell victim to unscrupulous con artists and avaricious domestic staff. She called me sometimes to demand large sums of money for them. Often, it was easier to just pay up than to refuse and listen to her weep or cope with her sulks.

And yet, for all this, she was my mother. I loved her very deeply. And she loved me. Her relatives were dead. Her husband had long gone. She had no other children and I was all she had. While I had my life ahead of me, a wife who made me happy, a son with whom I shared an exceptionally close relationship and a reasonably successful career, she had nothing.

And so we chugged along in a complicated but still, very loving relationship.

Each time I have sat down to write a personal chapter in this memoir, I have thought back to my father's death. I went from having my future mapped out for me to having to grow up very quickly when I was fifteen.

Did that contribute to making me who I later became? It changed my poor mother's life certainly. And logic suggests it must have affected me as well.

My principal at Mayo told my mother that he thought I had come back a very different person from New York after my father died.

'You may not like to hear this, Mrs Sanghvi,' he told her, 'but I used to find your son a little arrogant. But now I am surprised by how serious and responsible he has become.'

My mother who had a somewhat jaundiced view of my father's family retorted: 'I know what you mean. All Sanghvis are arrogant. I have lived with them and their arrogance for years. I am just glad that Vir is a little better now.'

The Principal who probably thought that this was too much information, moved the conversation on.

I can't really judge how arrogant I was as a child. But it is possible to conclude that my father's death when I was fifteen was the single defining moment of my youth. While I rejected many of his political views, I did embrace his basic ideals.

For instance, during his lifetime he was often asked by people, 'Your son is born in London; why don't you get him a British passport?'

He always refused, saying, 'The British took a lot from India: our wealth, our progress, our spirit. It is time for us to take something from them: their education, their popular culture, their language, their wealth. But we should never ever make the mistake of becoming them.'

This was an overstatement but he was of a generation that felt very bitterly about imperialism and took a perverse delight in having white people bow and scrape before him. On one occasion, I heard him refer to some of the people who worked for him as '*goray ghulam*' which shocked me at the time. (Frankly, it still does.)

And yet, some of those views have stayed with me. (Not the goray ghulam bit, obviously.) I refused to give up my Indian passport. I was always clear, both at school and university, that I was an Indian, would not stay on abroad after my studies and would make my future in India, the only country I really cared about.

Or take the subject of club memberships. My father loathed Raj-era clubs. In our house, places like the Bombay Gymkhana and (especially) the Breach Candy Club were treated as hell-holes, always to be avoided because they had, for years, refused to allow Indians to become members.

I found it a bit odd that my father who was a member of many swish London clubs should have such strong views about clubs set up by Brits in India.

'Well, the London clubs never refused to allow brown people to join, did they?' he would respond.

I am not sure that I fully agree with him. But all my life I have always resisted joining any Raj-era club.

So yes, my father's prejudices still proudly shine through in many of my views.

Did my life change in any other way when he died? Well because that loss was so sudden and so terrifying, I have gone through life holding on (often for much longer than I should have) to things that I should have just let go. That's been true personally and professionally. (I should have left ABP long before I did, for instance.)

I have also become more introverted, more self-contained, less willing to talk about myself and less keen on meeting people socially. I was always a loner. Now, my wife sometimes fears that I am turning into a misanthrope.

But life has taught me that nothing really lasts. Even sure things can turn sour or go wrong very quickly. Close friendships can suddenly become mere acquaintanceships. Jobs rarely stay very sweet for very long.

Did I expect that I would be out of NewsX in just ten months? Did I realize that so many of the publications I worked for would not outlast me? (*Bombay*, *Imprint* and *Sunday*, for example.)

And things that seem rock solid can turn out to be full of holes. In all the years that I worked at ABP, I was constantly assailed by rumours about the rift between Aveek and Arup Sarkar. I paid no attention to the rumours because the two brothers, both married to two sisters, seemed extremely close. Besides, ABP was notorious for the circulation of baseless rumours: even the durwan's love life was carefully dissected by the journalists.

I last met Arup Sarkar at Aveek's seventieth birthday celebrations at the Maurya. It was a grand party with an all-star guest list, organized by Arup. I knew Arup well during my ABP years and we always had a friendly, joshing relationship.

When I entered the party, Arup, who is, well, generously proportioned, said to me, by way of welcome. 'So you have put on some weight, eh?'

'I have indeed,' I retorted. 'Still trying to be more like you.'

It was all good fun, the evening was full of bonhomie and at the end Arup publicly touched Aveek's feet.

I have no idea what happened after that event but the brothers fell out extremely messily shortly afterwards. The rumour mongers claimed vindication, saying that they had been right all along (which I doubt) but clearly something had gone very wrong because Arup ousted Aveek from the company. Apart from being one of the most decent and honourable people I know, Aveek was solely responsible for the creation of today's ABP. And yet, after Arup's coup, he was out. The company tried to act like he had never been there.

If Aveek and Arup can fight, I thought to myself, anyone can.

And then there is the whole question of death. While this book was being edited, many people who were alive when I had written about them died (Kamal Morarka, Bhaskar Menon and others).

I still find death hard to approach. I avoid funerals and try my hardest not to go to hospitals. And sudden deaths always jolt me.

Take the example of K.K. Birla. He was not young, but he was full of energy and maintained his normal routine, including those formal lunches (complete with 'points for discussion' on his notepad) till his wife died.

I went to Calcutta to see him after her death and he seemed a different man, steeped in gloom, almost broken with grief. It was hard to see him like that but, I told myself, K.K. Babu is indestructible. He will bounce back.

He never did. He died around a month later, more out of grief than anything else.

On the other hand, a father's death has the power to change the lives of sons. Madhav Rao Scindia was one of my closest friends and my earliest memory of his son Jyotiraditya is of a small boy eating Chinese food with us at lunch at Chopsticks (then one of Mumbai's best restaurants).

Jyotiraditya grew up, went to Harvard, came back to India and became a successful investment banker. Then, without telling his father, he secured admission to Stanford for another degree and went off to California, where, from all accounts, he performed brilliantly.

He came back to Mumbai, resumed his career until his father suddenly died in a plane crash. I went to Gwalior with Jyotiraditya for the funeral where his father's old constituents and political associates begged him to stand for election to his father's old seat. I wondered how this Stanford and Harvard educated banker would put his life in Mumbai behind him and jump into the hurly burly of Indian politics.

I needn't have worried. He stood for his father's seat, won handily and went on to become a successful minister. You see him campaigning now in the dusty plains of North India and you would never guess that in another life, he was once a successful investment banker. One event changed his life. And he rolled with the changes.

Or take the case of Naveen Patnaik. I have known him since the early 1990s. He was what they would have called an aesthete in the 1930s. He was good on art, wrote books on cultural subjects (and one on the healing plants of India) which were published in New York by Jacqueline Kennedy Onassis.

His true calling though was as the jet set's ambassador to India. All the glamorous people who came to India from Camilla Parker Bowles to Mick Jagger to Robert DeNiro would gather at the small house he occupied on the grounds of his father Biju Patnaik's residence in central Delhi.

When Biju Patnaik died and it was announced that Naveen would take his place I was startled. Biju Patnaik had been the greatest political leader in the history of modern Orissa. What did his art-loving son know about Orissa politics?

But no, I was quite wrong. Naveen became an immensely popular chief minister of Orissa, abandoned his old life (he neither went abroad nor met his glamorous friends for years) and re-invented himself as probably the most successful chief minister of Orissa, at least as successful (if not more) as his father had been.

I went and spent three days with him in Bhubaneswar. He was the same old Naveen to friends but politics was his life now. He lived alone and spent most evenings having dinner by himself before watching an American or British TV show. What's more, he seemed happier and more content in Bhubaneswar than he had been in Delhi.

So, who knows how sons change when they lose their fathers? At least in my case, there were few outward changes but as a person? Who can tell?

What I do know is that I have learned to make some sort of peace with life. Possibly because I suffered a loss so early, I have never been a risk-taker or ever had the slightest entrepreneurial instinct. So I will never ever have the luxurious lifestyle my father had in the last years of his life.

But frankly, that's fine.

At least, I sleep peacefully at night like a good salaryman, knowing that my pay will be deposited in my account on the first of the month.

I have learned also that because life plays so many tricks on you, it is foolish to plan too much for the long term. Find happiness in small things. If you don't like spending cosy evenings at home with your spouse and always want to go out, then there is a hole in the centre of your heart. If you find a person who makes you happy just by being themselves, never let them go.

My father saw me as his link with the future. That's not how I see my son. Raaj gave us the greatest joy when he married Mallika Narvekar in January 2021. It is for them to find their own future. I am a link to his heritage. But his life is his own to live.

Because even if we are the sum of our experiences, each of us is still his or her own person. And we try and choose where we want life to take us.

As I have tried to do.

INDEX